*At This Time and In This Place*

# At This Time and In This Place

*Vocation and Higher Education*

———◦◉◦———

*Edited by*

## DAVID S. CUNNINGHAM

OXFORD

UNIVERSITY PRESS

# OXFORD
UNIVERSITY PRESS

Oxford University Press is a department of the University of
Oxford. It furthers the University's objective of excellence in research,
scholarship, and education by publishing worldwide.

Oxford   New York
Auckland   Cape Town   Dar es Salaam   Hong Kong   Karachi
Kuala Lumpur   Madrid   Melbourne   Mexico City   Nairobi
New Delhi   Shanghai   Taipei   Toronto

With offices in
Argentina   Austria   Brazil   Chile   Czech Republic   France   Greece
Guatemala   Hungary   Italy   Japan   Poland   Portugal   Singapore
South Korea   Switzerland   Thailand   Turkey   Ukraine   Vietnam

Oxford is a registered trademark of Oxford University Press
in the UK and certain other countries.

Published in the United States of America by
Oxford University Press
198 Madison Avenue, New York, NY 10016

© Oxford University Press 2016

Library of Congress Cataloging-in-Publication Data
At this time and in this place : vocation and higher education / edited by
David S. Cunningham.
pages cm
ISBN 978–0–19–024392–0 (hardback : alk. paper)   1. Vocation.
2. Education, Higher.   I. Cunningham, David S., 1961–, editor.
BL629.A8 2015
378'.013—dc23
2014049715

3 5 7 9 8 6 4
Printed in the United States of America
on acid-free paper

*Dedicated, with gratitude,*
*to the memory of*

## William C. Placher

*who, throughout his life,*
*responded faithfully to his own calling, which was:*
*to enable and encourage his students and colleagues*
*to respond to theirs*

# Contents

# *Foreword*

THE PUBLICATION OF this book marks an important milestone in a new effort within American higher education to use the intellectual and theological exploration of vocation as a pedagogical approach in college-level education. In several ways that are noted by the authors in this work, the resurgence of vocational exploration is a reclaiming of the basic purposes upon which American higher education was founded. These include an education that addresses big questions: the meaning and purpose of life, the role and place of oneself in the world, and the responsibility to contribute to the common good. The language of *vocation* has been extricated from its nearly-invisible recent existence among Reformation-era theological concepts and brought back into the common vocabulary. This book makes a valuable contribution to understanding the uses of vocation in higher education today, both as a theological construct and as an approach to teaching and learning.

It was the Indianapolis-based Lilly Endowment Inc. that gave birth to the resurgence of vocational exploration as an animating force in American higher education. In 1999, the Endowment launched its Programs for the Theological Exploration of Vocation (PTEV) to support independent colleges and universities in establishing or strengthening programs that would help students examine the relationship between their faith and vocational choices; provide opportunities for young people to explore Christian ministry leadership; and enhance the capacity of an institution's faculty and staff to teach and mentor students in this regard. The objective was to identify and nurture a new generation of highly talented and committed leaders for religious communities and for society. Over the subsequent years, Lilly generously supported the PTEV programs of 88 colleges and universities and a series of national conferences for representatives of participating institutions.

The Lilly Endowment also supported preparation of books and articles on vocation. William Placher's edited anthology, *Callings: Twenty Centuries of Christian Wisdom on Vocation*, has enjoyed wide use on campuses. Mark Schwehn and Dorothy Bass, two excellent scholars, prepared another robust collection, *Leading Lives That Matter: What We Should Do and Who We Should Be*. The Lilly Endowment insisted that a focus on teaching be built on the highest standards of scholarship and on students' engagement with significant—and demanding—texts. Indeed, texts from both these collections make regular appearances in the present volume.

The early success of the PTEV programs prompted a related request from college and university presidents. They were concerned about rapid change in the leadership of independent higher education that results when presidents and institutions are not well matched. In 2004 Lilly turned to the Council of Independent Colleges (CIC) to develop a program on Presidential Vocation and Institutional Mission. The program's premise is that better alignment between the "calling" of the president and the mission of the institution would result in a longer, happier, and more successful presidency. CIC established year-long seminar-based programs—one for presidents and a similar one for those aspiring to the presidency—that joined the reading of texts with periods of reflection and facilitated conversation. That initiative continues to this day with the Lilly Endowment's generous support. An extraordinary number of the "prospective" presidents who participated in the program have become college and university presidents.

By 2008, the majority of the 88 PTEV institutions that Lilly had funded were developing post-grant strategies to sustain their vocational exploration efforts. As the Lilly Endowment's active support concluded, college and university presidents were pleased with the positive results of these programs; but they also recognized the benefit of inter-institutional collaboration. Presidents pondered how this knowledge about the reframing of undergraduate education could expand and flourish beyond the PTEV grant years, and they asked CIC to help them develop a nationwide campus-supported network for the exploration of vocation. In early 2008, CIC laid the groundwork at a March 2009 conference. By fall 2009, the Network for Vocation in Undergraduate Education (NetVUE) was launched as a collaboration among colleges and universities. Within three months, 125 institutions had joined as dues-paying members of NetVUE; more than half of these institutions had not been a part of

PTEV. With vital support from the Lilly Endowment, a successor to PTEV had emerged.

Today NetVUE provides opportunities for a diverse group of 180 independent colleges and universities to strengthen institutional capacity for vocation, and the number continues to increase. NetVUE members include a majority of the former PTEV institutions plus a diverse mix of more than 120 additional colleges and universities that did not participate in PTEV. Members include smaller liberal-arts colleges such as Hendrix and Allegheny, as well as larger universities such as Baylor and Seton Hall. NetVUE institutions are located in rural, suburban, and urban settings in 38 states. Some member colleges and universities engage a variety of intellectual and theological traditions; others have a close affiliation with a particular one; and some have no religious affiliation. But all share NetVUE's goal to support vocational exploration among their students. NetVUE provides national and regional conferences, campus visit and consulting programs, program development grants, support for campus chaplaincies, and online resources.

The phenomenal growth of NetVUE in just a few years is due in large measure to the excellent leadership and tireless efforts of Shirley Roels, CIC senior advisor for NetVUE, who works out of a small office at Calvin College. Shirley has worked closely with David Cunningham, CIC's director of the NetVUE Scholarly Resources Project and a professor of religion at Hope College, to develop this book as the first in a projected series of three volumes. I want to express my appreciation to both of them for their significant contributions to this enterprise. I also want to thank my CIC colleagues, Hal Hartley and Barbara Hetrick, who oversee and support the NetVUE project. Finally, I want to convey gratitude to the Lilly Endowment for its generous support of the exploration of vocation on college and university campuses. In particular I am grateful to Craig Dykstra, former senior vice president for religion at the endowment, and Chris Coble, the program officer for NetVUE who has now succeeded Craig as head of the religion division at Lilly, for their vision to seize on vocational exploration as a means to revitalize higher education, and for their generous counsel and support.

This book, produced by twelve NetVUE Scholars with the editorial leadership of David Cunningham, is the first of three works to contribute to the body of scholarship that undergirds vocational initiatives. Not only does this effort mine the history of vocation and calling efforts; it also addresses the nature of current challenges to and opportunities for vocational exploration in independent higher education. I hope you will find this splendid volume to be a source of knowledge, reflection, and guidance for the path we all are following, on campuses today, of educating for vocation.

Richard Ekman
President
Council of Independent Colleges

# *Preface*

THIS IS THE first of three projected volumes to be published under the aegis of the Scholarly Resources Project of the Network for Vocation in Undergraduate Education (NetVUE). The goal of all three volumes is to deepen and broaden the current scholarly engagement with the themes of *calling* and *vocation*, understood in the broadest sense—including not only matters of employment and career, but also larger questions about meaning and purpose, and about the future direction of all facets of a person's life. These books are designed with a particular focus on the role that vocational reflection and discernment can play in undergraduate education. As will be made clear in the Introduction and at several points throughout this volume, a broader discussion of vocation and calling is particularly timely, given the current conversation on the state of higher education today. The contributors to this volume—all of them seasoned educators who care deeply about undergraduate life—are convinced that academic institutions have much to gain by attending to the scholarship on vocation and calling, and by expanding the role of vocational reflection on their campuses through a variety of educational practices.

This first volume of essays focuses on vocation in a general way, and particularly on matters of pedagogy. Can one "teach" vocation, or at least "teach about" it? If so, what exactly would this mean? Can educators cultivate conversations around vocation in ways that are productive for undergraduate students—conversations that lead to thoughtful discernment and, ultimately, to greater flourishing? What kinds of tools are needed to accomplish these goals? How are vocation and calling related to other important categories of moral and intellectual development, such as community, identity, relationship, narrative, and virtue? To what extent is the language of vocation tied to the theological assumptions with which it is often associated? How is it related to other academic pursuits, such as history, philosophy, psychology, and sociology? What educational practices are best able to support undergraduate students in their processes of vocational reflection and discernment? Should these activities take place within the classroom, beyond the classroom, or both?

This is, admittedly, a very long list of complex questions, and this volume will not answer all of them—at least not in any definitive way. Still, the collective goal of these essays is to make a significant contribution to the emerging scholarship on the topic and, in particular, to stimulate conversation about the pedagogical role of vocational reflection and discernment in the undergraduate context. We expect to follow this collection with two more volumes, to be published over the next two to three years, focusing on integrating vocation across diverse fields of study, and on the role of vocation in an inter-faith context.

I want to express my thanks to NetVUE, and especially to Shirley Roels, who has achieved a degree of balance that every editor hopes for: she has supported this project at every stage, yet has also managed to step back to allow the scholars the creative freedom needed to do their work. In the same balanced way, the Council of Independent Colleges has provided the budgetary, logistical, and organizational oversight that a project like this requires; my special thanks to Richard Ekman and Hal Hartley, with whom I have worked most closely. Thanks to Lynne Spoelhof at NetVUE and Shelly Arnold here at Hope College for administrative support, and to the administrators at Hope College who have allowed me the time and space to develop these three volumes and bring them to completion: President John Knapp, Provost Rich Ray, and Associate Dean Steve Bouma-Prediger have been unfailingly supportive at every turn. Thanks to Cynthia Read, Marcela Maxfield, and all their associates at Oxford University Press for their eager embrace of this project and their wise counsel. And many thanks to my wife Marlies, and to my (now adult!) children Nick and Lee; they have allowed me the time needed to complete this project, while also keeping me happily occupied during the times between.

My greatest debt of thanks is owed to this volume's brilliant contributors. As will be noted elsewhere, the process for assembling this book was not simply a matter of writing chapters and sending them to the editor. The contributors met on three different occasions for four to five days at a time; they engaged in deep and fruitful conversations about the topic in general and about one another's essays in particular; and they shared meals, walks, stories, and many, many laughs. Throughout this process, knowledge was generated, the ongoing scholarly conversation about vocation was enriched, and friendships were formed and strengthened. I hope that readers will not skip too quickly over these scholars' biographies, which we have titled "Vocations of the Contributors"; these pages provide some good illustrations of the twists and turns that a person's vocational journey can take, as well as offering a small taste of why this was such an enjoyable group of people with whom to gather, to break bread, and to write a book.

This volume is dedicated to the memory of William C. Placher. Bill was a mentor to many of the contributors over the years, and he played a major role in helping a number of us to discover, explore, and live into our various vocations. He was "present at the creation" of NetVUE and he helped to give it the depth, breadth, and scholarly character that it continues to exhibit today. We think he would have loved reading this volume; we hope you will as well.

David S. Cunningham
Professor of Religion and Director,
The CrossRoads Project
Hope College, Holland, Michigan

# Vocations of the Contributors

Quincy D. Brown has been fascinated with Marvel comic books since he was six years old. His enthusiasm first manifested itself when he began drawing the characters from the pulp pages, but it quickly blossomed into an imaginative journey, in which he filled in the stories "between the panels." Having often noticed the phrase "continued on next page" printed at the bottom of a page, he would reread the whole story, hoping that the adventure would never end. This early passion called him to a never-ending quest for imagination and meaning that led him into and among the worlds of engineering, theology, college administration (as Vice President for Spiritual Life and Church Relations at LaGrange College), and now church-planting. Ever the modern superhero, Dr. Brown's superpower is the ability to sort the through the whole range of human emotions and to determine what makes people tick, which he uses to help them give shape and meaning to the stories of their lives.

William T. Cavanaugh grew up in a devoutly Catholic home, where faith was so important that no one ever talked about it. He went to the University of Notre Dame with the intention of being a chemical engineer, but took a required Introduction to Theology course and got hooked. After declaring a theology major, he intended to be practical and go to law school after graduation, but one of his theology professors told him that "lawyers are a dime a dozen" and that he should go to graduate school in theology. Cavanaugh completed a master's degree at the University of Cambridge, then went to Latin America to look for the church that the books he studied were talking about. After a few years in Chile, he finished a Ph.D. at Duke, and has taught theology at the University of St. Thomas and DePaul University. He doesn't mind if a few of his students go to law school.

David S. Cunningham's parents bought him an electric typewriter when he was very young, mainly to distract him from tapping on his mother's Underwood while she was trying to write her master's thesis. He was soon recording for posterity his every waking thought, editing newsletters for the Boy Scouts, and typing up a (largely plagiarized) children's magazine. After a brief brush with the authorities for publishing an underground newspaper at his high school, he settled into more scholarly pursuits in the fields of communication studies (at Northwestern University) and Christian theology (at Cambridge and Duke). His ecumenical vocation has led him to positions at a Catholic university, an Episcopal seminary, and a Reformed college (Hope College), where he serves as professor of religion and founding director of the CrossRoads Project. He still has a few sheets of paper from a notepad that his parents bought him when he was ten years old; they are headed with the phrase, "From the desk of David S. Cunningham, Editor."

Douglas V. Henry grew up in Rogers County, Oklahoma, learning the lore of Oklahoma's favorite son—the cowboy/actor/political wit/newspaper columnist Will Rogers. Although he can't claim (as Rogers did) that "he never met a man he didn't like," he does like most people and he knows that God loves them all. Descended from farmers, printers, journalists, surveyors, cowboys, and ministers, he values the big questions of ordinary people. He was introduced to philosophy by a superb high school debate coach at Oologah High; and this, combined with the formative experiences of Baptist church life, led him to take up a calling to study religion (at Oklahoma Baptist University) and philosophy (at Vanderbilt). He now teaches "the best which has been thought and said" in the Great Texts Program at Baylor University, but he never has far from mind the plainspoken, hardworking, common-man roots of his northeastern Oklahoma heritage.

Thomas Albert (Tal) Howard considered several vocations before becoming a historian. Always a lover of the water, he began scuba-diving in high school and thought that life as a marine archaeologist would be the way to go. But the expensive nature of scuba-diving was driven home to him in graduate school, and his love of the water now manifests itself mainly in kayaking and in bodysurfing in the Atlantic with his children. The aforementioned graduate school was the University of Virginia, where he completed a Ph.D. in European intellectual history. Presently he teaches at Gordon College on Boston's North Shore, where he also directs Gordon's Center for Faith and Inquiry.

Kathryn A. Kleinhans is a fifth-generation Lutheran pastor. It was not obvious that she would follow in those ancestral footsteps, however, since she grew up in a denomination that did not ordain women. Under the influence of Perry Mason reruns (and because she likes a good argument), she also considered law—a vocational trajectory that she dropped when she realized that (a) not all her clients would be innocent, and (b) she would not win all her cases. As one of the few Lutheran adolescents who actually enjoyed confirmation class, her love of theology led her to Valparaiso University (B.A.), Christ Seminary–Seminex (M.Div.), and Emory (Ph.D.), and eventually to Wartburg College, where she happily continues to engage in good arguments with colleagues and students—but without the nuisance of winning and losing.

Charles Pinches arrived as an undergraduate at Wheaton College in Illinois with very little sense of where his life might be headed. After almost failing calculus in his first year, he decided he was not being called into a career in math. In a literature class he chanced upon Shakespeare, who went from "terribly boring and antiquated" to "incredibly perceptive and enlivening" in the space of just one play. After that, Pinches was mainly interested in reading books: plays and novels, but also philosophy and theology. He kept this up as long as people would allow it, and ended up with a Ph.D. in theological ethics from the University of Notre Dame. He landed a job teaching philosophy at a state school in Arkansas, where he came to recognize that he could not stop thinking theologically and needed to teach where such thinking mattered. He thus moved to the University of Scranton, a Catholic and Jesuit institution, where he has taught for the last 25 years.

Darby K. Ray spent more than a decade helping students discern their vocations at Millsaps College in Jackson, Mississippi, where she was professor of Religious Studies and founding director of the Millsaps Faith & Work Initiative. In 2012, she decided to heed her own advice about pursuing one's passion. Giving up tenure and sure-bet professional success (not to mention warm winters), she moved her family from Mississippi to Maine, where her full-time focus could be on equipping and mobilizing a college community for publicly-engaged learning and informed civic action. Now happily ensconced at Bates College as director of the Harward Center for Community Partnerships, she teaches occasional courses in religious studies, leads workshops and seminars in community-engaged learning and research, and delights in the daily challenges of developing college–community collaborations for the common good.

Caryn D. Riswold was taking that dreaded second-required-religion-course to fulfill the general education requirements at Augustana College. After class one day, the professor asked whether she had ever thought about going to seminary. She scoffed, assuming that the only people who did so were absolutely certain about their religious beliefs, or were extremely pious people, or both. She was (and still is) neither of these, so she demurred. The professor's simple response—"Well, you're asking the right questions"—eventually transformed what she thought it meant to study, and to teach, religion. She then set about pursuing questions and exploring answers, first at the Claremont School of Theology and then at the Lutheran School of Theology at Chicago. She has been inviting students along on this journey ever since, for two years as a postdoctoral fellow in the Lilly Fellows Program at Valparaiso University, and for twelve years at Illinois College in Jacksonville, Illinois.

Hannah Schell had her first experiences of community in Methodist Youth Fellowship and Girl Scouts, while growing up in the otherwise heartless San Fernando Valley in the suburbs of Los Angeles. As a student at the University of Redlands, she joined the Johnston Center—a living/learning community committed to the messy work of consensus-building. Her first-year seminar professor made her take a course on Asian religions and read Robert Bellah's *Habits of the Heart*; in these and other ways (including sending her to China in 1989), his wise mentoring changed the course of her life. She eventually graduated from Oberlin College with a major in philosophy and went on to study religion at Princeton University. She has taught at Monmouth College since 2001, where she has the good fortune of spending time with delightful students who mostly put up with her thought experiments and crazy ideas, including some of the ones presented here.

Paul J. Wadell's vocational journey, like any blessed adventure, has known a few surprises. It first took him from Louisville to a high-school seminary in a small town in Missouri, where over four years he experienced mentors and peers whose friendship and goodness changed his life. After college, he took vows in a religious community and headed to Chicago to study theology. Ordained a priest in 1978, he went to St. Louis to work in a retreat center and in campus ministry, and from there to Notre Dame for doctoral studies. That led to teaching Christian ethics at Catholic

Theological Union in Chicago for sixteen years. A very different chapter in his vocational journey began in 1997 when he left the priesthood and his religious community and taught for a year at the University of Scranton. He never expected his vocational journey to take him to Green Bay, but there he has been since 1998—teaching theology at St. Norbert College and, with his wife Carmella, wondering where the journey might take them next.

Stephen H. Webb quit the fourth-grade track team to write a novel. He remembers more about the coach's angry reaction than his novel. The coach, who was also the gym teacher, confronted him during recess while he sat on the end of a slide. Little Stevie stood (or sat) his ground; and while he never ran track again, he has been working on a couple of novels—though nothing has been published (yet). His Ph.D. is from the University of Chicago, and he has taught theology in one form or another for nearly thirty years at Wabash College, Semester at Sea, and Christian Theological Seminary. Raised in the independent wing of the Campbellite-Stone tradition, he migrated to the Disciples of Christ and then became a Lutheran before being received into the Roman Catholic Church in 2007.

Cynthia A. Wells is the great-granddaughter of traveling Bible lecturer turned nation's first female police officer, Alice Stebbins Wells—so perhaps the mixture of her life's callings shouldn't have taken her by surprise. She attended Occidental College, declaring a psychology major in her first year but slowly and surely taking enough religious studies courses to graduate with a double major. The intersection of these disciplines gradually found clarity, first through her doctoral work at Ohio State University, and then in conversations with college students who were grappling with the intersections of faith and personal experience. During her fifteen years in higher education, she has discovered that, much to her chagrin, not everyone shares her zeal for the transformative power of the liberal arts; still, she finds her deep joy in passing along her enthusiasm in the classroom. She has found, however, that in cocktail-party conversations, she should focus less on her love of general education, and more on her descent from the nation's first female police officer.

*At This Time and In This Place*

# Introduction

## Time and Place

### WHY VOCATION IS CRUCIAL
### TO UNDERGRADUATE EDUCATION TODAY

*David S. Cunningham*

IN THE AMERICAN CONTEXT, the topic of "higher education" has always elicited strong feelings and generated lively commentary. In recent years, however, the volume and pitch of that discussion have increased in magnitude, as has its generation of heat (though not always of light). The contributors to this conversation include not only experts in the field (whether self-proclaimed or otherwise), but also business leaders and sports reporters, parents and politicians, and the prospective, current, and former students of the motley array of educational institutions that are being identified by the designation *higher*. On this topic, it seems, everyone has an opinion; and perhaps rightly so, since we are all markedly affected by the colleges and universities that populate the higher education landscape.

Yet even though these conversations may be as perennial as the grass, the current round of discussion has taken on a more urgent quality. The debates range not only across the usual issues, such as cost and access, privilege and elitism, or administrative inertia, faculty politics, and student overindulgence. Rather, the current discussion seems to be asking deeper, more philosophical questions—questions that could have a greater impact on the future of higher education and on American culture more broadly. Among these questions are: what, exactly, is the *purpose* of higher education? Are colleges and universities the appropriate vehicles for the development of a well-functioning adult population? Should these institutions even continue to exist in their present form? Perhaps our culture could learn to do without them, just as it is learning to do without the items that once filled those institutions' libraries: physical newspapers, printed books, traditional-age students, and full-time faculty.

This conversation has gained particularly strong traction with regard to *undergraduate* education. While many concerns are also raised about graduate and professional training, these segments of the education sector are more closely aligned with particular fields of work and expertise; this means that they resonate with the longstanding American enthusiasm for all that is practical and economically relevant. But undergraduate education—with its lofty ideals and less-narrowly-defined goals—tends to come in for a great deal more scrutiny; concerns are regularly raised concerning cost, value-for-money, access, privilege, and "return on investment." This in turn encourages the public to leap on any research that even *hints* how little progress is made, over the course of a student's undergraduate career, in certain important areas of preparation for adult life. No surprise, then, that some commentators argue that the primary value of undergraduate education is its capacity for credentialing. But while all college graduates can proudly display a bachelor's degree, such documents only retain their worth if their value is accepted by all. As in the case of paper money, baccalaureate diplomas are radically endangered by any widespread loss of confidence in the institutions that issue them.

In the face of these circumstances, many colleges and universities are asking serious questions about their mission and purpose. These are not new conversations; the academy is one of the most self-reflective (some might say, "prone to navel-gazing") of all American institutions. But this internal analysis has taken on a new urgency as questions of confidence are raised on every side. Colleges and universities are eager to show that their graduates not only get better, higher-paying jobs; they also develop important skills in reading, writing, and critical thinking, not to mention various kinds of emotional and personal development. Skeptics argue that young people could make the same kind of progress if they spent those four years in a less leisurely, more rigorous enterprise (an apprenticeship, the military, or simply working in a lower-paying job), perhaps also enrolling in one of the many self-directed educational programs currently available online. This leads all sides back to the original question, which still bears asking: *What is college for?*

## *Focusing the discussion*

Interestingly, one important facet of undergraduate education seems to have been missing from the conversation—a facet that is, according to the authors of this volume, among its most important elements. In particular: as undergraduates, students are allowed, encouraged, and sometimes even forced *to think about their futures*. This thought-process may focus primarily on the world of work: the knowledge and skills students will need in the labor market, the first job that they will get after graduating, and the ways they will position themselves to move up the economic ladder. Such matters are indeed on the minds of students (and even more on the minds of their parents); nevertheless, a narrow focus on matters relating to future employment offers a highly attenuated picture of the ways that college students can and must think about their futures. Work is certainly part of it, and often an extremely vexed and neuralgia-inducing part; but it is hardly exhaustive of the concerns that students have as they look five, ten, or twenty years down the road. Instead, they face a panoply of opportunities and obstacles that will, to some extent, shape the entire course of their lives. These include: where and with whom they will live; how they will engage with the economic and political systems that will govern and limit them; what sorts of civic, philanthropic, and religious institutions will garner their time and attention; how they will be affected by the increasingly global nature of concerns that seemed more geographically limited only a generation ago; and how they will make the future decisions that they will inevitably face (some of which, they realize, cannot even yet be imagined). They are also aware, as they gaze into this complex and largely unknown future, that while their fellow students will have to face similar questions, they must do so in their own particular ways; there will be no magic formula that will demystify these matters for everyone at a stroke. Of course, these students' puzzlements in facing the future are intensified by the fact that they are still in the process of trying to understand themselves—that is, to determine what sort of persons they are and who they will become. In a world as complex as ours, twenty-year-olds remain relatively *unformed* individuals; they are already uncertain enough about who they are, let alone how they are going to manage the alarming-sounding complexities of the adult world awaiting them on the other side of that dignified-looking platform at commencement.

Which institutions are best able to help these gradually developing young people attend to the unknown future that they face? Many of us believe that, while colleges and universities are well positioned to carry out this very important work, it is too often eclipsed by the myriad tasks—most of them more immediate and more practical-sounding—that higher education has been assigned. Historically, colleges and universities sought to create the time and the space necessary for thoughtful and reflective consideration of one's future and one's own character in relation to that future. Such reflective consideration has traditionally been described as the exploration and discernment of one's *vocation*, which is to say, one's *calling* in life.

Words such as *vocation* and *calling* draw our attention to two important networks of concern, and to the interface between them. The first of these is the specific range of characteristics—personality traits, talents, abilities, judgments, and general approach to life—that is particular to each human being. This is why we typically speak of a specific *person's* callings or vocations, rather than to something more general; we recognize that every human being is marked by a unique combination of traits and talents, and that what might be an appropriate calling for one individual may be a totally disastrous path for another. But individual characteristics are only one side of the story; vocation is also about the specific context in which a person lives, which may open up or close off the opportunity to pursue some kinds of vocations. (Indeed, only in the modern era, and only within certain socio-economic strata, have most people even had the *opportunity* to explore their vocations.) The process of "discerning one's calling in life" requires an exploration, not only of one's own capacities and proclivities, but also of the world into which one has been "thrown"—and not just in its present state, but also the world of the future. To discern one's vocations with care, and to pursue them with energy and conviction, one must be in control of an enormous range of raw material: a clear-headed picture of one's own capacities and desires, a sense of how one can and should develop these in the years to come, and an almost preternaturally accurate account of the many facets of the future world with which one will be expected to engage.

It may seem obvious enough that the most appropriate time for undertaking this kind of discernment would be the years immediately beyond secondary education, when many young people move out of the family home and start to develop at least some degree of independence. This stage of life, which we have recently begun to call *emerging adulthood*,[1] seems to

---

1. Jeffrey Jensen Arnett, *Emerging Adulthood: The Winding Road from the Late Teens Through the Twenties* (New York and Oxford: Oxford University Press, 2004); see also

be lasting longer, and to be requiring more dependence on others, than was the case in previous generations; this extended period, marking the transition from adolescence to full adulthood, provides an excellent opportunity for vocational exploration and discernment. But this raises questions about the claim, already noted, that the outcomes of undergraduate education could be relatively easily duplicated among those who spend this period of life in another endeavor, such as an apprenticeship, the military, or an entry-level job. Filling the years of the late teens and early twenties with these kinds of activities could have tremendous value; it would also equip young people with a range of practical resources for the lives they will lead.

Nevertheless, in contrast to these alternatives, undergraduate education provides emerging adults with considerably more of two important resources that they need in order to explore and discern their vocations. The first of these is *time*: relatively unfettered time, time that does not put a person under immediate pressure to make a final and unrevisable decision. Discerning one's calling is, as noted above, a complicated business, so it cannot be resolved in an instant; it requires pointing oneself in a particular direction, giving it a reasonable trial run, and (often) discovering that something isn't quite right, which means a certain amount of backing up and starting over. This kind of process can be guided and directed and made more efficient, but it can't be rushed; the best way to find out whether some things work is to do them. And equally important to having adequate *time* is having what the late Bart Giamatti called "a free and ordered space":[2] a place where one can range widely, but that is also equipped with certain limits and safeguards, such that it can serve as a relatively *safe* space within which to undertake the experiments that are necessary to any thoroughgoing process of vocational exploration and discernment. In such a place, older adults are present in order to provide various kinds of guidance, to make sure that at least some obstacles are temporarily minimized, and to tolerate a certain degree of failure—so long as it is followed up by future efforts that have been tempered by the knowledge that is gained in the process.

---

Jeffrey Arnett and Nancy L. Galambos, eds. *Exploring Cultural Conceptions of the Transition to Adulthood* (San Francisco: Jossey-Bass, 2003), as well as Jeffrey Arnett and Jennifer Lynn Tanner, eds., *Emerging Adults in America: Coming of Age in the 21st Century* (Washington, DC: American Psychological Association, 2006).

2. A. Bartlett Giamatti, *A Free and Ordered Space: The Real World of the University* (New York: W.W. Norton, 1988).

All of these factors help us understand the importance of bringing young people together to spend a substantial period of time in a relatively safe place, and to be urged and helped to use this time and space to reflect on themselves and on their past, present, and future contexts. Of course, during this same time, we also want them to improve their ability to read with care, to think critically, to describe and analyze the world around them, and to write with clarity and grace. They also need to undergo certain kinds of emotional and personal development, progressing through an extended adolescence into the realm of emerging adulthood. But alongside these laudable goals of undergraduate education, students also need to make use of this relatively unfettered time, and this free and ordered space, to explore and discern their *vocations*: the callings to which they are truly called.

Needless to say, some institutions are better than others at providing students with the time, space, and necessary tools for undertaking such reflection. But some readers may be surprised to learn that an institution's ability to take on these tasks is not necessarily determined by the size of its student body, its student-faculty ratio, the size of its endowment, or any other of the common statistical measures that are increasingly used to rate and to rank colleges and universities. Nor does it always have much to do with the institution's "elite" status or its name recognition. It has much more to do with the degree to which the institution has thought carefully about questions of vocation and calling, has created opportunities for its students to undertake a process of exploration and discernment, and has institutionalized these structures as key elements of its programming and its ethos. Most significantly of all, it depends on a cadre of educators who, both inside and beyond the classroom, have learned how to entreat, cajole, encourage, and ultimately *inspire* young people to discern and explore their callings in life. Helping educators to undertake this work is the primary goal of this book: to promote, support, and sustain the *teaching* of vocational exploration and discernment in higher education today.

The contributors to this volume have all worked at colleges and universities that have embraced this goal—and that continue to seek out new ways of achieving it. We are, collectively, quite convinced that guiding and encouraging undergraduate students through this process is among the most important tasks of higher education today. It is, unfortunately, a task that is difficult to define, complicated to explain, and almost impossible to quantify; it does not show up on most of the charts and graphs that attempt to offer a statistical comparison of whether colleges succeed at achieving their goals or to specify how they rank among their competitors in this regard. Vocational exploration and discernment is a multifaceted activity that demands attention over an extended period of time, during which those who undertake it are being buffeted with a thousand other influences and demands; consequently, its role in undergraduate education cannot be easily isolated or assigned a numerical indicator of success. The best way to demonstrate the difference that this work makes, and to advocate for its importance in undergraduate education, is to describe it and to discuss it: to unfold its contours at considerable length, to account for the narratives on which it depends and the virtues that it cultivates, and to place it in the context of contemporary culture and current trends in higher education. That is precisely what the following thirteen essays seek to do.

At the outset, it seems important to offer a few paragraphs of reflection on the word itself: *vocation*. Unpacking this word's nuances will require us to venture into the fields of history, linguistics, philosophy, and theology. And while much of this work will take place throughout the volume as the authors seek to explain and illustrate the concept, some readers may appreciate a brief introduction to the word and its historical sojourn—even if this must necessarily be no more than a thumbnail sketch.

## *Defining the terms*

The word *vocation* derives from the Latin *vocare*, to call. Hence, the words *calling* and *vocation* are etymologically similar, though their English-language nuances are slightly different. Perhaps because of its more clearly Latinate origins, the word *vocation* is often seen as having a longer history, and one with more explicitly theological contours, when compared with the word *calling*. In fact, both words come into English in the 16th century; still, the perceived difference between them has some historical justification, since the Latin noun *vocatio* was, in the medieval era, largely restricted to what we would today call "religious vocations" (priesthood and the monastic life). This meaning still lingers, particularly in some Roman Catholic environments, where asking young people to "think about a possible vocation" is sometimes another way of saying that they should consider taking holy orders.

In cultural settings more strongly influenced by Protestantism, *vocation* tends to have a broader meaning, largely due to the Reformation tendency to broaden the reference of the word *vocatio* well beyond its previous range. As one of our authors will describe in detail (in chapter 4), this shift was largely the work of Martin Luther and his followers, who helped to endow the German verb *rufen* (to call) with a range of reference involving all walks of life—so much so that today, the closely related German noun *Beruf* means "occupation" or "profession" or even simply "job." This helps to explain why we tend to associate the English word *calling* with a person's work or career; as Luther would perhaps have put it, whether we are priests or farmers, tradespeople or homemakers, these various roles can be understood as *vocations*: our work and our various stations in life constitute the place to which God has called us.

This historical shift in the meaning of the word *vocatio* had, in part, an anti-clerical intention. It was designed to help offset the commonly held view that priests, nuns, and monks had a uniquely privileged relationship to God, a divinely appointed station in life (as opposed to all other stations, which were presumably merely inherited, or accidental, or in some cases chosen from among a fairly narrow range of possibilities). More positively stated, the word's revised meaning tended to accord a greater degree of dignity to a wider range of human occupations, marginally offsetting the more hierarchical structure of medieval life.

At the same time, however, this shift also had certain political and socio-economic implications that tended to ratify the status quo; if one's stations in life, broadly defined, were seen as appointed by God, then any self-motivated attempt to change one's status could be understood not only as politically revolutionary but also as rebellious against God. This problem might well be designated the "core danger" of using the language of *vocation* and *calling*: even today, these words still resonate with a certain degree of dramatic intensity and mysterious, quasi-religious power. Once we become convinced that this or that "station in life" is the one to which we are appointed by some powerful force outside ourselves, it can be difficult to accept the possibility that we might be mistaken about that notion—in other words, that we may not have discerned our callings with as much care as we might have. Admittedly, this tendency was mitigated somewhat by later strands of the Reformation; still, the language of vocation has often tempted people to use its resonances of divine sanction to encourage a certain kind of societal stability—and to discourage individuals from an ongoing consideration of shifts in their own vocational journey. This concern is addressed by several of our authors, and it is one to which any discussion of vocation needs to remain alert.

I have used the phrase "one's work and one's stations in life" as a reminder that, although we may associate vocation and calling primarily with a person's occupation or profession, its range is considerably wider. Since most adults spend a significant amount of their time undertaking some form of employment (either for subsistence or for wages), a person's work certainly plays a significant role within the broader concept of vocation. However, one's various stations in life can also be affected by a number of factors that we traditionally classify under the term *demographics*: age, marital status, level of education, location of residence, socio-economic class, race, sex, gender, sexual orientation. Are these factors determined by forces outside ourselves? Or do we choose them through the exercise of our own will? Obviously, the answers to these questions have generated a significant degree of debate (whether in the past, the present, or both). If we think more broadly about these categories, and think about them not merely as sociological statistics but as deeply important matters that individual human beings must face, we may find ourselves asking questions such as these: Where and with whom will I live? How will I engage with the economic and political systems that will shape my life? What sorts of civic, philanthropic, and religious institutions will garner my time and attention? How will I negotiate the larger global context that increasingly affects everything I do? How will I make the future decisions that I will inevitably face? It will not have escaped the reader's notice that these are the same questions that we listed, a few pages ago, as those which most urgently confront undergraduate students. To them, and to their own work of vocational exploration and discernment, we must now return.

## *Initiating a new conversation*

Precisely because the category of *calling* or *vocation* addresses not only the world of work, but also a wider range of questions about one's "stations in life," it provides us with particularly useful and effective language for carrying out conversations with today's undergraduates. Colleges and universities have always been eager to talk with students about their careers; institutions feature prominent, well-staffed offices with names like "Career Services" or "Professional Development" that help students think about their futures, and particularly their engagement with the job market. Often these offices even guide students through a process of discernment, providing a number of tools designed to help them assess their talents and skills, as well as helping them pair these with appropriate employment. But given the enormous range of questions faced by today's undergraduates, most colleges and universities are sensing a need to *expand* the kinds of conversations that they have with students about their futures. These conversations cannot be restricted to matters of future employment: they have to include every aspect of one's calling. This is why a recently published book insists that "colleges must talk to students about vocation."[3]

In fact, many colleges are already having that conversation. Some have been doing so since they were founded, while others have been making it a priority over the last several decades. Nationwide attention to the topic of vocation and calling took a quantum leap forward around the year 2000, due to an initiative undertaken by an important philanthropic foundation that focuses its initiatives in the fields of education and religion. Sensing the potential of the language of vocation to better address the aspirations and concerns of college students, the Indianapolis-based Lilly Endowment encouraged colleges and universities to develop programs in this area.

From the outset, this initiative had to consider whether, and to what degree, the programs that were developed by various colleges and universities would be expected to have a specifically faith-based character. On the one hand, some such orientation seemed necessary—not only because of the role that the word *vocation* has played in the history of religion in general and of Christianity in particular, but also because the Endowment sought (among other goals) to help students to examine the role of faith in shaping their callings, and to develop a better-prepared cadre of lay and ordained leadership for the church. On the other hand, however, the foundation's program officers were well aware that such concerns were not of paramount importance for all colleges and universities; even in the case of those founded by a particular denomination, many had since evolved away from, or deliberately downplayed, that part of their history. The Endowment hoped that these institutions as well—and not just those with strong ongoing relationships to a specific denomination—would be interested in developing programs for vocational discernment.

The solution that the officers of the Endowment hit upon was to describe its initiative as seeking to develop "Programs for the Theological Exploration

---

3. Tim Clydesdale, *The Purposeful Graduate: Why Colleges Must Talk to Students About Vocation* (Chicago: University of Chicago Press, 2015).

of Vocation" (PTEV). This meant that the conversation about vocation would be expected to have some kind of theological component, but the Endowment was careful not to specify just what shape this aspect of the program would need to take. Notably, one of the Endowment's officials, Craig Dykstra, posed and answered the question this way, in an address to representatives of the recipient institutions: "What does Lilly mean by 'theological exploration of vocation'? The honest answer to the question is this: we don't exactly know. That is what we hope *you* will figure out."[4] This left colleges and universities a great deal of latitude to shape these programs as befitted their institutions, and to accord them greater or lesser degrees of theological specificity. Many of the institutions that received grants had strong ongoing relationships with Christianity in general or with a specific denomination, but other grantees had weakened those ties many years ago or regarded them as being of primarily historical significance. At least a few were, or had become, the kinds of institutions whose constituencies would never have imagined them applying for anything with the word *theological* in its title.[5]

Over the decade that followed, the colleges and universities that were developing these programs met in various settings to compare their work and to discuss best practices. These events were typically attended by teams that included not only the program directors and other individuals in leadership roles within each institution's vocational discernment program, but also senior administrators, including (in most cases) the institution's president and its chief academic officer. This increased the likelihood that each program would gain a high level of visibility within its own institution and play an important role in its overall mission. In 2009, this ongoing conversation received additional impetus from the Council of Independent Colleges, which launched its Network for Vocation in Undergraduate Education (NetVUE)—a network that has grown steadily and now has roughly twice as many member institutions as were involved in the original PTEV program.[6]

---

4. Craig Dykstra, "The Theological Exploration of Vocation," address delivered at the 2003 Plenary Conference for Programs for the Theological Exploration of Vocation, October 1–3, 2003, Indianapolis, Indiana.

5. A complete listing of the original recipients of the PTEV grants, and the programs that they built with the grants they received, is archived at the program's website, www.ptev.org.

6. Up-to-date information about NetVUE can be found online at www.cic.edu/netvue. A more complete account of the origins and growth of NetVUE is provided in Richard Ekman's foreword to the present volume.

Clearly, *vocation* is a theme whose time has come. Given the current conversation about the purposes of American higher education, coupled with an increasing desire on the part of undergraduate students to reflect on their futures, a great many colleges and universities are cultivating programs for vocational exploration and discernment on their campuses. This volume is designed to support the constituencies of those institutions that are already taking part in this movement; to encourage others to do the same; and to engage the broader public in an ongoing conversation about the meaning, purpose, and relevance of higher education today.

## *Mapping the territory*

In order to offer a clearer picture of this book and the essays that it comprises, let us return to our discussion of the "two networks of concern" that were mentioned earlier in this introduction: the specific network of characteristics that each student brings, as well as the specific context in which each student will live. Discerning one's various vocations with care—and pursuing them with conviction—requires a careful account, both of one's own abilities and desires, and of the future world into which one is about to be launched.

A number of writers on the topic of vocation have found concise and poignant ways of expressing the dialectical relationship between these two orders of concern. Frederick Buechner, a writer often quoted on this subject, defines vocation in these terms: "The place God calls you to is the place where your deep gladness and the world's deep hunger meet."[7] This is, obviously, a strongly theological way of putting the matter, naming God as the author of the call and using religiously significant words like *joy* and *hunger* to invoke regions of our lives in which the material realm is invested with spiritual meaning and purpose. Still, Buechner's language is sufficiently broad and inclusive that a wide range of institutions have found it to be an appropriate motto for the kinds of conversations that they seek to generate among their students. In that respect, Buechner's phrase bears some similarities to the motto of the United States, which also invokes a rather unspecified notion of "God" in whom we claim to place the rather spiritual attitude of "trust."

---

7. Frederick Buechner, *Wishful Thinking: A Theological ABC* (New York: Harper and Row, 1973), 95.

Of course, precisely because this language is relatively generic, some institutions—especially, in this case, the more strongly church-related ones—have chosen to describe their engagement with questions of vocation in more explicitly theological terms. Some have used Christian language to flesh out the two "networks of concern" that vocational exploration involves—describing, for example, human life in terms of its relationship to Christ or to the Church, and describing the world into which one enters as created and sustained by God in ways that mirror the biblical narratives and/or Christian tradition more broadly. Most of these programs explicitly encourage conversations about the relationship of faith and vocation, and many include programming that is specifically designed to foster future church leadership, whether lay or ordained. Hence, vocation can be—and in many undergraduate institutions, very much *is*—a conversation vested with deeply theological resonances.

But this is not always the case. Indeed, many colleges and universities that have made quite widespread use of the language of *calling* and *vocation* have done so without invoking its theological roots, because this approach provides a better fit for their particular ethos and mission. Such institutions tend to avoid mottos that hint at "God" or make other theological references, instead preferring something like the following quotation from Hermann Hesse:

> There are many types and kinds of vocations, but the core of the experience is always the same: the soul is awakened by it, transformed or exalted, so that instead of dreams and presentiments from within a summons comes from without. A portion of reality presents itself and makes a claim.[8]

Like Buechner, Hesse seems to gesture toward the two networks of concern that have been described in this introduction: the inner world of the person who is exploring, discerning, and wrestling with his or her own vocations (Hesse here calls it "the soul" and speaks of something coming "from within"); and the outward realm from which one perceives something like an attraction: a summons, an urging, a call. Without identifying the precise nature of the "caller," Hesse is still able to imply that our

---

8. Hermann Hesse, *The Glass Bead Game (Magister Ludi)*, trans. Richard Winston and Clara Winston (New York: Holt, Rinehart and Winston, 1969), 58.

vocations are shaped not just by our own interior decisions, but also by the world that we encounter outside of ourselves.

The institutions that have implemented vocational discernment programs have adopted a relatively wide range of perspectives on the questions of whether, and to what degree, the exploration of vocation should be explicitly or implicitly *theological* in nature. One might well assume that a similar range of differences marks the potential readers of this book; and indeed, we can collectively state—with certainty!—that those differences also mark its *writers*. What can be expected, then, in the pages that follow? Is this a book about the *theological* exploration of vocation, in line with the Lilly Endowment's original language about the relationship of faith and vocation, or even more specifically about the *Christian* exploration of vocation? Or is it a book about *vocation* and *calling* in a broader sense—a more secularized version, focusing mainly on the kinds of career counseling that colleges and universities have traditionally done, but broadening this emphasis to include a wider range of questions that undergraduates are asking about their futures?

To answer the question directly: this book is neither of those two things, but some third option that is neither a synthesis of these two possibilities nor some compromise between them. Instead, this book seeks to initiate the next stage in the scholarly conversation about vocational exploration and discernment: a stage that both implicitly and explicitly interrogates the easy division of "sacred" and "secular" realms, a stage that raises questions about our tendency to locate the language of calling and vocation somewhere along a spectrum ranging from "narrowly confessional" on the one hand to "broadly public" on the other. Most of the authors of this volume find such a dualistic account to be not terribly descriptive of reality—more a leftover vestige of certain blind alleys of Enlightenment rationality than a genuine account of the actual workings of institutions of higher education and their various constituencies (including, most significantly, their students). Hence, in writing these essays, we have sought to avoid two highly unrealistic assumptions about these institutions and about their faculties and students (and therefore also about our readers): first, that they *necessarily* come into the conversation with specifically Christian perspectives and assumptions; and second, that they *are wholly unaffected by* those perspectives and assumptions. After all, Christian claims have, across history and also today, given a particular shape and texture to the language of vocation and calling (and indeed, to American higher education and to the broader culture in which it is ensconced). Our authors recognize that the language of *vocation* has a theological history and therefore takes on particular nuances for those who bring their faith into the conversation; but we are also convinced that the language has power, significance, and efficacy for those who approach it without those same assumptions. The language of vocation and calling is, perhaps, a post-secular phenomenon, dwelling in a land that lies beyond stale Enlightenment debates about "faith versus reason."

And a good thing, too—because American colleges and universities have become increasingly aware of the garden path down which they were led when they were urged to excise all mention of "religion" or "faith" from the ongoing intellectual conversation (as some certainly tried to do). The range of writing on this topic is far too vast to describe here, but it will perhaps suffice to note the energy generated by books with titles like *Education's End: Why Our Colleges and Universities Have Given Up on the Meaning of Life*[9] and *Cultivating the Spirit: How College Can Enhance Students' Inner Lives.*[10] Such books document the sheer absurdity of attempting to relegate religious faith and spiritual awareness to the scrap-heap of history. A good scholarly assessment of the current state of the question can be found in the essays collected in *The American University in a Post-Secular Age.*[11] While the present volume does not take up these questions directly, they surround and permeate its concerns.

## *Outlining the argument*

The time has now come to turn to those concerns directly, and to provide an overview of this volume. Despite the fact that it was not written by a single author, its contributors all share certain commitments; we have sought to make these commonalities salient, to link our chapters to one another, and to organize the book such that it achieves a fairly unified narrative arc. We were able to do so by meeting together on three occasions over the course of a year for extended seminars on the topic of vocation and higher education. We exchanged draft essays, commented on one

---

9. By Anthony T. Kronman (New Haven: Yale University Press, 2007).

10. By Alexander W. Astin, Helen S. Astin, and Jennifer A. Lindholm (San Francisco: Jossey-Bass, 2011).

11. By Douglas G. Jacobsen and Rhonda Hustedt Jacobsen (New York: Oxford University Press, 2008).

another's work, and reshaped the volume several times in order to give it the greatest possible degree of coherence. The proof of our efforts, will, of course, be in the reading; but in any case we hope that the productive conversations that we have had on this topic will resonate through the essays that we here offer.

Part One of this book provides the cultural and sociological background against which our account of calling and vocation will be constructed. It begins by casting the net as widely as possible, surveying the broad cultural conditions within which the concepts of vocation and calling must operate. In particular, the language of vocation has been strongly affected by the modern multiplication of individual choices, which helps to explain why undergraduate students often feel more and more overwhelmed when thinking about their futures: everything seems to depend on their decisions, and they have a seemingly infinite number of decisions to make. Their choices are further multiplied by the current realities of undergraduate education, which is often tempted simply to replicate the consumer-driven structure of the wider culture, rather than educating for the common good. Both of these contexts (of our culture in general and of higher education in particular) are always confronting our students—not only in the present moment, but also by enabling (or limiting) the ways that they can imagine their futures. Students can become frustrated when they are denied access to certain paths that their lives might have taken, while other paths—even those for which they may have little interest, ability, or enthusiasm—are somehow made to seem inevitable. In the midst of these cultural, educational, and structural realities, a recovery of the true contours of *vocation* has significant potential for reducing student anxiety, creating a more responsible and more hopeful educational environment, and ultimately helping students to live more fulfilling lives.

In Part Two, we attempt to unpack the heavily laden word *vocation* by exploring its historical, theological, and philosophical dimensions. This section begins with a more detailed account of the historical shift (mentioned in passing in this introduction and in several of our chapters) in which the word *vocation* lost its paradigmatic focus on the priesthood and religious orders, gradually becoming associated with all people and with many stations in life. We then turn to the claim that the language of vocation implies the existence of a *call*, and explore that call from two perspectives. Chapter 5 examines the nature of a call, and considers what counts as receiving and responding to one. According to the stories that are often told about discerning one's calling, a certain kind of bond is forged between the experiences that the recipients have had, and the work that they do (or will do); these stories help us to outline what we mean when we speak of a person's vocation. Then, in chapter 6, we turn to the vexed question of whether a calling, by its very nature, implies an agent, a "caller." If so, is this agent to be identified with God? What do we make of the fact that most of the language and literature of vocation is tied to various theistic traditions, and that its most common context is that of Christianity? We then conclude Part Two with an in-depth exploration of the role of *narrative* in the shaping of one's various vocations. After surveying the recent attention being given to the category of narrative in philosophical discussion and ethical reflection, this chapter goes on to describe the college years as a particularly important time for discerning the narrative threads that have constituted one's life and will shape it in the future. It also explores the significance of understanding oneself as being ensconced in larger "framing narratives" that are not of one's own making.

This exploration of narrative provides a fitting transition to Part Three, which bears the title "Vocation and Virtue." Attention to the framing narratives that shape our lives allows similar attention to the excellences of character that these narratives portray as worthy of praise and emulation. Such excellences of character, developed over time by the cultivation of good habits, are *virtues*—a category bequeathed to us by Aristotle, given deep and serious attention throughout the intellectual history of the West, and experiencing something of a renaissance today (in parallel to the renewed attention to narrative). Although the language associated with *virtue* and that of *vocation* can be seen as offering slightly diverging vocabularies for addressing larger questions of meaning and purpose in our lives,[12] the authors of this volume are convinced that these two fields of discourse are deeply intertwined—and that much is to be gained by putting them into conversation with each other.

We begin this part with an essay designed to introduce readers to the language of virtue and to illustrate it through a paradigmatic example. The essay explores the nature of virtue in general, its relationship to the

---

12. In a recent and important collection of readings on vocation, for example, the editors describe "three different categories" of authenticity, virtue, and vocation. However, the authors also note that these fields of discourse overlap and range around one another, such that the distinction among them is more heuristic than categorical. See Mark R. Schwehn and Dorothy C. Bass, *Leading Lives That Matter: What We Should Do and Who We Should Be* (Grand Rapids, MI: William B. Eerdmans, 2006), 40–46.

language of "happiness" and the good life, and its historical sojourn and present-day popularity. It then turns to the archetypal virtue of magnanimity ("greatness of soul") in order to demonstrate how this language might be used when thinking about vocational discernment and exploration. Our second discussion of virtue shifts the scene from ancient Greece to ancient Rome, and to the importance of *prudentia*, a difficult-to-translate term that is often described as "practical reason" and associated with wisdom and perspicacity. This chapter examines the natural relationship between *prudentia* and vocation, both of which are concerned with learning how to orient our lives to what is most important. Part Three concludes with a reminder that the language of virtue is not limited to the ancient world, but can be expanded and employed in helpful ways in the contemporary setting as well. Drawing on the work of the American philosopher Josiah Royce, this chapter explores the virtue of *loyalty* as one with particularly strong appeal among undergraduate students. It can help them fill the void created by broader cultural tendencies toward individualism, independence, and self-focus, all of which are intensified in the setting of higher education. Throughout Part Three, our authors are concerned with the ways that the particular virtues that they describe are both conducive to, and reinforced by, the exploration and discernment of one's callings in life.

While reflections on such complex categories as narrative, community, and virtue may provide excellent opportunities for vocational reflection within the setting of the undergraduate classroom, our authors are well aware that some of the most important work in this area takes place in other campus settings. The residence hall, the athletic field, internships, service projects, and a whole host of co-curricular programs provide students with many of the models, mentors, beliefs, and practices that will shape their processes of vocational exploration and discernment. Hence, in Part Four of this volume, we explore the importance of some of these regions of campus life for helping our students to consider their callings, to try on certain occupations and attitudes, and to explore their vocations in ways that make the best use of the "time and place" provided by their collegiate experience. The essays in this final part are ordered conversely to those in Part One. There, we began with a broad cultural focus and gradually narrowed down to the student experience; here, we begin with student involvement in co-curricular activities, focusing on the "rituals, contests, and images" of these venues as a key to their impact and to the reasons that they can, potentially, become active sites of vocational reflection. We then expand the focus to the physical reality of the college campus, attending to the geography and geometry of that "free and ordered space" and considering the degree to which it enables or inhibits vocational reflection and discernment. Attending to the physical features of our campuses may help us understand how these features affect our students' capacities for—quite literally—*listening to* their surroundings and *hearing* their callings. Our final chapter takes us not only beyond the classroom but beyond the campus as well, to the realm of *community engagement*. At its best, this work can engender precisely the character traits that we would most want higher education to instill, while simultaneously offering an extended period of time and a more expansive place in which students can reflect on their vocational choices and think about the shape that their future lives will take.

The book concludes with a brief discussion of how colleges and universities might initiate, or further develop, greater attention to questions of calling and vocation. We believe that we are at a key moment in this process, wherein a certain alignment of the planets has begun to generate the scholarship, resources, and energy necessary to acknowledge that vocational exploration is an essential element of the undergraduate experience. By engendering conversations among their various constituencies—faculty, staff, students, administrators, trustees, alumni, and supporters of all kinds—American institutions of higher education can prepare themselves for the conversations that they need to have with every student who passes through their hallowed halls. Our colleges and universities have an unparalleled opportunity, "at this time and in this place," to contribute more robustly to the flourishing of their students, both now and in the future—and, in doing so, to make the world a better place for us all.

# PART ONE

## *Vocation in the Current Cultural Context*

The first three essays in this volume focus on the broader landscape within which vocational reflection and discernment takes place, particularly among today's undergraduate students. Depending on the cultural context in which it occurs, the process of listening for (and responding to) one's calling can take very different forms. For example, as will be noted both in chapter 1 and elsewhere, the majority of human beings throughout history have not actually had the opportunity to undertake any significant degree of vocational reflection and discernment. Throughout much of history—and still today, for many people in the world—the range of truly viable paths is fairly narrowly restricted. Not all vocational paths are open to all people; our options are shaped by our socio-economic location, access to education, degree of political freedom, and a whole range of attributes determined by personal identity, by membership in certain groups, and even by matters as mundane as geography and demographics.

Thus, given that our range of vocational options is so highly dependent on our specific cultural context, the authors of this volume considered it important to analyze the conditions under which vocational reflection and discernment occur. These include, first of all, the broad shape of our economic and political culture, and especially the degree to which that culture depends upon providing us with an ever-expanding range of choices. To the extent that we have absorbed this central cultural reality into our lives, we are likely to think about our vocations largely in terms of choices that we make as individuals, thereby eliding the importance of other people, larger communities, and other significant forces that give shape to, and partially determine, the apparently free choices that we make. These cultural forces are, of course, present within higher education as well; and in that context, they take on a somewhat different shape. Thus, the various forms of vocational reflection that occur within academic institutions should be undertaken with close attention to that cultural context as well. And of course, within that context, the students who are listening for their callings and discerning their vocations have been shaped in significant ways by the rapidly changing cultural norms of the past two decades; these elements cannot be ignored, if we are to understand the nature and significance of the vocational reflection that takes place at colleges and universities today.

The following essays wrestle with these issues. Among the questions that they ask, and that readers will want to bear in mind as they read, are these:

- What are the most important cultural forces shaping today's undergraduate students?
- How do the assumptions of undergraduates differ from those of the two generations that preceded them into college, which now account for most of their teachers at these institutions?
- To what degree do today's students assume that they have a great deal of autonomy in determining their own futures, and that there will be a fairly direct correlation between the choices they make and the lives they will live?
- How have recent trends in higher education—particularly those related to funding mechanisms, academic specialization, curriculum design, and the use of technology—changed the background against which vocational discernment occurs?
- To what degree is the range of vocational options available to today's students expanded or contracted as a result of economic, political, educational, and sociological forces, often global in character, that are beyond their control?
- How can educators take all these factors into account when they seek to teach students about vocational reflection and to help students listen for, and respond to, their various callings?

The authors of these three essays—and indeed, all the contributors to this book as a whole—are convinced that academic institutions will be able to support the work of vocational reflection and discernment on their campuses only if they develop a capacity to read the signs of the times. Colleges and universities need to undertake deep conversations about the cultural context that has formed their students, so that their leaders can understand how that context shapes the range of callings that students can truly hear, and to which they can energetically and imaginatively respond.

*I*

# *Actually, You* Can't *Be Anything You Want (And It's a Good Thing, Too)*

*William T. Cavanaugh*

THE FOLLOWING QUOTATION is attributed to Abraham Lincoln: "You can be anything you want to be, do anything you set out to accomplish, if you hold to that desire with singleness of purpose." This message is constantly reinforced in education and entertainment directed at children. Disney movies often rely on a formula in which an anthropomorphized panda or plane or rat or monster or car believes in himself, overcomes his limitations and the restrictions of society, and fulfills his wildest dreams.[1] The protagonist along the way learns contempt for the unimaginative drudgery to which the majority of society remains captive; self-fulfillment is privileged over the common good. A disparagement of routine labor is accompanied by a disregard for hard work and the development of good habits. As Luke Epplin's recent article in *The Atlantic* puts it, "Turbo and Dusty"— the protagonists of the animated movies *Turbo* and *Planes*—"don't need to hone their craft for years in minor-league circuits like their racing peers presumably did. It's enough for them simply to show up with no experience at the world's most competitive races, dig deep within themselves, and out-believe their opponents."[2] Customs, community, rules, habituation—all are ignored in favor of spontaneous gratification of one's wants.

---

1. I use male pronouns here because in most cases (but not always), the character is male.

2. Luke Epplin, "You Can Do *Anything*: Must Every Kids' Movie Reinforce the Cult of Self-Esteem?," *The Atlantic*, August 13, 2013.

What happens when young adults who have been marinated in this type of cultural messaging come to the range of questions surrounding vocation? They are often told not only that they can and must *choose* their life, but that they must maximize that choice and choose their *best* life. Furthermore, the choice of their best life consists of knowing what they want and then seeking to attain what they want. It is no wonder that many young adults find this demand paralyzing. How many times has panic flashed across the face of a student confronted by the seemingly innocent question, "What would you like to do when you graduate?" Many, no doubt, suspect that what Abraham Lincoln and Dusty the animated airplane say is simply not true: you actually *can't* be whatever you want to be. But even if they accept some realistic limitations on the fulfillments of their wants, the deeper problem remains: do they even *know* what they want? How does anyone really know what kind of life one wants? Can people choose what sorts of lives are right for them before they have lived enough to know? The whole exercise of *choosing* one's vocation becomes fraught with anxiety.

Of course, this problem is not simply "the way life has always been"; rather, it has much to do with the peculiar type of economy and culture in which we live. Vocation must be understood against the cultural backdrop in which students are situated; in Western culture, vocation language has tended to center on individual choice. This chapter will offer a brief genealogy of some of the economic aspects of the problem of vocation to show that how we think about work and wants has changed. It will then examine some of the dynamics of choice in our culture. The chapter will conclude with a discussion of some resources for helping us think and act differently with regard to vocational reflection and discernment.

## *The social division of labor*

Sociologist Max Weber famously claimed that the way we think about vocation is integrally entwined with the rise of capitalism. Weber was right about this, but not necessarily for the reasons he offered. He argued that the rise of capitalism was facilitated in part by the Protestant development of the notion of a "calling" or vocation in one's everyday life.[3] Weber contended that there was a significant shift from the medieval

---

3. This development was mentioned briefly in the Introduction to this book; it will be taken up again in more detail in chapter 4.

Catholic view, which associated God's call paradigmatically with the otherworldliness of monastic life, and the Reformation's emphasis on responding to God within the context of one's station in life, no matter how mundane. As Weber writes, "The effect of the Reformation as such was only that, as compared with the Catholic attitude, the moral emphasis on and the religious sanction of organized worldly labour in a calling was mightily increased."[4] With the elimination of the Catholic sacramental system in Protestant Europe, says Weber, the "magical" means of attaining God's grace was eliminated; this motivated the search for God's blessing in the success that one found in commerce and industry.[5] Here the Calvinist doctrine of predestination played a crucial role, but rather than encouraging resignation to fate or faith in God's sovereignty, Weber thought it produced an anxiety about whether or not one was chosen—an anxiety worked out through ceaseless activity, which was taken as a sign that God was busily overcoming sloth and idleness in one's life. Thus was born what Weber called a "worldly asceticism," whereby hard work, frugal living, saving, and investing were given spiritual sanction.[6]

## Economics and theology intertwined

Even those who question Weber's famous thesis begin the story of the development of vocation at roughly the same time as the development of capitalism. Catholic theologian Edward Hahnenberg's excellent book on vocation begins with the Reformation and credits the Protestant reformers with discovering the notion that the call to holiness extends to all people—laity included—and to all aspects of human life, even the most mundane and tedious jobs that must be done.[7] Martin Luther thought of vocation as being called to one's stations (in German, *Stände*) in life, and such stations were generally fixed. The Puritans, however, introduced

---

4. Max Weber, *The Protestant Ethic and the Spirit of Capitalism*, trans. Talcott Parsons (New York: Charles Scribner's Sons, 1958), 83. Weber's view of the medieval period here is an overly broad caricature. The medieval guild system, for example, certainly fostered a strong link between one's worldly work and one's spiritual life.

5. Weber, *Protestant Ethic*, 105–6.

6. Weber, *Protestant Ethic*, 95–183.

7. Edward P. Hahnenberg, *Awakening Vocation: A Theology of Christian Call* (Collegeville, MN: Liturgical Press, 2010), 5–27.

the idea that "every person must *choose* a calling,"[8] one that most cru-cially enables the man (*sic*) to support himself and his family. Puritans and Anglicans over the course of the seventeenth century contrasted the notion of vocation with the supposed idleness of medieval Catholic monasticism. Talk of vocation among Protestant writers and preachers was permeated by emphasis on productivity, and there arose a whole Christian literature distinguishing the "deserving poor" who were unable to work due to illness, age, and disability, from the "idle poor," who *were* able to work but chose not to.[9] The former were to be given Christian char-ity, the latter condemned and punished. "Vocation" became synonymous with "employment" or "work." The result, as Hahnenberg puts it, is that "The sacred and secular split apart and vocation landed on the side of the secular."[10] God became increasingly superfluous to the notion of vocation as one's own choice took the place of God's calling.

Tracing the idea of vocation through the writings of the Reformers is interesting and important, but it can be misleading if it is done in isola-tion from a consideration of the actual economic conditions of the time. The notion that stations in life were relatively fixed was not just an idea that Martin Luther had; it was a reality of medieval life that carried over into early modernity. Men generally did what their fathers did, which for the majority was subsistence farming. Women generally married nei-ther above nor below their station. The exception to this general reality for both men and women was the choice to enter religious life, which is perhaps why the language of vocation was tied to becoming a nun, priest, monk, or brother. Unless she were royalty, joining a religious order was generally the one chance a woman had of becoming a public figure.

Likewise, the notion of "choosing" one's line of work was not simply a brainstorm that occurred between the ears of Puritan thinkers; it marked a major shift in the economic reality of developing capitalist economies. The industrial revolution meant the massive displacement of people from subsistence farming and craft industries to large factories. We tend to nar-rate this movement as a positive liberation of people from the narrow bonds of a life over which they had very little individual control. And for a certain

---

8. Hahnenberg, *Awakening Vocation*, 21.

9. Hahnenberg, *Awakening Vocation*, 20–22.

10. Hahnenberg, *Awakening Vocation*, 23.

class of people, it was indeed a liberation. As a middle-class American, I enjoy tremendous freedom of choice that my ancestors in Ireland did not; I am glad that I am not trying to scratch out a living from a small plot of potatoes. Still, this economic liberation (in connection with which our modern discourse of vocation developed[11]) has a negative side—one that is rarely mentioned in the literature on vocation. Examining these shadowy, unacknowledged realities can help us understand why the choices that young people face today, when reflecting on vocation, might not always be experienced as liberation.

## Forced into choice

People today are free to pursue the various lines of work that they choose because the development of capitalism required the existence of a large class of laborers—freed from ties to the land—who could work in factories. Capitalists supplied the means of production (machinery, raw materials, and networks of distribution) and collected the profits. Laborers, who no longer owned land or small cottage industries, had nothing to sell but their labor—which they did, for wages. Why would a person choose factory work over subsistence farming? We tend to assume that they did so freely, looking for an improvement in income or an escape from the boredom and stasis of rural life. The truth, however, is that the separation of capitalists from wage laborers in the early modern period was accomplished with deliberate and shocking brutality. Coercion was necessary because no sensible person would voluntarily exchange a life of dignified subsistence for the dehumanization of the factory.

Subsistence farming was the occupation of the majority in England until the industrial revolution, and it was made possible by the existence of common lands. In historian Joan Thirsk's words,

> people had to work together amicably, to agree upon crop rotations, stints of common pasture, the upkeep and improvement of their grazings and meadows, the clearing of the ditches, the fencing of the fields. They toiled side by side in the fields, and they walked

---

11. I am trying here to avoid causal language in either direction. I think it is misleading both to say that theological ideas caused the economic conditions and to say that economic conditions caused the theological ideas. The best we can do is to recognize their mutual influence, and try not to lose focus on either theology or economics.

together from field to village, from farm to heath, morning, afternoon and evening. They all depended on common resources for their fuel, for bedding, and fodder for their stock, and by pooling so many of the necessities of livelihood they were disciplined from early youth to submit to the rules and customs of the community.[12]

Common lands were common by custom, not belonging to anyone by legal title. Beginning in the sixteenth century and carrying on into the nineteenth, common lands were "enclosed" or privatized. This happened in many ways, with legal sanction and without. In many cases, nobles simply declared a piece of land to be theirs and met any resistance with armed force. In the Scottish Highlands, the heads of traditional clans began to think of themselves as owners of the clan's land, and drove off thousands of small tenant farmers by force in order to convert the land into sheep pastures. The Duchess of Sutherland evicted thousands of families from their ancestral lands between 1811 and 1820. On seeing many of her former tenants starve, she wrote to a friend in England that "Scotch people are of a happier constitution and do not fatten like the larger breed of animals."[13] In other cases, a Bill of Enclosure was issued by the House of Lords. Where outright fraud was absent, common lands were distributed to landowners in the area in proportion to the amount of land they already possessed. Those who did not already own land were excluded, and enclosure was often ruinous for small landowners as well. Even if they could afford the legal fees and fencing required by the Bill, they usually found that their small plot of land could not support a family without access to common pastures and woods. For many, their only remaining choice was to sell the land and find wage labor.

Two other sets of laws were instrumental in driving people off the land and into the factories. The Game Laws punished attempts to find food on property to which one did not have title; the severity of these laws increased over the course of the eighteenth century. Poachers were executed under the infamous Waltham Black Acts of 1722. A large proportion of those

---

12. Joan Thirsk, "Enclosing and Engrossing" in *The Agrarian History of England and Wales*, vol. 4, ed. Joan Thirsk (Cambridge: Cambridge University Press, 1967), quoted in Michael Perelman, *The Invention of Capitalism: Classical Political Economy and the Secret History of Primitive Accumulation* (Durham, NC: Duke University Press, 2000), 13.

13. Quoted in Janet Hilderly, *Mrs. Catherine Gladstone: 'A Woman Not Quite of Her Time'* (Sussex: Sussex Academic Press, 2013), 191.

exiled to Australia had been convicted of poaching. What seems like a minor offense to us was a matter of survival for rural people accustomed to feeding their families from the produce of the land. As a journalist wrote in 1826, it was "difficult to make an uneducated man appreciate the sanctity of private property in game [when] . . . the produce of a single night's poach was often more than the wages for several weeks' work."[14] Once traditional subsistence was made difficult, laws were enacted to ensure that people newly "liberated" from the land would not find other ways to avoid wage labor. Another set of laws was enacted against vagrancy; a typical 1572 law in England required flogging and branding for beggars over the age of fourteen. Repeat offenders over eighteen were to be executed if no one would take them into indentured servitude.[15] Classical political economists were at one with Puritan theorists of vocation in waging a war on the "idle poor." The great theorist of liberty John Locke recommended starting work at the age of three. Adam Smith's teacher Francis Hutcheson wrote that "Sloth should be punished by temporary servitude *at least.*"[16] Jeremy Bentham recommended that children be put to work at age four instead of fourteen, so to avoid those "ten precious years in which nothing is done! Nothing for industry! Nothing for improvement, moral or intellectual!"[17]

All of these measures were undertaken in the name of "modernization" and "improvement." Sheep replaced people on common lands because wool was needed to feed the growing Midlands clothing factories, and subsistence farming was seen as inefficient and not contributing to economic growth and national wealth. Most crucially, however, capitalism needed labor that is "free" to work for wages. As one observer in 1815 put it:

> Poverty is that state and condition in society where the individual has no surplus labor in store, or, in other words, no property or means of subsistence but what is derived from the constant exercise of industry in the various occupations of life. Poverty is therefore a most necessary and indispensable ingredient in society, without

---

14. Quoted in Perelman, *Invention of Capitalism*, 43.

15. Perelman, *Invention of Capitalism*, 14.

16. Francis Hutcheson, quoted in Perelman, *Invention of Capitalism*, 16, emphasis in the original.

17. Jeremy Bentham, quoted in Perelman, *Invention of Capitalism*, 22.

which nations and communities could not exist in a state of civilization. It is the lot of man. *It is the source of wealth,* since without poverty, there could be no labour; there could be *no riches, no refinement, no comfort,* and no benefit to those who may be possessed of wealth.[18]

The process by which some come to "be possessed of wealth," and others own nothing but their labor, is known as "primitive accumulation." Karl Marx famously wrote that we think about this process through the lens of the theological notion of original sin. We tend to think that, way back in the misty past, some people were hard-working and frugal and others were lazy and dissolute; the former became the owners of capital, the latter were relegated to work for others. In actual historical fact, however, the process of primitive accumulation is, as Michael Perelman writes, "an uninterrupted story of coercion."[19] That story is not limited to England and Scotland, but played out similarly on the Continent and especially wherever colonization took place—including the *encomienda* system in Latin America, the theft of Native lands in North America, and the use of African slaves. Nor is primitive accumulation a long-ago phenomenon that characterized only the early modern period.[20] Fred Pearce's 2012 book *The Land Grabbers* documents the ongoing efforts of governments, corporations, and wealthy individuals around the world to push subsistence farmers off their plots and into wage labor, enclose common lands, and convert them into large-scale agribusinesses—again, always in the name of efficiency and modernization, and usually with devastating effects.[21] The destruction of small-scale farming in the United States took place over the course of the twentieth century, and was in significant part due to deliberate government policies that favored large-scale agriculture as more "efficient." Similarly, the home has ceased to be a place of production and is now almost exclusively a place of consumption. Such basic

---

18. Patrick Colquhoun, quoted in Perelman, *Invention of Capitalism*, 23.

19. Perelman, *Invention of Captialism*, 15.

20. Thomas Piketty's much-discussed book *Capital in the Twenty-First Century* (Cambridge, MA: Belknap Press, 2014) shows how massive inequalities continue to be endemic in our economic system and are bound to get worse, barring decisive political action.

21. Fred Pearce, *The Land Grabbers: The New Fight Over Who Owns the Earth* (Boston: Beacon Press, 2012).

measures of self-sufficiency as preparing one's own food and raising one's own children have declined precipitously, as employment outside the home has come to occupy more of the average person's day. This in turn often compels people to spend their wages on prepared food, childcare, and many other services they once provided for themselves.[22]

In sum, then, the modern notion of vocation and the rise of capitalism were intertwined, but not only in the way that Weber thought they were. True, one's vocation was no longer given; it became a choice. Ironically, however, this "freedom" developed as a result of an enormously coercive process by which wage labor replaced self-sufficiency. The result, of course, has had tremendous benefits, at least for the winners in the process. The abundance and availability of material goods has reached undreamed of levels in developed economies. Millions have been pulled out of poverty. Individuals have escaped the limitations of local cultures, and for those with access to good education there is an enormous range of different kinds of employment from which to choose.

At the same time, however, as efficiency has replaced self-sufficiency, people entering the market feel increasingly at the mercy of larger forces that are beyond their comprehension and control. People seeking employment must try to conform to the ever-shifting demands of the job market. American colleges prospered on the promise of providing graduates a ticket to the managerial classes, but the opportunity to work in a cubicle is no longer guaranteed. Even when it is achieved, it is not always experienced as liberation; it is certainly not an automatic ticket into the ownership class. The role of the managerial class is still instrumental; its role is to produce wealth for shareholders, the ownership class. As a result, the notion of vocation can become a rather lonely and anxiety-producing business. Individuals who have successfully negotiated the educational system are thrust out onto the job market with the expectation that they must invent their own lives without traditional markers of identity and custom. This marks an enormous change in the way human beings relate to one another. As Thirsk notes, "Common fields and pastures kept alive a vigorous co-operative spirit in the community; enclosures starved it. . . . [E]very household became an island unto itself."[23] The argument here is not that we should attempt to go back in time or that we would necessarily be better off without enclosure. The point

---

22. Perelman, *Invention of Capitalism*, 34–35.

23. Joan Thirsk, "Enclosing and Engrossing," quoted in Perelman, *Invention of Capitalism*, 13.

is simply that enclosure happened, and we must deal with the consequences, both positive and negative.

## *The tyranny of choice*

Choice was created by coercion, and it can also be experienced as coercive. Psychology professor Barry Schwartz has explored this theme in detail and concluded that choice is not to be equated simply with freedom. Having some choice is essential to freedom, but as choices proliferate—"You can do anything!"—they can be experienced as coercive rather than liberating.

Schwartz begins his analysis by surveying the range of choices open to consumers today. His local supermarket offers 285 varieties of cookies, 360 types of shampoo, 230 kinds of soup, 175 different salad dressings, and so on. The electronics store has 110 different models of television; with cable one can watch hundreds of channels. Modern universities— "intellectual shopping malls," as Schwartz puts it—have often jettisoned common curricula in favor of student choice from among a bewildering variety of unrelated courses. "There is no attempt to teach people how they should live, for who is to say what a good life is?"[24] In keeping with the mall motif, dining halls at universities now resemble food courts, with a tremendous variety of options. Beyond stores and universities, we choose our electricity supplier, phone provider, stocks for our retirement plan, religious affiliation, even our own face and body (there are one million cosmetic surgeries in the U.S. each year).[25] Work is a choice as well, and that choice is not made only once. The "dynamism" of the global economy demands a flexible workforce. People must be (and therefore are) willing to change jobs and change cities with increasing frequency. As Schwartz notes, this "means that the questions 'Where should I work?' and 'What kind of work should I do?' are never resolved. . . . The Microsoft ad that asks us 'Where do you want to go today?' is not just about web surfing."[26]

With all of these choices open to us, we would expect to be happier, but Schwartz points out that that is not the case. By every major indicator—the doubling of the divorce rate since 1960, the tripling of the teen suicide

24. Barry Schwartz, *The Paradox of Choice* (New York: Ecco, 2004), 15. For more on this point, see chapter 7 and all three chapters of Part Three (chapters 8–10).

25. Schwartz, *Paradox of Choice*, 9–34.

26. Schwartz, *Paradox of Choice*, 36.

rate and the quintupling of the prison population in the same period, the tenfold increase in clinical depression since 1900, to name a few—more choice has not coincided with more happiness.[27] Schwartz offers a variety of reasons for thinking that more choice actually contributes to unhappiness. We have to devote enormous resources of time to sorting through the various choices before us. The stakes of our choices are thus increased, and we experience anxiety because we often lack the resources to separate good from less good choices. Even worse, the ideology of choice insists that we should strive to make not simply a *good* choice, but the *best possible* choice.

## Maximizers and satisficers

Schwartz and other psychologists use the term "maximizer" to describe the person who tries to live up to this ideal of the sovereign chooser by making the optimal choice from the range of options. The ideal is a corollary of the notion that having more choices is always better; as choice expands, some *even better* options may come into play, thus increasing the range of candidates for the "best" possible choice. Maximizers do not stop looking for a sweater or a job when they find one they like; there is always one more store or one more website they need to check to make sure that they don't settle for second best. The term "satisficer" is used to describe those who stop looking when they find what they were seeking. Maximizers are much less happy with life than satisficers, not because they make worse choices—after all, the maximizer might well end up getting a better deal on the same sweater—but because they can never be satisfied with the choices they make. Maximizers fantasize about living someone else's life, because the *best* life is always out of reach.[28]

The problem is not simply that we are limited in getting what we want; the problem is that we are limited in *knowing* what we want. Economic theory typically asserts that consumers are rational choosers who seek to maximize the fulfillment of their own wants; this claim, however, is increasingly questioned by psychologists. We base choices on previous experiences, but experiments have shown that people tend to judge their experiences in retrospect based disproportionately on how the experiences

---

27. Schwartz, *Paradox of Choice*, 108–9.

28. Schwartz, *Paradox of Choice*, 77–89.

felt at their peak (either best or worst) and how they felt at the end.[29] In addition, as Harvard psychologist Daniel Gilbert and his team have discovered, people are very bad at predicting how a future experience will impact their lives. We consistently overestimate how happy a positive choice—a new car, a new job, or a bigger house—will make us, and how long that happiness will last; this is called "impact bias." We likewise adapt more quickly to bad things that happen to us than we can predict. We get used to things, adjust to them, and start taking them for granted.[30] The proliferation of choices makes the problem of adaptation worse by increasing the amount of time and effort required to make a decision; if agonizing over a decision for months produced long-lasting results, that difficult process might be seen as worth the time and effort required, but such positive results are rarely forthcoming.[31] Moreover, evidence suggests that we are constantly surprised by our ability to adapt. We seem unable to anticipate adaptation and prepare for it. And so most people in our society stay on the "hedonic treadmill"; they continue to pursue novelty, new products, and new experiences—all of which promise happiness but inevitably disappoint.[32] Advertising and other kinds of cultural messaging exacerbate the problem by promising that we can exceed our limits and be anything we want to be.

## Bad decisions and anticipated regret

Psychologists have suggested that, among other factors that adversely affect our ability to make rational choices, we suffer from an "empathy gap": the inability to predict how we will behave in "hot" emotional states when we are in a "cold" state. We not only make bad decisions when we are in the heat of the moment, but we cannot consistently predict that we will do so and guard against the consequences.[33] When combined with the impact bias, we end up making all kinds of choices, small and large, that we will inevitably regret. Why did I think that working eighty hours a

---

29. Schwartz, *Paradox of Choice*, 48–51.

30. Jon Gertner, "The Futile Pursuit of Happiness," *New York Times Magazine*, September 7, 2003, 44–47+; here, 46.

31. Schwartz, *Paradox of Choice*, 176–77.

32. Schwartz, *Paradox of Choice*, 172–73.

33. Gertner, "Futile Pursuit," 86.

week at a law firm to earn more money would make me happy? Why did I think that taking a job far from my family would be a good idea? "You know, the Stones said, 'You can't always get what you want,'" says Gilbert. "I don't think that's the problem. The problem is you can't always know what you want."[34]

Regret occurs only when people feel sole responsibility for their choices; it is impossible to regret decisions other people have made. Regret also depends on a person being able to imagine a counterfactual alternative that might have been better. As Schwartz points out, the availability of more choices exacerbates both of these conditions. More choices would seem to increase one's chances that a good option is out there; given enough effort, a person should be able to find it. When a choice proves disappointing or when the impact bias kicks in, we regret retrospectively. We can have "buyer's remorse" over a past decision, becoming convinced that some option we rejected would have been better (or imagining there are options out there that we have not yet encountered).

The proliferation of choices also produces what is called "anticipated regret," in which we already despair of our inability to make the right choice before the choice is even made. Anticipated regret is worse; it not only produces dissatisfaction, but can also affect decisions currently in process. Both types of regret raise the emotional stakes of decisions (i.e., they produce more "hot" emotional states). Anticipated regret in particular can produce paralysis, the inability to make a decision. People can put off choosing a major or a career, or making a commitment to a partner or spouse, because the stakes are just too high.[35] Anticipated regret can also have an undue influence on any decisions that are actually made. To use Schwartz's example, "If you're trying to decide whether to buy a Toyota Camry or a Honda Accord and your closest friend just bought an Accord, you're likely to buy one too, partly because the only way to avoid the information that you made a mistake is to buy what your friend bought and thus avoid potentially painful comparisons."[36] This applies not only to decisions about material purchases but all sorts of major life choices.

---

34. Daniel Gilbert, quoted in Gertner, "Futile Pursuit," 46.

35. Schwartz, *Paradox of Choice*, 147–64.

36. Schwartz, *Paradox of Choice*, 158–59.

One proposed solution to the problem of regret is to try to ensure that all choices are reversible. Leaving our options open would seem to guarantee that we never experience serious regret. If we can bring our purchase back to the store and get our money back, then regret can always be fixed. But life does not work this way. Not only are the time, effort, and money invested in major choices (like college and career and marriage and children) nonrefundable, but leaving options open actually makes the problem of regret worse. If a decision is irreversible, we can stop thinking about it and get on with other things. If, on the other hand, we are always open to the possibility of dumping a spouse for another person, switching majors or jobs, or moving to another city, then we will always be considering the possibility that our choice of spouse or major or job or house was a mistake—or at least not the best decision we could have made. Our culture's ideology of choice is blind to this problem and thus makes it worse. We are constantly told that having more choices makes us happier; the more options open to us, the greater our freedom. But the opposite may often in fact be the case; for example, married people who consider their marriages reversible are less satisfied with their marriages than those who consider their vows irreversible.[37]

## Implications for vocation

Any examination of the question of vocation requires taking a serious and critical look at the cultural context in which people are asked to discern their calling. Particularly when the word *vocation* is used without nuance, it can sometimes lead to a focus on individual choice. Since choices have proliferated in the modern era due to a massive restructuring of economy and society, the ideology of choice has spread as well. As we have seen, this ideology considers individuals to be rational choosers who benefit from the proliferation of choices; the more choices we have, the better chance we have of choosing our best life.

The preceding analysis should give us reason to question this ideology, which will in turn have significant implications for how we think about vocational reflection and discernment. Admittedly, for those with access to good education and other resources, our society offers tremendous opportunities to live a good life. Innovation is often a good, and some

---

37. Schwartz, *Paradox of Choice*, 144–46.

choice is of course necessary and beneficial for human flourishing. As we will observe in chapter 3, constraints on choice due to race and gender and class are experienced as dehumanizing. The problems surrounding the matter of choice should not be used as an excuse to oppress others by artificially limiting their choices.

Still, we need to understand clearly why young people do not always experience the proliferation of choice as liberating. People who are in a position to make choices are often paralyzed by the choices they face. Which one of dozens of majors and thousands of careers is the right one for me? Where in the world should I live? Am I called to be married, and if so, who among millions is the right person for me? Given the mobility and flexibility of families, many young people cannot even count on family obligations to narrow down their options. The book *Quarterlife Crisis: The Unique Challenges of Life in Your Twenties* captures, through interviews, the anxieties of young people raised in a world where everything is up for grabs.[38] They experience intense self-doubt, in part because they are on their own when making decisions. In a world of individualized choosers, they have become convinced that, if their decisions disappoint, they will have no one to blame but themselves.[39]

## *Responses and resources*

There is no point to romanticizing the past or trying to recreate a lost world. Still, we can point to a number of resources—philosophical, literary, and theological—that can be of tremendous help when thinking about the process of vocational discernment under the cultural conditions of the present time. I will first discuss resources for making good choices, and then discuss resources for accepting the choices we have made.

### The limitations of human beings

The first and most important resource is a realistic assessment of human limits. You cannot be anything you want. This does not sound at first like

---

38. Alexandra Robbins and Abby Wilner, *Quarterlife Crisis: The Unique Challenges of Life in Your Twenties* (New York: Putnam, 2001); see the reference to this book in Schwartz, *Paradox of Choice*, 142.

39. Schwartz, *Paradox of Choice*, 211.

good news, and it poses a challenge for the marketing of our colleges and universities to prospective students. But it can be experienced by students as liberating, and it has the added advantage of being true. One of the most fundamental claims of Christianity, Judaism, and Islam is the notion that we are not God. This is established in the scriptures of all three faiths, wherein humans are created by God and therefore dependent on God for our being (Genesis 1 in the Hebrew Tanakh and Christian Old Testament; Sura 2:30–34 in the Qur'an). This dependency is not understood to be a problem or a burden; indeed, having one God instead of many seems to be *the solution* to a problem. Many scholars believe Genesis 1 to have been written in response to the Babylonian creation myth *Enuma Elish*, in which creation results from a war among the gods. In contrast, all creation, including humans, is declared repeatedly in Genesis 1 to be good, and humans are created to live in harmony with God and with the rest of creation. Being finite creatures of a good God is not a fallen condition; the fall occurs precisely when humans rebel against their limitations. They are tempted precisely by the (false) claim that if they eat of the tree, they "will be like God" (Gen. 3:5) or "become angels or such beings as live forever" (Sura 7:30).[40] The havoc that ensues shows how fruitless is any attempt to escape dependence on God and interdependence with other people, how self-deceptive it is to live as though one were self-sufficient. One need not consider these scriptural stories to be historical or scientific accounts of human origins in order to find here a compelling diagnosis of the human drama.

The human actors in these accounts are able to rebel because they are enough like God to have freedom. Like a child with a Chinese finger trap, however, the more they struggle to be free, the more they find themselves bound. They falsely imagine that freedom means being free from God, being the source of their own being. Sin and evil enter the world as a result of the freedom to choose to do what is against God's will. As Augustine explains, however, this type of freedom to choose anything at all, even what is bad, is not a strength but a weakness.[41] In an argument against the Pelagians, Augustine describes the freedom to do evil by using the

---

40. Here and throughout the book, unless otherwise noted, all biblical quotations are taken from the New Revised Standard Version. All quotations from the Qur'an are taken from the 1985 Saudi revision of the translation by Abullah Usuf Ali.

41. St. Augustine, *Confessions*, trans. Henry Chadwick (Oxford: Oxford University Press, 1991), 199 [X.xxiii.(33)].

metaphors of "slavery" and "sickness"—which, he notes, are hardly compatible with genuine freedom of choice.[42] True freedom, for Augustine, is not sheer indeterminacy; it is the fulfillment of what one is called to be.

In contrast, many current definitions of freedom are purely negative: freedom is defined as freedom from limits. In this sense, a heroin addict is free to shoot heroin if no one prevents him or her from doing so. Most people would recognize that this is not true freedom; they might in fact describe it using Augustine's language of weakness, sickness, or slavery to the drug. Negative freedom is a necessary ingredient for true freedom, but it is not sufficient. A positive account of freedom would define it as the ability to achieve a good goal. It is not enough to have negative freedom; it is not enough that, for example, no one is stopping you from playing the piano. Positive freedom is also necessary; you must learn how to play the piano, which requires a decision to pursue a particular goal, along with hours of practice to develop the necessary habits so that one's fingers move without thinking.

Augustine's intuitions on desire are remarkably similar to the findings of Schwartz, Gilbert, and other psychologists: the presence of more choices does not in itself make a person free, in part because people are not very good at knowing what they really want. Augustine describes this as a multiplicity within the self; in the *Confessions* he narrates the "struggle of myself against myself."[43] "I was neither wholly willing nor wholly unwilling. So I was in conflict with myself and was dissociated from myself."[44] Augustine intuits what true freedom might be, but finds himself unfree to choose it precisely because of the choices—*free* choices—that he has made. "I sighed after such freedom, but was bound not by an iron imposed by anyone else but by the iron of my own choice." Augustine explains the formation of this chain in this manner:

> By servitude to passion, habit is formed, and habit to which there
> is no resistance becomes necessity. By these links, as it were, connected to one another (hence my term, *a chain*), a harsh bondage

---

42. St. Augustine, *The Spirit and the Letter*, §52 in *Augustine: Later Works*, ed. John Burnaby (Philadelphia: Westminster Press, 1955), 236.

43. Augustine, *Confessions*, 152 [VIII.xi.(27)].

44. Augustine, *Confessions*, 148 [VIII.x.(22)]. The Latin translated here as "dissociated" is *dissipabar*, which suggests dispersal, scattering, or even squandering; other translations offer "fragmenting myself."

held me under restraint. The new will, which was beginning to be within me a will to serve you freely and to enjoy you, God, the only sure source of pleasure, was not yet strong enough to conquer my older will, which had the strength of old habit.[45]

For Augustine, sheer indeterminacy is not simply a bad way to live; it is impossible. Our choices inevitably dig a groove called habit, and habits color every choice we make. As Schwartz and Gilbert also recognize, the human person is never simply the sovereign consumer who stands back, surveys the options, and decides *ex nihilo* what path to take. The human person is a complex battleground of warring desires, and choices are constrained by human weakness and social forces that buffet the person from within and from without.

## Developing good habits

How does one find stability and vocation in such a conflicted condition? The goal cannot be to reject habit and seek indeterminacy. As we will see in chapter 8, habit is a way of relieving us from the burden of having to make choices. When we develop good habits—Thomas Aquinas called them "virtues"—we don't even need to spend time thinking about whether we might steal or commit adultery. For the person who has gotten into the habit of not doing these things, they rarely even come to mind. Habits are the way we achieve what is commonly called a "self," that is, the stable collection of characteristics that define a person. The nature of the self, and the moral world that it inhabits, is therefore not so much about *decisions* as it is about *formation*. If a person is well-formed in the virtues, then action will come naturally, and without the anguished and groundless deliberation that characterizes choice in the absence of any ground for choosing. The process might be compared to trying to walk on ice: a smooth surface that allows one to "go anywhere" is also one where falling and injury is likely, but habit digs a groove in the ice to give the walker some traction. Admittedly, our habits limit our options; but if they are good habits, they also make it possible to achieve the options that really matter.[46]

---

45. Augustine, *Confessions*, 140 [VIII.v.(10)].

46. For more on this point, see the reflections in Part Three, chapters 8–10.

The real question, then, is how to cultivate good habits. To distinguish good habits (virtues) from bad habits (vices), there must be a way of distinguishing good goals from bad goals. This requires that we come to know ourselves, and to orient ourselves toward some goal that is truly worth pursuing.[47] Given the ever-expanding range of choices and our relative lack of knowledge about them, our ultimate goals will need to be based on something other than subjective preference. Schwartz and Gilbert do not explain *why* humans are so bad at knowing themselves and orienting themselves toward good goals. Such explanations are offered by many faith traditions as a kind of estrangement from God, which they typically understand to be an estrangement from one's own self as well. For example, although Augustine says "I find my own self hard to grasp,"[48] he also says that God is "closer to me than I am to myself" (*interior intimo meo*).[49] The healing of our weakness depends on recognizing the source of our being outside of ourselves, but this source is simultaneously within us; we find ourselves precisely by finding God. Thus, vocation is both a call from outside the self that draws one outside the confines of the small self and it is also, at the same time, a discovery of our deepest desires and our true self.[50]

## The role of the community

Learning to desire rightly is not merely an individual endeavor. Just as learning the piano is facilitated by a teacher, so the acquisition of virtue requires the guidance of people who have already mastered those virtues. The isolation felt by the individual chooser in a modern context can only be overcome by acknowledging the ways that our vocations are not simply a subjective choice, but a response to a call that comes from outside ourselves. The call is mediated by professors and pastors and friends who let individuals know that their lives belong, in some significant way,

---

47. This point will be explored in some detail in chapter 7.

48. Augustine, *Confessions*, 193 [X.xvi.(25)].

49. Augustine, *Confessions*, 43 [III.vi.(11)]. Henry Chadwick's translation renders the passage rather woodenly as "more inward than my most inward part"; the translation offered here, using the word *closer*, attempts to capture some of the resonance between the Latin *intimo* and the English *intimate*.

50. An inquiry into the source of vocation is the primary focus of chapter 6.

to others who expect and need the individual to give his or her talents in a particular way. In a university context, for example, students may need less "Do anything you want!" from their professors and counselors; they may need more "You don't seem happy with your major. Have you ever considered majoring in x?" Ultimately, the call is not merely a lifestyle choice; it evolves through an encounter with objective realities. Some of these realities will likely take the form of obstacles, and some of these obstacles will not be surmountable simply by believing that we can be anything we want. Moreover, discerning one's calling is a communal effort; it must involve the wisdom of others to break through the confines of the individual self. Churches can be this kind of community; so can colleges and universities. Indeed, one of the reasons for sending students to college is that they might enter into a community where what is being proffered by their professors and other mentors and friends is not only *knowledge*, but *wisdom*.

Vocational discernment, then, not only *involves* others; these others need to help us *limit* our choices. We need others to tell us what we can give to the world, which is a quite different question from what will give us pleasure. We need families to make demands upon us, to limit the places that we will consider living. We need to prepare one another for suffering, for running up against limitations, for caring for a special-needs child decade after decade. We need to make commitments to one another that are not reversible. Marriage vows and religious vows are closely linked to the question of vocation precisely because they move in the opposite direction of the common logic of choice. Making a unilateral and binding commitment to another cuts off a whole range of choices. But as Schwartz observes, "what seems to contribute most to happiness binds us rather than liberates us."[51] As we have already observed, such binding actually wards off rather than encourages regret.

## Telling our vocational stories rightly

Yet even when we enter into vocational discernment in a communal context and attentive to our own limitations, the next step is of equal importance. Rather than focusing only on whether we have made the "right" choices, we need to learn to narrate the choices we have made in the light

---

51. Schwartz, *Paradox of Choice*, 108.

of our beliefs. What is perhaps most crucial is not so much making the right choices, but telling the story of our choices rightly. We will examine these stories in greater detail in chapters 5 and 7; meanwhile, however, we can encourage a step in this direction by noting the advantages of being a "satisficer" rather than a "maximizer." To be clear, being a satisficer is not the same as being lazy or weak, or accepting mediocrity; it is knowing what you want and stopping when you get it. This includes learning to accept "good enough" rather than judging our choices on the basis of what is "best." Even "good enough," however, is put in a different light when it is written as part of a larger story, which for many may mean: God's story. Vocational discernment is not just a matter of choosing well enough, but accepting the life you have; and this means learning to identify, retrospectively, the path that you did in fact choose as the right one. It may not be true that you can be anything you want to be, but you may find instead that you have become the person that you are called to be, even if you would not have chosen your life out of all the possibilities (had you even known what they were).

We must be careful here, because some choices are wrong choices, and we need others to help us discern when we need to repent and change. To tell the story of one's faults and failings and disappointments as "God's will" can also be turned into a resignation to cruel fate. The point is not at all to give up one's agency and become passive before events beyond our control. Rather than simply accept the hand that fate has dealt us—"I should have married someone else or chosen a different career, but now I'm stuck with it, by God's will"—the idea is to recognize that our story is *unfinished*, and to hold to this view until we transform what we have been given from fate into destiny. As Samuel Wells puts it, "one says, 'How can this gift be understood or used in a faithful way? What does the way we accept this gift say about the kind of people we are and want to be? What can (or has) this gift become in the kingdom of God?"[52] This is what Wells, borrowing a theatrical term, calls "overaccepting," which he defines as "accepting in the light of a larger story."[53] Wells illustrates this idea with a number of illustrations from improvisational theater, in which actors need to find ways of incorporating new ideas into a storyline that is already

---

52. Samuel Wells, *Improvisation: The Drama of Christian Ethics* (Grand Rapids, MI: Brazos Press, 2004), 130.

53. Wells, *Improvisation*, 131.

in progress. He also uses the image of a concert pianist who is interrupted by a child who begins banging on the keyboard. Rather than either having the child removed, or simply letting the child make noise, the pianist puts her hands around the child's on the keyboard and begins to play music that weaves the child's discordant notes into a larger, harmonious whole.

One need not simply resign oneself to fate; nor must one refuse it and try vainly to assert one's negative freedom to choose. Rather, one can try to discern what God, like the concert pianist, is doing with one's life; one can ask how one's life might contribute to, and fit into, the much larger story of the world. A Christian, for example, seeks to interpret the fog of his or her own imperfect individual decisions through the lens of the much larger story of God's creation and redemption of the world through the community known as Christ's body. Or, to return to the theatrical analogy, what I am describing involves seeing one's life ultimately as a comedy, not a tragedy; we are thereby relieved of the terrifying burden of imagining that we are alone responsible for our fates, that we need to make the best possible choices in order for our lives to come out "right."[54]

We cannot be anything we want, in part because we cannot know what we want. We are not sovereign rational choosers but fragmented selves. Our hope is that, in the crucible of our encounters with others, the fragments of our lives will be gathered up and used to tell a story that is broader, more nuanced, and much more interesting.

---

54. See the further reflections on "vocational humility" at the end of chapter 6.

## 2

## *Finding the Center as Things Fly Apart*

VOCATION AND THE COMMON GOOD

*Cynthia A. Wells*

COLLEGE LIFE TENDS to generate certain quintessential images. Admissions brochures prominently feature an engaging faculty member surrounded by a small group of students on a lush green lawn. Faculty members envision spending hours concentrating on research and guiding students through deep reading of consequential texts. Educators evoke portraits of students raising and pondering "big questions" about the meaning of life. Alumni recall studying together in the library and late-night conversations in the residence halls. The collegiate ideal is a perennial image that speaks to higher education's capacity to encourage contemplation and build relationships, to invite deep questions and create space for attentive response.

Of course, anyone familiar with the current context of American higher education knows that new developments are crowding out these prototypical portraits. Students read assignments on their laptops, tablets, and smart phones rather than in printed books. They study "together," but this may take place in digital environments rather than in physical proximity. The image of the college student quietly reading and writing in a library contends with the picture of one who fits in only a few moments to study here and there between other pressing demands. The image of faculty and students on the well-manicured lawn has been replaced by the individual student sitting in front of a computer accessing education via a portal, the presence of a teacher merely implied. These increasingly prevalent images have led many to wonder whether broader goals, such as the contemplation of purpose and the cultivation of relationships, are no longer matters of priority.

We must avoid the tendency to superimpose collegiate images from days past upon the realities of college in the present. At the same time, we cannot allow the particularities of the present to block our view of the longstanding and enduring promise of higher education. This moment in time calls for deeper attention, both to the phenomenal potential of colleges and universities to address questions of meaning and purpose, and to the pressures that these institutions feel as the realities of the contemporary world impinge upon them. Thankfully, the language of *vocation* and *calling* provides us with a way of attending to matters of institutional purpose that takes into account our particular place and time.

A context-specific interpretation of vocation is well articulated by Edward Hahnenberg, who draws on Karl Barth to argue that vocation involves responding as a "unique creation placed by God in a particular time, at a particular place, and gifted with particular abilities, disabilities, experiences, and associations."[1] Clearly, vocation is a matter of identity; it pays attention to *who* we are. In addition, vocation is lived out as a distinctive response to the particular context in which we find ourselves; it is heavily influenced by *where* we are. As we engage the idea of vocation in higher education, we need to address complex questions of identity among colleges and universities, even as we attend to the gifts and challenges posed by our time and our social context.

This chapter will suggest that, among the many purposes of colleges and universities, the call to *educate for the common good* stands out as particularly important. After an exploration of this claim, the chapter then examines the higher education landscape in our time, emphasizing how present realities impinge upon the ability of colleges and universities to fulfill this element of their collective mission. In particular, we will observe the *centrifugal* tendencies of our current context, in which the central focus of higher education seems to be spinning out in every direction. The third section argues that the language of vocational exploration and discernment can address some of these tendencies, thereby

---

1. Hahnenberg, *Awakening Vocation*, 119 (see chap. 1, note 7 *supra*).

helping us to re-imagine this central focus in ways that are attentive to the importance of educating for the common good. A concluding section examines two exemplary initiatives that have been implemented by specific institutions—initiatives that seek to create an environment in which vocational exploration and discernment can prosper, and to do so in ways that contribute to each institution's particular mission and purpose.

## Education for the common good

Higher education has a rich and dynamic purpose that flows from its identity and history and is grounded in its particular gifts and relationships. Fulfilling this purpose hinges upon colleges and universities realizing their distinct call to educate for the common good—a vision that undergirds and connects their commitment to the flourishing of individuals and of society as a whole.[2]

### The origins of the language

The notion of the common good is embedded in the Hebrew scriptures, and especially in the prophets. Jeremiah urged the Israelites to "seek the welfare of the city where I have sent you into exile, and pray to the LORD on its behalf, for in its welfare you will find your welfare" (Jer. 29:7). Jeremiah counsels the exiles from Jerusalem to care for the foreign land into which they have been displaced. Not only that: he implores them to recognize that their own well-being is interdependent with that of their place of exile. Similarly, after the exiles return from Babylon to the destroyed city of Jerusalem, Nehemiah gathers them and rouses them to action: "You see the trouble we are in, how Jerusalem lies in ruins with its gates burned. Come, let us rebuild the wall of Jerusalem, so that we may no longer suffer disgrace" (Neh. 2:17). When they agree to start building, he describes them as having "committed themselves to the *common good*" (Neh. 2:18, emphasis added).

Much of the current literature on colleges and universities suggests that higher education, like Jerusalem, is in ruins. Admittedly, higher

---

2. In the literature, the language of *common good* is sometimes employed as a synonym for *public good*; this parallel, however, would seem to align *common* with *public*, as though it were the antithesis to a "private" or "personal" sphere. This chapter's use of the term *common good* is meant to denote a region where individual and community goods overlap.

education does face many challenges (some of which will be discussed later in this chapter); yet it also holds great potential to attend to the common good, which emphasizes that the flourishing of each individual human being is inextricably linked to the thriving of others. In this light, the very nature of higher education—as responsible to both personal and social well-being—makes it an ideal locus for attending to the common good. By exploring and making use of the capacity of colleges and universities to educate for the common good, we can, like Nehemiah and his listeners, renew our own commitment to this important work.

From their earliest beginnings in the United States, colleges (and, later, universities) have nurtured the development of individual gifts while also seeking the good of the society.[3] Upon their arrival in the New World, the colonists quickly sought to found colleges in order to establish and distinctly shape a new society by educating people with the character of the desired society in mind.[4] The charters of the colonial colleges laid out a vision for educating young men for professions including, but also beyond, the "ministry" and "public officials."[5] This vision was grounded in an effort to "qualify a governing elite" in order to carry forward the society they were founding.[6] College served to prepare individuals for meaningful work but also functioned as "part of a large, important social, religious, and political vision."[7]

This interconnection has remained evident as higher education's history has unfolded. In a prominent report of the mid-twentieth century, *General Education in a Free Society*, a Harvard University committee

---

3. It is important to acknowledge here that the colonists' vision of leadership was limited by the focus on European white males. The view of Native Americans as "savages" is evident in many of the early charters and indicative of this limited and inhumane vision. In describing this early connection between individual and society as an asset, I do not mean to gloss over this particular failure in the way that connection was made manifest.

4. Frederick Rudolph, *Curriculum: A History of the American Undergraduate Course of Study since 1636* (San Francisco: Jossey-Bass, 1977); Frederick Rudolph, *The American College and University: A History*, rev. ed. (Athens, GA and London: University of Georgia Press, 1990); Richard Hofstadter and Wilson Smith, *American Higher Education: A Documentary History* (Chicago: University of Chicago Press, 1961).

5. John S. Brubacher and Willis Rudy, *Higher Education in Transition: A History of American Colleges and Universities*, 4th ed. (New Brunswick: Transaction Publishers, 1997), 6

6. Rudolph, *Curriculum*, 28.

7. John R. Thelin, *A History of American Higher Education*, 2nd ed. (Baltimore: Johns Hopkins University Press, 2011), 23.

wrestled with the meaning and purpose of undergraduate education against the moral backdrop of World War II.[8] The committee reaffirmed the interrelated ideals that undergraduate education was important for social relations in a democratic society as well as for individual preparation for occupation. The committee contended that the purpose of general education was to serve as the element of a "student's whole education which looks first of all to his life as a responsible human being and citizen."[9] This broad preparation was coupled with elements of undergraduate education that attend to the "student's competence in some occupation."[10] The committee was emphatic that these "two sides of life are not entirely separable, and it would be false to imagine education for the one as quite distinct from education for the other."[11] Education for individual advancement was thereby affirmed as inextricably bound to the needs of the society.

In a more recent example, The National Task Force on Civic Learning and Democratic Engagement argues in its report, *A Crucible Moment*, that civic learning must be a priority for "all of higher education" and that the betterment of the future of our society depends upon it.[12] The authors maintain that "if human beings hope to maintain and develop a particular type of society, they must develop and maintain the particular type of education system conducive to it."[13] *A Crucible Moment* argues for infusing a "civic ethos" into campus culture by cultivating civic knowledge, integrating "civic inquiry" into majors and general education, and cultivating capacity and commitment for "civic action."[14] Toward these ends, the authors argue that higher education requires both the "fullest preparation for economic success" and "education for citizenship."[15] Education

---

8. Harvard University, *General Education in a Free Society; Report of the Harvard Committee*, 15th printing (1945; Cambridge, MA: Harvard University Press, 1955).

9. Harvard, *General Education*, 51.

10. Harvard, *General Education*, 51.

11. Harvard, *General Education*, 51–52

12. National Task Force on Civic Learning and Democratic Engagement, *A Crucible Moment: College Learning and Democracy's Future, A National Call to Action* (Washington, DC: Association of American Colleges and Universities, 2012), 2.

13. Ira Harkavy, cited in National Task Force, *Crucible Moment*, 25.

14. National Task Force, *Crucible Moment*, 15.

15. National Task Force, *Crucible Moment*, 10.

for self and community are thus reaffirmed as mutually important and inseparable.[16]

These examples remind us that, particularly in the American context, higher education has intended (and has been expected) to be a positive influence on both societal and individual well-being. Moreover, merely by virtue of the large number of people who experience higher education, colleges and universities are granted a powerful ability to shape contemporary culture.[17] Still, the influence of colleges and universities cannot be measured solely by the sheer number of people they touch; what matters most is their social and cultural impact, to which we now turn.

## Expectations for higher education

First, with regard to individual flourishing, higher education has been tasked with *preparing emerging adults for meaningful work and service.* This involves helping them find meaning and purpose in their work and in their lives, not only for their specific occupation, but on a broader scale as well. Undergraduate students discern and develop individual talents, but fulfilling higher education's purpose requires more than simply amassing a sufficient range of individual gifts; they need to be understood as serving a purpose beyond the self.

Second, higher education has been entrusted with positively *influencing the character of society.* Colleges and universities wield a tremendous influence on society and its mores, infrastructure, and direction. They are not only tasked with preparing graduates with adequate knowledge, but also with the social and cultural development of students. The unique potential of a college education to help society flourish is an essential gift that undergirds higher education's role in establishing and promoting the common good.

Third, higher education has also been distinctively vested with *orienting emerging adults to the realities of the world.* Higher education serves as a "vital expression of vocation" in our contemporary context insofar as it is charged with the responsibility of "initiating young lives into a

---

16. See the further discussion of this point in the reflections on community engagement in chapter 13.

17. Sixty-six percent (66.2%) of 2012 high school graduates were enrolled in colleges or universities the fall following their graduation. U.S. Bureau of Labor Statistics, *College Enrollment and Work Activity*, 2013.

responsible apprehension, first of the realities and questions of a vast and mysterious universe, and second of our fitting participation in it."[18] Colleges and universities provide students with a way of understanding the world, so that they might see their own capacities and passions in light of their interdependent relationship with others. Higher education has inherited the responsibility to orient emerging adults into the realities of the world, and to help them acquire a sense of full and meaningful participation in that world.

In sum, to advance the commitment of educating for the common good, colleges and universities must help students connect their individual talents to the areas of our world that are broken and in need of those talents. Moreover, the common good—embedded as it is with commitments to individual and social flourishing—is not static. As Reinhold Niebuhr suggested, "each century originates a new complexity and each generation faces a new vexation in addressing the problem of our 'aggregate existence.' "[19] Advancing the common good depends upon seeing and responding to our shared realities in all their complexity.

## *Shared realities that shape higher education*

We are in a time of radical change and considerable disquiet in American higher education, in which dynamic and consequential transformations are fully in motion.[20] Even among those skeptical about whether this era marks some kind of fundamental revolution, urgent concerns are being raised regarding the contribution of higher education to individuals and to society. This section fleshes out the particularities that shape our context and considers their potential impact.

As a governing metaphor for the social realities that we face, we might describe the forces that dominate higher education as *centrifugal* rather

---

18. Sharon Daloz Parks, *Big Questions, Worthy Dreams: Mentoring Emerging Adults in Their Search for Meaning, Purpose, and Faith*, rev. ed. (San Francisco: Jossey-Bass, 2011), 16.

19. Reinhold Niebuhr, *Moral Man and Immoral Society: A Study in Ethics and Politics* (1932; New York: Scribner, 1960), 1.

20. Bobby Fong, "General Education: Connecting to Issues of Vital Importance—For Students, For Society," Keynote Address, Association of American Colleges and Universities, February 2013, unpublished manuscript; Jeff Selingo, *College (Un)bound: The Future of Higher Education and What It Means for Students* (Boston: New Harvest, 2013); Mark C. Taylor, *Crisis on Campus: A Bold Plan for Reforming Our Colleges and Universities* (New York: Alfred A. Knopf, 2010).

than centripetal: these forces create a tendency for things to fly apart in all directions, instead of referencing (and being oriented toward) a center.[21] Centrifugal forces work against the kinds of integrative work needed to educate for a "common good." Attending to our present context requires that we recognize these centrifugal forces and respond in ways that take these tendencies into account. The goal of the present section is to name and describe some of the centrifugal forces that higher education faces; in the section that follows, we will consider how a focus on vocational exploration and discernment might address some of these realities.

## The digital revolution

Among the social realities about which concern is most frequently voiced, the digital revolution is often identified as a disruptor to higher education's greater purposes. What, if anything, do we lose when learning becomes, at least in part, a "virtual" enterprise? Can knowledge be divorced from the contexts in which it is generated, and can learning be disengaged from the relationships that have traditionally constituted it? Certain elements of online learning change the nature of the relationships between students and faculty, as well as those among students. It is more difficult to communicate meaning when words on a screen are detached from the facial expressions and intonations that accompany face-to-face communication. Online forums provide avenues for shared discussion, but the contributions to the dialogue arrive piecemeal over time, rather than in the context of a shared classroom conversation. Learning online, in some fashion, decouples the educational process; students gain credentials, but without the embodied relationships and experiences that these credentials traditionally comprise.

The digital transition is one illustration of a broader obstacle that faces the academy: the tension between generations. Andrew Delbanco notes that "one of the peculiarities of the teaching life is that every year the teacher gets older while the students stay the same age."[22] It is indeed a

---

21. The language of "centrifugal forces" has been used with respect to higher education by a wide variety of voices. See, inter alia, Lynne Cheney, *50 Hours: A Core Curriculum for College Students* (Washington, DC: National Endowment for the Humanities, 1989); Andrew Delbanco, *College: What It Was, Is, and Should Be* (Princeton, NJ: Princeton University Press, 2012); Taylor, *Crisis on Campus*.

22. Delbanco, *College*, 9.

quirk of the academy that the past generation is perpetually responsible for educating the current one. This situation is fraught with tension, for the educators are forever one or more generations (and one or more sets of social realities) behind those being educated.

Of course, some of the most dramatic generational changes in the academic world have been technological ones. Summarizing the individual and organizational challenges associated with this transformation, Arthur Levine and Diane Dean put the matter bluntly: a generation of "digital natives . . . are being taught by digital immigrants in analog universities."[23] Students want more technology, and they want their faculty to adopt it effectively; faculty not only struggle to adopt technology (given that, for most, it is a "second language" at best), but also distrust the impact of technology on education in a way that often befuddles their students (since for students, technology simply *is*). The digital divide is therefore also a generational rift.

## Fiscal uncertainties

The range and impact of the digital revolution and its accompanying generational divide accelerates amid the fiscal challenges facing higher education. These challenges are real and coupled with a growing sense among many that accruing high levels of debt for college is no longer sensible.[24] We need to be cautious, however, about any overly simplistic attempts to determine a college education's "return-on-investment"— particularly when this is measured in terms of starting salary or other narrow monetary terms.[25] Should undergraduates really be pointed toward

---

23. Arthur Levine and Diane R. Dean, *Generation on a Tightrope: A Portrait of Today's College Student* (San Francisco: Jossey-Bass, 2013), 49.

24. Measurements of the educational debt of college graduates are fraught with complexity and often challenged in the literature. See, inter alia, Matthew Reed and Debbie Cochrane, *Student Debt and the Class of 2012* (Oakland and Washington, DC: The Institute on College Access and Success, 2013), http://www.ticas.org/files/pub/classof2012.pdf (accessed December 31, 2013); S. Georgia Nugent, "What Do We Talk About When We Talk About College Debt?" *The Huffington Post*, October 1, 2014, http://www.huffingtonpost.com/s-georgia-nugent/what-do-we-talk-about-whe_b_5909416.html (accessed November 5, 2014).

25. Various organizations have launched campaigns designed to help college students (and their parents) to think in broader terms about college affordability. See, inter alia, the Council of Independent College's "Power of Liberal Arts" website, http://www.liberalartspower.org/passion/afford/Pages/default.aspx (accessed November 5, 2014).

majors such as engineering or business, and directed away from history or music, for financial reasons alone? It is really wise, in the long run, to steer students away from their passions and inclinations, simply because they don't promise a sufficient monetary pay-off? Such approaches pay little attention to the particular ways of understanding the world that have dominated those fields and professions that are less well compensated in monetary terms. Needless to say, a business or engineering major may be ideal for some students; it may be precisely where their passions and inclinations lie. However, if such fields are pursued only for their perceived economic security, something very important is lost.

The cultural conversation on the value of higher education in our current context has grown myopic in its focus on economic outcomes, particularly those financial benefits *to the individual*.[26] The question as to whether college is worth the significant investment of time and money is an important one;[27] in the process, however, the full value of a college education can be skewed. In particular, an excessive focus on economic utility has too often displaced attention to broader questions of meaning and purpose that include, but also transcend, one's future occupation and earning potential.[28]

The vast majority of students place a higher premium on the employment-related outcomes of a college education than on the process of education itself. In fact, the percentage of incoming first-year students citing "to be able to get a better job" as a very important reason for attending college recently reached an all-time high.[29] This myopia is not limited to students. A recent poll suggested that gaining "skills and knowledge for a career" far outweighed gaining a "well-rounded general education"

---

26. Frank Donoghue, *The Last Professors: The Corporate University and the Fate of the Humanities* (New York: Fordham University Press, 2008), xiii.

27. William J. Bennett and David Wilezol, *Is College Worth It?* (Nashville: Thomas Nelson, 2013); Selingo, *College (Un)bound*.

28. Philip Eaton, *Engaging the Culture, Changing the World: the Christian University in a Post-Christian World* (Downers Grove, IL: IVP Academic, 2011); Anthony T. Kronman, *Education's End: Why Our Colleges and Universities Have Given Up on the Meaning of Life* (New Haven, CT and London: Yale University Press, 2007).

29. In 2012, this percentage was 87.9%, which is up from 67% in 1976. Kevin Eagan et al., *The American Freshman: National Norms Fall 2012* (Los Angeles: Higher Education Research Institute, 2013), 4. In 2013, this percentage showed a slight decline to 86.3%. Kevin Eagan et al., *The American Freshman: National Norms Fall 2013* (Los Angeles: Higher Education Research Institute, 2014), 35.

as a goal of higher education, not only among the general population, but also among college leaders.[30] Preparing graduates for employment is crucial, but not to the point that we neglect the longstanding commitment of higher education to nurture a sense of purpose and social responsibility.

## Specialization and silos

The current emphasis on individualistic economic indicators intersects with a longstanding trajectory toward greater specialization in higher education. This confluence poses a particular challenge for the advancement of integrated, holistic learning. The current academic culture both favors and furthers specialization; in particular, the "cultivation of increasingly specialized, mutually unintelligible languages" in increasingly specialized academic departments undermines the "ability of educated citizens to live in a common symbolic universe."[31] Faculty members on the same campus have a difficult time finding common educational ground. Students' educational experiences across campus are so divergent that conversation about texts or ideas is thwarted beyond those who share a major. We lack a common vocabulary that serves as a basis for integrative questions of meaning.

Historical developments in the undergraduate curriculum illustrate how the overemphasis on specialization has often crowded out more integrative goals. The widely adopted "distribution model" of general education exemplifies this reality, inasmuch as it allows individual academic departments to teach specialized content and have it "fit" within a model of general education. In this curricular design, students choose from a menu of courses created and taught by academic departments. This effectively introduces students to a variety of academic subjects, but falls short in helping students find connections across areas of knowledge. In fact, the only thread of integration across these distribution requirements is too often *the student,* who is sometimes expected to make sense of the connections without much help or guidance. The predominant idea that

---

30. Amanda Ripley, "College is Dead. Long Live College!" *Time Magazine* 180, no. 18 (October 29, 2012): 33–41; here, 41.

31. Donald Nathan Levine, *Powers of the Mind: The Reinvention of Liberal Learning in America* (Chicago: University of Chicago Press, 2006), 27.

general education is accomplished solely by being "distributed" is compelling evidence on its own that undergraduate education has been drawn away from a center.

Further evidence for disintegration can be found in the split between those responsible for classroom learning and those attending to out-of-class or co-curricular education. Specialization in the academy has not only perpetuated the development of disconnected academic silos;[32] it has also separated the people responsible for students' intellectual development—the teaching faculty—from those attending to social, emotional, and spiritual development.[33] Alongside the proliferation of increasingly specialized academic departments, specialists have arisen in spiritual formation, residential education, community service, and leadership development (and, for that matter, in vocational discernment!). What should be interconnected facets of the student—knowing, acting, feeling, and believing—have become separate tasks of increasingly specialized campus offices. The structure of the academy complicates the holistic formation of persons.

The concerns regarding overspecialization extend beyond internal critiques of educational coherence to the skeptical question in the public realm as to whether an overspecialized academy delivers the education necessary for success in the contemporary context. A growing "skills gap" has been attributed to the misalignment between college curricula designed to achieve discrete content knowledge and workplace needs for employees capable of collaboration and innovation.[34] Employers have voiced a need for graduates who are capable of teamwork and problem-solving, in addition to applying technical knowledge.[35] The college's aim should be to foster graduates who have *both* technical expertise *and* higher-order innovative capacities. In short, there is simply much more to be learned; and yet the pressures are also strong for institutions to take less time to accomplish this work.

---

32. Taylor, *Crisis on Campus*.

33. Julie Reuben, *The Making of the Modern University: Intellectual Transformation and the Marginalization of Morality* (Chicago: University of Chicago Press, 1996).

34. Economic Intelligence Unit, *Closing the Skills Gap: Companies and Colleges Collaborating for Change*, http://www.luminafoundation.org/publications/Closing_the_skills_gap.pdf (accessed October 5, 2014).

35. Hart Research Associates, "It Takes More Than a Major: Employer Priorities for College Learning and Student Success," *Liberal Education* 99, no. 2 (Spring 2013): 22–29.

## The dis-integrated degree

Financial constraints force students to spend less time in and on college, or at least to experience a diffusion or fragmentation of their study time. Students are increasingly attending multiple institutions and achieving college credits through a plethora of options.[36] Advanced placement credits and dual enrollment between high school courses and college have proliferated, largely intended to speed up and reduce the cost of a college education. College students today spend increasing amounts of time in paid employment while completing their education.[37] They often attend multiple colleges en route to a degree;[38] hence, a student is rarely shaped exclusively by any single institution of higher education over the course of four years. Taken together, these fiscal forces pull students away from full engagement in their undergraduate education and compromise the ability of any single college to serve as a formative influence on students.

The impact of current fiscal realities is not limited to students' experiences, but also affects faculty roles. The increasing need for colleges to rely on less expensive educational delivery models has substantially increased demands on faculty and increased the number of adjunct and contingent faculty.[39] Full-time faculty are doing more amid pressing institutional demands, leaving little time to prepare for teaching and even less time to relate to students or to one other. The image of faculty with ample time to meet with and mentor students may be as outmoded as that of the full-time student with time to linger in conversation.

Adjunct faculty are even more overworked, often teaching at multiple institutions in order to make ends meet. These faculty may very well be

---

36. Selingo, *College (Un)bound*.

37. Among full-time undergraduate students, 18% reported working twenty to thirty-four hours per week and 6% reported working thirty-five hours or more per week. See Susan Aud, et al., *The Condition of Education 2013* (NCES 2013-037) (Washington, DC: U.S. Department of Education, National Center for Education Statistics, 2013), http://nces. ed.gov/pubs2013/2013037.pdf (accessed December 30, 2013).

38. Selingo, *College (Un)bound*, 2013.

39. Adrianna Kezar, Daniel Maxey, and Judith Eaton, *An Examination of the Changing Faculty: Ensuring Institutional Quality and Achieving Desired Student Learning Outcomes*, Occasional Paper, Council for Higher Education Accreditation, January 2014, http://www. uscrossier.org/pullias/wp-content/uploads/2014/01/CHEA_Examination_Changing_ Faculty_2013.pdf (accessed October 4, 2014).

excellent teachers, but the very nature of adjunct instruction disconnects classroom teaching from institutional mission. Adjuncts often do not have the opportunity to contextualize individual courses in light of departmental curricula or the larger whole of the curriculum and are often isolated from students and other educators. Overdependence on adjunct and contingent instructors raises serious concerns, since it sometimes results in teaching that is disengaged from an institution's mission and its fulfillment through more active educational relationships between students and faculty. In short, adjunct instruction delivers the "part," but unplugs it from the whole.

Taken together, these "centrifugal" forces mean that aspects of higher education tend to move out away from one another, losing their center and their focus. This situation has led some observers to stake a claim in the past, mourning what has been lost as curricular models and educational practices have adapted over time. Others have fixated on perceived crises of the present, frenetically reacting to shifts in our midst. A better path might be to avoid succumbing to both these temptations and instead to try to pull the past and the present together. How can higher education attend to the successes of its past while reaping the benefits that may be hidden within the new realities that we face today? How might it resist the tendency for all the pieces to fly apart and perhaps recover a sense of "educating for the common good" at its core? In essence, we need to find a *centripetal* force that effectively mitigates the many *centrifugal* ones that we now face.

## *Higher education and the promise of vocation*

Fortunately, many of these pressing challenges can be addressed by greater attention to the work of vocational exploration and discernment. What is it about the language of vocation that facilitates this process? What does it mean to bring the language of vocation into the educational process for students and faculty? What does paying attention to vocation do for an institution? While these questions will only be adequately addressed by the work of this volume as a whole, it may be worth laying out some of the broad characteristics of vocational reflection. Three of these elements—vocation's enduring, mission-oriented, and holistic dimensions—suggest that it may well offer the kind of centripetal force that higher education needs in the present moment.

## Vocation is enduring

Simply put, vocation is not a fad. The language of vocation is as long-standing as education itself; its rich and dynamic history feeds its lasting quality and provides it with a wide relevance. As already noted in this volume (and as will be examined more thoroughly in chapter 4), vocation was once used narrowly to reference a very specific call to the priesthood or a religious order. Centuries later, vocation began to be used to refer to particular preparation for paid employment. While this inheritance might seem confusing at first, it can also contribute to the richness of the concept—inasmuch as vocation expanded to include nonreligious contexts but never lost its theological significance. Precisely because vocation applies to both spiritual calling and paid work—that is, both to broader queries of meaning and to specific career preparation—it can serve as an integrative concept for higher education in the present.

By way of illustration: vocation's enduring quality helps us remain attentive to the positive elements of specialization, even while serving as something of an antidote to some of its unintended consequences. After all, the problem facing higher education is not academic specialization per se, but rather those forms of it that go unmediated by integrative elements. Without specialized knowledge, higher education would not be able to fulfill its call to address the very pressing challenges facing our world today. Nevertheless, specialization without attentiveness to integrative questions of ethics and meaning would fail to faithfully address the technically complex but also fundamentally human dimensions of the world's deepest needs.

The language of vocation honors what is valuable in specialization while also stretching the concept in new directions. Rather than simply lamenting an overemphasis on specialization (particularly as this manifests itself in an excessive focus on the major field of study), vocational reflection encourages us to affirm the major while also opening it up to integrative questions. The notion of the "enriched major," an idea grounded in the work of Ernest L. Boyer and highlighted recently by Arthur Levine and Diane Dean, illustrates the way in which vocational queries can both affirm and faithfully stretch specialization.[40] The enriched major points to the importance of seeing educational fulfillment as more than

---

40. Ernest L. Boyer, *College: The Undergraduate Experience in America* (New York: Harper & Row, 1987); Levine and Dean, *Generation on a Tightrope*.

simply the knowledge of particular content and the expertise associated with an academic discipline. Knowledge of the discipline must be mindful of larger ethical concerns and challenges to which the discipline can attend: "What are the social and economic implications to be pursued? What are the ethical and moral issues within the specialty that need to be confronted?"[41] From this perspective, specific fields of study—as well as the professions—are given a broader purview through reflection on a more diverse range of issues. The advantages of specialization are maintained, even as commitments to questions about meaning and purpose are nurtured. One gift of vocation lies in its ability to affirm disciplinary expertise but also to situate knowledge within larger purposes. This brings us to a second characteristic of vocation—its ability to serve as a guiding principle.

## Vocation is attentive to mission

Vocation serves as an orienting principle that keeps us moving in the right direction even amid rapid change; it offers a north star that helps us navigate a frenetic educational environment. The fast pace of technological change tempts us to get lost in the immediate. The fiscal challenges facing higher education place more and more demands on the time of students and educators alike. For students, the culturally dictated overemphasis on employment as a college outcome often leads to viewing general education as an unnecessary and even annoying hurdle. For educators, the pressing demands of the twenty-first-century academy can lead to viewing the daily tasks of academia as distractions and disruptions. In the midst of these challenges, the language of vocation—which necessarily reminds us to give adequate attentive to the big picture—helps us to see how such apparently small matters as advising students, developing syllabi, and even participating in committee meetings can contribute to the whole. It thereby enables us to recognize how that larger whole can influence students and advance an institution's mission. In a manner of speaking, vocation asks us to "get out of ourselves," yet without ignoring the valued contribution that individuals make to shared goals.

Being attentive to vocation helps us to address, in a generative way, the concerns often raised about the excessive individualism evidenced in

---

41. Boyer, *College: The Undergraduate Experience*, 290.

colleges and universities. As noted above, higher education has clearly inherited an overemphasis on the individual; nevertheless, we should not ignore the ways that individual outcomes can be crucial. William Frame demonstrates that vocation facilitates the exploration of individual interests but places them in a shared context of social responsibility.[42] A robust pedagogy of vocation can accept the individualism that higher education has inherited and understand it as a new beginning point, rather than a fundamental hindrance to an authentic education. Indeed, a rich understanding of vocation takes the contemporary focus on the individual and opens it out to the "other."[43]

This expansive perspective is evident in Ernest L. Boyer's vision for undergraduate education. Boyer's work repeatedly raises questions about the balance between individual and communal outcomes for higher education without diminishing the importance of either. Boyer fully understood the challenges facing higher education in the late twentieth century, given its longstanding tendency to focus on the *parts* rather than the whole. His work effectively frames what it means to consider *individual* outcomes, but simultaneously to open them up to a *communal* perspective. Boyer's body of work suggests that undergraduates should wrestle with questions of identity, purpose, and community, and underscores the importance of significant questions such as "Who am I? What is the purpose of life? What are my obligations to others; what are theirs to me?"[44] Identity is a crucial concern for students, but it is embedded in a larger network of mutual responsibility. This prompts us to consider a third strength of vocation for our time and place: its attention to the whole person.

## Vocation is holistic

Vocation stakes a claim on the whole of a person—affecting ways of knowing, being, and doing.[45] As such, vocation is attentive not only to

---

42. William Frame, *The American College Presidency as Vocation: Easing the Burden, Enhancing the Joy* (Abilene, TX: Abilene Christian University Press, 2013).

43. Hahnenberg, *Awakening Vocation*, 175.

44. Ernest L. Boyer, "General Education: The Integrated Core," text of speech delivered as the Academic Convocation Address at the University of San Francisco, April 11, 1988, Catalog No: 1000 0000 9298 (Mechanicsburg, PA, The Ernest L. Boyer, Sr. Archives Collection, 1988), 33.

45. See the comments on the work of Hahnenberg, *Awakening Vocation*, note 1 *supra*.

what we know but also to who we are and how we act. This formative claim of vocation applies not only to students but also to faculty and staff. Indeed, vocation is generative for the academy precisely because it applies to both those being educated and those influencing and delivering the education. Moreover, the language of vocation stakes a claim not only on individuals within colleges and universities, but also on the institution itself—providing a means to pull together institutional structures, programs, and practices toward achieving shared aims. Vocational exploration and discernment can be embedded into the curriculum in general education and in the major; it can infuse career and academic advising. The language of vocation is similarly apropos for co-curricular education, in everything from residence hall programs to athletic team philosophy to chapel programs.[46] Moreover, vocation can serve as an avenue to pull these disparate parts of the institution together, creating space for relationships across apparent divides. On the whole, attention to vocation can address the disaggregation of the educational process that has occurred as a result of broader shifts in the academy.

Once again, Boyer's work helps to illustrate this vision for vocation. He surveyed a broad range of academic programs and campus offices, examining their contribution to institutional mission and suggesting how they might be redirected toward the greater fulfillment of that mission. Boyer emphasized the potential of the campus community *as a whole* to be educationally purposeful.[47] Moreover, he believed that the ideals of general education could and should be fulfilled in both the curriculum and the co-curriculum.[48] His work sought to expand and enrich our understanding of faculty scholarship in a manner that returned our attention to the ways that each form of academic work contributes to institutional mission.[49] Boyer's body of work reminds us that effective undergraduate

46. See the discussion of the importance of co-curricular conversations around vocation in chapter 11.

47. Carnegie Foundation for the Advancement of Teaching, *Campus Life: In Search of Community*, Special report, with a Foreword by Ernest L. Boyer (Lawrenceville, NJ: Princeton University Press, 1990).

48. Ernest L. Boyer and Arthur Levine, *A Quest for Common Learning: The Aims of General Education* (Washington, DC: The Carnegie Foundation for the Advancement of Teaching, 1981).

49. Ernest L. Boyer, *Scholarship Reconsidered: Priorities of the Professoriate* (Princeton, NJ: Carnegie Foundation for the Advancement of Teaching, 1990).

education involves bringing together seemingly separate arenas of the college or university on behalf of shared educational purposes.

## Vocation and the common good

The language of vocation provides just the sort of generative catalyst the academy needs to rouse attention to the rich promise and deep potential of higher education amid the complex and pressing realities of our time and context. It is conceptually broad enough to lead the academy into new territory—to encourage faculty and students to see beyond the narrow confines in which their respective academic disciplines and professional aspirations have been situated. At the same time, its perspective is not so novel or so intense as to make genuine progress unattainable. The language of vocation offers us a renewed sense of focus, thereby counterbalancing the impact of higher education's centrifugal tendencies that have left us feeling unmoored, while still honoring the gifts inherent in those forces.

Commenting on the work of William Perkins, Gilbert Meilaender describes vocation as integrally related to the common good. Employing the language of Aristotelian causation in the discussion of vocation, he describes the common good as the "final cause," or ultimate purpose, of our callings.[50] In our own time and place, being attentive to vocation helps us to see and be attentive to the "good" we hold in common without neglecting the individual talents and strengths that compose that shared good. Moreover, vocation offers us a common vocabulary that influences how we both use our specific gifts and to recognize the strengths of others as avenues through which we can both *see* and *seek* a common good. Responding faithfully to our present challenges means recognizing the elements of change for what they are: compelling realities that must find their place within a larger pursuit of the college or university's mission.

Of course, it is one thing to theorize that vocation serves as a means to addressing the challenges facing higher education; it is quite another to bring its potential to fruition. In the following section, I will describe how particular institutions have engaged the theory and practice of vocational discernment to address specific institutional challenges.

---

50. Gilbert Meilaender, *Friendship: A Study in Theological Ethics* (Notre Dame, IN: University of Notre Dame Press, 1981), 90.

## *Vocation in practice*

How have colleges and universities integrated the language of vocation into their educational programs in a manner that illustrates its value? Accomplishing this task requires strategically embedding the institution's mission and identity into the curriculum and using these elements to develop an ethos of vocation on campus. The remainder of this chapter is focused on how two promising vocational formation strategies, the *common curriculum* and a *mentoring environment*, have been utilized in particular campus contexts to redirect momentum toward institutional mission.

## Establishing a common curriculum

The common curriculum can productively advance vocational formation in the current context of higher education. Constituting a modest subset of the curriculum that is shared by all students, a common curriculum aims neither to replace distribution requirements nor to negate or usurp the major. Rather, it seeks to develop spaces for integration—a connective network of relationships across the educational experience. The work of vocation can find its impetus in individual gifts, but its fulfillment comes in allowing people to see their gifts in light of communal aims. The common curriculum is one way that vocation can serve as a means of educational integration.

Dominican University, located in River Forest, Illinois, illustrates how the work of vocation can enable colleges to recontextualize specialized study within larger integrative aims. By adopting a common core curriculum, Dominican has abated the decentering impacts of disciplinary overspecialization by fostering connections that complement, rather than diminish, the strengths of specialized study. A series of small, intimate, vocation-themed courses allow students to consider consequential and communal concerns, to ponder life's big questions, and to make connections between coursework and personal experience. The developmental design of these seminars allows students to begin with questions of the self and the particulars of their major and then to progress outward to broader questions of communal concern. Moreover, these seminars occur across the four-year curriculum, thereby providing intentional space for students to consider integrative questions as they progress in their major courses.

Students choose from a variety of seminars that explore a common theme. First-year seminars focus on the "examined life," with course themes addressing a variety of perspectives on the notion of knowing oneself. Sophomore seminars examine "life in community" and consider issues facing local, national, and global communities. Junior seminars focus on "a life's work," building on questions of the self and community in a manner that engages students in a deeper understanding of work itself. Finally, senior seminars focus on "the good life," fostering an understanding of the virtues as requisite qualities for living out one's vocations in the world.[51] Thus, the seminars guide students to make connections, which in turn compel them to discern and ultimately to live out their callings.

As the common curriculum was designed and implemented, Dominican made an intentional effort to equip faculty to deliver its constituent courses in a way that would be more likely to achieve their intended vocational aims. One of the genuine challenges of an overspecialized academic culture is that faculty are often not prepared to ask integrative questions. An initiative titled "Contemplating Life's Callings" prepared faculty to integrate contemplative practices for the discernment of vocation within the learning experience. To achieve this goal, leaders provided seminar instructors with faculty development opportunities that highlighted the Dominican tradition of contemplation. These included a three-day retreat for thirty to forty faculty members, followed by regular meetings throughout the year to integrate strategies and understandings from the retreat into the seminars.

The common curriculum at Dominican University preserves and infuses its distinct institutional mission. Claire Noonan, Vice President for Ministry and Mission at Dominican, speaks to how the common curriculum addresses the present-day realities of higher education: "As the marketplace culture tends to press in, the common curriculum has been a place where we've staked our claim."[52] These interdisciplinary seminars are required for all students, offering a somewhat countercultural perspective in a consumer-driven world where "choice" usually reigns.[53] Each

---

51. The important role of the virtues in vocational exploration and discernment is taken up in Part Three of this book.

52. Claire Noonan, personal interview, 2014.

53. See chapter 1 for further reflections on the role of choice and its (sometimes debilitating) effects.

seminar year is structured with common texts, a shared theme, and guiding questions. Building from these shared elements, faculty members create courses that fit their particular interests. Commonality and integration thereby build upon, rather than negate, the individual interests of students and faculty.

Dominican University has used its vocational efforts to strengthen its own sense of institutional mission, built on the claim that the language of vocation means something particular in the Dominican context—namely, that "in order to be a vocational person, one must be contemplative."[54] As a result of these initiatives, faculty members have become more conversant about the practices of contemplation and have sometimes been able to add contemplative practices into the classroom.[55] Moreover, faculty members and students gain greater familiarity with specific vocational practices, thus providing a space for shared conversation.

Creating a shared experience across the curriculum is one means to build an ethos of vocation. A complementary strategy is to attend to the campus culture, not only within but also beyond the curriculum. This approach is evident in our next illustration.

## Building a mentoring environment

What does it mean to develop a mentoring environment? It means to shape the ethos of an institution in intentional ways around the values and ideals that the college or university has designated as central. A mentoring environment involves infusing institutional mission into campus culture. Furthermore, for students who experience college as a fracturing experience (with various aspects of their lives being attended to by different parts of the academy), the mentoring environment can bring these pieces back together again. It can serve to counterbalance those centrifugal forces that pull the campus apart, yet without requiring radical restructuring of campus infrastructure or added demands that can make this goal difficult to achieve.

While many colleges and universities have recognized the importance of mentoring at all levels (of students, faculty, staff, and administrators), the designation of one individual as another's mentor can sometimes have

---

54. Claire Noonan, personal interview, 2014.

55. Claire Noonan, personal interview, 2014.

the effect of contributing to a culture of individualism. Even though mentoring relationships bring two people together, the mentee is still often expected to listen to *one* voice. Focusing instead on the creation of a mentoring *environment* can address this drawback, as well as deepen the formative influence of mentoring. Sharon Daloz Parks argues that, while a single mentor is sufficient for initiating emerging adults into a profession *as it is,* only a mentoring *community* is adequate to orient emerging adults into a profession (and the society it serves) as they *could become.*[56] A mentoring environment creates an institutional ethos that invites students into the work of vocational exploration and discernment.

Goshen College offers one illustration of the value of nurturing a mentoring environment. In order to assess the campus climate as it related to faith mentoring, the college conducted campus surveys. Results indicated that students yearned to hear more from both teaching faculty and administrative faculty[57] regarding their faith journeys. Further, the survey results suggested that while faculty were open to sharing their faith stories, they often didn't know how to do so; nor were they certain about when such sharing was appropriate. Moreover, the notion of being a "faith-mentor" turned out to be a loaded term; many felt that it should be someone else's responsibility and expected that it would demand considerable time and expertise for which faculty and staff were not well prepared.[58] These findings helped shape Goshen's emphasis on equipping *all* college employees to see their specific forms of work as contributing to a mentoring environment for faith and vocation.

Grounded in a three-part framework of "knowing, being, and doing," Goshen's efforts represent a college-wide focus on an important vocational practice. The "knowing" element describes the aims and qualities of effective mentoring and the variety of ways and spaces in which "mentoring moments" take place. The "being" element affirms the conviction that effective mentoring is grounded in one's own meaning-making and faith formation. Finally, the "doing" component identifies a wide variety of practices, both inside and outside the classroom, that advance vocational formation.

---

56. Parks, *Big Questions, Worthy Dreams,* 174.

57. At Goshen College, "administrative faculty" refers to such positions as residence hall directors, coaches, and chaplains.

58. Bob Yoder, personal interview, March 20, 2014.

In addition to equipping faculty both to share their faith stories and to invite student reflections on theirs, Goshen expanded its network for mentoring. Student chaplains in the residence halls were established to shape the residential context toward vocational reflection. A session was added to new employee orientation to allow the campus chaplain to help all employees recognize their contributions to the mentoring environment. Finally, campus-wide communications, both print and digital, were developed to build some degree of common vocabulary across a faculty and employee base with a variety of religious perspectives, thus increasing institutional capacity for mentoring. By equipping college employees to share their own faith journeys in their existing contexts and within the bounds of their existing responsibilities, a more interconnected mentoring environment was brought into being.

The faculty at Goshen College discovered, crucially, that inviting educators to contribute to a mentoring environment does not need to add to the workload of already overburdened educators. Sharon Parks astutely notes the impact of institutional context in considering the educators' responses to invitations to contribute to mentoring programs: "Pressured by the demands of financially stressed institutions, many professionals understandably wilt when the call to mentorship is added to a long list of musts."[59] Asking individual educators to take on mentees in one-to-one relationships can be overwhelming, particularly when educators are already doing so much more with less. Bob Yoder, Goshen College's chaplain, reflects that a "mentoring environment frees us up as a community," in contrast to the extra work demanded by individualized mentoring: "In a world with too much to do," he continues, "the pressure of being a mentor is too much."[60] As an alternative, the notion of "a mentoring environment" helps educators recognize existing places and contexts as mentoring moments, an idea to which hard-working employees can be receptive, even within a frenetic and demanding context. Yoder observes that "the beauty of the mentoring environment is that it's not all on you, it's on the whole of the environment."[61] That environment comprises many things, including individual relationships, course assignments, and brief conversations on the sidewalk. By focusing on the mentoring qualities of the

---

59. Parks, *Big Questions, Worthy Dreams*, 174.

60. Bob Yoder, personal interview, March 20, 2014.

61. Bob Yoder, personal interview, March 20, 2014.

campus environment, Goshen's efforts have helped to renew the promise of vocation, helping educators both to recognize the ways they are contributing to the whole educational process, and to apprehend how that process impacts every student.

## *Vocation as the* vocation *of higher education*

Higher education leaders cannot eliminate digitization, generational divides, individualism, fiscal constraints, or overspecialization; nevertheless, they should seek to mitigate the ways in which these have functioned as centrifugal forces. Precisely because higher education has inherited the task of educating for the common good, it can make use of the theory and practice of vocation as a means of addressing some of the forces that threaten to pull it apart. Indeed, by developing a capacity for providing students with the time and space they need to explore and discern their vocations, higher education may be fulfilling one of its *own* essential vocations. When colleges and universities adequately consider not only their unique potential but also the real dynamics of disruption, they will be well on their way to living more fully into their particular callings. This in turn will further enable institutions of higher education to contribute to the important work of vocational formation, for they will be even better positioned to help students discern and fulfill their own vocational paths.

## 3

# *Vocational Discernment*

### A PEDAGOGY OF HUMANIZATION

#### *Caryn D. Riswold*

> *"Malcolm, you ought to be thinking about a career. Have you been giving it thought?"...*
>
> *"Well, yes, sir, I've been thinking I'd like to be a lawyer." Lansing certainly had no Negro lawyers—or doctors either—in those days, to hold up an image I might have aspired to....*
>
> *Mr. Ostrowski looked surprised, I remember, and leaned back in his chair and clasped his hands behind his head. He kind of half-smiled and said, "Malcolm, one of life's first needs is for us to be realistic. Don't misunderstand me, now. We all here like you, you know that. But you've got to be realistic about being a n———. A lawyer—that's no realistic goal for a n———."...*
>
> *It was then that I began to change—inside.*
>
> —THE AUTOBIOGRAPHY OF MALCOLM X

THIS EXCHANGE BETWEEN young Malcolm and his teacher[1] reminds us of the tremendous power wielded by educators. Regardless of whether it occurred exactly as described here, we know that conversations like this have taken place—and that they still take place more often than we would like to admit. This encounter also reveals the influence of social and political systems on our daily interactions. The scope of, and limitations

---

1. *The Autobiography of Malcolm X as Told to Alex Haley*, introduction by M. S. Handler and epilogue by Alex Haley (New York: Grove Press, 1965), 43–44.

on, the potential of young people will be profoundly shaped by the culture in which they live and the relationships they have. Virginia Ramey Mollenkott describes her own experience of this shaping: "As a child and young woman, I was taught that if I wanted to please God and humanity, my place was secondary and my role supportive."[2] Like young Malcolm Little, Mollenkott understood the expectations that surrounded her; and also like him, she came to realize their flaws. These two stories reveal a wider truth: the process of development and discernment often includes stark encounters with socially and theologically constructed boundaries for human identity. Mollenkott describes these boundaries as creating a "frame of reference within which we think, live, move, and have our being—until some event or pressure forces a gap that opens the way to larger, more liberated thoughts."[3]

These culturally constructed obstacles and limitations can, at their worst, contribute to a process of dehumanization. Particularly for young people, whose identities are still in the process of being constructed and reconstructed, such encounters can undermine one's perceptions of oneself as a fully capable, fully human being. Some students, whether through direct interactions or less overt means, are encouraged to think of themselves as less than fully human. How can twenty-first-century educators play a stronger role in challenging these dehumanizing forces, and in helping students recognize their potential for living a more fully flourishing life?

My contention in this chapter is that the process of vocational exploration and discernment can play an integral role in this process. By exploring their various callings and by discerning the ways that they might live a more meaningful life, young people can gain a clearer perspective on the dehumanizing forces that shape both our material world and our perceptions of it. In his work with Brazilian peasants, educational theorist Paulo Freire argues that "concern for humanization leads at once to the recognition of dehumanization."[4] Freire also notes that "while both humanization and dehumanization are real alternatives, only the first

---

2. Virginia Ramey Mollenkott, *Omnigender: A Trans-Religious Approach*, rev. and exp. ed. (Cleveland: Pilgrim Press, 2007), xi.

3. Mollenkott, *Omnigender*, xii.

4. Paulo Freire, *Pedagogy of the Oppressed*, trans. Myra Bergman Ramos, foreword by Richard Schaull, introduction by Donald Macedo, rev. 30th anniv. ed. (New York: Continuum, 2002), 43.

is the people's vocation."[5] The work of "finding one's calling" thus operates in parallel with humanizing processes and practices. Freire talks about the people's yearning for freedom and justice, and a "struggle to recover their lost humanity."[6] College students may not be living under the conditions that Freire witnessed in Brazil, but they are struggling to lead a life that matters. Hence, to whatever degree their humanity has been lost or arbitrarily limited, they should be encouraged to find ways of recovering it.

Vocational exploration and discernment can help provide precisely this form of encouragement. Whether by articulating career goals, committing to serve a community, or exploring faith and identity, young people have much to gain by considering what it means to live a flourishing human life. This process takes place at the intersection of the personal and the political, the social and the theological; it happens in virtual spaces and in face-to-face encounters. It requires a recognition that human life is enmeshed in myriad systems and institutions that have bearing on who we understand ourselves to be, what we imagine we can do, and how we respond to the multiple callings we hear. These include governments, religious communities, cultural norms, changing technologies, and economic forces. They affect one's perceptions of one's humanity through a variety of identity categories; these include, in addition to those of race and gender highlighted above, elements such as social class, sexual orientation, and gender identity. Educators, both in the classroom and outside it, are in a unique position to help students examine—and sometimes to interrupt—these systems and institutions, and particularly their more dehumanizing aspects. The exploration of vocation invites us to consider questions of human flourishing alongside the constraints that our students face, whether appropriate or inappropriate. As William Cavanaugh observes in chapter 1, certain kinds of boundaries and constraints can and do serve a legitimate purpose. We therefore need to examine those structures of privilege and inequality that may *unjustly* impinge upon our flourishing, and to do what we can to prevent them from obstructing the process of humanization—"the people's vocation."

---

5. Freire, *Pedagogy of the Oppressed*, 43.

6. Freire, *Pedagogy of the Oppressed*, 44.

## *Reading the structures of the times*

In her work *Teaching to Transgress*, bell hooks suggests that education—including teaching, mentoring, and advising—is "a location of possibility." Here, she says, "we have the opportunity to labor for freedom, to demand of ourselves and our comrades, an openness of mind and heart that allows us to face reality even as we collectively imagine ways to move beyond boundaries, to transgress."[7] People are often called to move beyond established boundaries, which gives education the potential to free participants from an unquestioning acceptance of things as they are—whether social and political systems or digital and technological ecosystems. In calling education "the practice of freedom," hooks is informed by Freire's work. He makes a case against what he calls the "banking" model of education, insofar as it serves the interest of those already powerful. In this way of educating, students are to remain passive, so they might "simply to adapt to the world as it is and to the fragmented view of reality deposited in them."[8] This was Mr. Ostrowski's goal for young Malcolm: be realistic; adapt to this world as it is. This is an example of a student who needed to hear how and why to push beyond the socially established possibility: *Yes, you, too, can be a lawyer, even though there aren't any black lawyers in our town.* Imagining ways to move beyond limits is important, and yet, as hooks notes, facing reality is also part of this process. Some students might benefit from being reminded, not only that they can transcend certain limits, but also that their choices are not infinite: *You don't have to choose the one right thing from an unlimited and overwhelming set of possibilities; there are meaningful boundaries to your life.*[9]

Educators who are attentive to what a student needs must also attend to the context in which a conversation like this takes place. In his foreword to Freire's text, Richard Schaull notes that "there is no such thing as a *neutral* educational process."[10] This means that education is always formative—in one way or another. Though it was a negative encounter, young Malcolm was formed by his teacher. The hope articulated by Schaull, Freire, and

---

7. bell hooks, *Teaching to Transgress: Education as the Practice of Freedom* (New York: Routledge, 1994), 207.

8. Freire, *Pedagogy of the Oppressed*, 73.

9. This is especially important in light of the discussion of choice in chapter 1.

10. Richard Schaull, Foreword, in Freire, *Pedagogy of the Oppressed*, 34.

hooks is that education "becomes 'the practice of freedom,' the means by which men and women deal critically and creatively with reality and discover how to participate in the transformation of their world."[11] Knowing when the world needs to be lived into and when it needs to be challenged are equally important. To this end, Christine Clark and Paul Gorski suggest that we "must teach students to read the word—whether on a page or a screen—and the world."[12] We read the world so that we might recognize and challenge dehumanizing limits when and where they exist. My goal in the remainder of this chapter is to illustrate this process of "reading" some of these structures and systems, as a pointer toward how this process could be integrated into the work of vocational exploration and discernment.

## Technology

In the twenty-first century, the frame of reference for vocational discernment is shaped not only by identity categories but also by the way that we experience and perform them in connection to technology and social media. In a 2010 report from the Pew Research Center, those of the millennial generation are described as "leading technology enthusiasts." The report notes that technological "innovations provide more than a bottomless source of information and entertainment, and more than a new ecosystem for their social lives. They are also a badge of generational identity. Many millennials say that their use of modern technology is what distinguishes them from other generations."[13] The data bears this out, showing that young people "outpace older Americans in virtually all types of internet and cell use," including social media, texting, and sharing aspects of their lives online via photos and video. As part of the ecosystem, then, digital technologies and social media provide venues for humanizing as well as dehumanizing activity. In a 2001 article about how the technological generation gap affects teaching and learning, Marc Prensky coined the term "digital native" to describe those who had grown up in this world.[14]

---

11. Schaull, Foreword, in Freire, *Pedagogy of the Oppressed*, 34.

12. Christine Clark and Paul Gorski, "Multicultural Education and the Digital Divide: Focus on Socioeconomic Class Background," *Multicultural Perspectives* 4, no. 3 (2002): 25–36; here, 35.

13. Pew Research Center, "Millennials: Confident. Connected. Open to Change," http://www.pewsocialtrends.org/files/2010/10/millennials-confident-connected-open-to-change.pdf (accessed October 5, 2014).

14. Marc Prensky, "Digital Natives, Digital Immigrants," *On The Horizon* 9, no. 5 (October 2001).

More recently, he expressed optimism related to the ongoing integration of technology into all of our lives: "Let us hope that the technologies of the future will also be designed to protect that which is sacred, and that which is important in our own understanding of being human."[15] Technology has the power to protect, as well as the power to destroy.

In a theatrical performance piece called "Generation Sex,"[16] technology is threaded through monologues and performances about gender and sex and human relations among young people in the twenty-first century. This work, performed by *Teatro Luna* ("Chicago's first and only all-Latina theatre"), suggests that the effects of technology are both connective and corrosive, humanizing and dehumanizing. Prior to a performance at the *Instituto Cervantes* in 2014, audience members were enthusiastically invited to keep their cell phones on, to post pictures and responses throughout the show using the hashtag #WeAreGenerationSex. In this way, the artists were fully embracing the constant presence of technology, recognizing that it can meaningfully create community and connect people; for example, audience contributions are used during the performance and re-posted after the show. Throughout the performance, however, the ways in which technology becomes a tool of obsession and self-destruction for young women emerges: ignoring the person next to you so you can complete one more level of *Candy Crush Saga*; checking five different social media platforms to see who your most recent date has been with in the last forty-eight hours; managing anxiety because a text message isn't responded to after five whole minutes. The words to "Cyber My Space,"[17] a transitional rap piece performed with the artist projecting her own image behind her onstage with a hand-held video camera, include the following:

> *Cyber my space*
> *Book Time with my Face*
> *No finish line for this race*
> *No time for embraces*

---

15. Oliver Joy, "What Does It Mean to Be A Digital Native?" CNN.com, December 8, 2012, http://edition.cnn.com/2012/12/04/business/digital-native-prensky/ (accessed October 5, 2014).

16. *Teatro Luna*, "Generation Sex Summer 2014," http://teatroluna.org/season/season-13-productions/generation-sex-summer-2014/ (accessed October 5, 2014).

17. *Teatro Luna*, "Cyber My Space," Posted June 10, 2014, https://www.facebook.com/teatrolunachicago (accessed October 5, 2014).

*No emotions, just emojis*
*Abrazos y besos*
*No pen pals, just PayPal*
*Just BitCoin, no pesos*
*No huevos to call? Just text him and stall*
*Sext him, DM him, leave links on his wall.*

The terms used in this piece signify the virtual realities of human interaction in the twenty-first century for young people on our campuses. Note also what is not mentioned: physical space, face-to-face, emotions, literary texts, or the walls of home. Discerning how to use these virtual tools to forge connection and maintain threads of real relationship becomes part of the challenge of building a flourishing life. Opting out isn't always an option; however, opting in often means that one enters a race that has no finish line.

For some, technology becomes an inescapable part of what it is to be human; for all of us, it is part of our collective ecosystem, present with particular intensity on our campuses. It needs to be on the agenda in conversations about vocational discernment, if we hope to protect, indeed to develop, a better sense of human flourishing in the contemporary context.

## Race

The tragedy in the interaction described by Malcolm X in his autobiography and used at the beginning of this chapter lies in part with Mr. Ostrowski's response. Here was a teacher unable to see beyond his own assumptions and limitations, unable to be prophetic, himself fully a product of a dehumanizing racist and segregated time and place. As educators, we ourselves are enmeshed in the very same social structures that can serve to limit and dehumanize the students with whom we work. What should Mr. Ostrowski have done? An idealist might wish him to have been an enlightened white man, someone willing to support the high-achieving dreams of his young black student. This would have required him to resist every socializing impulse of early twentieth-century attitudes on race in the United States, to have learned somewhere along the way that race need not prevent one from becoming a successful lawyer. But Mr. Ostrowski wasn't idealistic; he was, in

Malcolm's word, realistic. He reflected the status quo of his time and encouraged his young charge to do the same.

What this teacher didn't do—and what we as educators today must do—is to read the world anew; we need to engage in critical analysis of the landscape we inhabit. This particular story might inspire us to do so through the way it names the problems inherent in a white racist society. In the late 1980s, Peggy McIntosh published some reflections on how and why white people in particular don't think about these things: "My schooling gave me no training in seeing myself as an oppressor, as an unfairly advantaged person, or as a participant in a damaged culture."[18] As participants in a damaged culture, we are part of structures larger than our individual selves. Recognizing this can help us get beyond them in order to encounter a student in her or his full humanity.

In short, we need to be able to see that which is invisible, that which we have been taught not to notice. For many, that includes race. As McIntosh observed, "I have come to see white privilege as an invisible package of unearned assets that I can count on cashing in each day, but about which I was 'meant' to remain oblivious. White privilege is like an invisible weightless knapsack of special provisions."[19] Seeing the unseen is only the beginning, and McIntosh also insists that "disapproving of the systems won't be enough to change them."[20] Here is a warning against moral self-righteousness; of course we are opposed to systemic racism, but the challenge is to live and act differently. McIntosh speaks to this challenge by asking, "What will we do with such knowledge?" She wonders whether we will "choose to use unearned advantage to weaken hidden systems of advantage, and use any of our arbitrarily awarded power to try to reconstruct power systems on a broader base."[21] This last challenge, to reconstruct power systems, echoes the call from Freire to envision education as serving the transformation of the world. In this case, it means transforming structures of racial inequality so that they might no longer dehumanize.

---

18. Peggy McIntosh, "White Privilege: Unpacking the Invisible Knapsack," *Peace and Freedom Magazine* 49, no. 4 (July/August 1989): 10–12; here, 10.

19. McIntosh, "White Privilege," 10.

20. McIntosh, "White Privilege," 12.

21. McIntosh, "White Privilege," 12.

This sounds daunting; consider, however, the degree to which it is already taking place in the regular cycles of activity on college and university campuses. It happens through classroom teaching that invites and instructs young people to think critically about what they hear and read on the page and see on the screen. It also happens through campus cultures that put students in conversation and contact with others who do not share their political views, their race, or their religion. It happens online, where professors and students can engage with a more diverse group of conversation partners than would be possible on their small, often somewhat homogenous campuses. It happens through individual mentoring and advising relationships, wherein we hear the textured complications of this young woman's life and of that young man's family. These can and should be relationships that serve as safe spaces to explore, challenge, wrestle, and discern.

Faculty can also model this with the content assigned in the classroom, making use of the insights of our particular academic disciplines. This means including voices that challenge the status quo and engage in the reconstruction of accounts that have made certain issues invisible. In my discipline of religion, James Cone notes that "white theologians would prefer to do theology without reference to color."[22] This concern is not limited to theology; nor is it limited to the classroom. Not talking about race is something that many people would prefer. And yet when we do talk about it in the classroom, it signals to students that *race matters*, and that critique is part of the public discourse into which we are inviting them. This is especially important when we are speaking with our students about their vocations and helping them to envision their future selves; as the opening quotation from Malcolm X reminds us, it is all too easy for peers and potential mentors to forget the degree to which questions of race affect a person's vision of what can or cannot be accomplished in a life. Attention to these questions can (and indeed should) happen across the campus in classrooms of every discipline, so that we become communities of lively critique—particularly as we address questions about calling. If we don't keep paying attention and keep interrupting them, the structures of racial inequality and privilege will continue dehumanizing us all—and will do so all the more insidiously for their relative invisibility.

---

22. James Cone, *A Black Theology of Liberation* (Maryknoll, NY: Orbis, 2010), 68.

## Gender

As Virginia Ramey Mollenkott's reflection indicated earlier, race is only one of many systems of privilege and oppression that dehumanize and therefore shape vocational discernment. The praise and criticism drawn by Sheryl Sandberg's 2013 bestselling book *Lean In*[23] reveals that we are far from done with discussing gender as a key component in the development of human beings as community members and leaders. In some ways, Sandberg's thesis was too simple. She more or less said this: *Patriarchy rewards and encourages women for being silent, stepping back, and submitting. Women! Stop doing that!* Some critics challenged Sandberg for putting the burden on women to "lean in," to show up, to sit at the table, to take on leadership roles, and to make demands in the workplace. Others rightly pointed out that her discussion and analysis was relevant almost only for white educated executive-class women who had or wanted families that included children. The lack of attention to women of color and working-class women's realities is fairly obvious in a book that talks about body language in the board room and is written by an executive billionaire. What about the women who see the inside of a board room simply because they are the ones cleaning it during the overnight shift? Her work was not meant as an analysis of systems of privilege and oppression; it draws general lessons from Sandberg's own extraordinary life in nonprofit work, the federal government, and the technology industry. Nevertheless, she rightly observes that patriarchy rewards women for taking a back seat in public, and that women are uniquely challenged to interrupt that social dynamic by claiming space and voice. This is a crucial part of their being fully human.

It shouldn't still be revolutionary to say that women are fully human, and yet the persistence of sexism is obvious in many places, including the underrepresentation of women in elective office at every level in U.S. government, the continued gap in wages between men and women in most professions, the pandemic of sexual assault in the military and on college and university campuses, and the fractured politicization of women's healthcare. These are dehumanizing realities. And it remains painfully clear in religion. In her 2012 book, *A Church of Her Own*, Sarah Sentilles transformed her own difficult experience with sexism in the ordination process of the Episcopal Church into a study of women across several

---

23. Sheryl Sandberg, *Lean In: Women, Work, and the Will to Lead* (New York: Knopf, 2013).

Christian traditions. Her goal was to determine, among those denominations that do ordain women, how well they are doing when it comes to gender equity. In short, the record is not stellar. Sexism remains a factor in every stage of the process, from education to job searches, from interviews to first calls.

In fact, Sentilles points out a compelling difference between her conversations with Catholic and Protestant women: "While many of the Protestant women I interviewed internalized their experience of sexism, taking it personally and believing, like I did, that what happened to them was somehow their fault, the Catholic women I interviewed understood sexism as institutional, not individual."[24] They recognized that these matters are not *personal* so much as they are *structural*—which, as Sentilles notes, made a tremendous difference for their survival and personal well-being.

In story after story, Sentilles describes unique challenges for women discerning a call to ordained ministry in Christianity, noting that "our ability—or inability—to realize our call and the calls of others is shaped by our context and by the limits we put on ourselves and each other."[25] The patriarchal frame of reference that Mollenkott bumped up against, decades ago, still remains. Despite the fact that many institutions no longer have formal limits on allowing women into ordained leadership, the dynamics that perpetuate male-only and male-dominated spaces are firmly in place. While Sentilles's work specifically focuses on the unique discernment, call, and employment processes in churches, her insight effectively describes the way that context shapes our ability to realize our callings beyond church. Sometimes, the inability to realize a call is a direct result of the limits that an institution or the culture has established.

How do educators equip students to respond to these challenges? If we are able to recognize that vocational exploration and discernment can be a process of humanization, we can better enable students to name the structures that dehumanize and to interrupt them. As with the earlier example (namely, including discussions of race in my theology classroom), it is possible to acknowledge gender issues in a wide variety of disciplines. In an economics class, analyzing the complex reasons for the wage gap between

24. Sarah Sentilles, *A Church of Our Own: What Happens When a Woman Takes the Pulpit* (New York: Harcourt, 2008), 4.

25. Sentilles, *Church of Her Own*, 36.

men and women, between white people and people of color, serves as both a disciplinary case study as well as an opportunity to call attention to persistent sexism and racism in society. In an advising session with pre-med students, providing examples of specialization and research agendas that disrupt the tendencies of some fields to be gender-segregated might crack open possibilities for the young biology major.

Young women are uniquely challenged in some ways, and young men in other ways. In *Lean In*, Sandberg tells a story about female employee she worked with at Google who wanted to talk to her for advice about being a working mother, what the company maternity leave policies were, and so on. Sandberg notes that in the course of the conversation she realized that this young woman not only wasn't pregnant or working on becoming so; she didn't even have a partner or intentions for parenting anytime soon. And yet she was making decisions about what projects and responsibilities to take on at work with her yet-to-exist children in mind.[26] We live in a culture that encourages young women to conceive of and plan weddings at age six, to spend inordinate amounts of time posting themes and accessories for said wedding online at age sixteen, and to make binding decisions about work and motherhood at age twenty-six, often without any actual life partner or child or job. We also live in a culture where young men struggle to embody a masculinity beyond video games and the locker room. Women and men are dehumanized by gender socialization that rewards deforming behaviors, demands conformity, and polices any deviations. It should be noted that much of this socialization and identity formation takes place in relationship to technology, whether it be social media or gaming systems. Those too are highly gendered spaces in which cultural expectations for women and men are mirrored and amplified. Navigating all of this requires skill, time, and mental creativity that isn't being spent on other forms of education and personal well-being.

A patriarchal culture rewards and celebrates women primarily when they speak and act in ways that lend support to the male-dominated power structure, whether that be corporate capitalism or someone's version of the "ideal family." As Sentilles and others note, patriarchal religions have supported and reinforced this ideology of female submission for millennia; critiques of it are not exactly new. In 1960, Valerie Saiving argued a twentieth-century Christian feminist version of *Lean In* when

---

26. Sandberg, *Lean In*, 92.

she suggested that the dominant theological view of sin reflected men's experiences, not women's. The traditional view is well summarized in Reinhold Niebuhr's notion that the fundamental human sin is pride, or too much a sense of self, wherein a human being is trying to be like God. Saiving showed that for women in patriarchal society, on the contrary, the fundamental sin is too *small* a sense of self, wherein a woman spends most of her time and energy serving and caring for other people, regardless of herself. This creates a crisis: "Her capacity for surrendering her individual concerns in order to serve the immediate needs of others . . . [can] induce a kind of diffuseness of purpose."[27] So when Niebuhr and the dominant Christian tradition called for Christians to give up their power and pride and sacrifice themselves for others as a corrective, Saiving invited the opposite. She noted that for women in a patriarchal culture, these theological ideas work against

> the woman who desires to be both a woman and an individual in her own right, a separate person some part of whose mind and feelings are inviolable, some part of whose time belongs strictly to herself, in whose house there is, to use Virginia Woolf's marvelous image, 'a room of one's own.' "[28]

In this way, Saiving was arguing that women need to "lean in" well before Sheryl Sandberg was born.

Patriarchal social and theological structures influence us all, especially young people who are in the earlier stages of framing their calls to family life, partnering, and parenting. Young men are pressured to abide by what Michael Kimmel calls "the guy code," in which "locker-room behaviors, sexual conquests, bullying, violence and assuming a cocky jock pose can rule over the sacrifice and conformity of marriage and family."[29] Young women are pressured to envision themselves as objects of sexual conquest and pleasing helpmates who always put other peoples' needs before their

---

27. Valerie Saiving, "The Human Situation," in *Womanspirit Rising: A Feminist Reader in Religion*, ed. Carol P. Christ and Judith Plaskow (New York: HarperOne, 1992), 31–48; here, 38.

28. Saiving, "Human Situation," 39.

29. From a description on http://www.guyland.net/ (accessed October 5, 2014) of Michael Kimmel, *Guyland: The Perilous World Where Boys Become Men* (New York and London: Harper Perennial, 2008).

own. Neither of these constitutes a fully human life. When cultural pressures like this become stifling, educators can help young people consider horizons that are a bit wider. By helping our students think about their vocations in ways that transcend inappropriate assumptions about the gender-specificity of certain roles, we open up new possibilities for them. They begin not simply to believe, but also to internalize, the idea that, for example, women are also skilled leaders, and men are also helpful partners. Our communities will be healthier if we are able to widen the stereotyped horizons of vocation, helping both women and men hear what they are called to do and who they are called to be.

## Social class

Race and gender decisively interact with social class and experiences of poverty in the United States. For young people, this shows up first in the quality of education and structural support they receive prior to college. It also shows up in the digital networks of which they are a part. In 2009, there was already a marked difference between the education and income levels of Facebook and MySpace users, and in 2011 research in the United Kingdom indicated that LinkedIn and Twitter have continued to stratify digital-social communities based largely on income levels.[30] This divide was present from the outset: Facebook originated in a Harvard dorm room and was originally only for Harvard students, and then expanded only to people with .edu e-mail addresses. As James Ball noted in his article in *The Guardian* on these trends in the United Kingdom, "Social media is just as capable of stratifying as every other part of society."[31] In the *NEA Higher Education Journal*, Theresa Capra summarizes data from a 2007 U.S. Census report showing how class stratification in the U.S. intersects with race and gender, and affects education.

Poverty does discriminate: 24.7 percent of the African American population and 20.7 percent of the Hispanic population are below

---

30. Breeanna Hare, "Does Your Social Class Determine Your Online Social Network?" CNN.com, October 14, 2009, http://edition.cnn.com/2009/TECH/science/10/13/social.networking.class/ (accessed October 5, 2014), and James Ball, "Social Media Has Its Own Class Divide," *The Guardian*, December 8, 2011, http://www.theguardian.com/commentis-free/2011/dec/08/social-media-blackberry-messenger (accessed October 5, 2014).

31. Ball, "Social Media."

the poverty line compared to 10.2 percent for Caucasians. . . . American poverty continues its discrimination by affecting single women at far greater numbers. Households headed by women are more likely to experience poverty than households headed by men. This statistic is, of course, indicative of the fact that women earn approximately 78 percent of what men earn.[32]

This data reflects the world from which students arrive on our campuses, as well as the world into which we are sending them to work and live. It can be dehumanizing insofar as it impacts their ability to learn and encounter the world, as well as their ability to envision a future beyond the one immediately before them; in short, it impacts their ability to discern. If a student is unable to afford to buy all of the required books, she will not be able to engage the coursework effectively. If a student must work overnight shifts at a nursing home in order to earn enough money for those books, his ability to be awake and alert in an afternoon class will decrease. When paying rent and buying food and getting a second job to help out her parents are important, being able to participate in campus programs is far down on a list of priorities, and an unpaid internship is not always a practical option. For many students, the hours of time that they need every day for reading and writing just don't exist.

Social class is determined by more than just wages and income. It also includes such things as access to education and other resources, power, authority within a social context, and occupational status. As Max Weber's classic definition has it,

> class situation means the typical probability of 1) procuring goods 2) gaining a position in life and 3) finding inner satisfactions, a probability which derives from the relative control over goods and

---

32. Theresa Capra, "Poverty and Its Impact on Education: Today and Tomorrow" *NEA Higher Education Journal*, Fall 2009, http://www.nea.org/assets/docs/HE/TA09PovertyCapra. pdf (accessed October 5, 2014). For more data, see Carmen DeNavas-Walt, Bernadette D. Proctor, and Jessica C. Smith, U.S. Census Bureau, Current Population Reports P60-235, *Income, Poverty, and Health Insurance Coverage in the United States: 2007* (Washington, DC: U.S.Government Printing Office, 2008), www.census.gov/prod/2008pubs/p60-235. pdf (accessed November 6, 2014).

skills and from their income-producing uses within a given economic order.[33]

Weber's writing here focuses on market activity—an important function of class but not the only one. In fact, the second and third element of his definition, "gaining a position in life" and "finding inner satisfactions," already suggest that social class depends on more than the ability to buy and sell material goods. The status of one's position, along with the ability to achieve satisfaction, connects to other social realities like race and gender, as we have already seen. Educators accompany students in their journey toward "gaining a position in life," in part through building a base of knowledge and skills, and in part through the work of advising that helps them determine what life and what work might bring "inner satisfactions."

And yet we do all of this within a corporate capitalist system that too often devalues human workers and sees them as purely interchangeable. The very idea that we can encourage young people to discern *meaning* and *purpose* in life and work seems countercultural. Social and economic forces are often beyond our immediate control and can be dehumanizing. Helping young people to see their lives as multifaceted can, in itself, enable them to survive and even to thrive amid these forces. If he can't get that job, he is still a valuable person. If she doesn't get into that graduate program, she can still learn and grow. This approach also broadens the horizon of what "inner satisfactions," or meaningful work and life, might look like.[34] If we allow our work to be informed by a critique of dehumanizing economic and social forces, we can help young people see beyond corporate success and salary as the only markers of a flourishing life.

While twenty-first-century U.S. higher education is notably different than struggles against political dictators and repressive regimes in 1960s-era Latin America, Paulo Freire's use of the concept of vocation, along with his willingness to frame the issue in terms of basic human dignity, suggest that a larger truth is at work from which we might glean

---

33. Max Weber, *Economy and Society: An Outline of Interpretive Sociology*, trans. Ephraim Fischoff, et al., ed. Guenther Roth and Claus Wittich (Berkeley: University of California Press, 1978), I: 302.

34. This point is more fully explored in chapter 1 of this volume.

insight. Students are dehumanized by a culture that that neglects the concrete needs of public education, defines a fulfilling life as one that includes a large salary, and neglects its poor in favor of the needs of corporations. In contrast, vocational discernment can have the opposite effect: it can humanize by encouraging students to recognize the connections between their skills and their passions, by giving them permission to take one step toward a goal without fully knowing the end, by placing a premium on satisfaction with one's chosen life for now, and by affirming the role of faith and service to one's community as part of a meaningful life.

It was in Freire's political and economic context that the Latin American Roman Catholic bishops gathered in 1968 in Medellín, Colombia, to consider the relevance and significance of the Second Vatican Council for their work with the poor. Likewise, Gustavo Gutiérrez suggested that we need to see the work of building a more just world as part of the process of salvation itself. "To work, to transform this world, is to become a human being and to build the human community; it is also to save. Likewise, to struggle against misery and exploitation and to build a just society is already to be part of the saving action."[35] Gutiérrez and other liberation theologians articulated one way that working against exploitation and dehumanization was part of the calling of the church in the world.

A more contemporary articulation of these ideas has been offered by Pope Francis, who made headlines with the November 2013 papal letter, *Evangelii Gaudium*. In it, he lifts up the Roman Catholic Church's focus on the consequences of economic inequality and call to work toward justice in this world:

> How can it be that it is not a news item when an elderly homeless person dies of exposure, but it is news when the stock market loses two points? This is a case of exclusion. Can we continue to stand by when food is thrown away while people are starving? This is a case of inequality. Today everything comes under the laws of competition and the survival of the fittest, where the powerful feed upon

---

35. Gustavo Gutiérrez, *A Theology of Liberation: History, Politics, and Salvation*, trans. and ed. Sister Caridad Inda and John Eagleson (Maryknoll, NY: Orbis, 1973), 91, translation slightly altered.

the powerless. As a consequence, masses of people find themselves excluded and marginalized: without work, without possibilities, without any means of escape.[36]

He goes on to argue that this culture is, as Freire named it, dehumanizing:

> To sustain a lifestyle which excludes others, or to sustain enthusiasm for that selfish ideal, a globalization of indifference has developed. Almost without being aware of it, we end up being incapable of feeling compassion at the outcry of the poor, weeping for other people's pain, and feeling a need to help them, as though all this were someone else's responsibility and not our own.[37]

Of course, the call to compassion transcends the boundaries of the Roman Catholic Church. We cannot avoid talking about social class on our campuses when economic inequality continues to form and deform the world into which we are sending our students. Talking about it is the first step; discerning what to do about it is the next step. Taking that step becomes more likely when we see vocational discernment as part of humanization and recognize that social class affects not only what one is able to do, but what one envisions is possible. To be the first in one's family to go to college—an ongoing marker of social class stratification—means that a student is already stepping into an unfamiliar culture. Educators must be aware of the tensions that this can produce and acknowledge their effect. Those of us who were ourselves first-generation college students do well to share that experience in mentoring conversations with young people, how it was perhaps cause for celebration as well as occasional consternation. When vocational discernment is part of the culture of education on our campuses, part of the work of a mentoring community,[38] these conversations and stories are made all the more possible, serving students who are often most at risk.

---

36. Pope Francis, *Evangelii Gaudium*, section 53, http://www.vatican.va/holy_father/francesco/apost_exhortations/documents/papa-francesco_esortazione-ap_20131124_evangelii-gaudium_en.html#No_to_an_economy_of_exclusion (accessed November 6, 2014).

37. Pope Francis, *Evangelii Gaudium*, section 54.

38. For more on mentoring communities, see chapters 2, 11, and 13 in this volume.

## Sexual orientation and gender identity

One of the most intimate and personal aspects of human life has, in recent decades, become one of the most politicized. Sexual orientation and gender identity have shown up on our ballots, in Supreme Court decisions, and at the denominational conventions of many church bodies. For students on our campuses, the issues are in some ways less controversial than they are for the generations to which their educators belong. Even before the Supreme Court's 2013 ruling that overturned the Defense of Marriage Act and reinstated California's marriage equality laws, a Pew Research Center report showed that, among millennials (those born after 1980), 70% support the legal right of gay and lesbian Americans to marry. That is almost twice the support voiced by 38% of baby boomers (born between 1946 and 1964) and notably higher than the 49% support from the Generation X cohort (born between 1965 and 1980).[39] Despite this support among younger generations, elections and laws continue to be influenced by the older generations who are still in power and who more frequently exercise that power through the vote. Moreover, despite notable shifts toward marriage equality in recent years, that institution is still governed by a patchwork of laws that differ from state to state.

How does this shifting landscape affect our conversations with young people trying to envision a fully flourishing human life? When a young person experiences a call to marriage and commitment to her beloved, she may live in a state that refuses to recognize it. Or, another student may learn that his civil rights will not be equally protected in every city in which he wants to take a job. These too are things that affect a person's ability to discern a path into the future.

Beyond the political issue of marriage equality, gender identity has emerged as a civil rights issue and theological question with which many institutions are wrestling. The American Psychiatric Association removed "gender identity disorder" from the fifth edition of its Diagnostic and Statistical Manual of Mental Disorders (DSM-V) in 2012, redefining a category now called "gender dysphoria" and reminding many people of a similar decision in 1973 to remove "homosexuality" from its status as

---

39. Pew Research Center, "Growing Support for Gay Marriage: Changed Minds and Changing Demographics," http://www.people-press.org/2013/03/20/growing-support-for-gay-marriage-changed-minds-and-changing-demographics/ (accessed October 5, 2014).

a disease. This is one example of how scientific views of sex and gender continue to change, inevitably affecting (and being affected by) social and political change. Jack Drescher, a member of the APA revisions committee, notes in *The Advocate* that "All psychiatric diagnoses occur within a cultural context. . . . We know there is a whole community of people out there who are not seeking medical attention and live between the two binary categories."[40] Making social space for those that live in-between binary gender options is part of ongoing cultural transformation. To that end, in February 2014, Facebook announced an expansion of the options for "gender" on an individual's profile page.[41] This was an attention-getting indicator of the ways in which identity is performed via social media,[42] along with the ways that public discourse about gender is moving beyond the binary male/female. The June 9, 2014, *Time Magazine* cover story was titled "The Transgender Tipping Point: America's Next Civil Rights Frontier," indicating that the momentum from the cascade of decisions making same-sex marriage legal in more and more states is now bringing attention to legal protections (or lack thereof) related to gender identity. Still, while changes are clearly underway, this does not mean that families, educators, and institutions readily understand and accept them.

Some college and university campuses are working on how, if at all, transgender students are welcomed in their communities. Allie Grasgreen notes that as of September 2013, "there are now about 150 colleges that offer gender-neutral housing, according to a running count by Campus Pride. Granted, that's out of more than 4,000 institutions—and it's taken more than 20 years to get to this point."[43] Housing is only one issue where transgender student rights emerge; access to bathrooms

---

40. Camille Beredjick, "DSM-V To Rename Gender Identity Disorder 'Gender Dysphoria,'" *The Advocate*, July 23, 2012, http://www.advocate.com/politics/transgender/2012/07/23/dsm-replaces-gender-identity-disorder-gender-dysphoria (accessed October 5, 2014).

41. Debby Herbenick and Aleta Baldwin, "What Each of Facebook's 51 New Gender Options Means," *The Daily Beast*, February 15, 2014, http://www.thedailybeast.com/articles/2014/02/15/the-complete-glossary-of-facebook-s-51-gender-options.html (accessed October 5, 2014).

42. See Erika Pearson, "All The World Wide Web's a Stage: The Performance of Identity in Online Social Networks," *First Monday* 14:3 (March 2009), http://firstmonday.org/article/view/2162/2127 (accessed October 5, 2014).

43. Allie Grasgreen, "Broadening the Transgender Agenda," *Inside Higher Ed*, September 18, 2013, http://www.insidehighered.com/news/2013/09/18/colleges-adopt-new-policies-accommodate-transgender-students#ixzz2nwlAIgQS (accessed October 5, 2014).

and the ability to use one's preferred name are others. Grasgreen also mentions a 2010 "Dear Colleague Letter" issued by the Department of Education's Office for Civil Rights, which "said schools must work to prevent gender nonconformity discrimination—when, for example, a student who is assigned a male sex at birth but does not act as a stereotypical boy (maybe by using female pronouns, or wearing dresses) is bullied."[44] Clearly, the ways in which issues around gender identity show up on our campuses are multilayered; they require conversation at administrative policy levels as well as at the interpersonal level among students and their faculty and staff educators.[45] We need to equip ourselves as well as our institutions to serve students when their vocational discernment, their process of becoming a fully flourishing human person, includes naming and claiming their own gender identity.

Some churches are addressing sexual orientation and gender identity in ways that educational institutions might explore. There, too, a basic identification of full humanity is a precursor to all else. At its seventy-seventh triennial General Convention in 2012, the Episcopal Church passed two resolutions that "granted transgender people protection against discrimination in the ordination process and in lay leadership in the Episcopal Church." In covering this event for *The Washington Post*, Becky Garrison noted that "such protections remain unavailable in the vast majority of religious and secular institutions as well as in most states and municipalities (only 16 states have transgender nondiscrimination laws on their books.)"[46] This is an additional dimension of the aforementioned patchwork of laws across the country.

On the issue of same-sex marriage, several denominations have taken positions to affirm their support of gays and lesbians who wish to marry, and allow pastors to perform those marriages. Others, like the Southern Baptist Convention, have restated their commitment to the model of

---

44. Allie Grasgreen, "Equal Access at all Levels," *Inside Higher Ed*, entry posted July 29, 2013, https://www.insidehighered.com/news/2013/07/29/settlement-favoring-transgender-student-has-implications-higher-ed (accessed November 6, 2014).

45. A recent case at George Fox University reveals how religious identification of the institutions also plays a role. George Fox University, "Transgender Student and Housing at George Fox University," http://www.georgefox.edu/transgender/ (accessed November 6, 2014).

46. Becky Garrison, "Episcopal Church promotes the "T" in LGBT equation," entry posted July 31, 2012, http://www.faithstreet.com/onfaith/2012/07/31/episcopal-church-promotes-the-t-in-lgbt-equation/10927 (accessed November 6, 2014).

marriage as between one man and one woman.[47] Similarly, the issue of whether or not gay and lesbian members can be ordained varies among denominations; in fact, the two issues are often intertwined. One recent example is the 2009 social statement, "Human Sexuality: Gift and Trust," adopted by the Evangelical Lutheran Church in America. In light of it, the churchwide assembly voted on ministry recommendations giving congregations the right to recognize same-sex relations and to allow gay and lesbian members to serve as rostered leaders of the church.[48] In doing so, it became "the largest Protestant church in the United States to permit noncelibate gay ministers to serve in the ranks of its clergy."[49] That being said, the United Methodist Church made national news when Rev. Thomas Ogletree was set to face canonical trial for officiating at the wedding of his gay son in 2012, in direct opposition to the church's position on same-sex marriage.[50] Thus, the landscape of religious traditions is no less a patchwork when it comes to this issue than are the states and their legal systems.

Socially, politically, and even theologically, issues related to sexual orientation and gender identity are among the fastest changing in our culture. In the meantime, dehumanizing limits continue to be imposed on those whose identities do not conform to the norm. As educators, we are challenged to equip the young people with whom we work to navigate this landscape authentically and carefully as they participate in the humanization process. Empowering them to understand who they are, and to acknowledge the impact these institutions and decisions have on their lives, is essential. Enabling them to be constructive participants in a

---

47. See Southern Baptist Convention, "On 'Same Sex Marriage' and Civil Rights Rhetoric," 2012, http://www.sbc.net/resolutions/1224 (accessed October 5, 2014).

48. Evangelical Lutheran Church in America, "Human Sexuality: Gift and Trust," http://www.elca.org/en/Faith/Faith-and-Society/Social-Statements/Human-Sexuality (accessed October 5, 2014).

49. Human Rights Campaign, "Stances of Faith on LGBT Issues: Evangelical Lutheran Church in America." *The Human Rights Campaign* maintains an ever-changing list of faith traditions and their policies and practices on its website at http://www.hrc.org/resources/entry/faith-positions (accessed October 5, 2014).

50. Sharon Otterman, "Caught in Methodism's Split over Same Sex Marriage," *The New York Times*, May 5, 2013, http://www.nytimes.com/2013/05/06/nyregion/caught-in-methodisms-split-over-same-sex-marriage.html (accessed November 6, 2014). The trial was eventually cancelled by New York Conference Bishop Martin D. McLee in protest of the church's prohibition on same-sex marriage.

fluid world continues to be our task. Gender and sexuality are aspects of self-understanding that are newly present in civic and religious discourse. In that way, our culture is perhaps at a tipping point, as *Time* suggested. We do need to talk about how living a flourishing life includes having access to legal protections and being able to live and love authentically. We do need to be institutions and educators who make this a part of the vocational discernment process.

## *Themes and conclusions*

In each section above—technology, race, gender, class, and sexual orientation and gender identity—one theme emerges as constant: we need to recognize how the social, political, and theological systems we have constructed often dehumanize. They do this when they prevent young people from hearing a call, discerning their vocations, and experiencing a fully flourishing human life. In our work with undergraduate students, faculty and staff educators are better able to accompany them through a discernment process when we recognize these structures and help students to negotiate them. Being in mentoring relationships with students allows us to help them think about which limitations need to be embraced and which boundaries need to be transcended. We need to help them see that work, *their* work, is part of their process of becoming more fully human.

Understanding our own biases and situatedness is also key in each area. Education is about the students, and it is about us as faculty and staff educators as well. Very few people working in twenty-first-century U.S. higher education have the luxury of the ivory tower ideal, wherein the sage on the stage holds court and spreads wisdom at his elite leisure. The work of educating today is practical, pressured, and involves messy work with young people navigating a damaged, fractured, digitized, and often dehumanizing culture. We can't pretend that they, or we, are immune to systemic pressure, interpersonal bias, and the influence of corporate capitalism. These challenges are not just facing our students; they face us as well.

Fortunately, however, social and theological resources exist in every area to help us do just this. For educators and institutions with religious heritage and commitment, exploring resources distinctive to that tradition will be part of the process. For all of us, engaging in the social and political discourse surrounding higher education and human identity is essential. Mining the resources of our own academic disciplines can also inform this work.

All of this leads us back, once more, to our opening scene between young Malcolm and Mr. Ostrowski. Might there have been another way of them being together in the midst of dehumanizing systems and structures? Perhaps not. But perhaps in our time and place, we have resources that were unavailable, or at least more difficult to find, for that teacher in that time and that place. We can also have renewed respect for a young man who was able, despite such blatant systemic impediments, to discern how to live a life that mattered. We are left where we began, standing at the intersection of this time and this place—but perhaps now with greater hope that vocational exploration and discernment can be part of a "pedagogy of humanization" that can lead students into a deeper awareness of the questions and challenges that inevitably emerge, and help them find meaningful resources to address them.

# PART TWO

# *The Contours of Vocation*

The language of vocation is rich and complex, with roots embedded deep in the history of the intellectual cultures that the modern university has inherited. Hence, to speak about vocation and calling is to open up a much wider inquiry into a range of topics that have been addressed by philosophy, literary studies, theology, sociology, and many other academic disciplines. Although this volume has set forth a number of provisional definitions of vocation and of the work of vocational discernment, its contributors are aware that no simple account of these terms will suffice. In order to offer some sense of what we mean when we use the word *vocation*, we need to approach the topic from a number of different directions. Only through the gradual collection and assembly of these varying perspectives will we be able to offer an adequate account of our use of this complex terminology.

As a result of lengthy conversations about calling and vocation, the contributors to this volume began to understand it as a very large and somewhat unwieldy object, like a monumental sculpture that can't really be framed by a single viewpoint. Viewed from one vantage point, it appears to be primarily about the choices that people make as they set a course for their future lives. But as soon as one moves around to another side of this very large entity, one discovers that those choices are heavily constrained (by, for example, the elements explored in part one of this volume), and that our range of vocational "choices" is often shaped by other people and by forces outside our control. From one perspective, vocation appears to be a deeply theological concept, inseparable from the ecclesial ramifications of "calling" from which it derives its very name; but again, one can look from a different vantage point at institutions that use this language in relatively secular contexts and that eschew theological language when describing it. When it comes to offering a clear definition and a concise account, vocation turns out to be a fairly elusive quarry.

Thus, we have chosen to speak of the "contours" of vocation: we seek to explore the shapes and textures of this large and complex entity, rather than to offer a one-paragraph definition that attempts to encompass the whole. In the four essays that follow, our authors trace these contours in various ways: historically, theologically, sociologically, and through the category of *narrative*. Along the way, they enter into conversations with still more fields of discourse, including drama and theatrical performance, literary analysis, the structure of communities, and the concept of revelation. While these may seem to be rather far-flung ventures, they are all designed to help readers address the following questions:

- What range of meanings and associations will typically be invoked when we use the language of vocation and calling?
- Does the language of "calling" presuppose the existence of one who calls, and if so, to what degree can we identify and specify the nature of this caller?
- To what degree is our understanding of a person's calling shaped by the stories that we tell about it, and how do these stories fit into the larger narrative frameworks that shape our culture?
- Do these larger narrative frameworks sometimes create certain assumptions (especially among undergraduates) that may limit their capacities to hear a call and respond to it?
- Does our ability to discern our own vocations depend on our willingness to trace the vocations of other people, with attention not only to how they were called, but also how they responded?
- Do the theological roots of the language of vocation and calling require that it be framed in religious terms, or is the concept sufficiently malleable that it can be adopted in contexts where less attention is given to explicit claims about faith and belief?
- Can we identify certain features of a call that are, if not absolutely essential, at least to be expected when one has rightly discerned a vocation?

The four chapters that follow will by no means answer all these questions; still, in wrestling with them, we believe that they have pointed us toward a more adequate understanding of the complex and multifaceted contours of vocation.

# 4

## *Places of Responsibility*

### EDUCATING FOR MULTIPLE CALLINGS IN MULTIPLE COMMUNITIES

*Kathryn A. Kleinhans*

SIXTEENTH-CENTURY REFORMER MARTIN LUTHER is credited with broadening the notion of vocation or calling to encompass all people rather than a select religious few. Luther inherited a medieval understanding in which the term "vocation" was reserved for clergy and those who took religious vows. Against this view, Luther articulated an understanding of "the priesthood of all believers," challenging a hierarchical understanding of the church in which some Christians pursued holiness in extraordinary ways and consequently were seen as holding higher status before God than others. But Luther's accomplishment with respect to the language of vocation was not limited to its spiritual aspects.[1] Luther also expanded the category of vocation itself to include all aspects of creaturely life, not just the identifiably religious dimension. Because Luther believed that everyone was called by God, he argued that vocation included all faithful work in service of one's neighbor, including

---

1. Nathan Montover argues that it is a misreading of Luther to think that the priesthood of all believers is primarily about providing individuals access to the divine. Rather, Luther's assertions that all Christians belong to the spiritual estate effectively eliminated the distinction of a spiritual estate separate from and higher than other forms of life. See Nathan Montover, *Luther's Revolution: The Political Dimensions of Martin Luther's Universal Priesthood*, Princeton Theological Monograph Series (Eugene, OR: Pickwick Publications, 2011).

responsibilities undertaken in the areas of domestic, economic, and civic life, as well as spiritual life.

Edward P. Hahnenberg describes in some detail how Luther's broadened sense of vocation becomes instrumentalized in the later strands of the Reformation. Both Luther and his contemporary, the Swiss reformer John Calvin, raised questions about the claim that clerics and monastics had a "higher" calling. Both reasserted the religious value of everyday life and work; their reasons differed, however. Luther criticized monastic life because it removed one from the concrete places where one's neighbor is to be found, while Calvin criticized monastic life because it replaced useful activity with contemplation and speculation.[2] While Luther affirmed almost all kinds of work, paid or unpaid, as *circumstances within which* one has a divine calling to serve one's neighbors, certain elements of the Calvinist tradition came to associate vocation with *the work itself.*[3] As noted in chapter 1, this theological claim was woven into concurrent developments in the economic and political conditions of the era, resulting in a dominant understanding of vocation as a calling to a particular form of work—namely, paid work. Hahnenberg notes with irony that Luther's "attempt to sanctify the ordinary led, in an unfortunate reversal, to a secularization of vocation."[4]

Contemporary discussion of vocation takes place between the two extremes shaped by this history: on the one hand, a narrowly religious view in which only the extraordinary life "counts" as vocation;[5] and, on the other, an equally narrow secularized view in which "vocation" is reduced to a synonym for "occupation." These days, one increasingly hears the language of vocation used to refer not just to any job, but to a job in which one finds a sense of meaning and purpose.[6] This is an improvement over

2. Hahnenberg, *Awakening Vocation*, 18 (see chap. 1, note 7 *supra*).

3. Hahnenberg, *Awakening Vocation*, 18.

4. Hahnenberg, *Awakening Vocation*, 4.

5. This limited use of vocation to refer only to specifically religious life and work is still reflected by such websites as www.vocation.org and www.vocation.com. Almost as narrow is the tendency to describe only certain (usually underpaid!) professions such as teaching and nursing as callings.

6. See, for example, such titles as Natasha Crozier, *Recovering Calling: Helping Millennials Connect Faith and Work* (Amazon Digital Services, 2012), Kindle e-book, and J. B. Wood, *At Work As It Is In Heaven: 25 Ways to Re-imagine the Spiritual Purpose of Your Work* (Denver: Patheos Press, 2012), Kindle e-book.

an instrumentalized understanding of vocation simply as paid work, in contrast to an avocation as something one does for pleasure rather than pay, but only a slight one. Missing from such discourse is Luther's expansion of the language of vocation to refer to multiple dimensions of life.

This chapter will explore the broad understanding of vocation developed in the thought of Martin Luther and of twentieth-century German Lutheran theologian Dietrich Bonhoeffer, thereby seeking to develop a richer, more complex account of vocation for our own time and place. Luther and Bonhoeffer offer a multifaceted understanding of vocation, in which we understand ourselves as having multiple callings simultaneously; moreover, these callings are situated within multiple dimensions of human life. This broadened understanding has renewed relevance and fruitful implications for the task of higher education; indeed, the college or university setting is an ideal place—and the undergraduate years an ideal time—for identifying and embracing multiple callings. The concluding sections of the chapter connect this broad Lutheran understanding of vocation to matters such as the diversity of the student body and the goal of educating whole persons, prompting educators to think constructively about the implications of these themes within their own institutional contexts.

## *Multiple callings in multiple communities: a theological foundation*

College students have multiple roles and responsibilities: as students, as family members, as workers, as athletes, and in many other facets of life.[7] Faculty members tend to privilege the academic roles and responsibilities of students, and it is true that these are at the heart of the collegiate enterprise. But students' other roles and responsibilities are very real—not only for the students themselves but also for their families, coworkers, teammates, roommates, and wider communities. When these roles and responsibilities come into conflict with one another, the tension in the students' lives is also very real. Insisting that intellectual pursuits are more important than other areas of life can sound a bit like the insistence that the contemplative life of religious men and women is higher than the

---

7. See particularly chapter 10 in this volume, concerning loyalty to social organizations, and chapter 11, on co-curricular activities.

ordinary life of others. Educators can best be attentive to our students' multiple communities (and the possible tensions that arise among them) by remembering that we are educating *whole persons*. There is not—and cannot be—an either/or distinction between the life of the mind and the rest of one's life.[8]

When students come to us, they are already participants in the complex structures that Sharon Parks describes as "networks of belonging." On the one hand, educators have the responsibility of helping students understand that they have a vocation as students, here and now, not just an awaiting future vocation in an eventual career.[9] On the other hand, we need to recognize that the academic vocation of students does not negate their other callings in domestic, economic, and communal life. We need to help them identify and affirm these roles and relationships as legitimate callings, and we need to help them learn to think and to act responsibly, as whole persons, within the complex intersections of lived human experience.

The historic Lutheran understanding of the plurality of callings within the various dimensions of human life can serve as a rich resource for this conversation and for this work.

## Luther: callings to steward the world

Martin Luther lived in a time of great social change. It was once common in Western Civilization courses to pose the question of whether Martin Luther was the last medieval man or the first modern man. The question posed a false dichotomy, assuming a clear and identifiable shift between one historical era and another; life in the early sixteenth century was not nearly so clear-cut. Luther's times were characterized by early forms of capitalism, growing social unrest, spiritual anxiety, and ongoing tension between political and religious authorities.

Luther inherited a narrowly ecclesial understanding of vocation rooted in a medieval social structure that had been divided neatly into three

---

8. See chapter 3 for a discussion of the relationship among vocational discernment, education, and embodied human realities such as gender and social class.

9. For an extensive discussion of this theme, see Korey D. Maas, "The Vocation of a Student," in a volume written by the faculty of Concordia University Irvine (Calif.), to be published in Scott Ashmon, ed., *The Idea and Practice of a Christian University* (St. Louis: Concordia Publishing House, 2015).

categories or "estates": those who work, those who fight, and those who pray.[10] Each group had one major responsibility, from which the entire community benefited. Those who labored (e.g., in agriculture) worked to feed all. Those who fought (a category including medieval knights but also, by extension, lords with responsibility for the protection of their vassals) fought for all. Those who prayed (priests and members of religious orders) prayed for all. While society depended on the existence and the contributions of all three estates, the spiritual estate claimed the highest status.

Luther recognized the existence of these three categories but radically reinterpreted them as areas of life in which each person participates simultaneously. Luther referred to them as "governances" or "hierarchies," understanding "the home, the city, and the church," or "the domestic, the royal, and the priestly," as organizing structures through which God's providential care of the world is exercised. Rather than locating specific individuals in separate categories, Luther believed that each person had roles and responsibilities within all three areas: domestic, political, and spiritual.[11]

Luther's identification of these dimensions of life as the places in which one fulfills God's calling served to critique the view that the spiritual estate was the most meritorious in God's eyes. It also served to redefine the kind of human activity that was seen as God-pleasing. Luther's signature theological claim—that human beings are justified by faith—rejected the view that the way to please God was through taking perpetual vows or doing designated religious activities such as praying, going on a pilgrimage, or giving alms. On the contrary, Luther insisted that God neither wanted nor needed human activity for God's own sake:

> For God does not deal, nor has he ever dealt, with humanity otherwise than through a word of promise, as I have said. We in turn cannot deal with God otherwise than through faith in the Word of

---

10. John Witte, *Law and Protestantism: The Legal Teachings of the Lutheran Reformation* (Cambridge: Cambridge University Press, 2002). See also William C. Placher, ed., *Callings: Twenty Centuries of Christian Wisdom on Vocation* (Grand Rapids, MI: William B. Eerdmans, 2005), 107.

11. Later Lutherans will identify economic life as a fourth discrete area of responsibility in daily life, but for Luther himself, work was simply how one served one's neighbors within any of the areas of daily life.

his promise. He does not desire works, nor has he need of them; rather we deal with other people and with ourselves on the basis of works.[12]

If one wants to know, then, what God would have us do, the proper recourse is not to look up toward the heavens but toward our neighbors. Responsible daily living within the areas of ordinary life provides us with a more than sufficient to-do list. According to Luther:

> Just look only at the home and at the duties it alone imposes: parents and landlords must be obeyed; children and servants must be nourished, trained, ruled, and provided for in a godly spirit. The rule of the home alone would give us enough to do, even if there were nothing else. Then the city, that is, the secular government, also gives us enough to do if we show ourselves really obedient, and conversely, if we are to judge, protect, and promote land and people.[13]

This understanding of the domestic and civic tasks to which God calls us is reflected in Luther's understanding and practice of confession. Luther replaced medieval penitential manuals, with their exhaustive delineation of levels of (and penalties for) sinful acts, with a simple formula: consider how you have behaved in the various roles in your life. In *The Small Catechism*, he provides several specific examples. A servant might confess quarreling or neglect of duty. The head of a household might confess setting a bad example for children. A merchant might confess, "I have injured my neighbor by speaking evil of him, overcharging him, giving him inferior goods and short measure."[14] Although particular sinful actions are mentioned, Luther emphasizes the damage done within human relationships as a consequence of these actions. The

---

12. Martin Luther, "The Babylonian Captivity of the Church," *Luther's Works*, vol. 36 (Philadelphia: Fortress Press, 1959), 42. Translation altered to inclusive language for humans.

13. "On the Councils and the Church," *Luther's Works*, vol. 41 (Philadelphia: Fortress Press, 1966), 177.

14. Martin Luther, *The Small Catechism*, V:23, in *The Book of Concord: The Confessions of the Evangelical Lutheran Church*, trans. and ed. Theodore G. Tappert (Philadelphia: Fortress Press, 1959), 350.

examples are not meant to be exhaustive but rather to stimulate the person making confession to consider his or her own daily life from the perspective of others.

Despite the inevitability of human failings, Luther understood our earthly obligations in the domestic, civic, and religious spheres as precisely how God continues to be at work in the created world. For Luther, to confess God as creator is to acknowledge not only God's original work, but also that God continually (daily!) sustains the creation by providing that which is necessary for life. Luther understands the necessities of life quite broadly. In his explanation of the first article of the Apostles' Creed, Luther asserts that God

> has given and constantly sustains my body, soul, and life, my members great and small, all the faculties of my mind, my reason and understanding, and so forth; my food and drink, clothing, means of support, wife and child, servants, house and home, . . . all physical and temporal blessings—good government, peace, security.[15]

In his explanation of the fourth petition of the Lord's Prayer, "Give us this day our daily bread," Luther defines "daily bread" to include not only food, clothing, and shelter, but also physical health, fiscal resources, stable government, and family, friends, and neighbors—"in short, everything that pertains to the regulation of our domestic and our civil or political affairs."[16]

Given this broad understanding of the scope of God's concern as Creator, it should come as no surprise that, for Luther, God's sustaining activity on behalf of the creation is mediated through various people and structures. God's providential care of the world occurs through tangible means—including not only natural structures (e.g., physical laws such as gravity and entropy),[17] but also the work of God's human creatures. According to Luther, God "wants to act through his creatures, whom he

---

15. Martin Luther, *The Large Catechism*, II:13, 15, in Tappert, ed., *Book of Concord*, 412.

16. Luther, *The Large Catechism*, III:73, in Tappert, ed., *Book of Concord*, 430.

17. As Luther writes in *The Large Catechism*, II:14: "Besides, he [God] makes all creation help provide the comforts and necessities of life—sun, moon, and stars in the heavens, day and night, air, fire, water, the earth and all that it brings forth, birds and fish, beasts, grain and all kinds of produce." In Tappert, ed., *Book of Concord*, 412.

does not want to be idle."[18] God now gives food through human labor, rather than through the miraculous appearance of manna, and God now creates human beings through sexual union rather than out of dust. In the words of twentieth-century Swedish Lutheran theologian Gustav Wingren, "With persons as his 'hands' or 'coworkers,' God gives his gifts through the earthly vocations (food through farmers, fishermen and hunters; external peace through princes, judges, and orderly powers; knowledge and education through teachers and parents . . . )."[19]

God works through human beings, not only by means of their individual efforts, but also through their social and political structures. In his explanation of the commandment to honor father and mother, Luther argued that parenthood[20] is the estate to which the highest honor is due and from which all other estates derive. Teachers, managers, and government officials, for example, fulfill the same functions as parents by providing for those under their care, but on a wider level. Luther frequently described such roles or positions as "masks of God"; he believed that God is at work precisely through these human agents. Thus, he claims, "God wants us to honor and respect these 'positions' as his masks or instruments through which he preserves and governs the world."[21] God's working through these "masks" is not unambiguous, however. On the one hand, Luther calls us to respect these "social positions or external masks" as God's "creatures, which are a necessity for this life."[22] But at the same time, he cautions against confusing God's human agents with God. Those who represent God as stewards of the created order are still sinners, even as they remain agents of God's creation.

---

18. Martin Luther, "Lectures on Genesis [Genesis 19:14]," in *Luther's Works*, vol. 3 (St. Louis: Concordia Publishing House, 1961), 274.

19. Gustav Wingren, *Luther on Vocation*, trans. Carl C. Rasmussen (Philadelphia: Muhlenberg Press, 1957), 27.

20. Luther's own language in this case is inclusive. "To fatherhood and motherhood God has given the special distinction, above all estates that are beneath it, that he commands us not simply to love our parents but also to honor them. With respect to brothers, sisters, and neighbors in general he commands nothing higher than that we love them. Thus he distinguishes father and mother above all other persons on earth, and places them next to himself." *The Large Catechism*, I:105, in Tappert, ed., *Book of Concord*, 379.

21. Martin Luther, "Lectures on Galatians, 1535 [Galatians 2:6]," *Luther's Works*, vol. 26 (St. Louis: Concordia Publishing House, 1963), 96.

22. Luther, "Lectures on Galatians, 1535 [Galatians 2:6]," 95.

American Lutheran theologian Robert Benne highlights three important features of these structures that order created life—structures Benne refers to as "places of responsibility." First, they are divinely sanctioned; that is, they are aspects of daily life that are part of God's intention for sustaining earthly existence. Second, they are dynamic. This dynamism "means a constant redefinition of our roles in our places of responsibility. Even when we resist change we redefine ourselves in relation to an environment that is changing."[23] Third, they are ambiguous. In part, this is because—as structures of the created world—they are fragile and finite. Moreover, our participation in these spheres is compromised by human sinfulness. Yet in spite of their provisional and potentially tainted character, Benne argues, these "structures of our common life . . . are the good vehicles of God's creative care for the world."[24]

To summarize, for Luther, the commandments and obligations of daily life replaced any sense of a higher calling and extraordinary deeds available only to a select few. He understood each of the three "orders" or arenas of activity—the household, the state, and the church—as having been established by God for the common good. Humans are called to exercise stewardship within these organizing structures, working to preserve the created world. Given the hierarchical nature of society in Luther's time, his insistence that one's callings are located within the same social structures as everyone else was particularly important. All people have genuine callings from God, and those callings are located within, rather than outside of, ordinary human experience.

## Bonhoeffer: vocation as resistance to the status quo

There is a danger implicit in the Lutheran emphasis on God-given structures through which humans exercise agency on God's behalf. As noted in chapter 3, social structures can be dehumanizing rather than empowering. Stewards are not always trustworthy, and the structures within which they work are not always healthy. According divine authority to social structures all too often results in justifying the status quo. When earthly

---

23. Robert Benne, *Ordinary Saints: An Introduction to the Christian Life* (Minneapolis: Fortress Press, 1988), 77.

24. Benne, *Ordinary Saints*, 79.

structures work against human flourishing, living responsibly may call for resistance to an unjust situation.

Dietrich Bonhoeffer makes an important contribution to this conversation by developing Luther's thought in his own time and place. While Luther's understanding of vocation developed in response to the excessive claims and abusive practices of the medieval church, Bonhoeffer was challenged by the excessive claims and abusive practices of the National Socialist state. In the context of Nazi Germany in the 1930s and 1940s, Bonhoeffer was particularly critical of theologians and church leaders who ignored the dynamism and the ambiguity of earthly structures of authority and treated these organizing structures as fixed "orders of creation" with unquestionable authority.[25]

In his posthumously published *Ethics*, Bonhoeffer consistently asserted that ethics is not abstract but concrete and contextual. "The good" is not a universal ideal; rather it is a reflection of being conformed to Jesus Christ in particular times and places. According to Bonhoeffer, God's grace lays hold of individuals in concrete, earthly circumstances, "be it a royal throne, the home of a respected citizen or a shanty of misery. It is a place of this world."[26] The call of God's grace comes to each of us in our particularity "as Gentile or Jew, slave or free, man or woman, married or unmarried. Right where they happen to be, human beings ought to hear the call and allow themselves to be claimed by it."[27] Bonhoeffer emphasizes personal engagement with one's context when he writes that "what is at stake are the times and places that concern us, that we experience, that are realities for us. What is at stake are the times and places that pose concrete questions to us, set us tasks, and lay responsibilities on us."[28] Wingren makes a similar point when he writes, "As soon as I think of my neighbor, all vocations no longer stand on a common plane, but a certain vocation comes to the fore as mine."[29]

---

25. For a Lutheran critique of a static interpretation of fixed "orders of creation," see Edward H. Schroeder, "The Orders of Creation—Some Reflections on the History and Place of the Term in Systematic Theology," *Concordia Theological Monthly* 43, no. 3 (March 1972): 165–178.

26. Dietrich Bonhoeffer, *Ethics*, Dietrich Bonhoeffer Works, vol. 6 (Minneapolis: Fortress Press, 2005), 290.

27. Bonhoeffer, *Ethics*, 290.

28. Bonhoeffer, *Ethics*, 100.

29. Wingren, *Luther on Vocation*, 65.

Bonhoeffer expanded Luther's three God-given spheres of responsibility to four: labor, marriage, government, and church.[30] In Bonhoeffer's understanding, human labor, like the human family, continues God's action of creation,[31] while government's function is to preserve what has been created.[32] For Bonhoeffer, as for Luther, the particularities of our existence are set within the broad organizing structures of domestic, economic, civic, and spiritual life within which God is at work ordering and preserving the world. Because these dimensions of life are both dynamic and contextual, what is mandated is responsible action within these arenas, not a specific form or arrangement. Indeed, Bonhoeffer rejects "the justification and sanctification of the worldly orders as such" as "pseudo-Lutheran."[33]

For Bonhoeffer, humans participate in these divinely mandated spheres simultaneously in our roles as workers, family members, and citizens. Bonhoeffer's concern was the whole person before God and the whole person living faithfully in response to God's call within God's world. This does not come easily, however. Bonhoeffer recognized the interaction—and, at times, the conflict—among our roles within these mandates. He gives the example of a physician, whose immediate task (in the economic sphere) is care of his or her patients but who also has a public responsibility (in the civic sphere) to speak out and to take action when scientific truth or human life is threatened.[34] He also recognizes the ambiguity inherent in these overlapping spheres, as well as the impossibility of living out one's callings perfectly, given "the unresolved conflict between

---

30. Both Bonhoeffer and Luther struggled with the best language to articulate this concept. While Luther tended to use the words like "orders" or "estates" [*Orden, Stände*], Bonhoeffer used the word "mandates" [*Mandate*] because he thought its connotations were less static. For both thinkers, the point is not the terminology per se but the facticity, the givenness, of these dimensions of life. Following Benne and others, this chapter uses the phrase "places of responsibility" as a less technical way of referring to these dimensions of vocation that are given rather than chosen.

31. It is worth noting that the word *economy* comes from the Greek words *oikos* (house) and *nomos* (rule, law, function, or structure). Thus economy literally is the rule of the household. It makes sense, then, to think of the arena of work as an extension of the domestic arena.

32. Bonhoeffer, *Ethics*, 68–75.

33. Bonhoeffer, *Ethics*, 289.

34. Bonhoeffer, *Ethics*, 293.

multiple obligations."[35] At times, this may even lead to "leaving a particular earthly vocation in which it is no longer possible to live responsibly."[36]

Bonhoeffer's own life is a powerful example of the costs of responsible engagement with one's context, especially when the status quo must be resisted. Bonhoeffer was one of the founding members of the Confessing Church, formed in 1934 by church leaders who believed that the "German Christian" movement, which collaborated with the Nazi agenda, was violating its God-given responsibilities. Bonhoeffer was also active in political resistance against the National Socialist regime. He worked undercover within military intelligence, was part of an operation to help German Jews emigrate to Switzerland, and was associated with the 1944 plot to assassinate Hitler. Although Bonhoeffer's many international contacts provided opportunities for him abroad, he chose to return to Nazi Germany in order to share the situation of his fellow Germans—a decision which led to his imprisonment and eventual execution.

## *Educating for vocation:*
## *some practical implications*

The multifaceted understanding of vocation that we have traced through Luther and Bonhoeffer offers a realistic awareness of the multiple roles and responsibilities we hold simultaneously. The recovery of the plural dimensions of vocation serves as a corrective to the instrumental view that equates vocation primarily with one's employment. The claim that one has multiple vocations simultaneously is consistent with the complexity of lived human experience. It is also liberatory, freeing people from the burden of feeling they need to find the one divine calling that is intended just for them, whether defined as the perfect job or the perfect mate. Another benefit of this more complex understanding of vocation is its ability to encompass those who are unemployed or underemployed, as well as to validate unpaid vocations such as parenthood, volunteering, and friendship. In whatever arenas of life one finds oneself occupied—work or play, paid or unpaid—all are suitable arenas for living out the divine calling

---

35. Bonhoeffer, *Ethics*, 292.

36. Bonhoeffer, *Ethics*, 291.

to serve the neighbor. Moreover, this dynamic understanding allows for change over time. For example, one's calling as a spouse may have preceded one's calling as a parent, but the latter does not supplant the former. The exercise of one's calling as the parent of adult children is different from the exercise of that calling when those same children were young. These developmental changes in no way suggest that the previous roles were somehow incomplete or lesser callings; rather, they reflect the dynamism inherent in the particularities of one's life at specific times and in specific places.

This attentiveness to the multiplicity and diversity of our context and our callings is particularly relevant in the setting of higher education. Both Luther and Bonhoeffer were educators as well as church leaders. It is appropriate, then, that their understanding of vocation generates some practical trajectories for the work of educating for vocation today. The remainder of this chapter sketches a few of these trajectories for our consideration. In particular, we will consider how educating for vocation is not just for a select few, not limited to a particular faith perspective, not limited to the physical and intellectual development of our students, and not limited to the classroom.

## Not just for a select few

Luther and his colleagues were revolutionary in calling for universal education, both for boys and for girls. Education was not seen as an end in itself. Their arguments for universal education were directly related to the Lutheran understanding of vocation. Both boys and girls needed to be educated so that they were prepared to fill the various roles that society needed. Of course, Luther's argument for the education of girls had to do with their roles in family life, including child-rearing and household management. Additional roles in economic, civic, and churchly life were open to boys, but all required a basic education. According to Luther, "Every community . . . must have in it many kinds of people besides merchants."[37] A broad general education was necessary in order to prepare people for roles they could not yet anticipate and for future needs that might arise in the community. Luther offers this almost prescient observation: "This is

---

37. Martin Luther, "A Sermon on Keeping Children in School," *Luther's Works*, vol. 46 (Philadelphia: Fortress Press, 1967), 215.

particularly true in our day, when we have to do with more than just the neighbor next door."[38]

The Lutheran reformers also attempted to limit the effect of social or economic status on access to education. Education was seen as a civic responsibility,[39] but Luther also recognized the challenges faced by parents and families. In his 1530 "Sermon on Keeping Children in School," Luther named the problem of parents encouraging their children to make a living rather than to attend school.[40] He argued persuasively for the long-term benefits of education. He then explicitly addressed the matter of educational financing, naming sources almost as diverse as a typical financial aid package today:

> Let *the government* see to it that when it discovers a promising boy he is kept in school. If the father is poor, the resources of *the church* should be used to assist. Let *the rich* make their wills with this work in view, as some have done who have established *scholarship funds*.[41]

Clearly, Luther was arguing against allowing a family's financial circumstances to prevent or delay the education of their children.

The evolution of many colleges and universities in the United States follows a pattern of moving from a very specific and narrowly constructed constituency to serving a wider public. As one example, Wartburg College was founded by German Lutheran immigrants in 1852. Initially a teachers college, it first expanded its scope to include a theological seminary (now a separately incorporated institution) and eventually became a comprehensive liberal arts institution. While Wartburg's structure and its programs evolved over time in response to the changing needs of the community, for the first 100 years of its existence its constituency did not; like most Lutheran colleges and universities, Wartburg was founded by a particular immigrant community to educate its own young people. Tom Christenson

---

38. Luther, "A Sermon on Keeping Children in School," 215.

39. See Luther's 1524 treatise, "To the Councilmen of All Cities in Germany That They Establish and Maintain Christian Schools," *Luther's Works*, vol. 45 (Philadelphia: Fortress Press, 1962), 339–378.

40. Witte, *Law and Protestantism*, 270, notes a dramatic drop in school enrollment in the 1520s, particularly in German universities.

41. Luther, "A Sermon on Keeping Children in School," 257, emphasis added.

describes this model as education "by Lutherans for Lutherans" or, more broadly, "for us/by us."[42] In today's pluralistic society and competitive educational environment, however, this kind of narrow focus is no longer viable.

Christenson suggests that vocation, rather than constituency, is the way to reframe the work of higher education—the vocation of the college or university itself as an educational institution as well as the vocations for which we educate our students.[43] A dynamic understanding of vocation in and for the world challenges institutions to widen the scope of the educational enterprise beyond their communities of origin.

What would it mean for an institution to be faithful to the spirit of its founders, even while it attempts to expand its mission to include constituencies that those founders never imagined? Undertaking this process requires asking a number of complex questions. For a college like Wartburg, these might include: Who are today's immigrants? Whose needs are not being well served by established educational systems? What kinds of educated citizens does our society need here and now? How do we make and keep higher education affordable? Even for private institutions, higher education serves a civic good; thus, institutions of higher education have a moral as well as a practical and financial responsibility to serve a broad base of constituents.

## Not just for Christians

Within the Reformed tradition, there is a history of distinguishing the general calling to faith in Christ from one's particular calling in life. This understanding that the general calling to faith grounds the other callings of one's life is useful when talking with Christians about vocation; however, this approach is limited if one wishes to talk about vocation with non-Christians. Does a non-Christian student have a calling? If so, from what or whom? When one cannot assume a shared faith, Luther is (perhaps surprisingly) a helpful resource, because he grounds vocation in created life rather than the life of faith. God, as creator, calls all people to live

---

42. Tom Christenson, *The Gift and Task of Lutheran Higher Education* (Minneapolis: Augsburg Fortress, 2004), 13; Tom Christenson, *Who Needs a Lutheran College? Values Vision Vocation* (Minneapolis: Lutheran University Press, 2011), 22.

43. Christenson, *Who Needs a Lutheran College?*, 24–31.

responsibly in the world God has made. Because God works in the created world indirectly, through natural and human agency, this is true regardless of whether or not the people themselves "hear" or acknowledge this call as coming from God.[44] Thus, Luther's understanding of vocation is particularly useful when dealing with a religiously diverse student body, since the contexts of family, work, and civic society are shared by all.

One the statements commonly attributed to Luther is, "It is better to be ruled by a wise Turk than a foolish Christian." While almost certainly apocryphal, this claim expresses a sentiment that accords with the Lutheran understanding of vocation. While Luther held that faith alone justifies the sinner before God, participation in the domestic, economic, and civic spheres of created life required—and still requires—essential knowledge and skills for which faith and good will are no substitute. It is reason, not faith, that is the appropriate criterion with regard to human relationships and actions within the created order, and reason is (pardon the pun) the raison d'être of institutions of higher education.

While Luther probably met no more than a handful of non-Christians in his life, the fact that his understanding of vocation is rooted in his doctrine of creation allows space for Christians and non-Christians to participate together in the preservation—and, indeed, flourishing—of life in this world. Luther's colleague at the University of Wittenberg, Philip Melanchthon, referred to schools as "civic seminaries."[45] This language points to the common good within the social order as the chief end of education, and the common good is something that people of differing faiths or no faith can work together to discern and to pursue.

Similarly, Bonhoeffer's discussion of vocation leaves an opening for religious difference. Bonhoeffer himself focused on the divine call of Jesus Christ, which leads into but ultimately transcends the other orders.[46] Nevertheless, he argued that this does not mean that the church can overrule the other orders within their own spheres of authority. The organizing structures of created life—family, work, and civic society—are constituted and authorized by God; they retain their God-given legitimacy, but they are penultimate. According to Bonhoeffer,

---

44. See chapter 5 for consideration of the phenomenon of hearing a call, as well as chapter 6 for reflections on the identity of the caller.

45. Witte, *Law and Protestantism*, 259, 271.

46. Bonhoeffer, *Ethics*, 290–291.

the *ultimate* responsibility of Christians is to proclaim the grace of God, but this does not exempt them from the penultimate—but no less real—responsibilities of daily life in the created order. As he notes, "The hungry person needs bread, the homeless person needs shelter, the one deprived of rights needs justice, the lonely person needs community, the undisciplined one needs order, and the slave needs freedom."[47] Here, Bonhoeffer reflects biblical injunctions for social action (see, e.g., Luke 4:16–21 and Matthew 25:31–40), while seeing them as something that human beings must claim as their own: "From Christ's perspective this life is now my vocation; from my own perspective it is my responsibility."[48] This affirmation of life as responsibility from the human perspective suggests that callings are not limited to a particular faith perspective, nor even to those who would identify the "caller" as God.

This approach raises several important questions for educators to consider and to wrestle with within the specificity of their own institutional contexts. How do we help students to recognize that they may experience a call, even a divine call, through earthly voices such as their parents or their peers rather than as a dramatic revelation? How can students come to recognize themselves as divine agents, participating in God's work of ordering created life? How do the custodians of an institution's heritage talk about religious or spiritual values in ways that are faithful to their own particularity without excluding those whose views differ? Can shared human and religious commitments to the common good create relationships and conversations through which students, faculty, and staff come to a deeper appreciation of the transcendent?

## Not just for head and hands

Those of us engaged in liberal arts education insist that the value of such an education is that it does not simply prepare a student for a desired job or profession,[49] but that it equips students with a set of intellectual skills and tools that will be useful in navigating a complex and changing world. A broad liberal arts education is ideally matched with an understanding

---

47. Bonhoeffer, *Ethics*, 163.

48. Bonhoeffer, *Ethics*, 290.

49. As noted in chapter 2 (note 29), 86.3% of entering college students rate the ability "to get a better job" as "very important" in their decision to attend a college. See Kevin Eagan et al., *The American Freshman: National Norms Fall 2013*, 35.

of vocations (plural), because it equips students to think and to act both critically and nimbly. Students in pre-professional majors (e.g., business rather than economics, or electronic media rather than communications) benefit from studying in a liberal arts context, which provides them with more than just the job skills and training they might receive elsewhere. The skills and habits of mind acquired in college will be even more essential, given the likelihood not only of job changes but of career changes in their future.[50]

Beyond this, however, undergraduate education—particularly in a liberal arts setting—provides a vital context for moral development and character formation. Higher education has always had a stake in personal and societal formation.[51] How much more should this be the case for those institutions committed to considering vocation as a dimension of education? For many students, the college years are a significant time of personal development. The typical undergraduate is between eighteen and twenty-two years old, a period now often referred to as emerging adulthood. College offers a time and place for students to explore their identity, distinct from (but still connected with) family of origin and peers. Residential colleges offer an enhanced opportunity for such development because students, together with faculty and staff, participate together in a relatively close-knit community. New relationships and new responsibilities in a new community can foster moral development as well as cognitive development.

Understanding and engaging family, economic, civic, and religious life as organizing structures of God's creating and sustaining activity is not a simple task. Living responsibly is not just a matter of who, what, and where, but ultimately of *how* one lives in response to God's call. Luther himself was careful to distinguish between the office, the office-holder, and how the office is exercised. With respect to family life, for example, the belief that God has established parenthood as an organizing structure is no guarantee that a particular parent will not be incompetent or abusive. With respect to civic life, the belief that God has established government as an organizing structure could never, in and of itself, justify

---

50. For example, no one working today as a sustainability manager, a patient advocate, or a social media strategist could have chosen—or even found—a pre-professional major twenty years ago to prepare them for the job they now hold, since these jobs did not yet exist.

51. See chapter 2 for a brief description of how colleges and universities in the U.S. were founded to shape specific visions of society.

a particular form of government or those who hold office in it (although Lutherans have often acted as though it did). Indeed, a healthy understanding of vocation as the human responsibility to serve the neighbor should lead to a willingness to call governments to account—especially when they fail to fulfill their God-given task of preserving created life and promoting human flourishing.

When these structures and the people in them fail to fulfill their purposes, more than intellectual skills and a knowledge of history are necessary for structural critique. Moral reasoning is necessary in order to determine the appropriate criteria for such critique. Character formation is necessary in order to become the kind of person who fills a role or holds an office responsibly, as God's steward for the common good, as well as to become the kind of person who is willing to act for the sake of one's neighbor despite the possibility of incurring negative consequences for him- or herself. How can education cultivate habits of mind that incline toward the common good, not just self-fulfillment? How do we equip educators to see their roles as formative, not just instructional? What educational experiences help students move from a dualism of clear cut "right" or "wrong" to a more mature understanding of moral complexity that equips them to wrestle with the ambiguities of life and with their own inevitable moral struggles? Part Three of this book will suggest that a focus on *the virtues* is central to these tasks.

## Not just in the classroom

Luther's understanding of vocation was forged through a combination of personal and social experiences outside the classroom. At the age of twenty-one, Luther abandoned law school in order to join an Augustinian monastery, motivated in part by fear for his soul. He had accepted the medieval view that the most valuable form of work was spiritual work, and that the best form of Christian life was that of a cleric or monk. When chastised by his upwardly mobile father, Luther insisted that his prayers would do much more for his parents than a successful law career. Luther was quite successful as an Augustinian friar, rising to a level of responsibility that involved supervising others and negotiating disputes on behalf of the order. Still, he struggled with the feeling that he could never do enough or be good enough to please God. Clearly, his personal experiences had undermined his confidence in the belief that, through religious vows, one entered a life closer to God and God's grace. As a result of theological reflection on his experience, in 1521 Luther wrote an extensive critique of the value of monastic vows.

The understanding of vocation that Luther inherited was inadequate, not only for the specific structures that he experienced, but also for the wider social changes brought about by the Reformation. In Wittenberg and elsewhere, Luther's critique of monastic vows quickly led to an emptying of convents and monasteries. An unintended consequence was the loss of vowed religious workers to perform some of the charitable and educational tasks on which late medieval society depended. Likewise, Luther's encouragement of doing the works associated with one's particular roles in life, rather than doing the specifically religious acts promoted by the church, resulted in a noticeable decline in almsgiving and thus a detrimental impact on those living in poverty. Those communities that adopted Luther's theological reforms quickly found themselves faced with the need to establish and maintain schools and to develop programs of social reform. Such developments pointed to the socio-political realm as a legitimate area for the exercise of Christian vocation—not only in meeting the concrete needs of real neighbors, but also in validating the civic roles of those involved in governance and social welfare as valuable Christian vocations.

Luther's experiences outside the classroom, both personal and communal, were thus essential in shaping his convictions about broader vocations in society and about the relationship between education and society. In fact, one of Luther's students recorded an offhand comment of Luther's about the importance of practical experience in education:

> Teachers of law can humble their students when the students try to put on airs about their learning, because they have a court and get practical experience. On the other hand, we can't humble our students because we have no practical exercises. Yet experience alone makes the theologian.[52]

Likewise, practical experience was a central component of Bonhoeffer's life and work. Bonhoeffer had significant international experience, including postdoctoral studies in New York City, ministry in Barcelona and in

---

52. Martin Luther, "No. 46: Value of Knowledge Gained by Experience, Summer or Fall, 1531," *Luther's Works*, vol. 54 (Philadelphia: Fortress Press, 1967), 7.

London, and frequent travel associated with his ecumenical work. This immersion in other contexts sharpened his ability to think critically about his own churchly and societal milieu. Consequently, Bonhoeffer stressed the importance of practical experience in education. Bonhoeffer was committed to community engagement, in part, as a result of his awareness that the predominant academic model of university education was inadequate for the dire circumstances of church and society in 1930s Germany, where the universities and many of the churches conformed to Nazi ideology. As he wrote in a letter to Karl Barth in 1936, "these young theologians need a completely different kind of training, training that absolutely should include such communal training experiences."[53] For Bonhoeffer, these "communal training experiences" included the nuclear life of the community of learners as well as outreach into the wider community.[54]

Luther's and Bonhoeffer's comments, as well as their experiences, suggest that an education that confines itself strictly to the classroom is inadequate for responding to the needs of world that education intends to equip students to address. This conviction raises questions with which today's educational institutions must also wrestle in our own time and place. What kind of practical experiences can and should we provide for our students, both in and outside of the classroom? How do we stimulate deep reflection on student experience? How do we shape experiential learning so that it becomes not just a matter of "What am I good at?" and "What do I enjoy?" but "Who is my neighbor?" and "What does my neighbor need?"

This emphasis on learning that extends beyond the classroom entails another observation, namely, that faculty are not the only resources in educating for vocation. Administrators, student life professionals, coaches, and others all play important roles in student education and formation. Educating students to live as whole (holy?) persons and responsible selves requires the resources of the entire college community. How do we equip all members of the college community to help students see the many aspects of their lives through the lens of vocation?[55]

53. Dietrich Bonhoeffer, *Theological Education at Finkenwalde: 1935–1937*, Dietrich Bonhoeffer Works, vol. 14 (Minneapolis: Fortress Press, 2013), 253; also excerpted in Introduction, 16.

54. It is no coincidence that Bonhoeffer's book about this alternative teaching-learning community was titled *Life Together*.

55. See chapter 11 on partnerships between faculty and administrative and professional staff, as well as chapter 13 on community engagement.

Residential campuses in particular have a rich possibility of educating students for the multiple, overlapping, and sometimes conflicting dimensions of life in the world. Education does not stop when the student exits the classroom. Many college students today are sharing a room with another person for the first time in their lives. How can the college years shape attitudes and interpersonal relationships that are not primarily self-serving but foster respect and a commitment to creating shared space and working for the common good? As educators, how do we instill in our students the awareness that college is already the real world, not a temporary alternative to it? As students work to balance study, work (whether on or off campus), residential life, and co-curricular activities, they are already living the challenges they will continue to face after graduation in their intersecting roles and responsibilities as workers, family members, and citizens.

## *Always reforming*

Focusing on vocation as response to the needs of the neighbor in the world also provides impetus for educational reform. The Lutheran Reformation was not limited to the church; the reformers also launched a comprehensive reform of the educational system in Germany. New schools were established, and existing schools adopted a humanistic curriculum grounded in the study of languages, literature, rhetoric, and history. As the Reformation spread beyond Germany, the establishment of schools and curricular reform continued to be a hallmark of Lutheran communities.

Bonhoeffer's life provides a more radical example of educational change in response to extreme circumstances and needs. An oppressive situation in which the government was not fulfilling—indeed, was violating—its God-given responsibilities required an educational approach willing to challenge the status quo. The Confessing Church provided an alternative to state-sanctioned theological education. Even after his license to teach was revoked for his opposition to the National Socialist regime, Bonhoeffer continued to educate leaders for the Confessing Church, first in an underground seminary at Finkenwalde, then illegally in small groups in local parishes.

The examples of Luther and Bonhoeffer call us to think critically about educational practices in our own place and time. Luther lived and worked in a context of widespread social change. Bonhoeffer lived and worked in a context of totalitarian oppression. For both men, the recognition of multiple callings in multiple dimensions of human life was essential to their work. Their emphasis on the plurality of our callings, however, should not be understood primarily in numerical terms, as if more were better. Rather, specific spheres of responsibility need to be identified as unavoidable givens. Such an approach challenges us to avoid focusing too narrowly on some dimensions of life to the exclusion of others. While we have choices about how to engage our families, our work, and our communities, we do not have the choice simply not to participate in the domestic, economic, and civic spheres.

College students today experience pressures and expectations from many directions. Recovering an understanding of vocation as our multiple callings to responsible relationships and action within the world—and educating students to engage these callings thoughtfully and with humility—are among the essential tasks of higher education.

# 5

## Stories of Call

### FROM DRAMATIC PHENOMENA TO CHANGED LIVES

*Charles Pinches*

WHEN BLACK ELK was a young man, he heard voices. "It was like some-body was calling me, and I thought it was my mother, but there was nobody there. This happened more than once, and always made me afraid, so I ran home." One day, when Black Elk had grown old enough to carry his grandfather's bow and ride on horseback, he saw a kingbird. As he prepared to shoot it, the bird spoke:

> "Listen! A voice is calling you!" Then I looked up at the clouds, and two men were coming there, headfirst like arrows slanting down; and as they came they sang a sacred song and the thunder was like drumming. I will sing it for you. The song and the drumming were like this: "Behold, a sacred voice is calling you; All over the sky a sacred voice is calling."[1]

Sitting in a cave at age forty, Muhammad suddenly felt a formidable presence telling him to "Proclaim! (or Read!) / In the name / Of thy Lord and Cherisher, / Who created— / Created man, out of / A leech-like clot: / Proclaim! And thy Lord / Is Most Bountiful,— / He Who taught / (The

---

1. As narrated to John G. Neihardt, *Black Elk Speaks* (Lincoln: University of Nebraska Press, 1932), 19. A phrase in this quotation becomes the title for John Neafsey's *A Sacred Voice Is Calling: Personal Vocation and Social Conscience* (Maryknoll, NY: Orbis Books, 2006), see especially pp. xi and 23.

use of) the Pen,— / Taught man that / Which he knew not" (Sura 96:1–5). Muhammad was terrified; in his horror, he ran from the cave but was unable to escape the strange presence. According to Ibn Ishaq's record of Muhammad's recollection of the event,

> When I was midway on the mountain, I heard a voice from heaven saying, "O Muhammad! Thou art the apostle of God and I am Gabriel." I raised my head towards heaven to see who was speaking, and lo, Gabriel in the form of a man with feet astride the horizon . . . I stood gazing at him, moving neither backward or forward; then I began to turn my face away from him, but towards whatever region of the sky I looked, I saw him as before.[2]

These two episodes illustrate the experience of "receiving a call." As the stories show, this experience can involve intense drama. It spans religious traditions—in this case, Islam and Lakota religious beliefs—but it also includes those traditions more familiar in the West, including Judaism and Christianity. In these traditions, too, a call can be dramatic: Moses is stopped in his tracks by the strange sight of the burning bush; Paul, at that time still known as Saul, is struck blind by a blazing light while traveling along the road.

These different cases of "receiving a call" can be investigated primarily as *phenomena*—that is, as narrowly circumscribed events in time and space that have common features. So, for instance, one might observe that for both Black Elk and Muhammad, voice and vision come together. In both cases, the sky is involved; a calling presence is spread out everywhere and cannot be escaped. Such an analysis, focused solely on the phenomenological experience, might prove fascinating.[3] However, in order to understand key elements of "receiving a call" displayed in these remarkable stories, we must proceed with caution. Accounts of receiving a call cannot be lifted from their context in religious traditions and separated from the lives and characters these traditions honor.

---

2. Ibn Ishaq, *Sirat Rasoul Allah*, Internet Archive, p. 21, http://www.archive.org/details/Sirat-lifeOfMuhammadBy-ibnIshaq (accessed November 8, 2014).

3. Rudolf Otto builds his famous *The Idea of the Holy* around the elements of mystery, fear, and fascination that he believes permeate encounters with the holy. His book is primarily a phenomenological exploration. In it he considers some biblical stories of call, such as Moses's at the burning bush. Rudolf Otto, *The Idea of the Holy*, trans. John W. Harvey (New York: Oxford University Press, 1958), 127.

Understood mainly as a remarkable phenomenon, call stands in danger of abstraction. Removed from its context in particular human lives and time-honored traditions, the phenomenon of "receiving a call" can be merely for show, of little use in our own processes of vocational exploration and discernment.

For instance, the story with which this chapter began comes from *Black Elk Speaks*, a book widely considered to offer deep wisdom about human life, especially a life lived in community. In this respect it is deeply embedded in the world of the Oglala Lakota, whose traditional ways were threatened in Black Elk's time. The story of this man's poignant words and actions contributed to the survival of his people through this time, as they looked for ways to carry their identity forward into a new world. Because we know of Black Elk, and something of the remarkable life he lived, we are interested in his account of the bird that speaks and the sacred voice that calls. Similarly, we listen to and are intrigued by Muhammad's account of what transpired in the cave precisely because Muhammad gave birth to the religion of Islam. But if we knew nothing of this, or didn't care, and were examining these accounts only as the record of strange but intriguing phenomena, the stories would likely strike us simply as dramatic bits of fiction or delusion.

Focusing too much attention on the experience of call as a phenomenon is a special temptation in our time. We are intrigued by the dramatic stories and experiences of the likes of Black Elk or Muhammad; however, their power remains locked in a distant world that seems very unlike our own. In effect, the stories intrigue us to the degree that they excite our imaginations—but they tend to do so only when we keep them at a safe distance. Like Cecil B. DeMille, we are tempted to pluck the drama from the story and use it as we like; we thereby insulate ourselves from engaging with the story itself. Such distancing is unfortunate, since in these stories—and this is true for every religious tradition in which call stories are told—those who are called fully enter the struggles of life, living them out in such a way that, later on, their call stories become worthy of our attention. Put another way, call stories are worth hearing if and only if they yield significant, enduring results in the life of the one called.[4] But

---

4. An exception to this rule is to be found in the biblical record in a few stories that focus attention on a call that is rejected by the one who is called. The rich young ruler, whose story is important in all the synoptic gospels, is the clearest example of this. The story is discussed below, in the section headed "Responding to the call."

we are tempted to ignore this when we look principally to the mere events, to the phenomenon alone. As a result, we tend to regard these stories as primarily about *someone else's experience*, and can thereby avoid having to think about what it might mean for *us* to be called.

Unsurprisingly, then, some have attempted to downplay the phenomenological details of their own call stories. Mother Teresa did this. She received what she called a "call within a call" while traveling on the train from Kolkata to Darjeeling on September 10, 1946. That she received the call at that time, and that it transformed her, was widely known; indeed, the date has been long celebrated as "Inspiration Day" by the sisters of the order she founded, the Missionaries of Charity. However, most of the details of this call remain hidden. For the nuns, "it was understood that the one thing you could not ask Mother Teresa about was the grace of the train. She would deflect the question and speak only of a divine 'command' to go to the slums to serve the poor."[5] Partly she kept silent about the experience because she could not put words on so intimate an exchange. But she also wished to focus her companions' attention on the shared work that came from the call—and this meant that she needed to discourage their curiosity about the call as a mere phenomenon.

Mother Teresa's caution shapes the contours of this chapter. Stories of receiving a call display important elements of what having a vocation might mean; however, they also can mislead. We should not imagine, for instance, that a dramatic call story is required in order for us to be called. As Mother Teresa saw, call is much more about the long work to be done than about the momentary encounter experienced. In our age, especially, we prefer the latter; hence we tend to neglect the training that prepares us for our calling. This chapter's first section examines this matter, extending some of the points just noted about our current culture's resistance to call. The second section attends to some of the common elements of these stories, considering especially what their logic might require—that is, what other related ideas and beliefs go along with the idea of call. The third section delves further into some of the biblical call stories, noting especially what they imply for one who seeks to respond to a call. The

---

5. Joseph Langford, *Mother Teresa's Secret Fire* (Huntington, IN: Our Sunday Visitor, 2008), 40. Fr. Langford became a close confidant of Mother Teresa's and co-founded with her an order of priests called the Missionaries of Charity Fathers in 1983. He spent many years puzzling over precisely how things went on the train to Darjeeling. Near the end of her life, he was able to obtain more information about these events from her, including (most importantly for him) that Mother Teresa had heard Jesus saying to her "I thirst."

chapter concludes with a very brief reflection on how call can lead to friendship.

## *Open to a call: humility and attention*

In the modern era, most of us doubt we will receive any sort of call that resembles those in the stories we enjoy hearing—whether ancient ones, like those of Moses or Muhammad, or relatively recent ones like Black Elk on horseback or Mother Teresa on the train. Of course none of these people expected they would receive the calls they did. Black Elk at first doubted the call, assuming that his mother was calling. The biblical judge Gideon was highly skeptical when he was called, asking for a sign (indeed, many signs) that "it is you [the Lord] who speaks to me" (Judges 6:17). Moses doubted as well: "Who am I that I should go to Pharaoh, and bring the Israelites out of Egypt?" (Exod. 3:11). Call, in other words, hardly eliminates doubt; indeed, the two are fairly consistent companions.

Still, the doubt that accompanies call in these classic stories is different from our modern doubt about call. The subjects seem to doubt their own ability or worthiness to receive a call, whereas modern people tend to doubt the very possibility of an audible or visible call. Moreover, in the great call stories, doubt is almost always accompanied by something else: *fear.* As already noted, Muhammad was terrified and ran from his call. Moses hears the Lord speak from the bush and hides his face, "for he was afraid to look at God" (Exod. 3:6). When the angel appears to announce the birth of Jesus to the shepherds in the field, "they were terrified" (Luke 2:9). A few verses earlier, the angel seems to assume that Mary's call will induce fear, insofar as it begins with the words "Do not be afraid" (1:30).

In contrast, in our time, this twinning of doubt with fear is relatively rare. If anything, modern doubt is more frequently mixed with confidence, the self-assertion of certain knowledge about what is or isn't possible. This is not to say that fear has disappeared from our modern world; if anything, it is more pervasive. John Paul II began his papacy with the phrase, which he repeated almost daily, "Do not be afraid."[6] He believed a spirit of fear characterized the modern age, concerned as it is with security and protection, and formed in the suspicions that accompany them.

---

6. See John Paul II, *Crossing the Threshold of Hope,* ed. Vittorio Messori (New York: Alfred Knopf, 1994), esp. 3–12.

As we doubt differently, so also do we fear differently. Moses's whole existence was not characterized by fear; according to the story he was busy tending the flock of his father-in-law Jethro, leading the sheep "beyond the wilderness" (Exod. 3:1). This small but vital task of daily life is interrupted by the burning bush and the voice of God, and the interruption causes Moses to fear. The same can be said of the shepherds or Gideon or Black Elk. In all these stories, the call is deeply close and personal; precisely this is what occasions fear. By contrast, pervasive fear in the modern age lacks a specific target. We do not know what we fear, or, perhaps better, we fear what we *cannot* know: the unnamed, impersonal abyss that is beyond our access.

The difference between these two types of fear can be tested by their relation to *love*. If we fear a personal presence that suddenly confronts us in the form of a burning bush or a talking bird, and then discover as we engage with it that it confronted us out of love, we lose our fear: "perfect love casts out fear" (1 John 4:18). Our dominant modern fear, however, is not so easily addressed, for how could the unknown, impersonal abyss confront us out of love?

Peter Berger spoke of a "sacred canopy"[7] that once shielded the whole world—from human life to the life of Jethro's sheep, and even the mountain of God that Moses traverses in the desert. The canopy placed human activity in the context of a mysterious, but meaningfully ordered, sacred universe. While the sacred purposes laced within the mystery remained largely hidden, they could blaze forth at any time. People knew this sacred order because they felt themselves participants in it. Jethro's sheep needed grass, and so Moses led them; Black Elk needed food to sustain his family's life, and so he hunted. In the case of each man's call, one purposeful and ordered activity is interrupted and transformed into another by a sacred voice that suddenly comes close and lays out a new unexpected direction.

Our ancestors tended to understand their everyday work—whether as hunters, shepherds, or seafarers—as part of a larger universe of order and purpose. In contrast, we typically conceive of our lives as enclosed structures that provide space for the meanings we ourselves make. Here, perhaps, lies the greatest modern impediment to the notion that a sacred

---

7. *The Sacred Canopy: Elements of a Sociological Theory of Religion* (New York: Anchor Books, 1967).

voice is calling each of us: we are less likely to experience the world as arranged according to larger purposes into which our smaller purposes need to fit.

Some will claim that our modern way of seeing is more accurate; for them, the sacred canopy was lifted for good reason, in that it was based upon a fiction. If held consistently, this view closes off the very possibility of a call. But before rushing to this view, we should consider whether our modern versions of doubt and fear have tended to distort our readings of call stories like those we have just briefly considered. For the modern age, any rigorous examination of "call" will require *preparation*, which includes some degree of "unlearning" certain impeding assumptions. Two capacities are of particular importance in this regard: *humility* and *attention*.[8]

Humility relates to *humus*; by it we are reminded that our lives arise from the ground, and will return to it. Humility has a de-centering effect, opening us to an awareness of the limits of our control; we begin to perceive how much of our life is consumed with the feverish attempt to build ourselves up into something larger than we are. "Attention," as Simone Weil describes it, opens us to communication with the divine, to prayer. Its awakening comes as we learn to give our close and undivided attention to something—for Weil, almost anything at all. This prepares the mind to turn in its highest reaches to its highest object: God.[9] As A. J. Conyers interprets Weil, attention means "the overthrowing of 'vain imaginations,' the disposal of a self-centered view of existence."[10]

For our purposes in this book, these two capacities are particularly important as we consider the idea of "calling" in the context of higher education. Arguably, the modern university is structured to keep humility at abeyance. If knowledge is conceived as something to possess, and if its possession is conceived as a means to power, then as the purveyor of knowledge, the university trains us to achieve in such a way as to dominate others. This is the very opposite of humility. Furthermore, the task

---

8. On humility, see the comments at the end of chapter 6; on attention, see the comments on "hearing" in chapter 12. Both of these capacities might also be understood as virtues, as that language is developed in Part Three of this book; see especially the comments on memory and teachability in chapter 9.

9. Simone Weil, "Reflections on the Right Use of Social Studies with a View to the Love of God," in *Waiting for God*, trans. Emma Gruafurd (London: Routledge and Kegan Paul, 1952), 51–57. This essay is excerpted in Placher, ed., *Callings*, 400–404 (see chap. 4, note 10).

10. A. J. Conyers, *The Listening Heart: Vocation and the Crisis of Modern Culture* (Waco, TX: Baylor University Press, 2009), 121.

of *study* in the modern university is in danger of coming uncoupled from the "attention" that Weil considers essential to it. So Conyers believes that, increasingly in our time,

> whether one receives something of value from the subject depends on whether it is instantly accessible to the mind. So the student who wants to convey the idea that he has a high "I.Q." claims hardly to study at all. . . . Or a student claims not to have an aptitude for something if it requires effort to understand. This is the obverse side of the same attitude—mental achievements are worthy in inverse proportion to the effort required.[11]

Such an attitude is the inverse of Weil's "attention."

Yet while this is a *temptation* of the modern university, it is not a *necessity*. If the college or university is rather a place where we are schooled in practices that open us to greater truths than we might imagine, it can still be a place of attention. It can also be a place of humility if, in presenting these truths, it can remind us that we are limited creatures, dependent on the wisdom of others, and that we can still fix our minds on things that are above us, coming gradually to know and even to love them.[12] As a place where we learn both humility and attention, the university can clear space in which to listen carefully for our calling.

But how do we start, particularly when we have been schooled in habits and attitudes that oppose both humility and attention? In one poignant biblical story we hear of Naaman, a Syrian general, who "was a great man," "in high favor," and "a mighty warrior"—but he was also a leper (2 Kgs. 5:1). The story of Naaman's healing from his leprosy is also a story of his humbling. And as he is humbled he learns to pay attention to voices he would have otherwise ignored.

Propelled by his need to be healed of his leprosy, Naaman listens to the advice of an Israelite slave girl in his service who tells him he can find healing in Israel. Armed with gifts and an official letter, he visits the king of Israel, whom Naaman presumes (through long-practiced habits related to his high status) must be running the show. But the Israelite king suspects a Syrian plot with which he will have nothing to do. Luckily,

---

11. Conyers, *Listening Heart*, 119.

12. See the comments on the relationship between love and knowledge in chapter 7.

Elisha the prophet catches wind of the matter and invites Naaman to visit his home. When Naaman arrives, however, Elisha does not come to greet him; instead, he sends a messenger to tell him to wash in the Jordan River. Naaman is incensed, convinced that there are many better, cleaner rivers back in his homeland; he thus "turned and went away in a rage" (5:11). Once again, he is saved by a servant who says, "If the prophet had commanded you to do something difficult, would you not have done it? How much more, when all he said to you was 'Wash and be clean'" (5:13). Naaman listens, washes, and "his flesh was restored like the flesh of a young boy, and he was clean" (5:14).

Naaman's healing, however, is not the end of this story. He attempts to offer gifts to Elisha for his health, but Elisha refuses, saying, "As the Lord lives, whom I serve, I will accept nothing!" (5:16). Elisha is adamant about this; he knows that what he has offered—life and health—is not something to be bought. But further, one suspects that his refusal is meant to remind Naaman that the old methods of using power, money, and valor to gain privilege have turned out in this story to be false and empty. This point is reinforced at the end of the story, when Elisha's servant Gehazi lies to Naaman and collects his money—and later, as a judgment, his leprosy as well. A key to Naaman's new life will be to recognize his dependency on the mysterious, life-giving gifts of others. So Naaman gathers some soil from Elisha's yard and returns to his home, pledging to worship only the Lord, the God of Israel (5:17).

We hear no more of how it all went back in Syria, but the implication of the story is that Naaman is reinstalled in his old life, himself a new man. His journey, propelled by his need, has led him to see the world in a new way; he has "overthrown his vain imaginations." A new story opens for him, because he has learned humility. Crucial in this learning was the recognition that he could not *achieve* his life and health. In the process of learning this, and propelled by his need, Naaman was opened up to communication from sources he would otherwise have shut out. By attending to these new sources, he learned to depend on them and to follow their sound advice. He learned to listen, to *attend*.

While Naaman's story does not relate any special call from God, it is especially instructive in our modern context. Naaman begins with the assumption that through his own effort and with the reputation and resources he has built with those in power he can guide his own life forward to success and security. The leprosy that touches him, though, turns out to be his salvation; it teaches him that what he loves, his life and health, is sustained by hands that are not his own. Following the advice of others whose lives of service have taught them a wisdom that Naaman's position has shielded from him, he takes his place in the Jordan, whose dirty waters are precisely what can make him clean.

In our time, we are likely to be guided by the narrative Naaman lived before his sickness. We spend our lives building up the means to secure success—and we counsel and educate young people to do the same. Yet cracks develop within this narrative. Indeed, perhaps we knew vaguely all along that they would—as our modern fears, unnamed yet pervasive, would suggest. Like Naaman, we need something to need—as well as servant voices to help us articulate that need, reminding us how prideful and, actually, silly is the story we are trying to live. We may need something like Naaman's lesson to develop the listening heart that can open to the sacred voice that is calling. If and when it comes, it will surely frighten us; but as the call stories in the next section suggest, that fear can recede, and even turn to love, as we come to recognize that we do not act alone. Rather, as Muhammad put it, we are (and always have been) in the hands of "the Sustainer, who taught us what we did not know."

## Call in context: location, logic, and scope

If our modern predispositions are not so strong as to close off the very possibility of a call, we can begin to notice its logic—particularly as this is displayed in important call stories of the great religious traditions. These stories do not simply record extraordinary phenomena; they spread out into the whole life of the person who responds to a call. Mother Teresa, for instance, lived the kind of life that supports the story of her call and makes it matter; if we are interested in her call, we must also be interested in her life.[13] The story of a call therefore reminds us to look, not simply directly *at it*, but *all around it*. In the case of Black Elk, this would mean recognizing that he had developed, even as a young child, an inchoate yet very real sense of a sacred realm that framed his life. That context helps

---

13. Fr. Langford was perhaps successful in bringing Mother Teresa to speak more openly about the actual experience of her "call within a call" because he came to her with the intention of founding an order of priests related to Mother Teresa's order of nuns. He wished to know the details precisely so that they could inform the charism of the new order. See Langford, *Mother Teresa's Secret Fire*, 38–47.

us understand how, later in life, he was able more fully to identify and embrace the sounds that came to him across the sky as a sacred voice calling.

As noted above, it is difficult to make sense of the notion of calling if one supposes there is no such realm from which a call might come. Or, put more precisely: *if someone is called, it seems that there must be a caller who solicits his or her attention.* While the next chapter will take up this question in more detail, we can here note that the story of a call functions in part to reveal something of the caller's character and purposes; this is necessary because the one who is called does not yet know who the caller is. This is why the occasion of the call elicits questions from the called to the caller about identity. "Who are you Lord?" asks Saul, when he is struck to the ground by a blinding light (Acts 9:5). If the one called holds suppositions about the caller, the call itself is sure to put them to the test. In this sense, a call is rightly positioned in the middle—partway between a settled denial of the existence of a caller, and complete certainty about the caller's nature.

This point helps uncover another feature of the logic of call. To whatever extent a call story is taken to imply the presence of a caller, its power to do so is based not in argument but in *personal witness in the form of a story.* For example, Saul had a particularly vivid experience of being called even while on his way, as a zealous young Jew, to arrest Christians in Damascus. This experience changed his life dramatically; as Paul, he became Christianity's chief evangelist to the Gentiles. In the course of his preaching, he frequently told the story of this experience; it was his way of witnessing to what he had come to believe. His call story matched his life—both supported the other. Again, call stories become worthy of our attention insofar as they are lived. And, indeed, if we notice a life (like Paul's or Mother Teresa's), we wonder what made it possible. In this way, call becomes plausible through the witness of a life.

Thus, call importantly *ties the experiences that we have to the work that we do.* We cannot know the significance of the call without the work to which it led; yet at the same time, we cannot know the significance of the work itself unless our understanding of it is informed by the call. This may become clear only in hindsight, and perhaps only as the call narrative is told or written. We should not assume that every call will lay out a precise path forward. Call must open *some* sort of path; if it does not eventually yield work, it is useless. However, not all call stories come with clear instructions for moving forward, and the relationship of the work and the call may take some time to emerge.

Religious traditions such as Christianity or Judaism carry along call stories, many of them quite dramatic. But the stories are not told and retold simply to inflame all believers with a yearning for similar call experiences. Rather, the stories are most valuable as they provoke a personal response that reaches out to do work that is both like and unlike the work of the one called in the story told. So a Christian might say: since Paul was called to preach to the Gentiles, perhaps God is also calling me to some related but also different work—one especially well suited to me at this time and in this place. This means that a call is tied, not principally to the experience of being called and its accompanying phenomena, but rather to how the experiences of our lives point (or pointed) to the work or tasks that are (or were) set before us.

Within a religious tradition, call stories encourage analogical thinking. The analogy assists in *the task of discernment*, which is a necessary feature of the call. Call implies discernment precisely insofar as it links inherited understandings of the one who calls and of the work that the call invites people to undertake. Discernment about call draws us into the tradition at the same time that it affirms our distinctive role within it.[14] So in discerning her call, a Christian can rightly say: since the same God who called Paul calls me, then the work that this God offers in my call will be like Paul's in some ways—but surely also unlike it, especially since so many differences stand between me (at this time and in this place) and Paul (in his time and place). The analogy emphasizes a connection between the two stories, but also allows for the unique, the particular. As Karl Barth has said, "vocation is the whole of the particularity, limitation and restriction in which each human being meets the divine call and command, which wholly claims him in the totality of his previous existence, and to which above all wholeness and therefore total differentiation

---

14. More than any other, St. Ignatius of Loyola, founder of the Jesuits, has codified the process of discernment as Christians might carry it out as they consider their decisions and callings. Indeed, when Pope Francis, a Jesuit, was asked how his Jesuit training most informed what he brought to his new papal role he answered with one word: "discernment." A variety of books trace how Ignatian discernment might inform our lives and callings. See, for instance, Timothy M. Gallagher, *The Discernment of Spirits: An Ignatian Guide for Everyday Living* (New York: Crossroads, 2005).

and specification are intrinsically proper as God intends and addresses this human being and not another."[15]

Barth here mentions a "previous" existence that is gathered up in all its particularity and specificity as one is called. In doing so he marks that *call signals a new beginning*. While it certainly is true that call looks forward to and is ratified in the work of our lives, call cannot be entirely merged with the various tasks we have simply in virtue of being human. On Barth's accounting, call opens us to a certain path of action or work set out for us in particular. Whether or not the identification of this path comes in a dramatic experience, it remains something we discover through call. Understood in this way, in any called life there is a certain "before" and "after" the call.[16]

In the biblical narrative, the call of Abram in Genesis 12 functions as the beginning—indeed, the beginning of all other beginnings related to call within the Jewish, Christian, and Muslim traditions. While we are given only a brief glimpse, it is important that there is a "previous existence" for Abram, the time spent in his father Terah's household. And, in a deeper sense, the stories of rebellion and dissolution of Genesis 3–11 also function as part of the context of that previous existence.[17] With Abram and his wife Sarai, God begins a new work that responds to this dissolution. God calls, instructing Abram to "go from your country and your kindred and your father's house to the land I will show you. I will make of you a great nation, and I will bless you, and make your name great, so that you will be a blessing" (12:1–2).

As Abram's call is the first term in a long redemptive work, his response similarly makes possible all other responses: "So Abram went as the Lord had told him" (12:4). Abram's assent to the call makes space for ours; indeed, as we respond to a call from this same God, we are participants in Abram's response. Of course, Abram's call is not ours; we are each different from him. Yet his call still relates to us analogically; in each age, a

---

15. Karl Barth, *Church Dogmatics* III:4 (Edinburgh: T&T Clark, 1985), 599–600; translation modified with attention to Barth's use of the German *Mensch* rather than *Mann*.

16. This is not to imply that to be called we must be able to identify the moment we were called. In fact, this is rare. Rather, the point is that since call always moves us to a certain work, we can tell a story of our lives that recounts how that work began for us, and how it has changed us.

17. Biblical scholars have pointed out the connection between the attempt at the tower of Babel to "make a name for ourselves" (Gen. 11:4) and God's promise in Abram's call to make his name great. The contrast is between human hubris and God's freely given blessing.

new call is issued that is continuous with the work begun in him, a call to participate with those who have gone before in God's full redemption begun in the one in whom "all the families of the earth shall be blessed" (12:3). Our call will be a new beginning for us, but it is also a continuation of the work already begun; thus, our call is an offer to contribute in our own unique way to work that is already long underway.

Mother Teresa spoke of her "call within a call" on the train to Darjeeling—by which she meant that her call to serve the poorest of the poor in Kolkata came in the context of an earlier call to join the Sisters of Loretto, who had sent her to Kolkata in the first place. Yet the expression transfers in another sense to all who are called within the context of a religious tradition. Earlier stories of call inform, and to some degree govern, what call can mean for those who follow in the same tradition. Their call is always to be placed within the context of the calls that have preceded it.

This logic is also illustrated by the approach to vocation in early Protestantism, as described in the previous chapter. Luther and Calvin accented the point that all Christians (not just "the religious") were called by God to particular callings: "each individual has his own kind of living assigned to him by the Lord."[18] In the generations following, Puritan theologians such as William Perkins came to identify two sorts of callings, general and particular. "The general calling is the calling of Christianity, which is common to all that live in the Church of God. The particular is that special calling that belongs to some particular men: as the calling of a Magistrate, the calling of a Minister" and so on.[19] The bifurcation between these two callings was unfortunate; indeed, as Max Weber argues,[20] soon enough the second calling—which urged the one called to take up some function within a social order such as magistrate or minister—broke off from the first calling and cleared a path to our modern circumstance in which "vocation" often stands free of the theological context that birthed it. This was not Perkins's intention. He held that "every particular calling

---

18. John Calvin, *Institutes of the Christian Religion*, ed. John T. McNeill and trans. Ford Lewis Battles (Philadelphia: Westminster, 1967), 724. For a recent defense and updating of Calvin's (and also Luther's) account of vocation, see Douglas J. Schuurman, *Vocation: Discerning our Callings in Life* (Grand Rapids, MI: Eerdmans, 2004), especially 48–75.

19. William Perkins, *A Treatise of the Vocations* (London: John Haviland, 1631), excerpted in Placher, ed., *Callings*, 265.

20. See Max Weber, The Protestant Ethic and the Spirit of Capitalism, trans. Talcott Parsons (New York: Charles Scribner's Sons, 1958), especially chapter 5, pp. 155–183. See also the discussions of Weber's work in chapters 1 and 3.

must be practiced in and with the general calling of a Christian."[21] Put differently, any claim to have been called by God to pursue this or that way of life, this or that work, cannot stand on its own authority but rather needs to be drawn within the long tradition of call carried along, at least by Jews and Christians, since Abraham.

This last point may seem to limit the applicability of "call" too narrowly for current conditions of religious pluralism. Yet in another very real sense it actually opens it, because calls arising within particular religious traditions can, and often do, *invite others from outside these traditions to join in the work of the call.* Mother Teresa's Missionaries of Charity serve as a case in point. Their website lists only one requirement for volunteering to help serve the poorest of the poor in Kolkata: "Hearts to love and hands to serve! (Mother Teresa)," and then adds "You are not required to call or write to the sisters ahead of time to go to Kolkata to volunteer. Simply 'show up' for Orientation and Registration at 3 PM on Mondays, Wednesdays and Fridays."[22] The Missionaries of Charity seem not the least interested in limiting the range of call to self-described Christians. For their part, they mean to pursue the particular work they have been called to do by God the Father of Jesus. What would be the reason to refuse others who want to join in the work? Indeed, since the sisters believe Jesus calls us all toward full communion with him "in his distressing disguise" as the poorest of the poor,[23] why not assume that the same call has been heard by anyone who shows up at 3 PM on Monday, Wednesday, or Friday?

In this way call stories that are sustained within various religious traditions can function as an invitation or witness, since they often involve someone whose life was dramatically changed through call. For those who long for such a change in their own lives, these stories attract. This longing is perhaps as present, even more present, in our modern world. So despite modern doubt and modern fear, the call of the Missionaries of Charity can respond to the promptings or yearnings that others may have, Christian or not. They witness to how the Christian tradition conceives of the good of human life and of the one who gives it, and invite others to come develop the skills they need, including attention and humility, to

---

21. Placher, ed., *Callings*, 269.

22. http://www.motherteresa.org/07_family/Volunteering/v_cal.html#1 (accessed October 5, 2014).

23. See James Martin's portrait of Mother Teresa in his *My Life with the Saints* (Chicago: Loyola Press, 2006), 163.

work in this way. The sisters do not do this abstractly, but rather by doing their daily work with the poor, gathering for prayer, and even by celebrating the story of Mother Teresa's call on September 10. Remembering her "call within a call" reminds them of why they work as they do, and locates that work firmly with a long tradition that, nonetheless, is open at many points for others who are called in various ways to join.

## *Responding to the call: conversation, language, future orientation*

The foregoing section has already opened the themes of this final part of the chapter, which concerns elements in the *response* to a call. An obvious feature of call stories is that they *assume call will be matched by response*. Call is surely dependent on the one who calls, the sacred voice; but it is just as dependent on the one who is called. A call is, at least sometimes, heard and responded to. The point is initially epistemological: how else could we know that there was a call unless someone listened and responded? But beyond this, the dependence of call on response suggests a certain vulnerability in the caller as well.[24] Within the dynamic of response lies the possibility of refusal.[25]

The Bible relates many stories in which the one who is called resists, or at least attempts to resist, the call: Moses, Gideon, Jeremiah, perhaps even Jesus in the garden. Only on occasion does it tell us of those who reject it altogether—fittingly, since the biblical story is carried by those who respond, not those who turn away. Yet we do hear such stories. Jonah is one such case, although God persists—calling in the form of a violent storm and a big fish. Most notable is the story of the rich young man who questions Jesus about what will bring him eternal life (Matt. 19:16–22). Their exchange winds around until Jesus tells the man to "sell your possessions, give the money to the poor . . . then come, follow me."[26] As

---

24. It is often assumed that power rests fully with the one in authority, in this case the one who calls. Yet if the logic of authority and obedience is fully probed, we can see a great vulnerability in an authority since it must await a willing response. With call coercion is not an option since it necessarily transforms authority into mere force. See Stanley Hauerwas and Charles Pinches, *Christians Among the Virtues* (Notre Dame, IN.: University of Notre Dame Press, 1997), 133–138.

25. This point will be discussed in more detail in chapter 6; see in particular its reflections on the grammar of the call.

26. Bonhoeffer, *The Cost of Discipleship* (New York: Collier Books, 1963), 84.

Dietrich Bonhoeffer notes, this brings the man "face to face with Jesus, the Son of God: it is the ultimate encounter. It is now only a question of yes or no, of obedience or disobedience. The answer is no." In rejecting the call the man rejects Jesus. So he goes away "sorrowful, disappointed and deceived of his hopes, unable to wrench himself from his past."[27] Jesus lets him go, aware of how heavy a weight he carries with all his riches. As Bonhoeffer notes, call ultimately requires surrender—an obedience that must be complete if it is to bring us into right relation with the one who calls. We should not be surprised when a call is rejected.

Yet as many stories in the biblical tradition suggest, even as it moves toward such a confrontation as this, *call invites, even initiates, conversation.* As just noted, Jesus and the rich young man go back and forth in their exchange.[28] The call of Moses extends this, to an almost comical degree: his discussion with God about call goes on for almost two full chapters, beginning with the appearance of a burning bush that is not consumed. As Moses moves towards it, God, the first to speak, says: "'Moses, Moses!' And Moses said, 'Here I am'" (Exod. 3:4).[29] This response suggests that the two parties have become fully present to one another as the call begins. They are mutually attentive. When God tells Moses who he is—the God of Abraham, Isaac, and Jacob—Moses begins to fear, heightening his attention, even if also bringing forth questions and worries. In response, God describes the suffering among the Israelites, as well as the plan to bring them out of captivity and into a land flowing with milk and honey. The explanation undergirds an assignment to do work. "So now, go. I am sending you to Pharaoh to bring my people the Israelites out of Egypt" (3:10).

But this is hardly the end of the conversation, which includes the well-known reply to Moses's concern about who he shall say sent him: "I am who I am." God then proceeds to lay out plans for Moses, including leading the people and confronting Pharaoh. But Moses pushes this off, offering various objections. God responds to each in turn, sometimes

---

27. Bonhoeffer, *Cost of Discipleship*, 84. For further reflections on Bonhoeffer's contributions to an account of vocation, see chapter 4.

28. Jesus's call of the disciples (e.g., Matthew 4:18–22) may seem perfunctory, involving very little dialogue. However, this is the exception that proves the rule, in the sense that this call is the beginning of a long conversation that, one might say, extends even until today.

29. Not infrequently the God of the Bible calls by name, sometimes using it twice. "Abraham, Abraham" calls God's angel as he stays his hand from plunging the knife into his son Isaac (Gen. 22). There, as here, Abraham's scripted response is "here I am."

doing tricks for Moses, such as turning his staff into a snake and back again. God seems to be attempting to convince Moses to come along with the plan. The call does not coerce; Moses does not finally refuse it, of course, but the long dialogue suggests he might. Indeed, through the course of the conversation Moses and God seem to begin a kind of friendship, although Moses' last objection provokes God's anger.

> "O my Lord, please send someone else to do it." Then the anger of the Lord was kindled against Moses and he said, "What of your brother Aaron, the Levite? I know that he can speak fluently; even now he is coming to meet you, and when he sees you his heart will be glad. You shall speak to him and put the words in his mouth; and I will be with your mouth and with his mouth, and will teach you what you shall do." (Exod. 4:13–15)

God's anger here seems to respond to the fact that Moses, after so much discussion about the particulars of the call, should now push it off to someone else. In effect, Moses threatens to break the presence, the attention that has held throughout the course of the call. Moses looks for a way to politely hang up, to end the call.

Yet God does not turn his anger to threat. Rather he contextualizes the call, reminding Moses of his place in relation to others, Aaron in particular, who presumably also has a call, although the Bible tells us no specific story of it. God returns, in effect, to the relations that hold Moses fast, and which support the call in the first place. Moses is an Israelite and shares in their plight. God's call of Moses is principally about the Israelites; to refuse the role God offers is, in effect, to refuse his place within his people, to pretend not to be their brother. God points to Aaron to remind him that his call is about a common plight. The work that accompanies it is also shared, not only by his brother Aaron, but by God as well.

This discussion between Moses and God can be understood as a very long message to Moses that his call is not principally about him. Indeed, *the call is for others*, a people whom God is inviting Moses to love as God loves them. Perhaps we can take heart in how long God works to bring this point clearly before Moses; it is especially difficult for modern people to comprehend since we conceive of ourselves principally as individuals.[30]

---

30. See the remarks on individualism, and how this affects our understanding of call, in chapters 1 and 6 of this volume.

(Indeed, this is why we have by and large replaced the language of "call" with that of "career.") Yet all biblical calls, as well as the calls of Black Elk and Muhammad, place the one called into a relationship of service to a people. They are called into participation in a larger plan that responds to the needs of others.

Another feature of call, one with important implications for our ability to respond to it, may seem obvious enough but is infrequently noted: *call comes in human language.* Call requires communication; only by means of language does the caller invite, discuss, and lay out a case. There is no biblical call that does not arrive in words; even the simplest, Jesus's "Come, follow me," comes in human speech.[31] This means that even if the call involves instructions that appear rather bizarre—for instance, the instruction that the prophet Hosea should marry the prostitute Gomer—it is nonetheless comprehensible to human beings since it follows the linguistic rules of speech, their manner of communication.[32] Call invites the one called to grow over time into its full meaning.

The fact that the call comes in language extends those points just reviewed about response, dialogue, and common connection. Furthermore, it locates the biblical story in terms of its oft-used title: the word of God. As Christians also say, the word became flesh and lived among us (John 1:14). This life of the Incarnate Word stands as witness, the articulation of the purposes of God for the world. And it speaks in human tongue. Like any communication in human language, we may listen, or, like the rich young man, we may turn away.

The call of Saul/Paul on the road to Damascus accents the specific words spoken, yet in complicated ways since different words are used in different accounts. Paul offers an extended recounting of his call before King Agrippa in Acts 26. In it he includes small details, such as that the voice he heard spoke in Hebrew (v. 14). The call here begins with a double address by name, followed by a question that is not merely rhetorical.

---

31. A possible exception comes in the call of Elisha. He was plowing with twelve pair of oxen when suddenly Elijah appeared and "threw his cloak around him." What could this mean? Elisha dutifully interprets it as a call, but asks if he might go say goodbye to his father or mother. In his only words in the passage, the caller Elijah dismisses the request with "Go back! What have I done to you?" (1 Kgs. 19:19–20).

32. And this extends beyond the biblical tradition: call, after all, involves a voice. For instance, even the birds speak to Black Elk in human tongue. Moreover, the words of the call must have meaning—not just individually, but together in phrases, if the one called is to be able to consider them and to know what it means to put them into action.

"Saul, Saul, why are you persecuting me? It hurts you to kick against the goads." Saul answers with a question: "Who are you Lord?" And the reply comes back,

> I am Jesus, whom you are persecuting. But get up and stand on your feet; for I have appeared to you for this purpose to appoint you to serve and testify to the things in which you have seen me and to those in which I will appear to you. I will rescue you from your people and from the Gentiles—to whom I am sending you to open their eyes so they may turn from darkness to light and from the power of Satan to God, so that they may receive forgiveness of sins and a place among those who are sanctified by faith in me. (Acts 26:15–18)

The words of this version of the call are very clear and specific; Jesus not only makes his intentions plain, he concludes with a reason that explains them: Saul is to do work that will open a place for the Gentiles in the community of the sanctified.

This can be contrasted with Luke's earlier account of the call in Acts 9. There Jesus's instructions are much abbreviated: "get up and enter the city, and you will be told what more to do" (9:6). The difference suggests something important about call.[33] The directives of the initial account meet Saul when he is not yet prepared to receive the reasons for it—reasons that follow in the account offered seventeen chapters later. In the intervening years, we can suppose, he received the formation he needed to understand his call. He received this formation as he lived out his call. In this way, *call commences a story that cannot be told until the call is lived out in response.* As such, call functions as an invitation into an unfolding adventure whose story can be better told as it unfolds, and fully told only eschatologically.[34] At the same time, the call also initiates a form of training into one's true identity. Those who are called may not know where the call will lead them, but they will be formed by the work that they are given to do, and will thereby learn to understand its significance.

---

33. It should be evident that our concern here is not which of these accounts more accurately reflects what was said on the road. Both are recorded by Luke; evidently he was aware of the difference, but generously gave us both.

34. Call looks to a future of completion, of perfection, and this cannot come fully come, as Aquinas notes, until the next life. See his *Summa Theologiae*, I–II, 5, 3, trans. Fathers of the English Dominican Province (Allen, TX: Christian Classics, 1981).

## *Vocation, formation, and friendship*

If we believe, with Black Elk, that the voice that calls is a sacred voice, then the interruption and reorientation of the story of the life that is called will lift that life up, pointing it toward divine purposes, as these apply in the world in which human life is lived out. The call in this way is not only an invitation to do a higher order of work, a particular work that is especially suited to the one called; it is also an invitation to become one who is worthy of being called, not so much by one's own efforts, but by the formation and friendship that comes in following the call. This formation involves our transformation; as we do the work we are called to do, we are also further schooled in the virtues necessary for the work, including the virtues of humility and attention that first opened our ears to being called. These virtues can deepen as we live out our call, and so we can come more fully to understand its purpose—in effect, we tap into the hidden reasons of the sacred. So it is that with three missionary journeys behind him, Paul can describe his call in the full language of Christ's purposes. Likewise, the disciples of Jesus, first called from their nets with the simple words "Come, follow me," later come not only to describe the new path on which the call has placed them, but also to call others to join it. Call, so mysterious when it first arrives, turns out to be nothing more nor less than God's coaxing us into a friendship wherein we are made capable, not only of following God's purposes in the world, but also of understanding the deeper reasons why following is the only thing that makes sense for us to do.[35]

---

35. The point here is little more than a paraphrase of what Jesus says to his disciples in his farewell discourse in the Gospel of John: "I do not call you servants any longer, because the servant does not know what the master is doing; but I have called you friends, because I have made known to you everything that I have heard from my Father" (John 15:15).

# 6

# "Who's There?"

## THE DRAMATIC ROLE OF THE "CALLER" IN VOCATIONAL DISCERNMENT

### David S. Cunningham

SCHOLARS WHO STUDY the works of William Shakespeare have observed that the structure of the plays often makes their opening and closing lines particularly significant. *Twelfth Night*, a play about music and love, begins with "If music be the food of love, play on" and ends with a song; *Macbeth*, a play about the bewitched quality of political power, begins with a witch's incantation and ends with the announcement of a coronation. So it seems fitting that the Bard's most existential play, the one most obsessed with the fluctuations of personal identity, would begin with a question—and perhaps the most pressing question of all: "Who's there?"

Out of context, it may sound like a line from a knock-knock joke; on the battlements of Elsinore, however, it's more likely to be a matter of life and death. When the question is asked by a guard, the answer will determine whether that unknown presence will receive a friendly greeting or a mortal blow. And in this particular case, Francesco's "Who's there?" is even more highly charged, for he knows that the castle walls have recently been visited by a ghostly presence whose identity has not yet been discerned. The questioner is not only asking whether the unseen visitor is friend or foe, noble or common, acquaintance or stranger; he is also asking whether it is human or superhuman, or perhaps wondering whether it even exists at all.

This famous first line sets up a question with which its characters will be obsessed throughout the play. It is the question Hamlet himself asks, when he finds himself spied upon while conversing with his mother or with Ophelia; similarly, Claudius tries to discern whether there is a God who will listen to his prayer; and even the play's minor characters seem preoccupied with trying figure out the nature and identity of those with whom they interact.[1] By making this a major theme of the play, Shakespeare was, as usual, onto something important about human character: that we know other people and other things imperfectly and that we often strive toward—and sometimes become obsessed with—knowing more. Whether in matters of religious faith, political structure, personal identity, or simple curiosity, we spend a great deal of time asking that very important question: "Who's there?"

Matters are no different when it comes to the topic of *calling* and *vocation*. Even though these words would clearly seem to imply an agent—someone who does the "calling"—they are often employed without any specific reference to that agent, or perhaps even in a way that explicitly avoids any talk about "the one who calls." A casual remark about "finding one's vocation," or about people who have "missed their calling," does not necessarily demand an existential inquiry into the causes and agency of the purported call. But once we move beyond the offhand remark—once questions are raised about what is actually meant by the word *vocation*, or about how one would go about discovering one's calling—matters become more complicated. Before very long, we begin to notice that the very grammar of these words involves an action (a call), and that a call would seem to imply a caller.[2] And suddenly we find ourselves swimming in some deep theological, psychological, and existential waters: Who controls our destiny? How much freedom do we have? Is there a God, and if so, to what degree does God shape our lives? If God is not involved, then who does the "calling" that we use to describe our own vocations?

These are questions about which reasonable people are likely to disagree; they are also the questions that motivate and guide this chapter. It argues, first, that many claims typically made about calling and vocation depend very heavily on the identity of the agent of vocation,

---

1. A feature of the play brilliantly explored by Tom Stoppard in his inside-out version of *Hamlet, Rosencrantz and Guildenstern are Dead* (New York: Grove Press, 1967).

2. See the reflections on these matters in the preceding chapter.

"the one who calls"; thus, we cannot ignore the question of agency. Nevertheless—and this is the chapter's second major point—many of the most important insights about vocation have a validity that does not depend upon universal agreement about identifying and specifying that agent. In other words: although we should pay attention to questions about the provenance of our callings, we are not required to be perfectly precise about "who's there" before coming to some agreement about the usefulness and impact of vocation. If we lack agreement on such matters, this does not negate the reality of the call. This leads to a third point: that all human beings have experiences that might be interpreted as instances of a calling, which makes it that much more important to engage in this conversation and debate. In a brief concluding comment, I will obseve that, because we will not attain universal agreement about matters of agency, we should employ the language of vocation with a certain degree of reserve. Here again, Shakespeare has something to teach us, so we will return to the text of *Hamlet*, as well as to *King Lear* and to *Romeo and Juliet*, for some of his insights on this matter. Along the way, I will make some reference to three theological concepts—mission, revelation, and creation—that may help us elucidate a more nuanced perspective on the language of calling and vocation.

## *The grammar of calling*

As noted in the Introduction to this book, the English word *vocation* is derived from the Latin *vocare*, to call. Thus, for the purposes of grammatical reflection, the words *vocation* and *calling* are roughly equivalent; both are nouns, denoting a state of being called. Both words are nominalizations, insofar as they are derived from verbs. This makes them relatively abstract; they designate a state or condition while avoiding any attention to the action that lies at their root. Nominalizations are very common in modern English; they allow us to speak abstractly of circumstances without reference to the agents that are responsible for them or the actions that brought about these states. So, for example, we use the noun *government* to speak collectively and abstractly of those who do the governing, or the noun *writing* to refer to things that have been written, without necessarily focusing on the activities related to writing, or on the people who undertake those activities.

An argument can be made, of course, for relying wholly on the nominalizations *calling* and *vocation* in all discussions of this topic. Doing so allows us to speak in conceptual terms without raising the grammatical (and philosophical) questions about *who* is doing the calling and about precisely *what* takes place when an agent issues a call. Because these questions are contested, avoiding them may make conversations about vocation easier to navigate and less likely to lead to argument and debate; still, this approach also has fairly serious disadvantages, three of which are worth mentioning here. These will be followed by a positive example, which may help to indicate what we stand to gain by risking some attention to agency and action in matters of vocation.

## The reification of the call

By relying exclusively on the nominalizations *vocation* and *calling*, and avoiding questions about agency and action, we create the same effect produced by all nominalizations: a tendency to *reify* activity, turning it from an action into a thing. As a result, the word and its referent lose some of their dynamic quality, their capacity for movement and change, and take on a fixed, stable quality. We know this from our use of other nominalizations; consider our use of the word *speech*. When a journalist reports that "tax reform was the main topic of the candidate's speech," the activity (the giving of the speech, the speaking) is set in the distant background and loses its character as *event*. The "speech" becomes a fixed entity—something that has definite content (in this case, its content is "tax reform"); it can be referred to and analyzed without making any reference whatsoever to the candidate as the agent, or to "speaking" as an activity that the candidate undertakes. We start to think of the speech as a relatively stable reality, unaffected by the various rhetorical contexts in which it might be delivered. The specific locations where the candidate has delivered the speech, the give-and-take that might have occurred between speaker and audience, and the ways that the speaker might have (on the spur of the moment) re-adjusted the speech's timing or volume or tone—all of these dynamic elements are minimized at the expense of the relatively stable elements of the speech. The *most* stable of these elements, of course, is the speech's *content*: the words that were spoken, and perhaps written down, which can then be passed along to others who were not present at the original event. While this increases the number of people who can gain access to the speech's content, it simultaneously strips the event of its dynamic, dialogical elements. Those who hear about the *content* of the speech believe that they have experienced the essence of the *event* of the speech, but of course they have not.

The concept of *vocation* can easily suffer the same fate. Our callings evolve throughout our lives, shaped and re-shaped by the contexts in which we carry them out, the people with whom we are in regular contact, and the new insights that we gain in the process. By treating vocation as a relatively stable entity—a "thing"—we may fail to recognize the extraordinary ways that our callings are being re-formed even as we undertake them. This can contribute to a common misconception about vocation—namely, that it is one (and only one) thing, a fixed reality that people either "find" or "miss," something that must be searched for and discovered, like a hidden vein of precious metal ensconced in layers of rock. By ignoring the agent(s) of vocation and the action(s) of calling, we reify vocation and may fail to recognize its dynamism and its propensity to change.

## Call as private interior disposition

This reified account of vocation begets another problem—namely, its interiorization and privitization. If we see vocation as a "thing," as some kind of duty or state of being that we feel bound to take up, it can be seen as just one more aspect of our consciousness—a state of mind that we may choose to grasp or set aside at will. As a noun, the word *vocation* can be easily modified by possessive adjectives such as *my* or *your*, and can start to seem like an item of property, like an article of clothing or a piece of furniture. Since it is "my" vocation, it is not fully accessible to others; I become the ultimate arbiter of its shape and dimensions. I begin to imagine that even the people who are closest to me would be incapable of fully understanding it or advising me about it, in the same way that they are incapable of fully understanding or experiencing my deepest emotions or my physical pain.[3] The nominalized form of vocation—a reified object that takes its place among the world of objects—makes it easy to put clear boundaries around our callings and turn them into a purely interior state, a private experience about which only its possessor can render authentic judgments.

---

3. Ludwig Wittgenstein, *Philosophical Investigations* (New York: Macmillan, 1953), § 302–3 (pp. 101–2).

If, on the contrary, calling is always understood in its verbal sense, as an activity with an agent who is other than the self, this kind of privatization and interiorization is much more difficult to sustain. I cannot be the sole arbiter of my vocation if its source is, in some ultimate sense, outside of me and beyond my immediate control. It is no longer merely an act of the will—a decision on my part to point my life in a particular direction—but rather a disposition to set out in the direction that has been suggested by someone or something exterior to me.[4]

Here, some additional attention to the character of drama can help to emphasize the distinction. In a novel, the author may tell us about a character's motivations, assumptions, and inner dispositions in a way that makes them sound as though these originated in that person's interior life. But a playwright does not have that option; the audience only learns about the lives of the play's characters by watching what they do and listening to what they say. The characters' actions, and especially their *interactions* with other characters, reveal their identities in ways that emphasize the communal structures though which those identities are cultivated. As we watch the play, we watch those identities (or, at the very least, our own perceptions of them) change and evolve in ways that neither we, nor the characters themselves, would have been able to predict with perfect accuracy. This reminds us of the difference it makes when one's interior state is exposed to the agency and actions of others, rather than simply being a private act of the will.

Consider the student who tells his advisor that his calling is to become a medical doctor. If his advisor notices that the student's talents are skills are somewhat misaligned for this particular profession—bad grades in organic chemistry, combined with certain habits that might create a less-than-ideal doctor–patient relationship—then she can certainly raise this question with the student. But if he insists that he needs to be a doctor because that is his vocation, and that only he can know that, the conversation may come to a quick stop. Under such a construal of vocation, what access does the advisor have to the student's inner life? If, on the other hand, the student can be encouraged to talk about the process through which he came to understand medicine as his vocation—the people, books, friends, and experiences that have led him in this direction—a more productive conversation might emerge. His devotion to the field may

---

4. See the comments on the "ideology of choice" in chapter 1.

have more to do with a relative's wishes or an idealized picture of how doctors actually spend their time. In any case, conversations about one's calling will be facilitated by an understanding that traces its sources, the channels through which it has been mediated, and the words and actions through which it came to be known—rather than understanding it to be an inner disposition that is the private property of the one who has been called.

## Vocation as merely instrumental

A final problem that arises from ignoring the complex grammar of calling (and treating it as a fixed entity, unaffected by others' actions) is the tendency to instrumentalize vocation as a mere means to some unrelated end. We see this in the well-documented tendency, already discussed in chapters 2 and 4 of this volume, to think of the English word *vocation* as a synonym for *profession* or even for *job*. This tendency has subsided somewhat over the last several decades, due in no small part to the ongoing academic conversation to which this volume seeks to contribute.[5] Still, the terminology lingers; "vocational training" still sometimes describes what one needs to do in order to get a job in a particular trade. Even the Reformation-era expansion of the language of *vocation*, beyond the clergy and religious orders to all walks of life, could sometimes participate in this tendency; whatever station in life one found oneself, that place could be named one's vocation.[6] On the positive side, this helped to elevate the dignity of the everyday work of the laity, describing it as part of God's call; but it could also serve as a useful instrument in the perpetuation of the existing social order. In that world, the everyday work of the workers—determined by economic forces far beyond their understanding or control—was "sanctified" by the claim that their wearisome lot was actually determined by God.[7]

---

5. See the brief history of these developments in the Foreword to the present volume, as well as in its Introduction (in the section headed "Initiating a new conversation").

6. For more on this point, see the discussion of the economic factors that have shaped our understanding of vocation in chapter 1, as well as the account of its theological development in chapter 4.

7. This concern is alluded to at several points in the volume, particularly in chapters 1, 3, and 4.

Obviously, the human desire to instrumentalize cannot be eradicated simply through the use of fewer nouns and more verbs. Still, by focusing on calling as an action—undertaken by a specific agent and directed toward us from outside ourselves—we can drastically reduce the temptation to use the terminology as a way of justifying whatever we might have chosen to do anyway. If, in referring to our callings, we are really doing nothing more than enacting our desires by force of will, then we ought not to disguise that assertion of the self by dressing it up in the language of vocation. If, on the other hand, we are willing to be open to perspectives other than our own—accounts of our lives that originate outside of ourselves—then we will have to pay attention to those who are offering such accounts, and why they have chosen to speak to us.

## Mission or *missio*?

Consider, in conclusion to this first section, a positive example: another word, often employed in the higher education context, in which a nominalization has slowly begun to regain some of its verbal qualities. Colleges and universities have found it useful, over the past several decades, to make use of the word *mission*. Most institutions have a "mission statement"; administrators describe particular aspects of campus life and culture as "central to our mission" or "relatively peripheral to our mission"; and in some contexts, faculty involved in search processes are reminded of the importance of "hiring for mission." All of these uses of the word—all of them nouns[8]—attempt to fix the institutional mission as a stable reality, obscuring the degree to which it has shifted over time and taken on different shades of meaning in various contexts and circumstances. Furthermore, this supposedly stable entity can become a kind of personal possession of various people on campus. They can use it to carry out other kinds of objectives, such as promoting one institutional goal over another by labeling their relative significance for the college's mission, when in fact the real reasons for prioritizing a particular goal might be primarily

---

8. One of them, in fact, is a participant in that particularly unpleasant use of nouns, the "noun string." By setting nouns up next to each other where we should be using adjectives (as in "mission statement"), we create a kind of compound nominalization in which multiple agents and multiple actions are all hidden from view. Still, even those who loudly denounce the use of noun strings have had to admit their occasional usefulness; for example, the phrase *noun string* is, of course, a noun string.

financial, political, or simply a matter of whim. The institution's mission becomes an instrument for carrying out other, less noble-sounding decisions.

However, this instrumental use of the language of mission can be usefully disrupted. At most institutions, the mission statement consists of one or more sentences, rather than just a list of nouns; it thus has some potential for reversing the reifying, privatizing, and instrumentalizing effects of a word like *mission*. At my own institution, for example, the mission statement has only one verb, but a good one: *educate*. Claims as to whether something is central to the college's mission can be tested, to some degree, by referring to that verb in its context in a sentence: does a particular practice or policy help the institution to "*educate* students for lives of leadership and service"? That's what the college's mission statement says that we *do*, and one can more easily evaluate whether something has been *done* than whether it *has* some particular quality. By attending to the agents and actions that are described in an institution's mission statement, we can get a better idea of what its mission might actually be.

Colleges could go further in this direction. The noun *mission* is rooted in the Latin verb *missio*, to send. To have a mission is to be sent: to be designated as having a particular purpose and to be expected to carry out that purpose. A mission therefore implies something more than a mere contract; it involves such intangible elements as duty, service, loyalty, and discipline. We tend to use the word when we are speaking of our more serious undertakings, or things to which we are particularly strongly devoted. Moreover, a mission implies an agent who does the sending, the commissioning: this is the person (or group or cause) for whom we loyally or dutifully carry out the task for which we have been sent.

Thus, institutions that take their mission statements seriously might reflect on the question: who has set us on this mission? Who is our "sender"? Such questions can push institutions to consider, not just their own histories (since most of those who have founded academic institutions thought they were doing something more than starting a successful business enterprise), but also their present-day networks of relationships. In order to understand, for example, the religious roots of a particular college or university, it may be helpful to consider what that institution and its constituencies believe about the role of the divine in its *commissioning*. Even those institutions that might prefer to avoid any talk of God can still give thought to how their missions originated, and why they consider themselves having been "sent forth" for particular tasks. In fact, colleges and universities might want to think about whether the language of *calling* or *vocation* might not apply to institutions as well.[9] What would it mean to think more about the college's *calling* than about its *mission?* That is a topic for another day, but it is also one in which these reflections might find a foothold.

## *The mystery of vocation*

Note that the argument thus far has been rather limited. It has not sought to identify the caller or to specify the caller's actions; it has only claimed that we should recognize that a call is an *action* (and not just a thing), that it comes from beyond ourselves, and that it involves others. Beyond these claims, we might be well advised to recognize the slight aura of *mystery* that surrounds the idea of vocation, and to leave at least some of that mystery in place.

Simply this recognition—concerning the "otherness" of the call's origins and the active, dynamic nature of our callings—is sufficient for attending to what has here been described as the *grammar* of calling. Determining the precise identity of the caller, and specifying the caller's actions, is a legitimate and valuable enterprise; moreover, offering some provisional accounts of these matters may be of great help to those who are seeking to discern their vocations. At the same time, however, these accounts are not ultimate. Conflicts among these accounts, though they may matter deeply to the persons who offer them, do not invalidate the significance of vocation in general; nor need these conflicts be fully resolved in order for various participants in the conversation to continue to make use of the language of calling and vocation in an active, agent-oriented way.

## God as the caller?

In the Christian tradition, the agent of the call is usually held to be God. God is the one who calls human beings, both to their general vocation of being human and participating in salvation, and to their specific vocations

---

9. See the remarks at the end of chapter 2, as well as David S. Cunningham, "Colleges Have Callings, Too: Planning, Programming, and the Politics of Institutional Vocation," keynote address delivered at the conference "Loaves and Fishes," Monmouth College, Monmouth, IL, March 2012. Publication forthcoming.

of work and action in the world.[10] Because of the long and venerable tradition of the language of vocation within its history, Christianity has rarely hesitated to identify God as the ultimate source of our callings. However, when it comes to specifying the precise way or ways that God acts in order to set forth these calls, accounts diverge widely. Even within the biblical narrative, we see a wide range of stories of call: these may involve the direct voice of God (either embodied or otherwise), but they often rely on others (angels as divine messengers or other human beings as prophets).[11] This divergence should remind us that, in specifying the origin of a call as "outside ourselves," we are not necessarily specifying the means through which it will be heard.

This, as noted in the previous section, is one of the most troublesome misconceptions about the notion of calling or vocation, and one that we need to identify as such. Many educators have remarked on the degree to which some students assume that they will only learn of their vocation when God speaks to them, in a recognizable form of speech: a voice that would come to them in the night.[12] Some would attribute these assumptions to the students' tendency to read the biblical stories in an overly literal way, but in my own experience, a different explanation is more likely. The tendency to speak about one's callings as involving the *vox Dei* can also arise from a felt need for definitive *certainty* about one's vocation. During the college years, practically everything is in motion: academic progress, personal development, and relationships with parents, friends, and potential partners. Students aren't sure what they will be doing for the rest of their lives—or where, or with whom, or with what degree of success. Thus, if all these matters are suddenly inflated in importance by designating them with the relatively serious-sounding word *vocation*, the uncertainties that surround these matters just seem that much more ominous. And these worries are further compounded by the issues described in the first section of this essay: if vocation is a relatively fixed and stable entity, and a relatively interior or private one, then who else could really know it, other than God? And who else could be entrusted to deliver it to us?

---

10. See, for example, the classic description of "general" and "particular" callings in William Perkins, *A Treatise of the Vocations*, excerpted in Placher, ed., *Callings*, 262–73 (see chap. 4, note 10).

11. See the various examples of biblical call stories mentioned in chapter 5.

12. This is not to suggest that no one ever hears a call in this way. For further reflections on the "audible" nature of our callings, see chapter 12.

Some observers might argue that this is exactly the problem that arises when we try to specify the agent of the call. At least some students will identify themselves as Christians, and some of them are likely to be quite serious about matters of faith and spiritual development; such students are probably fairly comfortable with the notion that God is the agent of the call and the ultimate source of their vocation. However, precisely because they are so quick to make this assignment, they might also be tempted to imagine that the call no longer has anything to do with them, with *their* needs and hopes and desires, but that it is the sole property of someone else, who will determine what shape their lives should take. One might argue that, if they were just to speak about calling or vocation in a more general sense—as related primarily to their own gifts and joys and without making reference to the one who calls them—then they wouldn't find themselves in such a fix.

## The interdependence of the caller and the called

On the other hand, the idea mentioned here—that it might be easier not to bring the question of the "caller" into the conversation—seems to misread the situation as a kind of either/or, or perhaps more accurately, as a zero-sum game. It suggests that, at least in matters of vocation, everything is determined *either* by an outside entity, the "caller" (whether that entity be designated as God, or as someone or something else); *or* it is determined by the person him- or herself. This perspective, however, once again fails to attend to the grammar of the verb *to call*. It is a transitive verb, so it requires an object; and, moreover, it typically requires an active object—an object with a will of its own, an object that is also a subject (and is thus able to respond to the call).

Consider our many uses of the verb *to call*. We use it to describe our efforts to get our pets to come to us; they may respond, but then again they may not. We call people on the telephone, but whether we will talk to them or to their voicemail messages will depend on whether or not they pick up the call. We "call out" to others to get their attention, but did we use a loud enough voice, and are the others in a place where they are able to hear? Practically all the instances of our ordinary use of this word involve at least two wills: that of the caller and that of the one who is called.

Once again, we can see this well illustrated on the theatrical stage. All drama originates in conflict, so practically anytime any character speaks a line, there are several ways in which others might react. If, as audience members, we already know the play, then we know what words will be used for this reaction (at least, if the director is following the script and if the actors remember their lines). Still, there is a great deal that we don't know until the response is actually delivered. Will the other character(s) respond quietly or loudly? Will they speak in a way that can be heard by the others in the room, or will they turn aside and speak in a way that makes it clear to the audience that the others don't hear them? Will they deliver their lines in a straightforward manner, or hypothetically, face-tiously, ironically? Even in something so heavily scripted as a stage play, the will of one speaker does not determine the response of an "other."

## Theatre and mystery

The theatre can also help us understand the importance of the strategy suggested at the beginning of this section: while affirming that our call-ings come to us from outside ourselves, it might be wise to leave the rest of vocation's mysterious quality in place. In academic circles, of course, the word *mystery* can be used as a means of obfuscation or as a crutch; this is particularly true in the field of religious studies. It can be tempting, any time we come up against a phenomenon that we don't understand or can't explain, to label it *a mystery* and to suggest that any attempt to offer anything so pedestrian as an "explanation" is to insult the grandeur of the enterprise.[13] But this term need not be used as a mere end-run around something that could be adequately explained if we just thought about it harder. It would certainly be possible for theologians, psychologists, soci-ologists, and even neuroscientists to offer explanations and descriptions of the origins of our callings and the nature of the "caller." These accounts would probably compete with one another; the dialogue that they might evoke could be productive and insightful. (Their reflections might even fill another volume of this size, and more.) But these competing accounts might not necessarily be of help to those who, like many of the students in our colleges and universities, are attempting to discern their own vocations.

---

13. At the very least, a positive invocation of mystery has to reckon with how it, alongside miracle and authority, is used by Dostoevsky to illustrate the obfuscations that the Christian Church has sometimes erected over the teachings of Jesus. See Fyodor Dostoevsky, *The Brothers Karamazov*, trans. Richard Pevear and Larissa Volokhonsky (New York: Random House, Vintage Classics, 1990), 250–62.

Thus, by recognizing the degree of *mystery* that will always be a part of vocation, we might help to counter the tendency to understand it as a fixed and stable reality—or as something that will always provide certainty. We might best serve our students by helping them recognize vocation as a fluid and dynamic reality, something that shifts and evolves across the course of one's life. In this regard, vocational discernment programs have often had success by organizing lectures and panel discussions among people whose life trajectories have changed over time.[14] By telling the stories of their own vocational journeys, they remind students that their callings are not fixed and eternal—except perhaps in some deeply metaphysical sense, in the mind of God. At the very least, our process of discerning our vocations is a lifelong journey, in which the purpose of each step along the way is to prepare us for the next.

Here again, the theatre has something to teach us. A play's audience typically comprises people who have widely varying degrees of knowledge concerning what they are about to witness. Some may have no idea whatsoever; for them, setting, plot, and characters are wholly unknown entities. In a few cases, they may never have experienced live theatre in any form and may have no concept of what is about to take place. At the other end of the spectrum are the theatre aficionados who have attended plays for decades and who may know this particular play very well indeed; they may have even memorized entire stretches of it. And of course, the cast and crew also bring a deep knowledge of the play, having worked through it dozens of times, in many different forms. At first glance, it is hard to imagine that people with such a widely diverse range of knowledge and preparation could all derive benefit from, and even enjoy, any one particular thing.

But the magic of theatre is that, regardless of their level of prior knowledge, everyone in the audience—as well as the cast and crew—will be surprised by something during the performance. Too many variables are at play for it to be otherwise: individual actors, interacting with others hundreds of times over the course of the play; technicians who must move thousands of switches, levers, and handles in every performance; and of course, the audience members themselves, whose actions and reactions will partially shape the course of the performance. When the entire enterprise depends on so many actions of so many human beings over the

---

14. See also the discussion of evolving vocations in chapters 5 and 7.

course of a relatively compressed period of time and in a single space, every performance will be different. Here, our only certainty is a negative one: that we can have *no degree* of certainty about what will happen. This is, of course, part of what we love about it—its slightly untamed quality, its instability. We can't quite shake the notion that the whole enterprise is always teetering on the edge of potential disaster, when one missed line or one forgotten prop could send the whole story off in a new and wholly unpredictable direction.

## Revelation and the mystery of vocation

The understanding of vocational discernment that is being offered here has certain resonances with the theological concept of *revelation*. When we use this word in ordinary circumstances, we are typically referring to a process by which something that is unknown, or imperfectly known, comes to be better known. The standard example is the unveiling of a work of art in a museum: the painting or sculpture is draped in a way that lets people know that something important is under there, but unless they have inside information, they don't yet know what it is. They gain this knowledge when the veil is removed. But although this example is frequently employed to describe the process of revelation, it suffers from a serious flaw: the object that is revealed—the work of art—is typically a stable, fixed entity; it may be understood and interpreted in a variety of ways, but the object itself doesn't change. Most of the things that are *revealed* to us, however, have a more dynamic character: a person's attitudes, a government's intentions, a teacher's knowledge, a friend's love. These personal attributes are neither stable nor fixed; thus, their revelation to another, as important as it may be at a particular moment in time, would not necessarily lead to the kind of permanent, intersubjective knowledge that is suggested by the more static example of the work of art revealed in a museum.

Three features of the process of revelation are worth noting here. First, the state of affairs that we come to know is typically situated *outside* the knower. We use the language of revelation, not for things that we investigate for ourselves, but for those things that we come to know because of what is offered to us by someone else. It may be a third party, as in our museum example; however, especially when the knowledge is about persons, those persons are themselves often the revealers of the knowledge. (Thus, when a friend tells us some new detail about her background, particularly if that detail seems to explain certain aspects of her personality, we might well say that the new information "was a real revelation.") Another possibility, and one that is especially relevant to our discussion of vocational discernment, is that another person will say or do something that will allow the recipients of the revelation to learn something new about *themselves*. In this case, the object of the new knowledge is oneself, but the catalyst for gaining that knowledge has come from outside oneself.

Second, revelation typically involves a complex relationship among various actors: the revealer, the new knowledge being revealed (which, as noted above, is often knowledge about persons), and the recipient of revelation. Thus, three or more people may be involved in the process, as when a person reveals something about her friend to her parents. Often, though, there are only two people involved—though this doesn't make things any less complicated, because whatever is being revealed will often have something to do with at least one of the persons in the relationship (either the revealer or the recipient). The complexity arises because, in the process of revealing something about oneself to another, the person doesn't just provide a nugget of information; the very process of revelation, the act of disclosure, can actually become a source of new knowledge as well. The recipient now knows, not just a new fact about the other person, but also that the other person is the *kind* of person who would reveal that *kind* of information. Thus, the act of revelation has a meta-revelatory quality that tends to expand interpersonal knowledge. This too has implications for vocational discernment, in that the experience of recognizing a call may provide us with further information about the caller.

Third, the knowledge produced by revelation is never complete. Even in our static museum example, only the visually discernible elements of the work of art are revealed; the removal of the veil tells us nothing about the artist's motivations, the process by which the work came to be in this particular spot in the museum, or any of a number of other interesting details, some of which would only come to be known through further revelations. And this aspect is only intensified when we consider the new knowledge gained about other persons, or about ourselves. The human person is a deep wellspring of thought, emotion, intention, and perspective; moreover, these elements are always changing—being shaped and reshaped in every encounter. An incident that strikes us as "particularly revelatory" about another person may be completely reversed a few minutes later, when some additional information comes our way that changes our perspective on what we have just learned, or when that person's attitudes or beliefs are suddenly changed by circumstances. This implies that vocational discernment, too, is an ongoing process, in which new information is continually coming to light; there is no point at which we have final and complete knowledge of our callings. This fact may help to offset some of the anxiety that our students often feel as they reflect on their possible vocations. By recognizing that this knowledge will never be complete, they may find themselves willing to take a few provisional steps in a particular direction, without assuming that they are therefore committing themselves to a single course of life.

## The universality of the call

The previous two sections of this chapter might well leave some readers feeling that they are being pushed in two opposite directions. While the first section emphasized the importance of the agent in calling, the second section seemed to minimize how much we should expect to know with certainly about the caller. As a result, it might seem as though the argument leads to the conclusion that vocation is a purely subjective reality, in which the caller is understood differently by each person who is called. To use a theatrical analogy: one might reason that, just as five hundred audience members at a play will have five hundred different reactions and opinions about what they saw, vocation might essentially be an interior dialogue with oneself, in which a person simply exerts her or his will in order to decide on a course of action. Even though someone else might act in a way that reveals some new information, what one *does* with that new information is essentially one's own decision, in which others need play no active role.

Before we venture too far down the path of a completely subjective account of calling and vocation, however, it would behoove us to return to our grammatical observations about the language of call. Taking this language seriously still means postulating a caller, even if we need to remain fairly clear about the fact that the one being called is ultimately free to accept or reject that call. If an external agent reveals something to me about myself, I am certainly free to ignore this new information and to carry on as though nothing had happened; but doing so will not cause that new information to go away. My thought processes have still been "intruded upon" by a force that is something other than me. This external reality has an objective existence of its own, regardless of how significantly my perception of it might differ from that of another person.

We can make a further claim: not only does this external reality exist; it confronts us all, and does so on a regular basis. Many people may well choose to deny the existence of a "caller" and reject the entire premise of vocation; but those individuals will still have experiences, will still be confronted with new information, and will still be pressed to choose among competing alternatives. They will be urged to read one book instead of another, declare this major instead of that one, plan for a career in one field instead of the one they had anticipated. They may receive invitations to parties, offers of employment, or proposals of marriage. And these encounters come in negative forms as well: closed doors, refusals of service, denials of opportunity. We can believe whatever we like about calling and vocation; still, unless we seal ourselves off from the world completely, we will all regularly be confronted by new experiences to which we will need to respond. This is why it is appropriate to describe calling as a nearly universal human experience.

## "This wide and universal theatre"

Returning to the theatre may help us more easily recognize the force of this claim. We might see a scene enacted on stage that presents, let us say, a certain view of married life. Obviously, the play does not tell us everything there is to know about that condition. Moreover, the particularities of this presentation will not apply identically to the lives of the all the members of the audience; for one thing, they will differ as to whether marriage is a direct part of their lives, or whether it is a past, present, future, or wholly absent reality for them. They may indeed have five hundred different reactions and opinions about what they saw. But this does not negate the fact that they all did, in fact, see something—that they received new information and were exposed to a new perspective. The play's presentation of the topic is now a part of their experience. They may forget it, ignore it, discard it as irrelevant, or actively campaign against it; but they can do nothing to rewind the clock and make the presentation vanish from their experience. It is now part of their mental scenery, even if it is shunted away or pushed down into the nether regions of the subconscious.

In fact, even when we react strongly against (or even reject outright) the information that we glean from any new experience, we still find ourselves having partially *incorporated* that experience into our lives. Just as one may reject a worldview that seems to have been presented on stage, one may also reject the validity of *any* new experience as having come from an unreliable source—even if it is a call to a new path in life. We might think back to the quotation that opened chapter 3, wherein Malcolm recognized that the person who was addressing him—who was actively calling him *away* from a particular course of life—was offering him a perspective that he could not adopt. Indeed, he seems to have felt called, even perhaps in that very moment, to work *against* that perspective: to change his own identity in ways that would bring the entire conversation into question. But this reaction did not obliterate his experience; indeed, his rejection of it may well have made it stand out more in his own account of his life story. Even a call that we dismiss, ignore, or actively work against is still, in some sense, a call. We may not even recognize it as such, but the reality of the call remains.

## Creation and universality

My reflections on the universality of vocation—its reality and existence, independently of our perceptions of it—has certain parallels in the theological idea of *creation*. In many faith perspectives, the existence of the physical universe, and especially of the world in which we live, is attributed to God or to the gods. The world is said to be brought into being at a certain moment in time: fashioned from some kind of primeval matter, or birthed from a divine womb, or—in the rather exceptional case of the Christian teaching on the subject—created out of nothing.

Of course, many of these accounts are in essential conflict with one another. They differ as to the causal agent of creation: God-in-general (deism), a particular God (various monotheistic faiths), or the gods broadly speaking (various polytheistic faiths); similarly, one may claim that no divine being of any sort was involved in the process, however remotely. In addition, these views differ as to what continuing forces of creativity are at work in the world at the present. Some describe a situation in which God continues to create the world, or in which physical and biological forces continue to shape it. Others argue that a divine watchmaker sets the whole thing in motion and leaves it alone, or that—particularly with respect to the creation of human beings—having brought into being a creature with a will of its own, its source is no longer responsible for it. These widely varying accounts compete in what James McClendon calls a "tournament of narratives";[15] we all insert ourselves at one place or another in the story, accepting some accounts and refusing others, inhabiting our own versions of these accounts and probably not agreeing with each other about every detail along the way.[16]

And yet, in spite of all these differences—and in spite of the essentially contested quality of the stories themselves—we all are faced with the reality of the world as it exists. We see it, hear it, and bump up against it all the time. It impinges on us in various ways, inviting us to bask in certain of its glories and often impeding our access to its less easily comprehensible parts. The world is simply *there*; no matter what story of creation we live with or live into—indeed, even if we deny that the world was created at all—we all still have to face the world, wrestle with it, share it, and inhabit it. Its very universality means that certain kinds of judgments can be made about it, even in the absence of complete agreement about how it came to be. At a minimum, we recognize that we did not create it ourselves.

These observations about the theological idea of creation help to corroborate our reflections on the universality of the call. Even if we disagree heartily about the source of a call (be it from God, other human beings, an accident of fate, or some combination of these), we still have to confront it. We will still be faced, on a regular basis, with manifold invitations to take up certain stations in life—not only with respect to paid employment but also in our leisure pursuits, family life, and engagement with governments and voluntary associations. These invitations will pose questions, invite reflection, and require discernment; and often, they will eventually demand decisions. Our disagreements about the provenance of these invitations do nothing to negate their existence, nor do they excuse us from responding to them (whether through acceptance or rejection).

## *Vocational reserve*

Calling is a universal experience and calling requires a caller. Yet the identity of that caller is not always clear, so every experience of calling is likely to leave us wanting to know more. Only by means of further experiences and events might some of those details be filled in; and even if that

---

15. James Wm. McClendon, Jr., *Systematic Theology: Ethics* (Nashville: Abingdon Press, 1986), 143.

16. A much fuller account of this notion is offered in the following chapter.

does occur, we may find ourselves in very different circumstances at those later moments. We may ultimately choose to accept or reject these calls, but they remain an ineluctable part of our experience. Indeed, even those vocational options that we forgo may haunt us for a very long time.

All these uncertainties surrounding calling would seem to demand that we exercise a certain degree of restraint when exploring and discerning vocations—whether our own or those of others. Here again, Shakespeare has something to teach us. The play with which we began these reflections—*Hamlet*—introduces us to characters who react to circumstances that they think they understand, with disastrous results. Hamlet thinks his uncle must be behind the curtain, but he ends up killing Polonius; Claudius prepares a poisonous drink for his nephew and ends up killing his wife. Their fault is not that they render judgment; that in itself is perfectly acceptable. Their fault is that, without pausing to confirm that judgment, they feel so convinced of its correctness that they are willing to use it as a basis for actions from which they cannot retreat. And this "point of no return" is not restricted to acts of murder; think of Lear, who misreads his youngest daughter's honesty for a lack of love, ignores his best advisor's remonstrations, and thereby sets in motion a series of events that will rob him of everything and devastate his kingdom. Think also of Romeo, who stakes everything on his belief that Juliet is dead. Throughout many of the plays, Shakespeare quietly counsels us to a certain kind of reserve: a willingness to wait, to think, to spend a few minutes "writing in the dust."[17] We need to consider carefully those assumptions that we take to be certain, in order to determine whether they can really bear the weight of the actions that we plan to undertake on their basis. Doing so will give us the amount of both time and space we need for such considerations—enough, as Rowan Williams suggests, "to allow some of our own demons to walk away."[18]

We might consider accepting a similar kind of counsel when it comes to claims about vocation—including the question of whom, in any given instance, we identify as the ultimate agent of call that we believe we have heard. We should not refuse to render a judgment on this question;

---

17. See the extraordinary reflections on this particular action, attributed to Jesus in the story of the woman taken in adultery (John 8:2–11), in Rowan Williams, *Writing in the Dust* (Grand Rapids, MI: William B. Eerdmans, 2002).

18. Williams, *Writing in the Dust*, 78.

indeed, if we are to avoid complete paralysis, we must not only judge but also act upon that judgment. Still, in doing so, we can exercise a certain degree of reserve; we can avoid staking everything on the assumption that our judgments are wholly without error. We can seek the wise counsel of others and compare our own accounts with theirs. Finally, we can take some comfort in the fact that, no matter how we respond to a particular call, it will probably not be the last such call to confront us, to require our attention, and to demand a decision. When we become attuned to vocation, we soon come to realize that there will always be another call waiting for us—somewhere in the wings, waiting for its cue, ready to "find its light" on all the stages of our lives.

# 7

# *Vocation and Story*

## NARRATING SELF AND WORLD

*Douglas V. Henry*

VOCATION HAS A *narrative* quality. Hearing and responding to a calling stands within a story in which we act as characters alongside others, adopt goals that provide our lives with their plots, and remember our story in order to make sense of our decisions. We tell stories to make our lives intelligible, and those stories can play a role in whether we are able to hear—and perhaps respond to—a calling. Teaching for vocation thus invites questions about our personal stories and the framing narratives within which they fit. Which narratives and what kinds of moral imagination do we need? Within which narratives are we already actors, and in which do we hope to act? Should we accept the culturally ascendant narratives of our time? What guidance, modeling, and avenues of vocational discernment shall we offer, as students frame their stories and listen for their call?

Exploring such questions can help us prepare students for what James McClendon aptly calls a "tournament of narratives."[1] McClendon invites us to understand our time as one in which competing narratives vie for attention. Consider the metaphor. Tournaments are rule-governed contests among players seeking to win recognition through admirable competition. Tournaments call forth excellence from participants; they also invite judgments about excellence by officials and observers. Tournaments

---

1. McClendon, *Systematic Theology: Ethics*, 143 (see chap. 6, note 15).

recognize talent, preparation, and fair play; they divide winners from losers; and, as with all things human, fortune plays its part as well. Among other things, therefore, a tournament of narratives showcases contending stories of varied quality, each rehearsed more or less proficiently. Storytellers secure or squander allies, gain or overcome adversaries, and emerge with or without honorable mention. Thus, for students to relate their own stories confidently and well—and discern their vocation therein—they first need help in recognizing the tournament of narratives that constitutes our world.

Scholars have long explored the relation of narrative to character and action. This chapter begins by invoking three of them: Iris Murdoch, Alasdair MacIntyre, and Nicholas Wolterstorff. A second section examines the importance of the college years for learning to narrate one's life. The following section explores three dominant framing narratives at work in modern colleges and universities (and in the broader culture), offering literary examples of each. The fourth and final section offers practical counsel for helping students discern their calling within worthy self-narratives.

## *The revival of narrative*

Iris Murdoch exhibited a sophisticated grasp of the Enlightenment's abstract moral theories; however, she deemed them inadequate. She especially faulted two dominant theories—those based on duty and on utility—for their preoccupation with right action instead of good character. Right action is better than not; yet admirable deeds depend upon character, imagination, and vision. She argues that moral vision is enriched or impoverished by the stories we hear, read, and enact. She writes, "I can only choose within the world that I can see . . . [and] clear vision is a result of moral imagination and moral effort."[2] Our choices, in short, emerge from our possibilities, and our possibilities are governed by our narratively shaped vision of life. Murdoch not only wrote penetrating philosophy[3] but also—unsurprisingly, given her outlook—celebrated novels.[4] She shaped

---

2. Iris Murdoch, *The Sovereignty of Good* (New York: Routledge & Kegan Paul, 1970), 37.

3. These include, inter alia, *The Sovereignty of Good*; *The Fire and the Sun: Why Plato Banished the Artists* (Oxford: Clarendon Press, 1977); and *Metaphysics as a Guide to Morals* (New York: Allen Lane, Penguin Press, 1992).

4. She wrote 26 novels in all, including award-winning titles such as *The Black Prince* (New York: Viking, 1973), *The Sacred and Profane Love Machine* (New York: Viking, 1974), and *The Sea, the Sea* (New York: Viking, 1978).

others' imaginations through both philosophical argument and stories whereby readers might see more perspicaciously and live more admirably.

Acknowledging his indebtedness to Murdoch, Alasdair MacIntyre explored the narratively constituted self in *After Virtue*. He argues that our character—our very self—arises through the stories we inchoately assume or explicitly rehearse. In our actions, practices, and fictions, each of us is "essentially a story-telling animal."[5] One might confirm MacIntyre's insight through empirical study of how ordinary people make sense of personal action; MacIntyre's argument, however, is a philosophical one. Intelligibly accounting for human action depends upon discerning intentions. Because it is impossible adequately to "characterize behavior independently of intentions," and because intentions only make sense within a causally and temporally ordered story, "narrative history . . . turns out to be the basic and essential genre for the characterization of human actions."[6] He concludes: "narrative form is neither disguise nor decoration. . . . Because we all live out narratives in our lives, and because we understand our own lives in terms of the narratives that we live out, . . . narrative is appropriate for understanding the actions of others."[7]

On MacIntyre's appraisal, having a narrative that makes sense of life is of fundamental importance. "The unity of a human life is the unity of a narrative quest"—one that, despite vulnerability to tragedy, moves toward a goal or purpose.[8] Crucially, the narratively constituted self is not merely *self*-narrated. No one simply makes up his or her own life story; our narratives must ultimately conform to the realities of the world we inhabit. Moreover, "the narrative of any one life is part of an interlocking set of narratives," so that each person's story is shaped by a host of others.[9] In naming human beings as "story-telling animals," MacIntyre thus also retains Aristotle's view that we are "social animals."

Religion often powerfully influences one's narrative. Consider Nicholas Wolterstorff's Christian reflection on the interplay of personal stories and

---

5. Alasdair MacIntyre, *After Virtue: A Study in Moral Theory*, 2nd ed. (Notre Dame: University of Notre Dame Press, 1984), 216.

6. MacIntyre, *After Virtue*, 207, 208.

7. MacIntyre, *After Virtue*, 211, 212.

8. MacIntyre, *After Virtue*, 219.

9. MacIntyre, *After Virtue*, 218.

the Bible. He first identifies human life's unremitting narrative shape, noting that "we all live story-shaped lives. The issue is not whether we will do so; the issue is rather, which are the stories that will shape our lives?"[10] Following Erich Auerbach, Wolterstorff then notes the biblical narrative's extraordinary scope.

> Far from seeking, like Homer, merely to make us forget our own reality for a few hours, [the Bible] seeks to over-come our reality: we are to fit our own life into its world, feel ourselves to be elements in its structure of universal history. . . . Everything else that happens in the world can only be conceived as an element in this sequence.[11]

As the Bible's all-encompassing narrative shapes Christians' life stories, so also the Hebrew Bible influences Jewish self-narratives and the Qur'an informs Muslims' personal narratives.

Wolterstorff recognizes that "living within a text" such as the Bible or the Qur'an defies simple characterization. One cannot avoid "a great many points of collision" between ancient religious texts and modern life, and sometimes "our modern Western mentality ought to bend and give."[12] For instance, Jews, Christians, and Muslims may agree that the rapacious destruction of God's creation for private benefit should give way to divinely inspired narratives of gift and stewardship. On the other hand, modernity's reading of reality gets many things right. Where the biblical narrative seems to suggest a single week sufficient for God's creation of the cosmos, many believers still feel compelled to accommodate their reading of the text to modern cosmology. Wolterstorff sees that "allowing oneself to be shaped by the biblical narrative is only one facet of a complex picture. For the shaping has to be a *discriminate* shaping."[13] Whatever the religion within which one's personal narrative takes shape, believers need both critical acumen and humility before texts and traditions that tower over their lives.

---

10. Nicholas Wolterstorff, "Living within a Text," in *Faith and Narrative*, ed. Keith E. Yandell (New York: Oxford University Press, 2001), 211–212.

11. Wolterstorff, "Living within a Text," 202. Wolterstorff's citation is Erich Auerbach, *Mimesis* (Princeton: Princeton University Press, 1968), 15–16.

12. Wolterstorff, "Living within a Text," 212.

13. Wolterstorff, "Living within a Text," 212.

Murdoch, MacIntyre, and Wolterstorff help us recognize the narrative quality of human life. They commend renewed attention to the framing narratives that constrain or enlarge our imagination, making possible more or less meaningful stories, characters, and actions. They also underscore the mutual interdependence of our life stories. We learn to relate our narratives by hearing others' stories. As we apprehend the characters, settings, plots, reversals, and denouements of family, friends, saints, and scoundrels, we acquire raw material for interpreting our own narratives. Wolterstorff especially explores Christianity as a ground out of which believers' personal stories grow. His insights apply, mutatis mutandis, to other religious traditions.

Together these authors identify the lineaments of a narrative approach to life. We now turn to the question of when and where one might most productively explore the narratives that constitute one's life.

## *College as a time and place for telling one's story*

Of all the times and places of our lives, the collegiate years offer one of the most auspicious occasions to discern the narrative threads running through otherwise episodic and disconnected life experiences. College invites the rehearsal of one's story and the hearing of others'; such rehearsals begin in de rigueur accounts of hometown, year, major, and aspirations. By moving past superficial summaries, and by recognizing the qualities of good life stories, students are better prepared to hear a genuine calling.

Undeniably, however, students must *learn* the nature of worthy narratives and *practice* the virtues that sustain them in their quests. Consider what Sharon Daloz Parks and Jon Moline attest regarding college students' desire for meaningful life stories, along with the challenges of nurturing their worthy dreams. Parks frankly acknowledges that students can flounder in the tournament of narratives:

> In the eighties and nineties, I watched emerging adults . . . seeking a place in a new global commons that ambivalently welcomed, encouraged, exploited, and discouraged their participation. . . . I continue to watch young adults . . . reach for a place of belonging, integrity, and contribution . . . while the tides of globalization, cynicism, polarization, and consumerism, coupled with an uncertain

economy and a shifting social-political milieu, play big roles in charting their course.[14]

If college students settle for small questions and neglect worthy dreams, it is partly because they are finding it difficult to negotiate the tournament of those narratives that our culture has generated.

Parks calls on us to encourage students for whom big questions and worthy dreams beckon. She advises attention to two facets of vocational exploration. First, she calls for space to explore the big questions and answers that religious faith raises.[15] By extending hospitality to the questions and to the students asking them, we validate both. Second, she emphasizes the importance of questioning the master narratives of our age. She observes that "each of us lives into and through a host of narratives, each narrative differing in its scope and explanatory power."[16] Based on the narratives we tell and inhabit, we "make our lives bigger or smaller, more expansive or limited."[17] The exploration of vocation "requires that we recognize and interrogate the master narratives that shape our lives."[18] Because "stories stick" and "take up lodging within us," much depends upon who tells the most compelling stories.[19]

Jon Moline similarly credits undergraduates with seriousness of purpose, even though it may not always be apparent. With respect to college classrooms, he grants that students may not always "say what they seriously think."[20] However, in settings like residence halls, campus restaurants, sports events, parties, and places of worship, undergraduates

14. Sharon Daloz Parks, *Big Questions, Worthy Dreams*, 4.

15. Sharon Daloz Parks, "Big Enough Questions? The Search for a Worthy Vocation—From Coffee to Cosmos," lecture given at biennial conference of the Network for Vocation in Undergraduate Education (NetVUE), Indianapolis, IN (March 14, 2013), 5–6, www.cic.edu/Programs-and-Services/Programs/NetVUE/2013-NetVUE-Conference/Documents/Parks.pdf (accessed August 20, 2014).

16. Parks, "Big Enough Questions," 7.

17. Christine Baldwin, *Storycatcher: Making Sense of Our Lives through the Power and Practice of Story* (Novato, CA: New World Library), ix; quoted in Parks, "Big Enough Questions," 7.

18. Parks, "Big Enough Questions," 6.

19. Parks, "Big Enough Questions," 8.

20. Jon N. Moline, "Words, Deeds, and Words about Deeds," in Yandell, ed. *Faith and Narrative*, 168.

routinely ask and answer questions about who to be, how to respond to others, and what to do. Many "are grappling personally with the question, 'How should one live?' "[21] Moline comments that most students are "far more confident of what a good roommate is than of what a good theory is"; still, they are "capable of bringing [their] enacted, applied, and hence serious views about roommates to bear on general questions about the way one ought to live."[22]

Moline also shares Parks's view that collegiate educators should extend hospitality to students, invite good questions of them, and point them toward plausible answers. They need "guidance on the major questions of life. . . . If they do not inherit terminology that helps them in responding to these questions, they will struggle to develop their own."[23] Again like Parks, Moline identifies the importance of narrative. Taking a cue from ordinary life, he observes that

> the popularity of gossip is often thought to be a discreditable thing, but the telling of illustrative and cautionary anecdotes has always been one of the chief tools of moral education. . . . These are stories—micronarratives, if you will, of *choices*. . . . [Undergraduates] share stories of people who are worth choosing or worth avoiding in key roles such as friend, teacher, advisor, fiancée, roommate, mate, or even parent.[24]

The "micronarratives" of students' everyday conversation call for a larger story, a framing narrative that contextualizes their meaning and interprets their significance.

Parks and Moline acknowledge what should be obvious: alongside other worthy aims, colleges and universities bear responsibility for shaping students' lives. Whether or not we want this responsibility, we influence students by the curriculum we prescribe, the practices we reward, and the lives we lead. We contribute to students' self-narratives by rehearsing,

---

21. Moline, "Words, Deeds, and Words about Deeds," 168.

22. Moline, "Words, Deeds, and Words about Deeds," 168. See chapter 11 for a broader discussion of how student life outside the classroom affects, and is affected by, vocational discernment.

23. Moline, "Words, Deeds, and Words about Deeds," 169.

24. Moline, "Words, Deeds, and Words about Deeds," 171.

inhabiting, and commending the framing narratives they observe, consider, and often adopt.[25]

What framing stories are on offer? Which narratives do we enact? Where do we find recounted the compelling narratives of our time? Such questions require a complex response; a beginning may be made by surveying three culturally legitimized narratives that many of our educational institutions simultaneously reflect and shape.

## *Three framing narratives*

American higher education is governed by wildly varying narratives, and competing narratives commonly divide individual institutions. Nonetheless, three major framing narratives appear repeatedly, shaping institutional rhetoric, curricula, and politics. College students often locate their life stories within them, for not only do their schools legitimate these three ways of being in the world, but the wider culture reinforces them through art, film, literature, and music. The whole culture, higher education included, inducts the young into its master narratives.

Grasping these narratives' imaginative power calls for more than *saying* what they are, but also *showing* what they are. For this reason we will examine three popular works of literature emblematic of distinct ways of life and concomitant educational visions. Written on epic scales, commanding vast audiences, and adapted into film, each author's work has narratively embodied correlates in higher education. Ken Follett's *Pillars of the Earth*, George R. R. Martin's *Game of Thrones*, and J. R. R. Tolkien's *Lord of the Rings* portray radically different approaches to education and life. Careful readers see an education *in* them, as characters learn crucially important lessons. They also can discern an education *of* the novels. The stories form imaginations and orient readers in particular ways. In their reading, the music they listen to, and the films they watch, students encounter these framing narratives—whether in these three illustrations or in other works. Helping students with the process of vocational exploration and discernment means paying attention to which narratives are honored in institutional rhetoric, curricular design, and professorial example.

---

25. For one example of refusal to acknowledge the responsibility of mentoring students, see Stanley Fish, *Save the World on Your Own Time* (New York: Oxford University Press, 2008).

## "A man is always better off for understanding something"

Ken Follett's *Pillars of the Earth* was published in 1989, translated into 30 languages in over 25 million copies, and recently adapted into a critically acclaimed miniseries.[26] It begins and ends with the same somber line: "The small boys came early to the hanging."[27]

The first hanging, in 1123, befalls a penniless French minstrel accused of stealing a silver chalice.[28] Jacques Cherbourg, we later learn, is the only surviving witness of the sinking of the White Ship, in which perished the heir of King Henry I; Jacques' hanging secures his silence and ensures prolonged political intrigue in England. The hanging that ends the book, in 1172, is of William Hamleigh, a sadistic nobleman involved in the murder of Thomas Becket, Archbishop of Canterbury. Hamleigh's death ends a terrible life and provides a semblance of justice for countless crimes. The first hanging dooms an innocent commoner; the final one, a guilty aristocrat. Between them Follett traces the lines of a soaring cathedral while exploring the foundations—the pillars of the earth—upon which life, longing, and love are built, whether well or badly.

The human drama of a thousand pages grips readers' hearts, but few of the book's human characters rival the importance of a nonhuman one: the cathedral of Kingsbridge. For its sake lands are won or lost, careers made or broken, and lives saved or destroyed. It rises from a ruinous fire's ashes, first taking Romanesque shape according to the Norman conventions of master architect Tom Builder and later receiving Gothic form at the hands of Jack Jackson, Tom's gifted stepson. *Pillars* also portrays the surrounding town's transformations, from a sleepy priory village into a major commercial center. Hundreds of cathedral builders contribute to Kingsbridge's initial prosperity, but savvy civic planning ensures long-term vitality. The cathedral and the town, both underwritten by Prior Phillip's patronage, constitute the heart of the book. People live and die, kings rise and fall, generations come and go, but monumental feats of human ingenuity like cathedrals, and sophisticated social forms like cities, last forever. Or do they?

---

26. See ken-follett.com/bibliography/the_pillars_of_the_earth (accessed on October 15, 2014).

27. Ken Follett, *The Pillars of the Earth* (New York: William Morrow and Company, 1989), 11, 963.

28. Follett, *Pillars of the Earth*, 13.

*Pillars* expresses a way of life well described as *tragic optimism*. Horrid events take place en passant—murder, pillage, thieving, usurping—and yet, ploddingly, human know-how makes the world more secure. Cathedrals are made beautiful, spacious, and safe when architects study problems, think imaginatively, test designs, and learn from mistakes. Trade becomes profitable when markets are open, rationally designed, and operated under just laws. Urban life is improved when leaders serve goods other than mere self-interest, when roads are well planned and underwritten by fairly collected taxes, and when professional expertise guides public decisions. Fewer people die when the sick are isolated from the healthy, hygienic precautions undertaken, and treatment records kept.

Follett's book encourages confidence in the claim that thought, transformed into action, can solve problems. Consider the example of Aliena, the dispossessed daughter of the late Earl of Shiring, who comports herself admirably despite misfortune. Without land or money, she thrives through a combination of good luck and hard work, becoming a profitable wool merchant. As her trade grows, she encounters new difficulties. Traders want felted wool, and felting "is backbreaking work." But her friend Jack Jackson wonders whether the ingenuity that built mills to grind grain might also build a machine to felt wool.[29] Jack's stepsister argues that if it could be done, someone would have already done it. He perseveres nevertheless; he makes Aliena her fulling mill, and her trade grows even more profitable. Clever people employ reason to solve problems—especially problems that no one else has even recognized.

In another instance, Jack lauds Euclid's recently translated *Elements of Geometry*. Most of his friends question the value of abstractions about right angles and inscribed figures, but Jack extols their practical import for designing bridges, roofs, and cathedrals. One optimistic colleague agrees: "A man is always better off for understanding something!" In addition, Jack explains, "now that I understand the principles of geometry, I may be able to devise solutions to new problems."[30] Follett's narrative underscores the exhilaration of understanding, the human mind's competence, and confidence in reason to resolve problems.

But the narrative's optimism is ultimately tragic. Death opens and closes *Pillars of the Earth*; readers repeatedly encounter life's fragility. The

29. Follett, *Pillars of the Earth*, 556–557.

30. Follett, *Pillars of the Earth*, 679–681 passim.

innocent and the guilty, young and old, parents, children, friends—all suffer loss and die. To be sure, some deaths are better than others; and just as plainly, knowledge makes some lives more pleasant than others. Airy, lighted Gothic cathedrals are better than dark Romanesque ones. Water-powered fulling mills produce felt better than fuller's bats. Yet art, industry, technology, and the skill that enable them confront limits. Technological mastery, economic productivity, sound public administration, and good medicine cannot solve the riddle of human existence. Education makes possible lovelier spaces, safer lives, and more efficient labor, but then what? An easier death after longer delay?

*Pillars* and its sequel, *World Without End*, take no refuge in the consolation of achievements that outlast individual lives. Kingsbridge and its cathedral stand at the heart of the story; people come and go, while the cathedral city gathers greatness. Yet Follett avoids making it invincible; tragedy tempers his vision of what human minds imagine and hands create. The cathedral collapses (more than once). A splendid bridge built to grow trade washes down the river. The Black Death decimates the population. Fire destroys public buildings and cozy homes. Hopes, dreams, labors, and struggles are vanquished, even when people aspire to a legacy that outlives them.

Follett rightly celebrates education and progress; more admirably, he acknowledges the tragic limits of technical prowess. Bertrand Russell, a kindred spirit, captured tragic optimism's spirit especially well:

> blind to good and evil, reckless of destruction, omnipotent matter rolls on its relentless way; for man, condemned today to lose his dearest, tomorrow himself to pass through the gate of darkness, it remains only to cherish, ere yet the blow fall, the lofty thoughts that ennoble his little day.[31]

Tragic optimism is heady stuff for those able to bear it. However, few can embrace tragedy, and students do not rally around tragedy-riven callings. Hence, the framing narrative embodied by Follett's novel bears upon the pedagogy of vocation in two key ways.

First, like other contemporary institutions, colleges and universities easily put too much stock in technophilic fantasy. Powerful corporate interests,

---

31. Bertrand Russell, "A Free Man's Worship," in *Why I Am Not a Christian and Other Essays*, ed. Paul Edwards (New York: Simon & Schuster, 1957), 115–116.

savvy marketing, and lucrative research grants, combined with real problems for which technology provides useful remedies, make utopian dreams
seem plausible. Successful technological exploits foster optimism that still
better possibilities lie ahead, even in tradition-bound higher education where
a long view comes more naturally. As Anthony Kronman observes, "All we
can imagine is more technology: new and better gadgets that permit us to
do what we want at greater speed and lower cost. That is for us today the only
imaginable future, and we embrace it both because we want it and because
we believe it is inevitable."[32] Wittingly or not, we can find ourselves caught
in the grip of a narrative in which know-how reigns supreme. Worse, we
sometimes induct students into that narrative through exuberant, uncritical
accounts of the natural and applied sciences.

Technophilia can bend the narrative arc of human life toward sham
optimism, leading us to forget that no technology can banish tragedy.
Underwritten by science, technology gives us "unprecedented powers of
control," but it also "discourages the thought that our finitude is a condition
of the meaningfulness of our lives."[33] When curricula, rhetoric, and example
nurture students into a narrative in which technology solves all problems,
we ill prepare them for callings responsive to the human soul's deep needs.[34]
Of course, technophobia provides no solution either; the point is that authentic vocation unites know-how with self-knowledge and knowledge of others
under the ambit of divine providence.

Second, unyielding tragic optimism—expressed narratively by Follett
and philosophically by Russell—does not suit a pedagogy of vocation any
better than sham optimism. Given a choice, people do not devote themselves
to hopeless tasks, as in the absurd life of Albert Camus's Sisyphus whose
"whole being is exerted toward accomplishing nothing."[35] For good reason,
university recruiters do not distribute glossy admissions brochures citing

---

32. Anthony T. Kronman, *Education's End: Why Our Colleges and Universities Have Given
Up on the Meaning of Life* (New Haven, CT: University of Yale Press, 2008), 209.

33. Kronman, *Education's End*, 233.

34. See Edward O. Wilson's technophilic claims in *Of Human Nature* (Cambridge,
MA: Harvard University Press, 1978), 202–203. He mocks reticence before God's questions in Job 38 by insisting: "Jehovah's challenges have been met and scientists have
pressed on to uncover and to solve even greater puzzles. . . . Could the Old Testament
writers have conceived of such activity? And still the process of great scientific discovery
gathers momentum."

35. Albert Camus, *The Myth of Sisyphus and Other Essays*, trans. Justin O'Brien
(New York: Vintage Books, 1991), 120.

Lord Russell. Even if one could consistently adopt tragic optimism's narrative (an arguable point), it represents a framing narrative that no one embraces, cherishes, or finds fulfilling in the ways that a calling—even a difficult calling—entails. No doubt, a collegiate education should temper student idealism with the sobriety appropriate to a world marred by tragedy. Yet unremitting tragedy crushes aspirations for a meaningful vocation. In extreme forms, as with Follett, Russell, and Camus, we find what Josef Pieper calls the "nadir of despair . . . the affirmation of nonfulfillment as though it were fulfillment."[36]

## "When you play a game of thrones you win or you die"

George Martin's *Game of Thrones* debuted in 1996, the first installment of a fantasy epic now totaling two million words.[37] Transcending the world of fantasy aficionados, its fourth and fifth books reached the uppermost rungs of *The New York Times* bestseller list. HBO has adapted it into a critically acclaimed television series, landing thirteen Emmy nominations and winning two in its first season. Martin's intricately spun world and wild success prompted *Time* to name him one of "the most influential people in the world," a recognition of outsized influence presaged by Lev Grossman's proclamation, also in *Time*, that Martin is "the American Tolkien."[38]

"Westeros" is a world of lords, ladies, knights, squires, and sellswords. Oaths bind lesser lords and "bannermen" to greater lords, as they bind great lords to kings (except when they don't). As the books' titles suggest, the land is riven by conflict in which the stakes are life and death. One devilish power-monger says, "When you play a game of thrones you win or you die. There is no middle ground."[39]

Indeed, two predominant themes of Martin's novels are *death* and *power*. Death is implacable, but those wielding power have some say about

---

36. Josef Pieper, "On Hope," in *Faith, Hope, Love* (San Francisco: Ignatius, 1997), 123.

37. It includes *A Game of Thrones* (1996), *A Clash of Kings* (1998), *A Storm of Swords* (2000), *A Feast of Crows* (2005), and *A Dance with Dragons* (2011). Two forthcoming titles completing the series have been announced: *The Winds of Winter* and *A Dream of Spring*.

38. Lev Grossman, "The American Tolkien," *Time* vol. 166, issue 21 (November 21, 2005): 139.

39. George R. R. Martin, *A Game of Thrones* (1996; repr., New York: Bantam Books, 2011), 488.

when and how death arrives. The poor, weak, and vulnerable—called "smallfolk" by the powerful—will, likely as not, suffer horribly and die early. Even if close kin mourn them, the novels present them as nameless and valueless. The rich and powerful also die, and when they play the game of thrones poorly, they die in torment too. Provided they play well, though, they can inflict death rather than suffer it. Robert Joustra, writing in perhaps too casually dismissive a tone (given the work's popularity and influence), describes its "thematic arc . . . [as] pretty basic: Violence, rape, devastation. Repeat. Sprinkle in some dragons and frozen zombies."[40]

Great narratives often confront death and power. Homer's *Odyssey* hinges on the hero's reclamation of his long-vacant throne; in the process, all of his men die. Sophocles' *Antigone* gives us Creon, who issues dubious commands leading to multiple deaths, even while he grieves holding the reins of power. In Shakespeare and Joyce, Willa Cather and Albert Camus, Marilynne Robinson and Cormac McCarthy, artful stories swing upon the drama of death and power. Thus, Martin's attention to death and power represents nothing new. Enthralling fantasy is not unprecedented either. What, then, does one of the world's most influential people offer? In a word: *cynicism*. His work may not be distinct in this respect either, but it is surprisingly stark in the cynicism with which power grinds human lives into oblivion.

"Cynicism" means multiple things. It names an ancient philosophical movement; the Cynics believed that reconciling human excellence and nature required abandoning Athenian social conventions. Because of their crudeness, they were called *kynikoi*—"dog-like."[41] Cynics such as Antisthenes and Diogenes rejected money, power, and fame, seeing them as impediments to happiness. They lived simply, naturally, and self-sufficiently. Although the Cynics would probably repudiate much of Martin's narrative, their spirit—including the repudiation of convention and emphasis upon self-sufficiency—animates his story.

"Cynicism" also bears a colloquial meaning. The cynical do not trust others. They expect the worst and they deride what others value. Cynicism

---

40. Robert Joustra, "The Return of the Dragons" *Books & Culture*, April 2012, www.booksandculture.com/articles/webexclusives/2012/april/returnofdragons.html (accessed October 15, 2014).

41. The word survives in English both in *cynical* and more obliquely in *canine*, from the Latin *canis*.

takes no delight in generosity, hospitality, humility, or wonder. Cynics, scornfully secure, have little to offer others; avoiding the vulnerabilities of expectation, they anticipate barren desolation. Martin's novels offer these qualities too.

The cynicism in *Game of Thrones* is not a pose. Martin's implicit claim to show the "honest-to-God" truth about life, conjoined with his finely wrought story, makes his books spellbinding. Answering criticism that "his books were too cynical, Martin simply responded 'they are realistic.' "[42] Joustra observes that Martin's

> barren world unapologetically mirrors the experience and expectation of Millennial culture. What's missing is not just kindness or innocence, although those are relentlessly bled from Martin's imaginary world. The most salient absence is hope. . . . [I]t puts words to that malaise of modernity that erodes the foundations of hope.[43]

Martin's cynical stories sell millions of books because they match our age's rising cynicism.

Consider three brief examples. In *A Clash of Kings*, Jon Snow is stricken by the plight of Gilly, a teenager taken as a wife by her vile father. Jon wants to rescue the brutalized girl. His superior, however, curtly forbids him: "We cannot set the world to rights. That is not our purpose."[44] Second, when the heartless King Joffrey publicly strips his betrothed, Sansa, shaming and humiliating her, his uncle cautions: "Wanton brutality is no way to win your people's love." But Joffrey responds by saying that "Fear is better than love"—and then, pointing at Sansa, adds, "*She* fears me."[45] Finally, we witness the "education" of the same twelve-year-old Sansa by a monstrous force of power, Sandor Clegane (who is nicknamed the "Hound" and thus serves as a human dog or "cynic"). Minutes before a battle, Sansa asks what Clegane will do amidst combat. He responds: "Fight. Kill. Die, maybe." She wonders aloud if the gods might punish him, but he denies their existence; when she protests that there are, at least, true knights who protect the weak, he denies this as well. "If you can't protect yourself,

---

42. Joustra, "Return of the Dragons."

43. Joustra, "Return of the Dragons."

44. Martin, *A Clash of Kings* (1999; reprint, New York: Bantam Books, 2011), 375.

45. Martin, *Clash of Kings*, 489.

die and get out of the way of those who can. Sharp steel and strong arms rule this world, don't ever believe any different." Sansa runs away, telling herself that there are gods and that there are true knights: "All the stories can't be lies."[46] Yet nowhere in Martin's stories do we see Sansa's hope vindicated.

Cynicism denotes a way of life frequently chosen in our time, and it affects students. Indeed, even within colleges and universities, some seek to demolish all intuitions about good and bad, right and wrong, virtuous and vicious. They teach in a cynical spirit (yet often without the ironic wit represented in Woody Allen's pronouncement: "Marxism is dead, feminism is dead, humanism is dead and frankly, I don't feel so good myself."[47]) Every age produces cynical teachers, those whose repertoire is exhausted by sneering and irony. Joustra notes that Martin's approach mirrors "that of Plato's Thrasymachus: there is no right, there is no honor, there is only the advantage of the strong."[48]

Our time and place are shaped not just by Socrates' interlocutors in Plato's dialogues, but also by Machiavelli, the original *modern* teacher of those who would be powerful. Marcus Schulzke argues that Martin's story "illustrates many of Machiavelli's most important lessons."[49] Regrettably, its central idea—that morality is a fiction forced by the powerful upon the unsuspecting weak—informs wide swaths of contemporary economic, political, social, and intellectual life. No less is it the case, sadly, that colleges and universities can exemplify Machiavellian struggles for power. When the quest for truth, beauty, and goodness is supplanted by skillful exercises in marketing, utility, and management, the university becomes a cynical place; it jades rather than inspires, slackens instead of stirs, and reinforces manipulative, self-serving aims instead of an aspiration to greatness that seeks and accomplishes worthy things.

Of course it does not follow that anyone should suppress study of Machiavelli's political realism—or, for that matter, any other less-than-

---

46. Martin, *Clash of Kings*, 757.

47. Quoted in Ewan Morrison, "Cynicism and Postmodernity," review of *Cynicism and Postmodernity*, by Timothy Bewes, *Variant* 2, no. 5 (Spring 1998): 29.

48. Joustra, "Return of the Dragons."

49. Marcus Schulzke, "Playing the Game of Thrones: Some Lessons from Machiavelli," in *Game of Thrones and Philosophy: Logic Cuts Deeper than Swords*, ed. Henry Jacoby (Hoboken, NJ: John Wiley and Sons, 2012), 34.

savory theories of our life together. Much may be learned from such views, and one's calling can be constructively and critically shaped by them. Still, hearing and responding to a call demands a framing narrative that regards seriously the possibility of noble, self-transcendent service. For this, the cynicism embodied in *Game of Thrones* will not do—even though grappling with its manifold expressions remains important.

## "I will trust you once more"

A quarter-billion copies of Tolkien's *Lord of the Rings* and *Hobbit* have sold in languages around the world. Ralph Wood notes that in three polls, the British proclaimed it "the most important book of the twentieth century."[50] W. H. Auden regarded it as a "masterpiece" and favorably compared it to Milton's *Paradise Lost*.[51] Readers quickly see the justice of such high praise, for they enter a story of extraordinary imaginative detail. Tolkien invented languages, millennia-old histories, and complex cultures for his books. His heroes inhabit a remarkable world in a theologically superintended cosmos, and many readers find themselves rooting for their victory.

At the heart of Tolkien's narrative lies *charity* or love. Here, we need to heed a prompt cautionary note: fully grasped, both "charity" and "love" mean much more than is suggested by culturally debased uses of the terms. Charity entails more than do-goodism and love involves more than a feeling. The *virtue* of charity or love names a habit acquired through grace that shapes one's character, and thus that transforms one's moral vision, emotions, understanding, motivation, and action. Theologically considered, charity is the friendship of human beings for God.[52] It is a "special virtue" that "joins us to God," gives shape to "the acts of all the other virtues" and "to this extent is said to be the form of the virtues," and thus "extends not merely to the love of God, but also to the love of

---

50. Ralph C. Wood, *The Gospel According to Tolkien: Visions of the Kingdom in Middle-earth* (Louisville, KY: Westminster John Knox Press, 2003), 1.

51. W. H. Auden, "At the End of the Quest, Victory," *The New York Times Book Review* (January 22, 1956), 5; www.nytimes.com/1956/01/22/books/tolkien-king.html (accessed October 15, 2014).

52. Thomas Aquinas, *Summa Theologiae: Latin Text and English Translation, Introductions, Notes, Appendices, and Glossaries*, 61 vols., trans. Fathers of the English Dominican Province (London: Eyre and Spottiswoode; New York: McGraw-Hill, 1964–1981), II–II, questions 23–27 (English text, 34:5–183).

neighbour."[53] Practically regarded, charity takes shape in corporal and spiritual works of mercy. Corporal works of mercy include such things as attending to the hungry, thirsty, sick, and imprisoned; spiritual works of mercy include the offering of instruction, counsel, forgiveness, and comfort. The virtue of charity, in short, initiates one into a distinctive way of being in the world, seeing oneself, and regarding others; all of these things make a difference for *vocation*. And although charity is the highest of Christian virtues, it figures in Western theology more generally.[54] Even the academy privileges charity. To speak of someone's interpretation as "uncharitable" is a rebuke; conversely, we praise those who read, write, and critique "charitably." Perhaps charity's wide acclaim, combined with its central status in Tolkien's epic, account for the lavish celebration of his books.

Nowhere are charity's implications clearer than for Frodo and Sam, small-statured hobbits upon whose quest the fortunes of Middle-earth hang. In them we witness an education in charity. This virtue transforms their imaginations so that they sympathetically understand a world that is more complicated than they first think. The test case is Gollum, a twisted creature whose life of solipsistic self-preferment has monstrously diminished him. Absent charity for Gollum, Frodo doesn't really see or understand him; in fact, Frodo believes that Gollum deserves death, and thoughtlessly calls it a "pity" his Uncle Bilbo didn't kill him when chance allowed. The wise wizard Gandalf admonishes Frodo: "It was Pity that stayed his hand. Pity, and Mercy: not to strike without need."[55] Similarly, Sam's hatred perniciously warps his understanding of Gollum. On seeing Gollum, Sam's "eyes, filled with anger and disgust, . . . fixed on the wretched creature."[56] Wood writes: "Sam is determined not to find even a sliver of good in Gollum. He treats him with utter contempt, repeatedly

---

53. Thomas Aquinas, *Summa Theologiae* II–II, 23, 4 (English text, 34:19); II–II, 23, 3 (34:15); II–II, 23, 8 (34:33); and II–II, 25, 1 (34:83).

54. I have in mind *khesed* and the practice of *tzedakah* among Jews and Muslims' praise of *zakat*.

55. J. R. R. Tolkien, *The Fellowship of the Ring* (New York: Quality Paperback, 1995), 68. At the beginning, Frodo thus falls short of Bilbo's charitable compassion toward Gollum. Wood observes that "the pity of Bilbo may rule the fate of many" is the only "declaration to be repeated in all three volumes of *The Lord of the Rings*," and Gandalf's speech "lies at the moral and religious center of the entire epic" (*Gospel According to Tolkien*, 150).

56. Tolkien, *The Two Towers* (New York: Quality Paperback, 1995), 220.

calling him a 'nasty treacherous creature' . . ., and giving him multiple unsavory names: 'Slinker' and 'Stinker' and 'Sneak.' "[57]

Through charity, however, Frodo and Sam see revealed what otherwise would remain hidden. Frodo's charity helps him eventually see Gollum as more than an unambiguous evil. It helps him apprehend the tragedy of Gollum's warped inner life, thereby uncovering and illuminating what he is. Traveling in uneasy companionship, Frodo tells Gollum, "I will trust you once more. . . . it seems that . . . it is my fate to receive help from you, . . . and [it is] your fate to help me."[58] In the wake of Frodo's charity, readers thereafter glimpse hidden possibilities within Gollum: "For a fleeting moment, could [they] have seen him, they would have thought that they beheld an old weary hobbit, shrunken by the years that had carried him far beyond his time, beyond fields and kin, and the fields and streams of youth, an old starved pitiable thing."[59] Charity more clearly reveals Gollum for who he is. The lesson is plain: we cannot understand what we hate; conversely, loves kindles the desire to know.

Sam experiences two beautiful epiphanies, though Gollum has no direct role in them. In the first revelation he looks upon Frodo sleeping, and seems to see a light shining within him; his face looks "old and beautiful, as if the chiseling of the shaping years was now revealed in many fine lines that had before been hidden." In this moment, he finds himself murmuring, "I love him. He's like that, and sometimes it shines through, somehow. But I love him, whether or no."[60] The second epiphany happens as Frodo and Sam approach Mordor and all seems lost; the fellowship is broken and their quest has broken them. In this valley of the shadow of death, Sam's eyes catch a solitary, faint star: "the thought pierced him that in the end the Shadow was only a small and passing thing: there was light and high beauty for ever beyond its reach."[61] Sam is a simple gardener, but love uncovers wondrous things. Charity empowers him to see what others do not: another soul's luminous shining and the heavens' wondrous glory which the darkness has not overcome.

---

57. Wood, *Gospel According to Tolkien*, 132.

58. Tolkien, *Two Towers*, 248.

59. Tolkien, *Two Towers*, 324.

60. Tolkien, *Two Towers*, 260.

61. Tolkien, *The Return of the King* (New York: Quality Paperback, 1995), 199.

Tolkien's world of humble hobbits and wise wizards inspires because it calls forth our longing for love. Its framing narrative teaches us that love opens the mind's eye. Dostoyevsky similarly expresses charity's power when he has Father Zosima say,

> Love all of God's creation, both the whole of it and every grain of sand. Love every leaf, every ray of God's light. Love animals, love plants, love each thing. If you love each thing, you will perceive the mystery of God in things. Once you have perceived it, you will begin tirelessly to perceive more and more of it every day. And you will come at last to love the whole world with an entire, universal love.[62]

Whether in Dostoyevsky or Tolkien—or in the gospel narrative that inspires them both—charity is the greatest of all. When divine charity undergirds one's personal narrative, sacrifice for the sake of one's calling makes sense.

The tournament of narratives within contemporary higher education should privilege charity for a variety of reasons. Most obviously, it stands at the heart of one of the great narratives produced by the West. No adequate understanding of art, education, history, literature, medicine, philosophy, politics, and certainly theology is possible without acknowledging charity's sway.

In addition, charity governs the intellectual life prized within colleges and universities. Mark Schwehn writes: "As with the life of the spirit in general so too with the life of spirited inquiry: love or charity is the greatest of the virtues."[63] The reason why is clear; "charity both enriches and enlivens the quality of thought."[64] Tragic optimism's halting, self-preserving conquests and cynicism's debilitating bleakness foreclose intellectual

---

62. Fyodor Dostoevsky, *The Brothers Karamazov*, trans. Richard Pevear and Larissa Volokhonsky (New York: Random House, Vintage Classics, 1990), 319.

63. Mark R. Schwehn, *Exiles from Eden: Religion and the Academic Vocation in America* (New York: Oxford University Press, 1993), 50.

64. Schwehn, *Exiles from Eden*, 51. Schwehn applauds nontheistic expressions of charity and praises Jeffrey Stout as an instance of it; however, he expresses concern that Stout "might be living off a kind of borrowed fund of moral capital" (53). Schwehn worries whether or not charity "can be sustained over the course of several more generations absent the affections, practices, and institutions as well as the network of beliefs that gave rise to [it] originally" (56).

vision and moral imagination; charity, on the other hand, enables the intellectually blind to see and the morally lame to walk. The aforementioned examples of Frodo and Sam in Tolkien's story express the insight nicely, but it is easy to identify academic instances as well. Absent Rachel Carson's charitable regard for nature, *Silent Spring*'s courageous findings would have remained silent. As she notes, having experienced "a sense of the beautiful, the excitement of the new and the unknown, a feeling of sympathy, pity, admiration or love—then we wish for knowledge about the object of our emotional response."[65] Similarly, when Barbara McClintock quipped of her plants, "I know them intimately, and I find it a great pleasure to know them," the Nobel Prize winner hearkened to attentive love as a wellspring for her astonishing cytogenetic discoveries.[66] McClintock's biographer observes, "Both literally and figuratively, her 'feeling for the organism' has extended her vision. . . . Good science cannot proceed without a deep emotional investment on the part of the scientist."[67] Intellectual charity enables scholars to serve their subjects, attend patiently to them, regard them in their integrity, and understand them sympathetically. Whatever one's subject—Carson's songbirds, McClintock's corn plants, Homer's *Iliad*, hungry children, international politics—the general claim holds true: love deepens knowledge.

Not least of all, a narrative of charitable inhabitation of the world, together with the admirable virtues it calls forth, is responsive to college students' longing. They can hold technophilic fantasies, capitulate to tragedy, and succumb to cynicism, especially when so tutored. Yet they really yearn for honest, hopeful, worthy lives; they anxiously watch to see charity crowned champion in the tournament of narratives, and they inwardly grieve when it falters before other narratives. In a world governed by charity, students will rally around a calling, even to a life of hardship and sacrifice, because they possess confidence that their vocation truly matters.

65. Rachel Carson, *The Sense of Wonder* (New York: Harper & Row, 1965), 45. Cf. Lisa H. Sideris, "The Secular and Religious Sources of Rachel Carson's Sense of Wonder," pp. 232–250 in *Rachel Carson: Legacy and Challenge*, ed. Lisa H. Sideris and Kathleen Dean Moore (Albany: State University of New York Press, 2008).

66. Quoted in Evelyn Fox Keller, *A Feeling for the Organism: The Life and Work of Barbara McClintock* (New York: W.H. Freeman, 1983), 198.

67. Keller, *Feeling*, 198. She adds, "Over the years, a special kind of sympathetic understanding grew in McClintock, heightening her powers of discernment, until finally, the objects of her study have become subjects in their own right; they claim from her a kind of attention that most of us experience only in relation to other persons" (200).

Colleges and universities concerned with the exploration of vocation must challenge students to a way of life that is bolder than tragic optimism and more vulnerable than cynicism. If our students are learners with the amplitude of mind and aspiration of heart for it, and if we are teachers with the openness and sensitivity for it, then we will undertake to read, listen, speak, and write charitably, humbly, reverently, and hopefully. Therein we begin to inscribe our personal stories within a framing narrative of charity that makes sense of our callings.

## Discerning vocation amid contested narratives

How do we learn to tell coherent, truthful, and sensitive narratives of ourselves and our world? What practices can allow charity, rather than tragic optimism or cynicism, to frame our life stories? Where in our stories might we hear and respond to God's call? All such questions invite more discussion than present space allows, but here are four practical approaches.

First, we can help students interpret the epic stories of our age. This chapter has sought to exemplify such an effort by considering three popular epics that create worlds of meaning, which in turn shape readers through their metanarratives. Follett's tragic optimism, Martin's jaded cynicism, and Tolkien's self-sacrificing charity present persuasive ways of regarding our place in the world, the life to which we are called, and the virtues needed for heeding that call. But Follett, Martin, and Tolkien are not alone in offering compelling narratives. Students read Philip Pullman's *Golden Compass* trilogy, Suzanne Collins' *Hunger Games* trilogy, J. K. Rowling's *Harry Potter* series, and countless others long before they encounter more sophisticated stories. Whatever the literature du jour, students need help reading intricately developed works of moral imagination with critical understanding and pleasure.

Second, we can teach great works of confession and autobiography. Students should study the charity-suffused narrative of Augustine's *Confessions*; the dispirited cynicism of Rousseau's *Confessions*; and the tragic optimism of Henry Adams's *Education*.[68] They can thereby see how

---

68. Cf. David Mazella, *The Making of Modern Cynicism* (Charlottesville: University of Virginia Press, 2007) and Gary Wills, *Henry Adams and the Making of America* (New York: Houghton Mifflin, 2005).

significant personal narratives hold together (or not), they can learn the arc and ethos of such stories, and they can identify the practices, virtues, and difficulties of saints and sinners through the ages.

Third, in selected courses we can guide students in writing—provisionally and fallibly, to be sure—their own memoirs. Especially when a structured, iterative process guides memoir-writing, and particularly when the assignment includes an invitation to vocational reflection, students may gain great insight into who they are, better understand the vocations to which they are called, think about why these things matter, and consider how they might "write ahead" a worthy narrative to enact.[69] In the process of editing and revising their memoirs, students are also encouraged to explore alternative interpretations of the important episodes in their lives, seeing them as openings into (or foreclosures of) possible life callings.

Fourth, we can explore with students the framing narratives assumed within our guilds, at work within curricula, and inscribed within the texts they read. For instance, where, why, and to what extent do natural science curricula endorse unsustainable narratives of optimism? Can rigorous method and new technologies really solve humanity's fundamental problems? How might the charity-sustained virtue of humility facilitate greater openness to a divine call? Correlatively: where, why, and to what extent do the humanities legitimate narratives of cynicism? How might the charity-enabled virtue of magnanimity undergird responsiveness to God's call instead of the despairing cynicism sometimes apparent in the humanities?[70] Yet again, where in our guilds and institutions may be found charity's legacy? Plato, Augustine, Dante, Teresa of Avila, Kierkegaard, Murdoch—all of them and many others affirm the mutually interdependent qualities of love and understanding. Do our curricula, texts, lectures, and assignments bind love and understanding together, or divide them from one another? Do we invite our students to love what they study, dispose themselves in charity toward the intricacies of the persons, problems, and puzzles they encounter academically, and open themselves to a vocation prompted by love?

---

69. See the comments in chapter 5 on the relationship between call stories and changed lives.

70. See the account of magnanimity in chapter 8.

## Charity and vocation

Through its narratives—whether articulated or implied—education invites us to cherish some things and discount others. Education fits us for lives inhabiting particular framing narratives; our story-constituted selves take shape within these worlds. Educators concerned with helping students to explore their callings must therefore attend thoughtfully to the explicit and implicit narratives that they teach and model. While honoring the power of science and technology, we should not endorse overbold fantasies of control ending in tragedy. While prizing the interrogative mood of much academic discourse, we ought not capitulate to cynical narratives of self-assertion and power. Within a narrative of charity we can meet humankind's deepest questions and greatest problems without succumbing to either presumption or despair.

In postmodernity's tournament of narratives, charity possesses tremendous advantages. As with all great narratives, it incorporates the best its competitors offer and goes beyond them. Charity's aim isn't to conquer either tragic optimism or cynicism, but to transform them by making space for them and then locating what they get right within their proper context. Charity takes tragic optimism—with its imperative to improve life here and now—and transforms it into genuine hope beyond human ingenuity. Charity takes cynicism—with its sobriety about the world's scars, wounds, and ugliness—and transforms it into companionship and mercy. It sees equally well the world's evils, but it does not succumb to despair and fatalism. For all of these reasons, when we give pride of place to charity, we esteem the framing narrative best suited to the reality in which we live and move and have our being—and thus the one also best suited to our students' nascent lives, fledgling stories, and hope-filled callings.

# PART THREE

# *Vocation and Virtue*

Over the past half-century, conversations among philosophers, theologians, and ethicists have been increasingly attentive to the ancient category of *virtue*. The word translates the Greek term *aretē*, which denoted an excellence of character; a person of virtue was someone who not only did good deeds, but whose character was such that one would expect good deeds to issue forth from such a person. Of course, what counted as "good" in any particular context was highly dependent on the culture within which it operated; in ancient Greek culture, character traits that made a person good at fighting wars or deliberating about the city-state were typically held in higher esteem than traits that made a person compassionate toward the needy or capable of raising children well. Still, the moral terminology that we have inherited from the Greeks—including the names of specific virtues, such as courage, temperance, justice, and wisdom—have been defined anew in every age, and have therefore continued to exercise a significant influence on moral and ethical reflection.

What does virtue have to do with vocation? The contributors to this volume found themselves returning, again and again, to the claim that vocation is a *teleological* reality—that is, it has something to do with one's *telos*, one's goal or purpose. Discerning one's vocation is tantamount to discerning one's purpose in life, the ends toward which one feels compelled to act. But this in turn requires making some judgments about what would count as a good goal, a worthy purpose, a form of life that is really worth pursuing. That goal will, in turn, determine the actions that one will take in order to pursue such a life. All of this suggests that vocational discernment is essentially a *moral* enterprise; it requires moral judgments about what kind of life is worth living. Unfortunately, most undergraduate students (and indeed, most people in general) have not had that much experience deliberating about these kinds of questions; they tend to possess a rather meager vocabulary for discussing and assessing the moral worth of purposes and goals, whether their own or someone else's. Hence, many discussions of vocation can devolve into merely instrumental assessments of which potential directions in life will offer some level of security, a reasonable level of income, or simply the fewest obstacles. At this point, reflecting on and discerning one's vocation lapses into a rather uninspiring conversation about what seems practical under the circumstances.

The contributors to this book are convinced that there is a better alternative. By helping our students to develop a richer and more complex moral vocabulary, we provide them with the tools to reflect on and to evaluate potential vocations in ways that are not merely instrumental. We enable them to think about the relationships among a particular calling, the means by which one might respond it, and the purposes or goals for which it might be pursued. We help them to think about those goals in a more nuanced way, considering (for example) which directions in life might make them better people. The three chapters that follow are each focused on a particular virtue—magnanimity, prudence, and loyalty—but all three authors also point to a wider range of moral judgments that are involved in vocational discernment, and they introduce the reader to some of the terminology and the thought processes that might help us make those judgments.

Equipped with the language of virtue, our students will be able to ask a different set of questions about their potential vocations. These might include:

- What are the excellences of character that I hope my own life will exhibit?
- To what degree have I seen these character traits at work in other people, and what criteria do I use to evaluate whether a particular life is a "good" life?
- What will I need to do in order to be truly happy in life—not just in the sense of a passing emotion, but in the sense of living a truly fulfilled and fulfilling life?
- Does a particular vocational direction encourage me to develop excellences of character that will make me a better person?
- Conversely, does an apparent calling to which I feel particularly compelled have some (perhaps partially hidden) features that might actually obstruct my own moral development, or that might curtail my progress toward the good?

- What are my own character strengths at the present moment, and how will they contribute to the vocational direction that I'm considering?
- What other character traits are necessary if I am to respond well to the particular calling that I am discerning, and how will I develop these?

Clearly, the ways that students will define and internalize some of this moral language will vary greatly, just as our modern assumptions about "courage" or "compassion" might differ greatly from that of the ancient Greeks. But this is not an argument against developing a better vocabulary for addressing moral questions; indeed, as they begin to demonstrate greater facility with this language, students will be better positioned to shape their own definitions and find their own examples of people who exhibit good character and have lived lives of virtue. As such, they may also find ways of entering into their own work of vocational reflection and discernment with an eye to its *telos*. Our hope is that they will not only focus on what seems practical, but will also consider what goals and purposes can truly be called *good*—and how these might be rightly achieved.

## 8

# An Itinerary of Hope

CALLED TO A MAGNANIMOUS WAY OF LIFE

*Paul J. Wadell*

PERHAPS THE MOST compelling argument for inviting students to think about vocation is that it can be a path to fullness of life: an itinerary of hope. Vocational exploration and discernment can lead us into a way of being and acting—and of understanding ourselves and our place in the world—that gives us meaning, purpose, and direction; it can orient us toward our life's journey. Seen through the lens of vocation, human beings are not bemused tourists leisurely taking in the sights, but moral agents uniquely enabled to make a gift of their lives by generously using their time, energy, and talents to do good in all the creatively insightful ways it can be done, and in all the compellingly beautiful ways it needs to be done.

Thus, to think rightly about vocation we ought to begin by helping our students ask the right questions: not only "What should I do with my life?" but also "What kind of life is truly worth living?" A vocation is a call to shape one's life in a way that is fully commensurate with human flourishing and excellence. No one has a vocation to waste one's life; no one is summoned to live stupidly or self-destructively. Hence, any adequate understanding of vocation requires some account of a good life, some substantive articulation of the disciplines, habits, and practices conducive to a life of genuine fulfillment and happiness. Put more strongly, there is an inescapably *moral* dimension to educating for vocation; a called life means becoming a particular kind of person and acquiring specific qualities of character, so that we can make progress in our journeys toward happiness, excellence, and flourishing.

Unfortunately, however, many of our students have been formed in less hopeful ways of being in the world. They have been swayed by counterfeit understandings of happiness and have been initiated into highly dubious accounts of what constitutes a good life. Educating for vocation may have to begin by nurturing some degree of healthy disenchantment with these inadequate accounts, freeing our students to undertake a more fulfilling journey through life. If this kind of evaluative language makes us uneasy, this may be due to our loss of the connection between happiness and moral excellence. We tend to think of happiness and excellence as something that each of us is free to determine for ourselves; often it means little more than having what we want whenever we want it.[1] Alternatively, we may equate happiness with pleasure, an uplifting feeling, or a positive emotional state—which we again tend to connect with the timely satisfaction of our wants and desires. It is hard not to be captured by these views; after all, corporations spend billions to encourage us to think this way.

There are, however, much more promising accounts of happiness, including those that connect it directly with the idea of the *good*. On this view, being truly happy means cultivating virtues—"those good moral habits, affections, attitudes and beliefs that lead to genuine human fulfillment, even perfection, on both personal and social levels."[2] We admire persons who are just and generous, loyal and patient, truthful and courageous, because in acquiring these and other virtues, they have nurtured the most fundamental calling of every human being: the call to recognize, respond to, and grow in the good. To do this faithfully, courageously, and insightfully is to become a *magnanimous* person, aspiring to excellence in every dimension of life.

A vocation can be understood as a summons to a magnanimous way of life. It is a call to respond to, embody, and witness goodness in all the exquisite ways that can be done. This chapter explores the close connections among vocation, happiness, and the moral life, beginning with an account of the virtues. We will then examine a particular virtue—magnanimity, or "greatness of soul"—as having a uniquely important relationship to vocation;

---

1. See the discussion of this approach to choice and happiness in chapter 1.

2. Russell B. Connors, Jr. and Patrick T. McCormick, *Character, Choices and Community: The Three Faces of Christian Ethics* (New York: Paulist Press, 1998), 25.

it is characterized by a willingness to move beyond self-centeredness and to live for something greater than ourselves. In the third part of this chapter, we will observe that although vocations are promising adventures, they are also costly and difficult ones; we will sometimes be tempted to forsake the journey for less demanding options. Vocational challenges impinge upon our willingness to grow, to risk, and to persevere. The ancients called this the vice of *pusillanimity*. Prolonged challenges can even lead to malaise and disengagement, the lack of desire to do much of anything, which is called *acedia*. Overcoming these vices will be essential if we are to experience the fulfillment and joy that come from living magnanimously and from being faithful to our vocations. The chapter will then conclude by considering one additional virtue and one important practice that can help us avoid these vices, live into the virtue of magnanimity, and thus sustain our vocations as itineraries of hope.

## *Virtue as vocation: called to a good life*

The past several decades have witnessed a renewed interest in the virtues.[3] During the Enlightenment, the focus of ethics had shifted away from the language of goodness and virtue and character to concerns about moral autonomy, freedom, and conscience; about moral rules, principles, duties, and obligations; and especially about strategies for resolving nettlesome moral dilemmas. These are obviously important concerns, but focusing

---

3. In philosophy, the rediscovery of virtue ethics can be traced to Philippa Foot, *Virtues and Vices* (Berkeley: University of California Press, 1978); Iris Murdoch, *The Sovereignty of Good* (chapter 7, note 2 *supra*); and perhaps most of all, Alasdair MacIntyre, *After Virtue* (chapter 7, note 5 *supra*). In theology, the work of Stanley Hauerwas was pivotal. See especially *Character and the Christian Life: A Study in Theological Ethics* (San Antonio: Trinity University Press, 1975); *Vision and Virtue: Essays in Christian Ethical Reflection* (Notre Dame, IN: Fides Publishers, 1974); *A Community of Character: Toward a Constructive Christian Social Ethic* (Notre Dame, IN: University of Notre Dame Press, 1981); and, with Charles Pinches, *Christians Among the Virtues* (see chapter 5, note 25 *supra*). Other theologians who contributed to the renewal of virtue ethics include Romanus Cessario, O.P., *The Moral Virtues and Theological Ethics* (Notre Dame, IN: University of Notre Dame Press, 1991); David S. Cunningham, *Christian Ethics: The End of the Law* (London: Routledge, 2008); Jennifer A. Herdt, *Putting on Virtue: The Legacy of the Splendid Vices* (Chicago: University of Chicago Press, 2008); Joseph J. Kotva, Jr., *The Christian Case for Virtue Ethics* (Washington, DC: Georgetown University Press, 1996); Gilbert C. Meilaender, *The Theory and Practice of Virtue* (Notre Dame, IN: University of Notre Dame Press, 1984); Jean Porter, *The Recovery of Virtue: The Relevance of Aquinas for Christian Ethics* (Louisville: Westminster/John Knox Press, 1990); and Paul J. Wadell, *Happiness and the Christian Moral Life*, 2nd ed. (Lanham, MD: Rowman & Littlefield, 2012).

on them too exclusively tended to sever morality from a more fundamental matter: "the planning of human life so that it could be lived as well
as possible."[4] Put differently, if the moral life is largely learning how to
navigate our way through difficult decisions, what do we do on those days
when no troublesome dilemma confronts us? How should we live on those
ordinary days—days when we are not being stymied by problems that fill
the pages of a typical ethics textbook?

A singular focus on rules, principles, and dilemmas also overlooks an
important fact: the ways that we approach these matters, and even what
we are able to recognize as a moral rule or a moral dilemma, will depend
on our character—the kind of persons we have become.[5] The turn to virtue ethics acknowledged that the choices and decisions of our lives (as
well as our attitudes, perceptions, desires, and emotions) can only be properly understood in light of our character, which is determined by our most
deeply ingrained habits and practices. This is exactly what the virtues
are: they are habitual ways of being and acting that shape our character
and therefore affect every dimension of our lives.

But perhaps what most fueled the renewal of virtue ethics was the
realization that the heart of the moral life—and the heart of human
existence—requires an ongoing process of change and transformation.
We are called to become more than we already are; we are not yet who we
need to become. Such transformations occur through the virtues because
they are habits—characteristic ways of being and acting—that form
persons in courage, justice, truthfulness, compassion, and other expressions of goodness. Instead of picturing habits as routines we unthink-
ingly fall into, the virtues remind us that habits develop over time through
consistent ways of being and acting. Virtue is what results from being
changed by good ways of being and acting, so much so that they become
second nature to us.[6] Furthermore, growing *into* particular virtues often
means growing *out of* their corresponding vices. Thus, as the philosopher

---

4. Edmund Pincoffs, "Quandary Ethics," in *Changing Perspectives in Moral Philosophy*, ed.
Stanley Hauerwas and Alasdair MacIntyre (Notre Dame, IN: University of Notre Dame
Press, 1983), 93.

5. On this point see Stanley Hauerwas, *The Peaceable Kingdom* (Notre Dame, IN: University
of Notre Dame Press, 1983), 116–17.

6. For a similar analysis of the relationship between habits and moral formation, see the
closing section of chapter 1 in this volume. As that chapter emphasized, our selves are not
*given*, but emerge through the habits that define us.

Edmund Pincoffs summarizes, giving adequate attention to the virtues will mean that moral quandaries and dilemmas "are given their due but are by no means stage-center. The question is not so much how we should resolve perplexities as *how we should live.*"[7]

Thus, the question that should drive ethical reflection (and vocational discernment as well) is not only "What should I do?" but "How can I live my life as well as possible?"[8] These are foundational questions that those of us in higher education should regularly pose to our students. Regardless of what each student's particular calling might be, it should enable the living of a good and beautiful life—a life of substance, purpose, and moral achievement. The philosopher and theologian Herbert McCabe wrote that one studies ethics in order to learn "how to be good at being human."[9] And McCabe insisted that the business of ethics is not simply to teach people how "to *talk* about being good," but, more importantly, "to *make* people good as well."[10] Educating for vocation must share this goal; its fundamental objective is not to guide our students to promising careers or lucrative professions, but to enable them to become "good at being human." That is the basic vocation every human being shares: the calling to discover and achieve what it would mean to live a good life.[11]

## Aristotle on happiness and virtue

Aristotle's account of a good life is an essential starting point. He begins by observing that all human beings seek happiness (*eudaimonia*), by

---

7. Pincoffs, "Quandary Ethics," 94, emphasis added.

8. For an expanded account of the factors that have created a renewed interest in virtue ethics, see Paul J. Wadell, *Friendship and the Moral Life* (Notre Dame, IN: University of Notre Dame Press, 1989), 1–26.

9. Herbert McCabe, O.P., *The Good Life: Ethics and the Pursuit of Happiness* (New York: Continuum, 2005), 9.

10. McCabe, *Good Life*, 49.

11. While this section of the chapter explores the importance of educating students in the virtues during their college years, a college or university is obviously neither the first nor last setting that this occurs. Students come to college already having been formed by their families, friendships, religious communities, and other individuals and groups; when they leave college, their moral formation will continue. Moreover, attending to the pivotal role of the virtues in vocational discernment and formation is much more likely to succeed when it is supported and reinforced by the other moral communities of which students are a part.

which he means not a passing feeling of pleasure, but the more substantive understanding of happiness mentioned at the beginning of this chapter. For Aristotle, happiness is a way of being that "makes life something desirable and deficient in nothing."[12] A person is happy when she lacks nothing that is necessary for human flourishing, nothing that will help her live a truly good, fully human life.[13] This is why Aristotle calls happiness our "highest good" and our "final end."[14] But he also notes that we will never be happy unless we develop the particular function or purpose that distinguishes us from other creatures. Just as the function of a harpist is not just to play the harp but to play it well, human beings have a special function through which they achieve the particular excellence for which they were made.[15] For Aristotle, this "lifetime job description" is to grow in goodness, thereby cultivating our most distinctive and promising potential and becoming truly happy and fulfilled as human beings. We grow in goodness only by acquiring and becoming skilled in the virtues—the quintessential elements for a truly good and happy life. Without the virtues, we cannot flourish; we cannot live wisely or well. Aristotle thus insists that "happiness is some kind of activity of the soul in conformity with virtue."[16]

A life of happiness, a fulfilled and flourishing life, is a *good* life, and this goodness is given specificity through the virtues. For example, justice is an expression of goodness and is thus part of a good and happy life. Loyalty and faithfulness embody goodness and thus contribute to our flourishing, as do courage and perseverance, trustworthiness and honesty, and all the other virtues. In forging an intrinsic connection between happiness and a virtuous way of life, Aristotle is not suggesting that the virtues are merely a *means* to the *end* of happiness, as though happiness were some long-awaited reward for a life of sacrifice and self-denial. Aristotle does not see happiness "as some ideal final state, realizable only

12. Aristotle, *Nicomachean Ethics*, trans. Martin Ostwald (Indianapolis: Bobbs-Merrill, 1962), 1097b15, p. 15.

13. As chapter 7 makes clear, how one understands what constitutes a truly good human life depends on the "framing narrative" that guides one's life.

14. Aristotle, *Ethics* 1097a25–1097b10, pp. 14–15.

15. Aristotle, *Ethics* 1098a12, p. 17.

16. Aristotle, *Ethics*, 1099b25, p. 22.

in the distant future. For happiness is not so much the end, but the *way*. Happiness comes *as we acquire and live the virtues*."[17] The most satisfying life for humans is the virtuous life embraced as completely as possible every day.[18]

The language of virtue is subject to certain common misperceptions. We sometimes picture a virtuous person as someone afraid to enjoy life—overly cautious, a bit uptight, and far too respectable. We imagine a person who plays by the rules and never takes chances.[19] But as we grow in the virtues, we discover that, far from repressing us, they are liberating ways of being and acting. They are the attitudes, intentions, feelings, and ways of acting we need to develop in order achieve happiness.[20] Julia Annas notes that, as people grow in the virtues, they come to see that happiness is not just a pleasurable state, something that we

> struggle to achieve and then relax, as though we were working at an uncongenial job in order to retire and forget about the work we did to get there. Rather, happiness, living happily, is always . . . an ongoing project, and so very different to accounts in terms of feeling good or getting what you want or being satisfied. This is an account of happiness which emphasizes activity and engagement rather than passive experiences.[21]

As we grow in the virtues, our understanding of happiness becomes deeper and richer and more certain, and our enjoyment of happiness intensifies.

The language of "growth" alerts us to the fact that virtues, like all habits, are only gradually acquired. We have an initial capacity for virtue because human beings are oriented to the good; however, no one is instantaneously or naturally virtuous. In order to acquire true expertise in goodness, this orientation has to be developed into a habit: a

---

17. Hauerwas and Pinches, *Christians Among the Virtues*, 13, emphasis added.

18. Portions of this section are taken from Paul J. Wadell, *Happiness*, 28.

19. This stereotype is particularly present with regard to the virtue of *prudence*; for considerably more on this point, see chapter 9 of this volume.

20. On this point see Paul J. Wadell, *Happiness*, 52–54.

21. Julia Annas, *Intelligent Virtue* (Oxford: Oxford University Press, 2011), 164.

persistent, stable, and reliable way of being and acting.[22] Moreover, a virtuous person does the good not only consistently, but also skillfully and insightfully, and with a certain amount of ease and joy. Just like the process of becoming a skillful athlete or an accomplished musician, becoming this sort of person takes time and practice. But also like the athlete or the musician, the effort is worth our while because the outcome is so greatly desired.

Virtues must flow from our character and accurately communicate who we truly are. Thus, they must be habitual—not something we might occasionally do, or do only when we set our minds to it, but rather something we would *characteristically* do. This is why, for example, when someone we have come to know as patient inexplicably explodes in anger, we are surprised and recognize that she acted "out of character." Her anger shocks us because we had understood patience to be a core dimension of her identity, an essential feature of her self. As Annas elaborates, "a virtue is a disposition which is *characteristic*—that is, the virtuous (or vicious) person is acting in and from character when acting in a kindly, brave or restrained way. This is another way of putting the point that a virtue is a *deep* feature of a person."[23]

Virtues are acquired through practice and repetition—just like the skills necessary to being a great athlete or musician. Consider, for example, the virtue of justice: We become just persons only by *practicing* justice in all the different relationships of our lives—whether with a family member, an intimate friend, a student, a stranger, or even an enemy. By repeatedly taking actions that are just, our inclinations to consider our responsibilities to others—occasional though they may be, at least at first—will gradually develop into an abiding characteristic of our essential selves, such that we become genuinely and reliably just. That transformation occurs because, by acting justly often enough, it becomes a habit. Consequently, the quality of justice in our actions becomes an ever-deepening and enduring quality of *who we are*. This example demonstrates the circular relationship between actions and character—a key element of Aristotle's account. If we act a certain way often enough, eventually the quality of that action becomes a resilient quality of our selves; it begins to characterize us. And the more it

22. Aristotle, *Ethics*, 1103a24–25, p. 33.

23. Annas, *Intelligent Virtue*, 9.

becomes an abiding quality of our character, the more we will practice it in our actions.[24]

## Implications for vocational exploration

We can appreciate the relevance of Aristotle's claims for vocational exploration and discernment when we reflect on the necessity of certain virtues for carrying out this kind of work. Vocational reflection compels us to think about ourselves in relation to the other significant people in our lives; yet without the virtues of *justice* and *faithfulness*, we will lack the relationships necessary for discovering and growing in our vocations. Vocational discernment also demands a certain willingness to venture into new territory, to try on various callings to see whether they fit; yet without *courage*, we would never be able to risk, to take chances, or to explore. Since many callings demand something new of us, it may take time to live into them fully; hence we need the virtue of *patience* to work through frustrations and difficulties in order to achieve important goals. As these examples illustrate, it would be difficult to guide students in thinking about their callings without also teaching them about the importance of the virtues for both discovering and living into those callings.

In addition to our need for particular virtues in the work of vocational exploration, four specific aspects of this work make the language of virtue particularly useful in conversations about calling. First, if the one universal vocation is the calling to live a good life—to become "good at being human"—then we need to show our students that this is something they can do each day and at any stage of their lives. Embracing a called life is not something they need to postpone to the future when other major decisions of their lives have been made; the good summons them every day. If we limit our discussion of vocation to particular careers or professions, or to particular states of life (such as marriage), students may assume that they are not yet "called" at all, and will not be until they have committed to

---

24. Aristotle captures the circular relationship between our actions and our character when he writes: "Strength is produced by consuming plenty of food and by enduring much hard work, and it is the strong man who is best able to do these things. The same is also true of the virtues: by abstaining from pleasures we become self-controlled, and once we are self-controlled we are best able to abstain from pleasures. So also with courage: by becoming habituated to despise and to endure terrors we become courageous, and once we have become courageous we will best be able to endure terror." Aristotle, *Ethics*, 1104a30–1104b2, p. 36.

a particular career or state of life. Not only is this a far too narrow under-standing of vocation; it also encourages students to overlook the relevance of calling during a pivotal time in their lives. They do not need to be clear about their futures in order to begin thinking and living vocationally; they can still embrace and enter into their core vocation of responding to the appeal of the good. Indeed, doing so may be an important step toward discerning their future vocations.

Second, if the virtues themselves constitute a good and joyful life, educating students for vocation means introducing them to a more substantive, and indeed more challenging, understanding of happi-ness and of a good and flourishing life. Our students tend to be swayed by individualistic accounts in which each of us is free to determine the meaning of happiness, which usually involves little more than the immediate satisfaction of our desires.[25] We cannot rightly educate stu-dents for vocation without first prying them free of such flaccid (and ultimately hopeless) understandings of happiness and a good life. We need to show them why such fraudulent conceptions make us less human rather than more, and why they lead not to our flourishing but to our moral and spiritual diminishment. Of course, the best way to demonstrate the truth of these claims is by the witness of our lives. Our students are far more likely to recognize the beauty of the good and to appreciate the delight and joy that inhere in lives of virtue and integrity when they not only hear someone talk about it, but when they see it enacted in another person's life.

Third, without the virtues, we will find it difficult to *persevere* in the various callings of our lives. We have already suggested that answering a call is like going on a journey; some journeys are brief and unevent-ful, but others are prolonged, baffling, and filled with challenges that we never anticipated. Moreover, a vocational journey is not the kind where we reach our destination simply by following clear and sensible direc-tions; it is more like a quest, the meaning of which can only gradually be fathomed as we experience it. Living into this uncertainty requires character traits that allow us to adjust our itineraries as new opportuni-ties and obstacles arise—traits such as prudence, courage, and persever-ance, but also imagination and the ability to improvise. As Renee LaReau writes,

---

25. This point is explored in greater detail in chapter 1.

One of the biggest misconceptions about vocation is that the discovery of one's vocation is a momentary happening, an instant epiphany, or a lightning bolt that illuminates the rest of our life's path. The discovery of our vocation is, rather, a process, a journey. There may be significant, discrete moments of clarity along the way, but there is always more to be discovered and discerned. On the vocational journey we never "arrive." We are always "arriving."[26]

Consider, for example, a vocation that all college students share: the calling to study and learn. This would seem easy enough for those who are engaged, inquisitive, able, diligent, and confident. But a semester is a long time; if the student struggles with the material of a course, does poorly on an exam, or wrestles with indifference, a once-stalwart confidence can diminish day by day. Discouragement, illness, or a family tragedy can imperil the goal of successfully completing a semester, as can a professor with high expectations or a text that seems impossible to read. Overcoming these obstacles requires courage, along with patience, perseverance, and hope—and perhaps even a certain boldness of spirit. Armed with such character traits, the disconsolate student in a stormy semester has a much better chance of finishing the course successfully.

This example can be easily extended because, as we observe throughout this book, college students explore and discern their callings both in and out of the classroom; moreover, they face a wide range of new challenges as they do so. They meet people whose background, viewpoints, and experiences are very different from their own; they negotiate the diverse and sometimes conflicting responsibilities that accompany emerging adulthood; and they often experience loss, disappointment, and abandonment, even among those on whose support they thought they could safely rely. In the midst of such challenges and potential obstacles, persevering in one's calling will require a whole range of virtues: hospitality and humility, practical wisdom and self-control, loyalty and kindness and generosity. A life of virtue is a life well-equipped to keep taking the next step in an adventurous journey—recognizing that it is unscripted and unpredictable, and thus remaining open to surprises and to new possibilities.

---

26. Renee M. LaReau, *Getting a Life: How to Find Your True Vocation* (Maryknoll, NY: Orbis Books, 2003), 143.

Fourth, while our callings are unfolding journeys or adventures, they are journeys going somewhere in particular and adventures with a purpose. Vocation implies a *teleology* (from the Greek *telos*, "purpose" or "goal"), insofar as our callings are meant to achieve some goal or purpose. That purpose may be quite focused and immediate, such as attending to a person in need or being available to a friend; or it may shape the overall trajectory of our lives, such as being faithful in love and committed to justice. But in all cases, our callings ask us to become something more than we already are; this implies movement, change, and transformation in light of the goods we are trying to achieve. And the virtues themselves imply a teleology; they are excellences of character, and any achievement of excellence requires movement toward a goal.

Academics may be skeptical of talking about a *telos* or purpose to which our lives ought to be oriented. Yet students inevitably ask teleological questions when they wonder about meaning and purpose, or when they think about their own narratives and wrestle with how those stories should best be told. The students who are entrusted to us do not expect us to answer all of their questions about purpose and meaning, nor about the goods to which they should direct their lives; however, they do look to us for guidance and for wisdom as they discern these matters in the crucible of their souls. They seem to recognize, often quite intuitively, that their callings can truly be itineraries of hope only when their destination is one worth reaching.

## *The shape of a magnanimous life*

A vocation entails making ourselves available to something good. It reminds us that to be human is to want our lives to count for something worthwhile, while to live only for our own gratification depletes us.[27] Regardless of its duration or depth or significance, every calling of our lives is a summons to fully inhabit our best selves—to become the people that we ought to be. Perhaps surprisingly, we become *most fully ourselves* when we focus, not *on* ourselves (through lives of careful calculation and strategic self-promotion), but on something greater than ourselves.[28] This

---

27. Jack Fortin, *The Centered Life* (Minneapolis: Augsburg Fortress Publishers, 2006), 8.

28. Such as, for example, the calling to work for the fuller humanization of all persons that is set forth in chapter 3.

dynamic is the heart of every calling; when we say yes to a calling, in whatever way it presents itself, we grow into "the fullness of who we each have it in us to be."[29] This process—growing into our best selves—is closely related to our discussion of the virtues, and in fact to a specific virtue: that of magnanimity, or "greatness of soul."

Thomas Aquinas (1225–1274) defined the virtue of magnanimity as "a certain aspiration of spirit to great things" and said that a magnanimous person is one who has "the spirit for some great act."[30] This also describes a life lived with attention to vocation—when we understand ourselves as called to the great work of attending to the world around us, rather than focusing only on ourselves. Today we often connect greatness with wealth, power, and celebrity; in contrast, the defining characteristic of magnanimity is a love for the good. The magnanimous person aspires not for fame and material wealth, but for the good. And yet, as with any virtue, this is not an isolated undertaking, as though we could simply wake up one day and decide to achieve "greatness of soul." Rather, we become magnanimous by faithfully embracing all the myriad callings of our lives, including the most mundane ones. Hence, a magnanimous life is possible for anyone—no matter what his or her circumstances might be.

Magnanimity is a steadfast orientation to excellence in every dimension of our lives. Many of us may doubt whether we could be truly magnanimous, but we may be surprised. The teacher who prepares well for every class, who looks for ways to improve her teaching, and who is available to her students and committed to their good, is living magnanimously. The student who cares enough about his friends to be honest with them—or who follows his conscience, even when doing so might evoke the disapproval of others—is aspiring to the excellence that characterizes the magnanimous. On the campus of St. Norbert College, for example, if students were asked who had the most impact on them during their years at the college, they might well say Agnes—a cashier at a deli on campus who, in her brief interaction with students, let them know that she cared for them. In what many would consider a very ordinary job,

29. Mark A. McIntosh, "Trying to Follow a Call: Vocation and Discernment in Bunyan's *Pilgrim's Progress*," in *Revisiting the Idea of Vocation: Theological Explorations*, ed. John C. Haughey, S.J. (Washington, DC: Catholic University of America Press, 2004), 119.

30. Thomas Aquinas, *Summa Theologiae* (see chap. 7, note 52 *supra*), II–II, 129, 1; English text, 42:99.

Agnes exemplified magnanimity and in doing so made herself a blessing to every person she encountered. So did Tom, a professor of sociology who died in 2010. His death was a tremendous loss to the college community, not only because he was a skilled and passionate teacher who was steadfastly committed to his students, but also because he saw the good in everyone and looked for ways to affirm it. He was an uplifting presence who undeniably believed that one very important calling of his life was to support and encourage others, to be an attentive listener and a healing presence, and to delight in the achievements of his colleagues and his students typically more than they did themselves. In all of these ways and more, Tom each day demonstrated "a certain aspiration of spirit to great things."

Magnanimity is a beautiful virtue, but it does not have to be a rare one.[31] There is nothing elitist about a life of magnanimity; indeed, it is absolutely egalitarian, available to anyone willing to commit to a good and beautiful life. We regularly encounter students for whom succeeding in college will not come easily; yet we know many of them, by working hard, being diligent and responsible, and persevering, have been magnanimous students. Similarly, a professor who may never receive the acclaim awarded his colleagues, but who nonetheless is happy for their successes and refuses to succumb to envy or jealousy, exhibits the "greatness of soul" that characterizes magnanimity. These examples again illustrate that a magnanimous life is not measured by possessions, fame, or even by the list of one's achievements; it comes from a willingness to grow in goodness, to be persons of honor and integrity, and to do the best that

---

31. Aristotle, of course, would contest this claim. His account of magnanimity is hardly democratic. The "high-minded man" looks down on others because he knows he is better. Moreover, he is "the kind of man who will do good, but who is ashamed to accept a good turn, because the former marks a man as superior, the latter as inferior" (*Ethics* 1124b5–10). For Aristotle, magnanimity or "high-mindedness" characterizes those who strive to be self-sufficient, who are utterly mindful of their accomplishments, and who seek to put others in their debt rather than acknowledge their dependence on them. By contrast, Thomas Aquinas maintained that a magnanimous life was possible for everyone because its basis was charity, the befriending love that God lavishly extends to all. Thus, unlike Aristotle's high-minded man, humility, gratitude, and an unyielding awareness of having been blessed would, for Aquinas, characterize the magnanimous person. One of the reasons for this difference, of course, was the different "framing narratives" according to which Aristotle and Thomas Aquinas lived their lives; for more on the importance of such narratives and their relationship to the virtues, see chapter 7. For an insightful critique of Aristotle's "high-minded man," see Robert C. Roberts, *Spiritual Emotions: A Psychology of Christian Virtues* (Grand Rapids, MI: William B. Eerdmans, 2007), 137–39.

we can in light of our gifts, our shortcomings, and the unique (and often not ideal) circumstances of our lives. This is why a magnanimous person is not one who always succeeds (at least, according to broadly defined notions of success), but one who knows how to deal with failure, learn from it, and move on—and in doing so, demonstrate "a certain aspiration of spirit to great things."

A magnanimous life is highly appealing, but that appeal can quickly fade once we realize how difficult it can be to "aspire to greatness" not only occasionally, or when we feel energized and really inspired, but regularly and even habitually. As we have already noted, to say yes to a calling—to follow one's vocation—is to enter a journey that may be immensely promising, but will unquestionably involve moments of doubt and uncertainty, periods of disillusionment and darkness, and times of hardship, suffering, and perhaps considerable loss. Even the callings to which we are most wholeheartedly committed comprise numerous routines that can be both boring and exhausting. And our callings may lead to misunderstanding, rejection, and even hostility by people who may be troubled—even threatened—by the decisions we make about our lives. Moreover, as some of the call stories chronicled in chapter 5 indicate, our initial impulse may be to reject or refuse a calling, precisely because we realize it will demand more than we think we could give. It may involve sacrifice, adversity, and sometimes more sorrow than joy. If we are to take up such arduous callings, we need to be aware of these difficulties and to consider how we will manage them. This is the goal of our next section.

## *Threats to the magnanimous life*

When zeal for the callings of our lives erodes, we are particularly prone to *pusillanimity* and *acedia*—two strange-sounding (but especially dangerous) vices that sabotage any possibility of a magnanimous life. If they are not recognized and reckoned with, these two vices can diminish the happiness and excellence that is most properly our own. What makes these two vices especially pernicious is that we can so easily settle into them without realizing it, such that we slowly lose the "aspiration of the spirit to great things" that characterizes a magnanimous life. We may find ourselves unwilling to undertake the great work that each of us is called to do, each day, in the ordinary circumstances of our lives.

## Falling into a smallness of soul

If a magnanimous man or woman is a person of "great soul" or "great spirit," a pusillanimous person is the man or woman of "small soul" or "puny spirit." In his analysis of this vice, Thomas Aquinas begins by noting that everything has "a natural tendency to undertake action commensurate with its capability."[32] Thus, pusillanimity causes us to fall short of our capabilities when we refuse to extend ourselves to achieve an aim that is "commensurate with" our powers; we refuse to be "who we have it in us to be." This can result from a number of possible causes: fatigue, trials and tribulations, fear of failure, the conviction that our callings ask too much of us, or simply a desire to gain what we desire on easier terms. We see pusillanimity at work in students who look to do the least amount of work possible for a course. We see it in tenured professors who withdraw or who never revise their courses. We see it in administrators who are much more interested in what is good for them rather than for the institution. As these examples indicate, pusillanimity means shrinking our horizons, shirking responsibilities, and abandoning our most noble and compelling aspirations; in short, we betray our callings.

If magnanimity involves looking to what is best, those tempted by the vice of pusillanimity tend to lower their sights by opting for what is easier or more immediately appealing. A pusillanimous person has puny hopes, dreams, and goals—in short, too small an expectation about one's self and one's life. Pusillanimity is a dangerous habit to acquire; through it, we not only lose our taste for what is truly good and promising, but also grow comfortable with mediocrity. We begin to think that we never need to grow, never have to change or be challenged; we avoid any goals or commitments that would call us beyond ourselves in sacrifice, goodness, or love for the sake of another. The pusillanimous person plays it safe, preferring comfort and complacency to the demands of excellence. Of course, a magnanimous person does not suddenly become a pusillanimous person; rather, one gradually "withdraws from what is good,"[33] and often, as mentioned above, in ways that one does not recognize. Thus, this particular

---

32. Thomas Aquinas, *Summa Theologiae* II–II, 133, 1, English text 42:161. Thomas uses the gospel story of the servant who, on account of fear, buried the money his master had entrusted to him as an apt example of pusillanimity.

33. Thomas Aquinas, *Summa Theologiae* II–II, 133, 2 ad 4, English text 42:167.

vice can be very hard to detect, yet relatively easy to fall into; its harvest is always harm and diminishment both to ourselves and to others.[34]

## Falling into a lethargy of soul

Acedia, which means "not to care," has traditionally been listed as one of the seven deadly or capital sins. It describes the moral and spiritual lethargy that descends on a person who has lost all aspirations for the good, either because that person no longer believes it matters or no longer believes it is possible.[35] This pervasive malaise is debilitating because it gradually leads a person to disengage with life and to lose affection for what is truly good and worthwhile. Thomas Aquinas spoke of acedia as a "spiritual apathy" that results in "a kind of oppressive sorrow which so depresses us that we want to do nothing"—the clearest sign of which is that the work that used to enthrall us no longer holds any interest for us.[36] That "work" meant not only one's occupation or profession, but *all* the callings of one's life and their accompanying responsibilities. Eventually the despondency characteristic of acedia expands from an emotional state into the deliberate decision to flee from what we are called to do.

Josef Pieper insightfully describes acedia as "a perverted humility" and says that a person caught in acedia, instead of being grateful for all our gifts and talents, expressly wishes to have been left in peace.[37] That is why acedia can be described not only as sorrow about the good but also, more seriously, as *loathing* the good.[38] As the vice of acedia grows in us, we move from disillusionment and disenchantment about what is best, to despair of ever attaining it, and finally to an almost vehement disgust for it. This sounds like a dramatic shift, yet—as with pusillanimity—one can begin to slide into acedia without even being aware of it. This is

---

34. Portions of this paragraph were taken from Wadell, *Happiness*, 61–62.

35. On this point see Paul J. Wadell and Darin H. Davis, "Tracking the Toxins of *Acedia*: Reenvisioning Moral Education," in *The Schooled Heart: Moral Formation in American Education*, ed. Douglas V. Henry and Michael D. Beaty (Waco, TX: Baylor University Press, 2007), esp. 134–41.

36. Thomas Aquinas, *Summa Theologiae* II–II, 35, 1, English text 35:23, altered (Thomas uses the third person singular; I have translated it here using the first person plural).

37. Josef Pieper, *Faith, Hope, Love*, trans. by Richard and Clara Winston and Sr. Mary Frances McCarthy, S.N.D. (San Francisco: Ignatius Press, 1997), 119–20.

38. Thomas Aquinas, *Summa Theologiae* II–II, 35, 3, English text 35:31.

especially true when we avoid the demands of our callings not so much through idleness or laziness, but by the restless busyness and endless activity that enables us to flee the demands of love and ignore the appeal of the good.[39]

Acedia may be more pervasive than we would like to admit. The cynicism that characterizes acedia tends to dismiss anything noble or honorable as impossibly idealistic and to avoid investing in anything truly excellent, anything genuinely transcendent.[40] It manifests itself in the arrogance that prevents us from receiving constructive criticism or correction (behavior not unknown in academic circles). Moreover, acedia is fostered by a culture that encourages us to be constantly entertained, enticed, and distracted, that continually urges us to set aside substantive and enriching goods for the sake of lesser ones, and that teaches us to see our lives as little more than a series of disconnected events going nowhere. Such a culture seems to proclaim that there really is nothing noble and excellent to which one might aspire.

Educating for vocation requires opening our eyes to the reality of acedia, recognizing its dangers, and helping our students—as well as ourselves—to discover ways to resist it. This isn't easy, because often the very things we are told to see as the most important elements of a good and successful life (wealth, possessions, power, status, achievements) can be paths into acedia rather than ways out of it, especially if we allow desire for these things to rule us. Ancient Christian writers called this "worldliness," and described it as being so enamored with the things of this world that we shut the door on higher things, on better things. Charles Pinches captured well the baneful effects of acedia when he said that it "casts down our spirits so that we cannot imagine any higher good for ourselves, any better path to travel. We become mired in small pleasures, shrunken creatures with . . . low horizons."[41] A path of drudgery and a low horizon are not very conducive to undertaking a journey—especially

---

39. Rebecca Konyndyk DeYoung, *Glittering Vices: A New Look at the Seven Deadly Sins and their Remedies* (Grand Rapids, MI: Brazos Press, 2009), 94. For a very personal account of the nature and perils of acedia, see Kathleen Norris, *Acedia & Me: A Marriage, Monks, and a Writer's Life* (New York: Riverhead Books, 2008).

40. On this point see the analysis of cynicism in chapter 7.

41. Charles Pinches, "On Hope," in *Virtues and Their Vices*, ed. Kevin Timpe and Craig A. Boyd (Oxford: Oxford University Press, 2014), 361.

a journey so complex, eventful, and potentially exciting as the exploration and discernment of our vocations.

## *Virtues and practices to sustain a magnanimous life*

How can we confront and overcome these vices in order to flourish in our callings and to grow in the joy of a magnanimous way of life? While many virtues and practices could be suggested as helpful in this regard, two will be discussed here: the virtue of hope and the practice of friendship. These are offered as two archetypical examples in the hope that readers will want to consider and explore others as well.

### "A future that is difficult, but possible, to attain"

In his analysis of the virtue of hope, the philosopher Josef Pieper begins by noting that human beings are oriented toward a fulfillment we can anticipate (and, in some way, already experience), but that we cannot yet completely enjoy.[42] This is why, Pieper says, to be human is to be "on the way": journeying toward a destination at which we have not yet arrived. This, as we have seen, is also a good description of living out our callings. This means, in turn, that *hope* is a quintessential virtue for our vocational journeys and for a magnanimous way of life.[43]

Hope can fittingly be described as a *bridge* between the "already" and the "not yet."[44] If human life is a pilgrimage toward the good or goods through which we become complete, and if these goods come into being through our callings, hope sustains us on that journey by keeping us

---

42. Pieper, *Faith, Hope, Love*, 92–93.

43. For a beautifully compelling analysis of a Christian theology of hope, see Douglas V. Henry, "Hope's Promise for Christians in the Not Yet and In Between," *Logos* 14, no. 3 (2011): 104–32.

44. That hope can be seen as a "bridge" between the "already" of the good we now experience and the "not yet" of our perfect possession of it was suggested to me in a paper by Fr. Lambert Hendriks, "How God Is Hoped for in the Moral Life: The Virtue of Hope as the Bridge between 'Already' and 'Not Yet,'" presented on December 12, 2013, at a conference entitled "Faith, Hope and Love: Thomas Aquinas on Living by the Theological Virtues," Utrecht, Netherlands, December 11–14, 2013.

focused on those elements of our vocations that are best and most promising. It does so by reminding us of the value of our callings, especially
when we are tempted to doubt it. By drawing the future into the present,
hope assures us that what we have set our lives on will not disappoint
because we are already participating in it now.[45] Through hope, the future
good—the fullness of which we already anticipate—breaks into the present, touches and inspires us, and thus continues to orient our lives to
its inevitable fulfillment. Or, to put it another way, we move toward the
complete good for which we hope, and we do so through acts that already
embody it, in the here and now.[46]

Thomas Aquinas wrote that "hope's object is a good that lies in the
future and that is difficult but possible to attain."[47] Note that, unlike
some common assumptions about hope (which associate it with pie-in-
the-sky impossibilities), Thomas emphasizes that the object of our
hope can, in fact, be attained. However, he continues his definition by
explaining how this possibility can be realized: "either through personal
effort or through help from others."[48] His comment raises two important
considerations about hope that are pertinent for guiding students on
their vocational journeys. First, his claim that hope requires "personal
effort" suggests that, as with any virtue, we must work at it. Even if, as
Christians believe, hope is a gift of God's grace, that gift has to be nurtured and strengthened and deepened. This can occur when we "place
ourselves on the side of the good"[49] and progressively seek to conform
our lives to the good through acts of kindness, love, justice, generosity, and service—and perhaps especially through the active compassion
by which we console anyone who is suffering. In short, hope requires
a particular way of life, a virtuous life, and grows through virtuous
actions: "All serious and upright human conduct is hope in action."[50] We
can *live* in hope when we truly have been *habituated* in hope, and in the

---

45. On this point see Benedict XVI, *Spe salvi* (Boston: Pauline Books & Media, 2007), 7.

46. For this insight I am indebted Lambert Hendriks, "How God Is Hoped for in the Moral Life."

47. Thomas Aquinas, *Summa Theologiae* II–II, 17, 1, English text 33:5.

48. Thomas Aquinas, *Summa Theologiae* II–II, 17, 1, English text 33:5.

49. Benedict XVI, *Spe salvi*, 36.

50. Benedict XVI, *Spe salvi*, 35.

other virtues; and this helps to fortify us against the mediocrity of pusil-lanimity and the desolation of acedia.

## "Good people help keep each other good"

The definition of hope offered by Thomas Aquinas also observed that sustaining hope may require "help from others." Hope has an undeni-ably social character, which Thomas captured when he noted that we are much more likely "to be hopeful when we have friends to rely upon."[51] For Thomas, our primary companion in hope is God, but we need other com-panions as well. This is why *friendship* is necessary not only for a hope-ful life, but also for sustaining us in our respective vocations and in the promise of a magnanimous life. Thomas—along with Augustine, Cicero, Aristotle, and Plato before him—had a richer and fuller understanding of friendship than we are accustomed to today. For these writers, friends were far more than a loose network of persons with whom we could occa-sionally share the tidbits of our lives; rather, friends were the people who made a good and happy life possible for us. There are several reasons why they believed friendship is essential for a good life, but two seem espe-cially pertinent for understanding and living our callings.

First, friends want what is best for us; they are not only devoted to our well-being, but also committed to doing what they can to bring it about. Friends support and encourage us, they offer guidance and coun-sel (sometimes by speaking uncomfortable truths that we need to hear), and by their presence and availability, they let us know we matter to them. We absolutely need such people if we are to live our callings with a sense of hope and promise, enthusiasm and joy. Vocations are not soli-tary ventures, each of us solemnly trudging down lonely paths on our own; rather, they are inescapably social. Our callings draw us out of our-selves and place us in relation to others; they help us see the beauty of *sharing* everything that is good about our callings, rather than treating such features as merely private possessions. Hence our vocational jour-neys require the presence of friends who can accompany us, friends who are willing to help us along our way. Anyone who works with students befriends them "along their way" by offering an encouraging word, by taking time to ask how they are doing, and perhaps especially by letting

---

51. Thomas Aquinas, *Summa Theologiae*, II–II, 17, 8, English text 33:27.

them know that, in the time they are with us, we want what is best for them—as any friend would.

Second, friends help us to *persevere* in our callings and to sustain the demands of a magnanimous life—even in the wake of temptations to smallness of soul and lethargy of soul. Perseverance can be described as "prolonged endurance in any good which is difficult."[52] Our callings are the pivotal goods with which we have identified our lives, but they can also be very difficult goods to pursue. Perseverance enables us to continue in the commitments that are important to us. But it is much easier to persevere when others accompany us and support us, and share in the very same goods with which we have aligned our lives. Friendships are built around shared goods and purposes, around common commitments and concerns. Friends help us in living out our callings because what is important to us matters to them as well. Anything difficult is more easily managed when others share in it with us. Friends help us persevere by their presence and companionship, by their support and encouragement, by their counsel, and even by their humor. Moreover, friends help us persevere because they not only care *about* what we care about, but care *about us* caring about it. If we grow discouraged or disillusioned in our vocations, they help restore our confidence in our callings; they help us to remember why a particular vocation once appealed to us, and why we first chose to embrace it. All of this again confirms that, while callings are deeply personal adventures, they are not solitary ones. To continue on the journey, we need the "communal virtue" of perseverance or constancy, which is "not something one of us possesses alone, but something we share and into which we help each other grow."[53] Or, to give a more compact summary of the point: "good people help keep each other good."[54]

## *An itinerary of hope*

What kind of life is truly worth living? That question lies at the heart of educating for vocation, and it summons us to think about our work with students differently. Yes, we should help them grow in knowledge and in

---

52. Thomas Aquinas, *Summa Theologiae*, II–II, 137, 1, English text 42:209.

53. Hauerwas and Pinches, *Christians Among the Virtues*, 36.

54. Hauerwas and Pinches, *Christians Among the Virtues*, 36.

the skills of critical thinking and analysis. But we should also offer them some account of what would constitute a truly good and beautiful life, a life that would lead to genuine flourishing and fulfillment for themselves and others. At a time when they are bombarded with so many dreary and vacuous accounts of a good life, our first task might be to shake them "out of stultifying habits of thought and life"[55] so that we might offer them something better—something exquisitely more promising. That is found in the appeal of the good, in the virtues, and in a magnanimous life. No matter what the particular callings of our lives might be, answering the call of the good is every person's vocation. Only by taking this path do we experience a truly fulfilling journey and a truly fulfilled life—for it provides us with an itinerary of unabashed hope.

---

55. Douglas Henry uses this phrase in his account of the importance of Christian hope in "Hope's Promise," 106.

# 9

# Seeing with All Three Eyes

## THE VIRTUE OF PRUDENCE
## AND UNDERGRADUATE EDUCATION

### Thomas Albert Howard

IN CANTO XXIX of the *Purgatorio*, Dante presents an allegory of the Church Triumphant with a sumptuous profusion of symbolic references. Next to the central image of the Chariot, symbolizing the Church itself, dance seven ladies (*donne*):

> *Then came three ladies dancing in a round*
> *Near the right wheel . . .*
> *Four other ladies, dressed in purple,*
> *Were dancing at the left, keeping to the cadence*
> *The three-eyed one among them set.*[1]

The commentary tradition on the *Divine Comedy* speaks with one voice in identifying these ladies as the three theological virtues (faith, hope and love) and the four classical or cardinal virtues (prudence, justice, temperance, and courage).[2] In this chapter, we will focus on the "three-eyed one," the virtue of prudence. Why does she have three eyes?

---

1. Dante, *Purgatorio*, trans. Jean and Robert Hollander (New York: Anchor Books, 2003), 651.

2. Giuseppe Costa, *Virtù e vizi nella Divina commedia, tomisticamente coordinati* (Vicenza: Tip G. Consonni, 1964), 7.

Why does she set the cadence for the others? Where does prudence fit in the broader scheme of moral philosophy, of which it is a part?

These questions are of course tethered to the broader aim of this book: what role might the language and practice of "vocation" play in present-day American higher education? I seek, therefore, to explore the relevance of the tradition of the virtues, and of *prudence* in particular, for the purpose of re-envisioning how we think of undergraduate pedagogy—and, relatedly, how undergraduates might think of the arc of their lives, their unfolding sense of identity and purpose, during their college years. Toward these ends, I will also offer an account of certain potentially effective pedagogical practices, drawn in this case from a "great books" honors program.

Permit three additional preliminary reflections. First, I write as a historian, as someone convinced that decisions in the present about the future suffer when made without knowledge of the past. Happily, this is precisely why prudence is sometimes depicted with three eyes: a well-ordered individual or society understands the *past* to promote the well-being of the *present* and *future*. As a medieval proverb puts it, "From past experience the present acts prudently less future action be vitiated."[3] Second, while I am interested in engaging, even recovering, an older moral vocabulary, this is not an exercise in nostalgic retrospection; I have little patience with appeals to lost Golden Ages of one sort or another. But lacking powers of clairvoyance, we have only the past to orient us to the road ahead and the road beneath our feet. Finally, I am persuaded that the virtue of prudence possesses relevance today for helping students and their mentors reflect on vocation during their college years. If I may cut briefly to the chase, prudence means marshaling accurate knowledge about the world for the purpose of living rightly in it.

## *Prudence among the classical virtues*

Writing about prudence in contemporary culture requires certain qualifications and clarifications. Today, the word is more likely to be understood as caution, timorousness, small-mindedness—perhaps not even as a positive characteristic at all, but as an instinct toward self-preservation that is not particularly compatible with more ambitious schemes of social justice

---

3. *Ex praeterito—praesens prudenter agit—ni futura actione deturpet.*

and charity, and certainly at odds with the distinctly modern goals of authenticity and self-actualization. *Saturday Night Live* deftly parodied the apprehensiveness of President George H. W. Bush by having him repeatedly say of a particular course of action, "Not gonna do it. Wouldn't be prudent." "To the contemporary mind," the neo-Thomist philosopher Josef Pieper has noted, "the concept of the good rather *excludes* than includes prudence."[4] Or, as a colleague of mine once quipped, prudence for most people means the humdrum advisability of buying a Toyota Corolla instead of a BMW.

This is a singularly unhappy development, for in an older scheme of virtue, prudence occupied a distinguished position. It was regarded as "the mother and mold" of the cardinal virtues and the indispensable ally of the theological virtues; it was equated with the searching wisdom, the fully orbed perspicacity, that was necessary for living well and in service to things that truly mattered.

In the Middle Ages—as attested by the quotation from Dante with which this chapter began—the seven virtues (four cardinal, three theological) were widely represented, in print and image. A prayer by Thomas Aquinas, "To Acquire the Virtues," is illustrative:

> Grant that I may abide on the firm ground of faith, be sheltered by an impregnable shield of hope, and be adorned in the bridal garment of charity. Grant that I may through justice be subject to You, through prudence avoid the beguilements of the devil, through temperance exercise restraint, and through courage endure adversity with patience.[5]

In more recent times, Josef Pieper has eloquently articulated the medieval template of the virtues, defining *prudent* individuals as those who do not allow their view on reality to be subject to the will, but who instead make the will "dependent upon the truth of real things."[6] Taken together,

---

4. Josef Pieper, *The Four Cardinal Virtues: Prudence, Justice, Fortitude, Temperance* (Notre Dame, IN: University of Notre Dame Press, 1966), 5 (emphasis added).

5. *The Aquinas Prayer Book: The Prayers and Hymns of St. Thomas Aquinas*, trans. and ed. Robert Anderson and Johann Moser (Manchester, NH: Sophia Institute Press, 2000), 33–35.

6. Josef Pieper, *Kleines Lesebuch von den Tugenden des menschlichen Herzens* (Ostfildern: Schwabenverlag, 1988), 20–21. I have consulted a translation of this book made by Paul

these two authors suggest that prudence equips one to avoid the malice and deceit that Christians have traditionally associated with the devil, the human will, and "the world"—instead seeking to live according to "the truth of real things."

While prudence in the Middle Ages was incorporated into a specifically theological vision of the virtues, it did not originate in Christianity's sacred texts. Rather, in the language of Augustine, it was one of those "spoils of Egypt" that merited Christian appropriation.[7] To be sure, it resonated with Christian Scriptures—particularly with Hebraic wisdom literature and with the Bible's many injunctions in praise of wisdom and against folly—but it itself was a child of "Athens," only subsequently incorporated into "Jerusalem" in the complex process of cultural "mergers and acquisitions" that characterized the world of late Antiquity.[8]

While traceable to Plato, the language of virtue and prudence as integral to ethical theory owes most to Plato's pupil, Aristotle. In several of Aristotle's works, we find lists of virtues that, while regularly enumerating more than the four cardinal virtues, ritualistically include prudence (the Greek word is *phronēsis*, sometimes translated "practical wisdom" or "practical reason"). Aristotle's most extensive and influential discussion of prudence comes in his *Nicomachean Ethics*, in which he identifies it as an intellectual virtue and proceeds to distinguish it from other forms of knowledge, including science, comprehension, and wisdom (*sophia*). Scientific knowledge is that of facts "that do not even admit of being otherwise." Comprehension is the art of judging well in imprecise things—things "about which we might be puzzled," or about which rational people can disagree. And wisdom or *sophia* is the goal of all knowledge: a contemplative, superlative knowledge about "what it all means" and what constitutes the human person's highest good.[9]

---

Duggan (San Francisco: Ignatius Press, 1988), but the final responsibility for the translations in this chapter are my own.

7. Augustine, *On Christian Doctrine* (New York: Dover Publications), 75–76.

8. Ivor J. Davidson, "Ambrose's *De officiis* and the Intellectual Climate of the Late Fourth Century," *Vigiliae Christianae* 49 (1995): 313–33.

9. Aristotle, *Nicomachean Ethics*, trans. Terence Irwin, 2nd ed. (Indianapolis: Hackett Publishing, 1999), 95. Cf. Andreas Lückner, "Klugheit und Orientierung: Historische-systematische Ortsbestimmung," in Arno Scherzberg, ed., *Klugheit: Begriff, Konzepte, Anwendung* (Tübingen: Mohr Siebeck, 2008), 8–9.

What then is prudence (or, to use Aristotle's term, *phronēsis*)? In his *Commentary on Aristotle's Ethics*, Thomas Aquinas offers a helpful analogy: prudence is to wisdom what the art of medicine is to health.[10] It is the capacity by which human beings seek knowledge and make decisions that lead them toward true wisdom and true goodness—two sides of the same coin for Aristotle. At the heart of prudence, in Aristotle's judgment, is the ability to "deliberate well," not as an end in itself, but to lead to right decisions concerning one's proper course of action. In a felicitous phrase, Aristotle elaborates that "good deliberation is correctness that accords with what is beneficial, about the right thing, in the right way, at the right time." This applies to the three types of prudence that Aristotle identifies: civic prudence, determining what is correct for a polity; domestic prudence, determining what is correct for a household; and individual prudence, determining what is correct for oneself. But ultimately these are inseparable: what is good for the whole must be good for the parts and vice versa. What is more, prudence is always prescriptive, leading one to the best course; "its end is what action must or must not do, whereas [mere] comprehension only judges."[11]

Unlike scientific knowledge, which admits precision, prudence must reckon with the foggy world of human motivation, desire, vice, and emotion. It is at once absolutely necessary and exquisitely imprecise. In search of the good, it must navigate myriad complexities and deliberate well about them. As Aristotle writes, "prudence . . . is about human concerns, about things open to deliberation. . . . Deliberating well is the function of the prudent person more than anyone else; but no one deliberates about things that cannot be otherwise, or about things lacking any goal that is a good achievable in action."[12] Put differently, prudence presupposes some opacity about the situation and some uncertainty about what course to take; but it implies the skill to size up the situation nonetheless, and to foster clear-sighted action toward the good. In two words, prudence must be *insightful* and *prescriptive*.

Of particular interest to historians, Aristotle insists that the prudent person must not only have knowledge of "universals" (what Thomas Aquinas

---

10. Thomas Aquinas, *Commentary on Aristotle's Nicomachean Ethics*, trans. C. J. Litzinger (Notre Dame, IN: Dumb Ox Books, 1964), 406.

11. Aristotle, *Ethics*, 95–97.

12. Aristotle, *Ethics*, 91–92.

calls "the first principles of Being"), but also of "particulars," the specific make-up of the present situation—which, by implication, can only be known by ascertaining how that situation came to be. For this reason, Aristotle values "experience" and suggests that older people will more often be more prudent than younger ones, for they have a repository of past experience from which to draw. When good deliberation, knowledge of universals and particulars, and experience are all brought to bear on determining the proper course of action, then the virtue of prudence manifests itself. This capacity is indispensable for human goodness: "we cannot be fully good without prudence, or prudent without virtue of character." Prudence is nothing less, Aristotle concludes, than "the eye of the soul"—a suggestive phrase given the subsequent iconographic representation of prudence with three eyes.[13]

The virtue tradition continued apace in the Roman world. To offer but one influential example, the philosopher and statesman Cicero (106–43 BC) often limits the list of virtues, or at least the principal virtues, to four (as did Plato).[14] Prudence is also discussed at some length in Cicero's *On Duties*; and in his "Discussions at Tusculum" we are told that "an essential element in every virtue is prudence."[15] Following Aristotle's contrasting of *phronēsis* and *sophia*, Cicero regularly makes a distinction between *prudentia* (knowledge that leads to right action) and *sapientia* (a more contemplative knowledge of first principles). For him, *prudentia* presupposes some amount of *sapientia*—even as the accretion of prudent decisions expands the breadth of one's wisdom.

## *Christianity, virtue, and prudence*

During the Roman Empire and early Middle Ages, both Jewish and Christian thinkers drew from the classical virtue tradition. Already in several deuterocanonical books, the influence makes itself felt. In the Book of Wisdom (8:7),[16] for example, we read that *sophia* (the personification of wisdom) "teaches temperance, and prudence, and justice, and fortitude,

---

13. Aristotle, *Ethics*, 91–92, 98–99. See James Hall, *Dictionary of Subjects and Symbols in Art*, rev. ed. (New York: Harper & Row, 1979), 254–55.

14. See Cicero, *De Inventione*, books II and LIII, trans. C D. Young, http://www.classicpersuasion.org/pw/cicero/dnv1-1.htm (accessed on April 16, 2014).

15. Cicero, *On the Good Life*, trans. Michael Grant (New York: Penguin Books, 1971), 59.

16. All scriptural quotations in this chapter are taken from the Revised Standard Version (RSV), with some slight alterations.

which are such things as human beings can have nothing more profitable in life." Elsewhere we are told that "the kinds of wisdom are right judgment, justice, courage, and self-control. Prudence [*phronēsis*] is supreme over all of these since by means of it reason rules over the emotions" (4 Maccabees 1:18–19).

While key early church figures did not speak with a single voice on moral matters, they were conversant with, and many actively promoted, the classical virtue tradition. In fact, it was Ambrose, Bishop of Milan, who first coined the expression "the four *cardinal* virtues," for upon these virtues, he believed, the whole of the moral life "hinges" (from the Latin *cardo*, hinge). He used Cicero's treatise on ethics, *On Duties*, as a model for his own work on ethical obligations and even employed the same title. In his judgment, significant overlap existed between the classical virtues and the moral injunctions of Scripture; prudence in particular resonated with Hebrew wisdom literature.[17] Ambrose's most famous pupil, Augustine, appropriated the classical virtues, too, but was also among the first to subordinate them to the theological virtues of faith, hope, and love. From the standpoint of Christian theology, in Augustine's judgment, true prudence cannot deploy its services for just any goal, but ought to promote the expansion of Christian *caritas* (self-giving love[18]). "Prudence," he says, "is love distinguishing with sagacity between what hinders and what helps it."[19] Without prudence, love would slacken and/or grow disordered. Therefore, for Augustine, prudence possesses the ability "to discern between what is to be desired and what is to be shunned. . . . It is the role of prudence to keep watch with most anxious vigilance, lest any evil influence should stealthily creep in upon us."[20]

Clement of Alexandria, Gregory the Great, and many lesser-known figures reasoned similarly. In his *Psychomachia*, Aurelius Prudentius Clemens (348–c. 413) dramatically depicted the virtues and the vices as two armies warring against one another. By the early Middle Ages, abetted by a numerological mysticism hallowing the biblical number seven,

---

17. *Commentary of Saint Ambrose on the Gospel According to Luke*, trans. Ide M. Ni Riain (Dublin: Halcyon Press, 2001), 138.

18. See the discussion of this virtue in chapter 7 of the present volume.

19. Augustine, *On the Morals of the Catholic Church (De moribus ecclesiae catholicae)*, http://www.ccel.org/ccel/schaff/npnf104.toc.html, chap. 15 (accessed April 16, 2014).

20. Augustine, *On the Morals of the Catholic Church*, chap. 24.

the list of four cardinal and three theological virtues became a fixture of the Christian moral imagination.[21]

In the thought of Thomas Aquinas (and among subsequent thinkers carrying on a "Thomistic" perspective), the cardinal virtues—and prudence in particular—have received their most extensive elaboration. This tradition makes manifest two characteristics of prudence that are particularly important for the purposes of this chapter: the relevance of prudence for vocational exploration and for historical thinking. Examining these two characteristics will put us in a better position to consider the applicability of prudence to undergraduate education today.

The prudent person, for Aquinas, must enlist relevant knowledge of universals and particulars for the purpose of making good decisions. These decisions might concern minute matters, but they are often about much bigger ones. For this reason, prudence is especially relevant to vocational questions: what should I do with my life? What course of study should I pursue? What gifts and abilities do I possess? Where have I come from and where ought I be going? To be sure, many other virtues and habits of mind come into play in posing and asking such questions. But the "charioteer of the virtues" (*auriga virtutum*), as prudence is sometimes called, deserves a distinguished place in vocational reflection and discernment.[22]

Aquinas would agree, I'd like to think, because he accords to prudence a particularly significant role in thinking about the arc of one's whole life. In fact, he felt that prudence was the anchor of all the other virtues—even the theological ones. Good actions, in his view, quite simply could not contravene an accurate understanding of reality and deliberation based on this understanding. Accordingly, as he phrased it, "all virtue is necessarily prudent."[23] Or, as James F. Keenan has summarized Aquinas' views,

> Prudence has a privileged place among the cardinal virtues; it recognizes the ends to which a person is naturally inclined, it establishes the agenda by which one can pursue those ends, it directs the agent's own performance of the pursued activity, and,

---

21. Adolf Katzenellenbogen, *Allegories of the Virtues and Vices in Mediaeval Art* (New York: W. W. Norton, 1964), 14.

22. *Catechism of the Catholic Church* (New York: Doubleday, 1995), #1806, 496.

23. *omnis virtus moralis debet esse prudens*, noted in Pieper, *Four Cardinal Virtues*, 35.

finally, it measures the rightness of the actions taken. Prudence, in short, guides the agent to living a self-directed life that seeks integration.[24]

Prudence entails a sober-minded view of reality—an accurate, unsentimental measure of how the world and human nature *are*. It is a matter of being, of ontology, of predicating both understanding and good action on how human reality is in fact constituted. As Josef Pieper puts it, "All duty is grounded in being. Reality is the foundation of the ethical. Goodness must correspond to reality."[25] Therefore, he explains, those who want to know and do the good must direct their gaze toward the objective world, not toward their own sentiment or toward arbitrarily established ideals; they must look away from their own deeds and look upon reality. Pieper continues:

> The "health" of justice, of fortitude, of temperance, of fear of the Lord and of virtue in general is in the fact that they are *appropriate to objective reality, both natural and supernatural*. Conformity to reality is the principle of both [intellectual] soundness and [ethical] goodness. The priority of prudence means that the achievement of goodness presumes knowledge of reality.[26]

Following Aristotle, the Thomistic tradition has insisted that prudence cannot be content with knowledge alone, of simply understanding human reality; rather it seeks to render accurate knowledge *relevant* to good action and human flourishing. In the words of Pieper again:

> Prudence . . . [seeks to] transform . . . knowledge of reality into the accomplishment of the good. It encompasses the humility of silence, i.e., unbiased understanding, memory's faithfulness to being, the skill of letting things speak for themselves, the vigilant composure before the unsuspected. Prudence means hesitant

---

24. James F. Kennan, S.J., "The Virtue of Prudence," in Stephen J. Pope, ed., *The Ethics of Aquinas* (Washington, DC: Georgetown University Press, 2002), 259.

25. Pieper, *Kleines Lesebuch*, 21.

26. Pieper, *Kleines Lesebuch*, 21–22 (emphasis added).

seriousness, . . . the filter of reflection, and *yet also the daring courage for definitive resolution.*[27]

Given its comprehensive significance for the well-lived life, it is not surprising that Aquinas went to great lengths defining the integral parts of prudence. Many of his words have become terms of art in scholastic thought, and they are highly germane to questions of vocational exploration. They include:

- Intelligence (*intelligentia*), a correct understanding of first principles;
- Shrewdness or quick-wittedness (*solertia*), the ability to size up a matter quickly;
- Discursive reasoning (*ratio*), the ability to consider and compare alternative possibilities;
- Foresight (*providentia*), the capacity to estimate whether a particular action will lead to the realization of a goal;
- Circumspection (*circumspectio*), the ability to take relevant circumstances into account;
- Precaution (*cautio*), the ability to mitigate risks and avoid foolish outcomes;
- Teachableness (*docilitas*), a disposition of mind that seeks out and recognizes reliable authorities;
- Accurate memory (*memoria*), the ability to remember what is true to the reality of the past.

Each of these terms has received extensive commentary and elaboration by Aquinas himself and by his many subsequent disciples.[28] For the purposes of this chapter, two of these components—*memoria* and *docilitas*—seem particularly relevant to vocational reflection, to historical understanding, and to the relationship between these two endeavors.

*Memoria* is important for thinking about one's vocation. To chart a course for life, individuals must possess a clear-eyed understanding of their personal past, but also of the particular events and forces that

---

27. Pieper, *Kleines Lesebuch*, 26–27 (emphasis added).

28. For more recent commentary, see Daniel Mark Nelson, *The Priority of Prudence: Virtue and Natural Law in Thomas Aquinas and the Implications for Modern Ethics* (University Park: Pennsylvania University Press, 1992) and Thomas S. Hibbs, *Virtue's Splendor: Wisdom, Prudence and the Human Good* (New York: Fordham University Press, 2001).

constitute the present, in which they must act.[29] Any undergraduate course on the philosophy of history or historiography will likely make reference to George Santayana's quip that those who forget history are doomed to repeat it. That same course would also be likely to discuss the thought of Leopold von Ranke, the founding father of modern historiography, and his famous reversal of the traditional role of historical analysis: "History has been assigned the high office of judging the past, of instructing the present for the benefit of future ages. To such high offices this work does *not* aspire: it wants only to show what actually happened."[30] In effect, Ranke sought to drive a wedge (an unhappy wedge, from our current vantage point) between an older humanist tradition of historical inquiry, which connected knowledge of the past with moral philosophy, and a distinctly modern one, which shunted this connection and sought simply to render a disinterested, "objective" representation of the past.[31]

Prudence, rightly understood, carries with it the fortunate consequence of bridging this divide. An individual engaging in knowing the past is never a mere "spoiled idler in the garden of knowledge," in Nietzsche's felicitous phrase;[32] rather, that person is always a moral agent, embedded in a web of relations, circumstances, politics, and duties that require deliberation, decision-making, and action. For this reason, Aquinas highly values "memory of past things." He elaborates by observing that "experience

---

29. In the words of Oliver O'Donovan, "Reflection on things remembered, anticipation of things projected, feed and shape my actual deliberations, for prudence, the virtue proper to deliberation, weighs up existing states and projected outcomes." But deliberation and action can both go wrong, he continues, when they "lack reference to the available moment of *time*, and so fail to concentrate upon what is fit to be done in this time and this place." See his *Self, World, and Time: Ethics as Theology*, vol. 1 (Grand Rapids, MI: William B. Eerdmans, 2013), 16–18.

30. *wie es eigentlich gewesen ist*. Leopold von Ranke, *Geschichte der romanischen und germanischen Völker von 1494 bis 1514*, 2nd ed. (Leipzig, 1874), vii.

31. Ranke's legacy, to be sure, is vast and its interpretations conflicted. For an entry into the literature, see Georg Iggers and James Powell, eds., *Leopold von Ranke and the Shaping of the Historical Discipline* (Syracuse: Syracuse University Press, 1990). Cf. Peter Novick, *That Noble Dream: The "Objectivity Question" and the American Historical Profession* (New York: Cambridge University Press, 1988). On the older humanist tradition, see Anthony Grafton, *What Was History? The Art of History in Early Modern Europe* (Cambridge: Cambridge University Press, 2007).

32. ". . . verwöhnte Müßiggänger im Garten des Wissens . . ." Friedrich Nietzsche, *Vom Nutzen und Nachteil der Historie für das Leben* (Stuttgart: Philipp Reclam, 1969), 3.

and time generate and increase intellectual power. But experience comes from memory of many things. And so memory of many things is required for prudence." Accordingly, "forgetfulness" is an especially befouling danger of prudence: "forgetfulness can hinder prudence, since the command of prudence [viz., to act rightly] is the product of some knowledge, which forgetfulness can take away."[33]

Obviously, no single person could master all relevant "particulars" that have led to the present; this is an impossible task. For that reason, a spirit of teachableness (*docilitas*) is also needed. In an academic culture in which young people are herded to submit everything to "critical inquiry," this aspect of prudence can be a particularly hard sell. For Aquinas, however, it was integral to prudence. *Docilitas* is a disposition of mind that allows one to draw on the experience and wisdom of others in forming judgments and making decisions. Only fools set out by their own lights bereft of guidance; such a person is pilloried in Sebastian Brandt's *Ship of Fools*:

> *The man of stubborn, willful mind*
> *To prudent counsel's ever blind,*
> *Of gracious fortune he is void*
> *And prematurely is destroyed.*[34]

Sadly, in our time, the word *docile*, like the word *prudence*, has lost its older connotations and suggests for most people something more akin to sheep-like tractableness bordering on stupidity. But for Thomas Aquinas, it meant a willingness, indeed a yearning, to seek out and find appropriate authorities and gain instruction. It denotes an energetic and scrutinizing teachableness, an eagerness for knowledge, rather than a hapless passivity before whatever comes across one's path. Students who develop such an eagerness for knowledge—and, alongside it, an active attention to the past—are well positioned to enter into a thoughtful and productive exploration of their various vocations.

---

33. All of the above on Thomas Aquinas comes from *Summa Theologiae* (see chap. 7, note 52 *supra*), II–II, 47, 16 (English text, 36:49–51); II–II, 48, 1 (36:53–59); II–II, 49, 1 (36:61–65); and II–II, 53, 3 (36:129–31). Cf. Thomas Aquinas, *The Cardinal Virtues*, trans. Richard J. Regan (Indianapolis: Hackett Publishing, 2005), 9–11, 22.

34. This comes in chapter eight, "Of Not Following Good Advice." Sebastian Brandt, *The Ship of Fools*, trans. Edwin H. Zeydel (New York: Dover Publications, 1944), 79.

## *Prudence, vocation, and the classroom*

The language of prudence may sometimes seem too thoroughly anchored in the past to be of use in the contemporary setting of higher education. Perhaps surprisingly, however, students can be drawn into conversations about prudence; moreover, they often discover that it affords them an opportunity to consider large issues of meaning and purpose. Significantly, it also leads directly into conversations about vocation. In order to illustrate how this is possible, most of the rest of this chapter will focus on the way that the language of prudence is used in a particular course at a particular institution.

Gordon College is a four-year liberal-arts college located north of Boston. Established in 1889 by a Baptist minister, the college has maintained close connections to its religious roots. I have the privilege and pleasure of teaching in its honors program, which I helped found in 2003. Because of the college's religious roots, we reached back into the Christian past and adopted as the title of the honors program the "Jerusalem and Athens Forum." While some continue to mistake it for a study-abroad program, *cognoscenti* know that the name derives from the second-century Church Father Tertullian's famous question: "What does Athens have to do with Jerusalem, the Academy with the Church?" The program's mission statement observes that Tertullian's

> questions have resonated over Christian learning for centuries, focusing the mind on the relationship between faith and intellect, piety and thought. . . . The two-semester program is founded on the premise that the present and future suffer when the wisdom of the past is neglected. A major objective of the program is to assist students in cultivating a tradition-informed and morally reflective sense of personal vocation by reading and discussing classic texts, explicitly Christian ones but also others that raise questions of abiding significance for present-day Christian intellectual and moral life. The program is interdisciplinary in nature and welcomes students from all majors and backgrounds.[35]

At a general level, one might say that the whole program rests on a premise of prudence; we felt that the prudential action called for, in light of the opportunity afforded us, was to establish a program grounded in the virtue

---

35. See the program's website at http://www.gordon.edu/jaf (accessed November 8, 2014).

tradition and in prudence in particular. Prudence called for prudence, as it were, and particularly for *memoria* and *docilitas* as discussed above. One sees this in the program's goal of cultivating a "tradition-informed" sense of vocation and "seeking out the wisdom of the past." The program aims to give students, in Jaroslav Pelikan's pithy locution, "a new sense of the old"—not out of antiquarian or nostalgic interest, but to help them (as prudence would have it!) to develop historical and moral perspicacity about their lives. This in turn can allow them, at the same time, to pursue vocational questions and decisions from a deeper reservoir of inquiry and reflection.[36]

More specifically, the Jerusalem and Athens Forum helps familiarize students with the virtue tradition itself (and prudence in particular) that this chapter has sought to describe. A teacher, of course, cannot make prudent decisions *on behalf of* students, for we can never know our students the way they know themselves. In a classroom context, the best one can hope for is to render accessible to students the moral grammar of the virtue tradition and suggest some of its implications for vocational inquiry. In other words, teachers can try to equip students with the formal elements (but not the specific content) that will enable them to think carefully and to speak well about their own path—including its present obstacles and opportunities, as well as any foreseeable forks in the road. Educators can also provide young people with a supportive community of fellow inquirers. Of course, the decisions themselves, in the final analysis, reside with the student; still, much can be accomplished through the student's external relationships, both inside the classroom and beyond it. Consider four examples of how this particular program has made a difference.

First, quite simply and as a matter of both *memoria* and *docilitas*, the program aims to put students in conversation with helpful voices from the past. Some of the thinkers discussed in this chapter—Aristotle, Augustine, Thomas Aquinas—are standard fare in the program, along with many more. But Dante's *Divine Comedy* deserves to be singled out. Viewed as a whole, the poem is about a person "midway in the journey of life" in search of his true vocation, after finding himself "in a dark wood / for the straight way was lost." Perhaps surprisingly, given that Gordon College is largely Protestant in its student make-up, Dante's *Purgatorio*

---

36. Jaroslav Pelikan, *The Vindication of Tradition* (New Haven: Yale University Press, 1984), 15.

tends to evoke the most penetrating questions and insights. The seven virtues, allegorized as ladies or stars, appear at several points in the poem, and examining them provides rich food for thought and discussion.[37] Of course, Mount Purgatory is ordered according to the medieval notion of the Seven Deadly Sins, beginning with pride, followed, in rank of their displeasure to God, by envy, anger, sloth, avarice, gluttony, and lust.[38] A particularly fruitful exercise is to have students list the seven virtues and vices in Dante's day and then have them, in groups, come up with a comparable list for American culture today. Typically, this reveals a yawning gap between the ages—even as it also makes clear that contemporary culture, for all its celebration of do-your-own-thing individualism, remains rife with strident moralisms and instances of powerful group-think. To offer a recent example, students defined the seven virtues of today as freedom, opportunity, tolerance, education, success, service, and self-reliance; the present-day vices were oppression, lack of ambition, intolerance, violence, censorship, apathy, and cowardice.[39]

Second, a rather simple but rewarding exercise used in the program is to have students write a paragraph-length response to a question asking them to identify what helps and what hinders the acquisition of a particular virtue. With respect to the argument of this chapter, two particularly relevant questions presented to students are: "What are the hallmarks of a prudent person?" and "What prevents one from becoming a prudent person?" To the latter, one student opined "fear of the future—it you're scared about what you're going to do next in life it can be easier to avoid it and only think of the present," while another commented that prudence is hindered because life today "is sort of a rat race and people don't take the time to slow down and think about what it is they are doing." Other impediments students have listed include naiveté, peer-pressure, information overload, "passionate emotion," obsession with past missteps, excessive optimism, anxiety, not learning from mistakes, "spiritual blindness,"

---

37. The actual word prudence (*prudenza*) appears only once in the entire *Divine Comedy*; when Thomas Aquinas speaks of King Solomon to Dante and Beatrice in the *Paradiso*, he remarks: *"regal prudenza é quel vedere impari / in che lo stral di mia intenzion percuote"* (regal prudence is that peerless vision / on which the arrow of my purpose strikes). *Paradiso* XIII, 104–5. See Costa, *Virtù e vizi nella Divina commedia*, 127.

38. On the origin and history of the tradition of vices, see Keven Timpe and Craig A. Boyd, eds., *Virtues and Their Vices* (New York: Oxford University Press, 2014), 115–16. and DeYoung, *Glittering Vices* (see chap. 8, note 39 *supra*), 25–44.

39. Drawn from an in-class assignment (November 12, 2013).

and—particularly insightful on the part of the students—"lack of empathy to think outside oneself and one's time" and "the vastness of wisdom and information to be grasped versus the limits of ourselves."[40]

For the third example, recall that prudence is sometimes portrayed with three eyes: past, present, and future. How can students be encouraged to think *forwardly* about the arc of their own lives? A common classroom device is to ask the standard-fare question, "Where do you see yourself in ten years?" When such a question is asked on the first or second day of class, students focus preponderantly on career paths and future desires, without much attention to (for example) growth in virtue or piety, religious faithfulness, or the future shape of their family lives. Such is the vision generated by the eyes of the present, gazing into the future. But what if, like three-eyed prudence herself, students were able to gaze *from the perspective of the future* back onto their own imagined pasts?

In order to encourage such "three-eyed" vision, I have frequently asked students in the Jerusalem and Athens Forum (sometimes over Christmas break!) to write the eulogy that they would hope to hear at their own funeral. What is especially revealing about this exercise is that, while students make known likely career paths, they almost inevitably focus more attention on traits of character, moral dispositions, faithfulness to religious beliefs, or devotion to family and friends. "She lived beautifully by trying to understand the varied and marvelous world around her," as one student wrote. His life was an accumulation of "small deeds in the noble cause of peace," wrote another. Above all, wrote a third, she was "a loving daughter, sister, friend, wife, mother, and follower of Christ."[41] By imagining themselves into their own future and looking at their lives *as a whole*, students are quickly drawn to larger questions of meaning and purpose—much more so, it seems, than when they simply imagine where they might be at some point in the hazy future.

Finally, I'll recount a rewarding opportunity from several years ago that I had with a group of students, all alumni of the honors program. We set out on a "study trip" to Italy, staying in the lodging of Gordon College's study-abroad program in Orvieto, Italy, an hour by train north of Rome. We chose as our topic "Explorations in Virtue and Vice in Renaissance Italy" and took as our guidebooks Dante's *Purgatorio* and Josef Pieper's

---

40. Drawn from an in-class assignment (November 14, 2013).

41. Drawn from a class exercise done over Christmas break (December 2013–January 2014).

*The Four Cardinal Virtues.* The particular quarries that we sought were allegorized representations of the virtues (and vices) in late-medieval and Renaissance art and architecture. Needless to say, opportunities for this kind of immediate, on-site exploration of illustrations of the virtues will not be available to all students or all courses. But even for those who view works of art and architecture through photos and videos, much is to be gained from the opportunity to compare textual descriptions of the virtues with their visual representation.

When students know what to look for, such illustrations jump out at them from frescoes, stand silently on the facades of palaces and churches, and dutifully serve as moral reminders on doors, windows, and sarcophagi. Often these representations are missed by tourists and art-history students alike, since they often compete with other (sometimes more well-known) works in the same space. For example, in the room that holds Raphael's famous "School of Athens" in the Vatican museums, the intentional observer can find ceiling frescoes of the seven virtues—to which most passers-by are oblivious.

Two particularly arresting examples of all seven virtues come from Florence. In the so-called "Spanish Chapel" of Santa Maria Novella (an erstwhile leading Dominican house in Florence), there appears a fresco, usually dubbed "The Triumph of Thomas Aquinas." The Angelic Doctor himself appears in the center of the fresco holding open *The Book of Wisdom*. Beside him are several biblical figures; under him are personifications of the the Seven Sacred Sciences and the Seven Liberal Arts. And, not least, surrounding him, depicted as angelic beings, are the Seven Virtues. Appropriately enough from the standpoint of Christian theology, the cardinal virtues are at a lower level; the theological virtues at a higher one. To Aquinas' right hovers prudence, carrying a book symbolizing this virtue's dependence on knowledge, and temperance with an upright branch of peace. To his left, one sees justice, holding a scepter and crown, and fortitude, outfitted with armor and a sword, and carrying a large fortress. Above the cardinal virtues come the theological ones: faith clutches a fiery light-bearing shield; hope holds an olive branch; and charity, highest of all and dressed in red, holds her arms open, welcoming all comers.[42]

Also in Florence, not far away, is the city's cathedral, with its famous octagonal baptistery where Dante was baptized. The building is best known for the

---

42. Joachim Poeschke, *Wandmalerei der Giottozeit, 1280–1400* (Munich: Hirmer Verlag, 2004), 362–79.

so-called "Doors of Paradise" by Lorenzo Ghiberti on its north side; however, in the south-side doors, by the lesser-known Andrea Pisano, the eight lower panels depict the seven virtues. Predictably enough, the four cardinal virtues are on the lowest level, as they represent the virtues obtainable without the aid of special revelation. Above them come the three theological virtues, but also the New Testament virtue of humility (Pisano had an eighth panel to fill!). On the bottom row, prudence appears with a Janus face in the back of her head, such that she is looking both into the future and into the past; this symbolizes the retrospective *memoria* needed for this virtue. She also holds a snake, a reference to the biblical exhortation to be as "innocent as doves but as wise as serpents" (Matthew 10:16). Next comes justice, holding scales and a sword. Temperance is portrayed with a sheathed sword (symbolizing anger restrained), while fortitude holds a raised mace and shield. From left to right on the row above, one finds charity holding up a flaming heart, symbolizing the burning love one ought to have for God and also a cornucopia, a symbol of earthly charity. Faith holds a cross and Eucharistic chalice, while hope is portrayed reaching for a "crown of righteousness" (2 Tim. 4:8), and humility, with lowered gaze, holds a rod of discipline.[43]

The virtue of prudence has attracted an especially interesting set of iconographic representations over the centuries. In addition to the symbolism of eyes, Janus faces, books, and snakes, the virtue is sometimes portrayed as a figure staring into a mirror, suggesting that the prudent person must observe the Delphic dictum, "know thyself." The woman allegorized as prudence in the Raphael rooms in the Vatican museums, in fact, is looking at herself in the mirror. Less frequently, prudence will hold a compass, suggesting measured judgment and precise calculation; or she will appear with a stag—a creature shrewd in eluding its pursuers. Furthermore, prudence will sometimes appear alongside one of her opposite vices, folly (*stultitia*), often portrayed as a jester with a bauble, a clown, or a man crowned with feathers and holding a cudgel.[44] Finally, the virtue is sometimes depicted with three heads; a famous example by Titian, found in the National Gallery in London, actually has *two sets* of

43. I am grateful to John Skillen of Gordon College for first discussing these doors with me.

44. See Katzenellenbogen, *Allegories of the Virtues and Vices in Mediaeval Art*, 55–56; Hall, *Dictionary of Subjects and Symbols in Art*, 169, 254–55. Cf. Clifford Davidson, ed., *Fools and Folly* (Kalamazoo, MI: Medieval Institute Publications, 1996). Guidance to various images of prudence can be found in Colum Hourihane, *Virtue and Vice: The Personifications in the Index of Christian Art* (Princeton: Princeton University Press, 2000), 278–83.

three heads. The lower ones are animal heads, while the higher ones are human—suggesting that the threefold nature of prudence (memory, present awareness, foresight) applies both to our "animal" or "natural" selves and to our "rational" or "spiritual" selves. Accompanying this painting is the medieval inscription, mentioned earlier, that "from past experience the present acts prudently lest future action be vitiated."[45] Such examples from art and architecture might not immediately seem to apply to vocational exploration; however, I am persuaded that such visual encounters with the virtues help students think about appropriating them in their own lives. Images have a different, more palpable power than words. When images and words about prudence are combined for the student, not only does an interesting pedagogical environment result, but the larger "life questions" of vocation come more easily to the discussion. Reflecting together on the "the past, present, and future" as it applies to representations of the virtue of prudence, for example, readily facilitates questions to students such as: what past experiences or past skills learned are important to consider in charting a course for your own future? Or, what from your educational experience would improve an understanding of the etiology of a contemporary social problem or a problem anticipated in the future?

A student who has spent years learning Arabic might *prudently* conclude that a future path ought to involve further study in and about the Middle East. The unsustainable debts and looming fiscal crises of many Western welfare states might lead one *prudently* to consider graduate work in economics or politics. A student who knows first-hand the realities of an underprivileged background might *prudently* feel called to social work or some form of ministry to those living in poverty, at home or abroad. For a student who has cultivated the virtue of prudence, selected areas of study (as well as other life experiences) will often suggest specific vocational paths.

In the final analysis, the three eyes of prudence are not simply bygone, interesting decorations in medieval art or beautiful words on the pages of Dante. They are far more; they touch deeper realities. They have the potential to help us view our lives, our gifts and abilities, and the times in which we live—as well as the potential for a life calling.

In seeing them, they may well help us see ourselves.

---

45. See the discussion of the work in Simona Cohen, *Animals as Disguised Symbols in Renaissance Art* (Boston: Brill, 2008), 166–76.

# Commitment and Community

## THE VIRTUE OF LOYALTY AND
## VOCATIONAL DISCERNMENT

### *Hannah Schell*

UNDERGRADUATE STUDENTS LIVE in the midst of multiple and competing narratives. These form them in understanding who they should be and what they should do, both during their collegiate years and beyond. Most students have only recently left their family homes, yet they suddenly find themselves overwhelmed by a number of possible candidates for goals that they could pursue and ends that they could seek to achieve. Often the messages they receive are contradictory. Upon arriving on our campuses, they are advised to make academic study their priority, but then are barraged with opportunities to join clubs, pressured to rush a fraternity or sorority, and pushed to participate in the many ever-present social events on campus. While their first-year-seminar professor may be encouraging them to appreciate the importance of a liberal, broad education, and perhaps to hold off on declaring a major, they are asked "what's your major?" every time they must introduce themselves in a new setting. In short, college students are thrust into an unstructured universe, populated by dissonant voices, and the voices that most capture their attention will help to determine which stories they will live by, the kinds of happiness they will pursue, and the goals toward which they will direct their lives. As Mark Schwehn and Dorothy Bass note in *Leading Lives That Matter,* "sorting out the character and worth of many voices is a crucial matter," not only for students but for anyone experiencing a time of transition—since those voices inform our identities and "continue to be present all our lives long."[1]

The uncertainties faced by undergraduates can complicate their work of vocational exploration and discernment. They are unsure about whom to consult or whether their calling is simply a matter of "finding themselves." The vagaries of where to begin the process can lead to deferral and postponement, and they may feel so disconnected that making a commitment seems arbitrary. Hence, the first part of this essay explores some of the complexities in the vocational discernment of young adults and identifies four conundrums faced by contemporary undergraduates. It then turns to the work of the American philosopher Josiah Royce (1855–1916), introducing his philosophical perspective and briefly tracing the sources from which he drew. This section then discusses Royce's exploration of what it means to develop a "plan of life"; it also explores his focus on the virtue of loyalty, highlighting his attention to the significance of both the individual and the community. The third and longest part of the essay returns to the four conundrums and suggests how the language of "loyalty" might help to address them when they arise.

The overall goal of this chapter is to suggest some elements of an approach that might help mentors and students negotiate some of the complexities that attend vocational discernment, particularly during this highly uncertain period of our students' lives. As we will see at several junctures, the language of "loyalty to a cause" provides an approach to the exploration of vocation that does not rely on theological categories, yet without approaching its topic in an anti-theological way. This is significant, and needed, if we are to mentor *all* of our students—and to do so regardless of their formation in, or even knowledge of, a particular faith tradition. While the language of loyalty challenges students to think about what is most important to them (and this may, of course, include their religious faith), it is simultaneously neutral and capacious with respect

---

1. Schwehn and Bass, *Leading Lives That Matter*, 360 (see Introduction, note 12 *supra*). For a thoughtful treatment of the role that narrative plays in vocation, see chapter 7 of the present volume. While I agree with and am inspired by much of this chapter, I have shied away from its use of the phrase "tournament of narratives"—both because it invokes images of battle, and because it suggests a winner at the end of what can indeed be an agonistic process, even though it does not necessarily yield a singular operating narrative.

both to their belief in God and to whether they understand their callings as coming from God.[2]

## *The conundrums of undergraduate life*

Undergraduates are bedeviled by uncertainty. They are unsure about how and whether to think about their lives as a cohesive whole. On one side stands an overdetermined view that claims that discerning one's calling allows for only one correct outcome—a single trajectory for a life that must be discovered and correctly planned out, once and for all. This creates an enormous amount of stress for young adults, a sense of anxiety that they might discern their calling incorrectly; their response is often to try to put off the discernment process, indefinitely if possible, for fear of getting it wrong. At the other extreme is the view that life is a disconnected series of situations with nothing harmonizing them; we just bumble our way along, making choices for no particular reason beyond immediate satisfaction or instrumental value. In this case, it can be difficult to get students to think beyond the here and now in a way that takes seriously their larger, more sustained commitments.

Our students are both products and agents of their culture. Their vocational discernment is infused with a strong sense of individualism and what Charles Taylor has called "expressivism": the most important element driving their discernment is the sense that, whatever they choose as their vocation, it must first and foremost express their true selves.[3] In the "expressive view of human life," Taylor writes, "fulfilling my nature means espousing the inner *élan*, the voice or impulse" that is then made manifest.[4] The eighteenth century bequeathed to us the idea that "each individual is

---

2. For a more specific inquiry into the agent of the call, see chapter 6; with respect to the present volume's efforts to situate itself with respect to the role of theology and religious belief, see the Introduction, particularly the subsection headed "Mapping the territory."

3. Schwehn and Bass explore the multiple and contending vocabularies for how we think about a meaningful life and suggest that there are three dominant paradigms in our contemporary culture, including the paradigm of authenticity, which they find usefully diagnosed in the writings of Charles Taylor. Taylor is part of a group of contemporary thinkers who have raised thoughtful and serious questions about our modern forms of individualism and self-individuation. Schwehn and Bass, *Leading Lives that Matter*, 39–46. See also the comments in the present volume's Introduction, note 12 *supra*.

4. From "The Expressivist Turn," in Charles Taylor, *Sources of the Self: The Making of the Modern Identity* (Cambridge, MA: Harvard University Press, 1989), 374.

different and original, and that this originality determines how he or she ought to live"; modern forms of expressivism add to this the idea that we have an obligation "to live up to our originality."[5] Under these conditions, the pressures on young adults to make the right vocation-relevant choices are immense. How can one choose? And what if the choice is wrong? Given that these choices are dependent upon their sense of identity, which is still in flux, how could they possibly know what they are called to do? In what follows, I will call this conundrum the "problem of expressivism."

A second concern that affects vocational discernment, particularly during the young adult years, is the conflict between self-assertion and the claims of others upon one's life. College students find themselves affirming, and being encouraged to affirm, *both* their own unassailable ability to determine the shape of their own lives *and* the greater degree of experience, expertise, and wisdom of the parents, mentors, and educators that populate their social worlds. The work of trying to find one's calling is thus haunted by the type of self-expressive individualism that insists "I just have to be me." But, at the same time, the dictates of various authorities can have such a powerful impact on the discernment process that young adults can end up unreflectively following whatever is offered to them—whether it comes in the guise of mere suggestion, considered advice, or implied obligation. Young adults experience enormous pressure from the various authorities in their lives and hear these claims as "you must do this," thereby creating a conflict that they experience in an acute way. Hence, "to whom should I listen?" is a live question for young adults. As Schwehn and Bass note, our students' wariness about taking advice stems from the contemporary ideal of authenticity. They may feel that the only real answers must come from within themselves. And yet,

> other people matter immensely in the choices we make. When we look within ourselves, we find a medley of voices from important others in our lives—parents, grandparents, siblings, teachers, pastors and friends—that we have internalized. . . . The distinctive individuality so prized by contemporary people is in fact fashioned in a lifelong series of conversations with significant others such as these.[6]

---

5. Taylor, *Sources of the Self*, 375.

6. Introduction to Chapter 5, "To Whom Should I Listen?" in Schwehn and Bass, *Leading Lives that Matter*, 360.

There is a paradox at work in the simultaneous desire for autonomy and need for the advice and guidance of others.

A third, and related, conundrum arises as students begin to think about the various communities to which they belong, and how these groups bind them to certain commitments. The significance of these communities (and the possible conflicts among them) can be revealed during a discernment process. Some of these communities are important and enduring constituents of their identity, while others are temporary and evanescent, yet still significant (including athletics, Greek life, and even one's choice of major). Helping students realize and adjudicate among these different communities is an important part of the guidance we can offer in their vocational discernment process. Their choices will, we hope, be guided by those commitments and communities that already are constitutive of who they are and where they may be headed in life.

Finally, given the age and stage of life of most college students, they can expect to confront moments of transition, change, or even crisis in their lives—and not least with respect to their vocations. Students are often focused on and exercised by what they will do following graduation, and they will certainly experience moments of change and crisis on the other side of the platform at commencement; but they are likely to experience such moments during their college years as well. How can educators equip young adults to be able to handle these experiences and to realign their vocational outlook over the whole arc of their lives?

In the next section, I want to consider how Royce's understanding of the self, as well as his sense of the importance of loyalty for a meaning-filled life, can provide us with insights that may help college students negotiate the conundrums delineated here—as well as other complexities of their undergraduate lives—through a guided process of vocational exploration and discernment.

## *Royce, his tradition, and his account of loyalty*

Josiah Royce is part of an American tradition stretching back to Ralph Waldo Emerson (1803–1882) that celebrates the capacities of individuals to create lives of significance and meaning. Like his friend and colleague William James (1842–1910), Royce was committed to exploring those capacities in the broadest possible terms, taking into account a wide range of values and practices. But whereas James began with the religious experiences of individuals in *The Varieties of Religious Experience* and elsewhere, Royce believed in the primacy of the *community* as a source of meaning and insight.[7] Like John Dewey (1859–1952) in his work *A Common Faith*, Royce was attuned to the role that values play in guiding human action and was interested in expanding the range of ideals that animate our choices beyond merely traditional religious options. For Dewey and others of his generation, such expansion was entailed by a robust democratic sensibility. Such "natural piety," according to Dewey, does not depend upon belief in a supernatural realm; yet neither does it require a "fatalistic acquiescence" to the world. Instead, it recognizes that humans, as a part of nature, "are marked by intelligence and purpose, having the capacity to strive . . . to bring conditions into greater consonance with what is humanly desirable."[8] This line of American thinkers took religion seriously but did not write as theologians confessing or promulgating a particular religious worldview.

This naturalistic (as opposed to supernatural) form of piety is further expressed in the thought of contemporary thinkers writing self-consciously as inheritors of the tradition of Emerson, James, and Dewey.[9] This is a trajectory that looks back to Aristotle, but does not then

---

7. For Royce's critique of individualism, see especially the second chapter of Josiah Royce, *The Philosophy of Loyalty* (1908), reprinted with a new introduction by John J. McDermott (Nashville: Vanderbilt University Press, 1995), 25–47, as well as chapter 2 of *Sources of Religious Insight* (New York: Charles Scribner's Sons, 1911), where he specifically addresses James's views. Royce went on to develop the idea of the "beloved community" in what many consider his most important work, *The Problem of Christianity*, 2 vols. (New York: Macmillan Company, 1913); this concept later figured prominently in the thought of Dr. Martin Luther King, Jr. An electronic version of *Sources of Religious Insight* is included as part of Project Gutenberg and can be found at http://www.gutenberg.org/files/33677/33677-h/33677-h.htm (accessed November 9, 2014). For a helpful overview of Royce's understanding of community, see Jacquelyn Ann K. Kegley's entry on Royce for the *Internet Encyclopedia of Philosophy*, which can be accessed at http://www.iep.utm.edu/roycejos/ (accessed November 9, 2014), as well as her longer monograph, *Genuine Individuals and Genuine Communities: A Roycean Public Philosophy* (Nashville: Vanderbilt University Press, 1997).

8. John Dewey, *A Common Faith* (New Haven, CT: Yale University Press, 1934), 25.

9. See especially the work of Richard Rorty (1931–2007), Jeffrey Stout (1950–) and Cornel West (1953–). In a provocative essay, Rorty adopts the term "romance" for the "fuzzy overlap of faith, hope and love" that best captures what it is to have a "faith in the future possibilities of mortal humans, a faith which is hard to distinguish from love for, and hope for, the human community." Romance, in this sense, Rorty claims, "may crystallize around a labor union as easily as around a congregation, around a novel as around a sacrament, around a God as easily as around a child." Richard Rorty, "Religious Faith, Intellectual Responsibility and Romance," *American Journal of Theology and Philosophy* 17, no. 2 (May

follow the explicitly Christian theological strand through Augustine and Thomas Aquinas (and thence through modern and contemporary authors who have explored Christian virtue ethics).[10] It does not depend upon the idea that only certain religious beliefs and commitments make live worth living; yet, with some exceptions, it is quite sympathetic to those beliefs and commitments and understands them as part of the pluralism that is one of the important hallmarks of American culture. Virtues such as flexibility and imagination, intellectual humility and collaboration, creative intelligence and solidarity are what make robust democratic culture possible; this language is woven through this tradition. And, as I hope to show, virtues such as these are highly relevant to the difficult work of vocational discernment.

## Royce's view of the self

Before we turn our attention to the particular virtue of loyalty, we must briefly consider Royce's view of the self.[11] We often imagine ourselves as static entities and disconnected monads, when in actuality the self is *dynamic*: our inner life is in a state of Heraclitean flux. The self is also essentially *relational*. Royce was well attuned to human beings as social creatures who live alongside and with others. His thought was grounded in the insights of the emerging discipline of social psychology, which

---

1996): 121–40; here, 96. This essay is included in *The Cambridge Companion to William James* (Cambridge: Cambridge University Press, 2006) and can also be found in Rorty's *Philosophy and Social Hope* (New York: Penguin, 2000). More recently, Stout has explored what it means to think of the democratic sensibility invoked by Dewey as itself having a tradition. See his *Democracy and Tradition* (Princeton: Princeton University Press, 2009) and *Blessed Are the Organized: Grassroots Democracy in America* (Princeton: Princeton University Press, 2012). Nearly all of Cornel West's writings touch upon the importance of Emerson and Dewey; for a focus on democratic virtues, see especially *Democracy Matters* (New York: Penguin Books, 2005). Without intending to downplay the moments of contention that can be found in the writings of these thinkers, my point here is to suggest that Royce is a part of a tradition worth our considered attention when exploring the relationship between the virtues and vocational discernment.

10. See chapters 7, 8, and 9 in this volume for detailed and thoroughgoing accounts of this tradition.

11. For a useful introduction to Royce's approach to the self, see Jacquelyn Ann K. Kegley, "Mind as Personal and Social Narrative of an Embodied Self," in *Josiah Royce for the Twenty-First Century: Historical, Ethical and Religious Interpretations*, ed. Kelly A. Parker and Krzysztof Piotr Skowronski (Lanham, MD: Rowman & Littlefield, Lexington Books, 2012), 227–244. Royce addressed the self as dynamic in his Gifford Lectures of 1899–1900 entitled *The World and the Individual*.

understood humans as embedded in relationships with others. While autonomy is an important feature of human activity, Royce highlighted and even celebrated the role that living within a community plays for meaningful human existence. We cannot be selves without communities.

Royce was also very perceptive with regard to the role that *time* and *narrative* play in human life. We are unavoidably temporal and narrating creatures—living in the present, we make sense of things with reference to a past and oriented toward a future. We have the capacity for *self-evaluation* and *reflection*, and judge ourselves over and against a vision of our "ideal self," adding an additional dynamic to self-consciousness. Finally, we must think of the self as inherently *teleo-logical*, as oriented toward plans and purposes. If asked the question "who are you?" Royce suggests that we will answer in terms of some sort of statement about the plans and purposes of our life, in terms of our deeds and our ideals.[12]

Royce was well attuned to these features of the self. They form the backdrop of his understanding of loyalty, as well as his rationale for why it should be understood as a principal virtue. Communities come together around certain ideals or causes; worthy causes, Royce insists, are super-personal because they involve more than just the individual's pref-erences or concerns.[13] Royce's philosophy of loyalty, then, both depends upon and celebrates an understanding of the self as socially embedded, dynamic, relational, reflective, and teleological. And yet, loyalty as a virtue is complicated and potentially problematic. We therefore need to examine its contours in more detail.

## The virtue of loyalty

In 1916, Sophie Bryant noted in her entry on "Loyalty" for the *Encyclopedia of Religion and Ethics* that the English word *loyalty* has its etymological roots in the word *law* (through the French *loi* and the Latin *lex*). However, as she went on to observe, loyalty means "much more than 'law' in the limited sense of a definite written code." While a legalist merely follows the "letter of the law," a loyal person puts "his whole mind into his duty" and "forms his spirit in accordance with the spirit of the purpose to be served."

---

12. Royce, *Philosophy of Loyalty*, 78–79.

13. Royce, *Philosophy of Loyalty*, 11.

The truly loyal have the spirit of the cause "written on their hearts, as the Scripture says, and incorporate in their will."[14] They are in turn bound by the cause; and it is this binding quality it what helps inform and give meaning to a life, even as one's loyalties may seemingly limit one's freedom.

While we rightly value loyalty in our friends and family members (and they value it in us), loyalty is a complicated virtue and has had its critics and detractors. Loyalty's excesses, in the form of unreflective allegiance to a group or to a pernicious cause, are notorious; with good reason do we worry about zealousness and "blind loyalty." But, as R. E. Erwin has argued, expressions of loyalty—like expressions of sympathy, compassion, fidelity, and love—stem from our inherent sociability; they imply a relationship that is more than merely contractual. Erwin concludes his essay on "Loyalty and Virtues" with the observation that loyalty, understood as the affective connection one feels toward a group, is in fact the basic foundation for the virtues. It involves taking "the interests of others as one's own" and a "willingness to bear some cost for that."[15] If we are suspicious about this kind of devotion to a particular group, Alasdair MacIntyre has argued, it is because the dominant strand of modern moral thought assumes that such particularity or partiality is a problem—and that morality requires comprehending moral rules as "universal and general."[16] And yet, MacIntyre argues, there is an important rival perspective that suggests that "detached from my community, I will be apt to lose my hold upon all genuine standards of judgment. Loyalty to that community, to the hierarchy of particular kinship, particular local community and particular natural community, is on this view a prerequisite for morality."[17] In a similar vein, Josiah Royce embraced the particularity that is signaled by

14. Sophie Bryant, cited in Matthew Foust, *Loyalty to Loyalty: Josiah Royce and the Genuine Moral Life* (New York: Fordham University Press, 2012), 43. Foust offers a detailed and helpful analysis of Royce's project and applies some of Royce's insights to contemporary issues such as whistle-blowing and the Enron scandal.

15. R. E. Erwin, "Loyalty and Virtues," *Philosophical Quarterly* 42, no. 169 (October 1992): 403–419; here, 419.

16. Alasdair MacIntyre, "Is Patriotism a Virtue?" The Lindley Lecture, University of Kansas, March 26, 1984, http://kuscholarworks.ku.edu/bitstream/handle/1808/12398/Is%20Patriotism%20a%20Virtue-1984.pdf (accessed November 9, 2014), 9. For more on moral rules and their problems, see chapter 8 in the present volume, particularly the subsection headed "Virtue as vocation."

17. MacIntyre, "Is Patriotism a Virtue?" 11. For a brief review of the contemporary debates about whether justice and partiality are incompatible, as well as a discussion of

loyalty to a cause. Royce approached loyalty not just as one in the family of virtues, but as constituting "the fulfillment of the whole moral law."[18]

## Royce on loyalty

Royce's discussion of loyalty was shaped by his appreciation for the importance *and* limits of individualism. Like Alasdair MacIntyre, Royce was frustrated by the ways in which the modern understanding of the atomistic self has limited our ability to talk about what matters most. Like Charles Taylor, however, Royce also appreciated the power of an ethic that embraces a subtle understanding of authenticity.[19] In 1908, Royce wrote:

> A self is a life in so far as it is unified by a single purpose. Our loyalties furnish such purposes, and hence make of us conscious and unified moral persons. Where loyalty has not yet come to any sort of definiteness, there is so far present only a kind of inarticulate striving to be an individual self. This very search for one's true self is already a sort of life-purpose, which, as far as it goes, individuates the life of the person in question, and gives him a task. But loyalty brings the individual to full moral self-consciousness. It is devoting the self to a cause that, after all, first makes it a rational and unified self, instead of what the life of too many ... remains,—namely a cauldron of seething and bubbling efforts to be somebody, a cauldron which boils dry when life ends.[20]

For Royce, becoming persons with lives of integrity, meaning, and purpose entails reflecting upon our commitments and devoting ourselves

---

the significant affinities between Royce and MacIntyre, see chapter 1 of Foust, *Loyalty to Loyalty*, 10–25. Jacquelyn Ann K. Kegley (in *Genuine Individuals and Genuine Communities*) explores four concepts from MacIntyre with reference to Royce: "virtue," "narrative quest," "tradition," and "practice."

18. Royce, *Philosophy of Loyalty*, 9. The *Philosophy of Loyalty* was first presented as a set of lectures at the Lowell Institute in November and December 1907. Much like William James's Lowell lectures, delivered the previous year and published as *Pragmatism*, Royce hoped to lay the foundation for "a new way of thinking through old problems" by examining the often-overlooked and occasionally maligned virtue of loyalty.

19. See Charles Taylor, *The Ethics of Authenticity* (Cambridge, MA: Harvard University Press, 1991).

20. Royce, *Philosophy of Loyalty*, 80.

to those causes (broadly understood) that deserve our loyal attention and devotion. When we act upon a sense of commitment to a cause, our lives have a needed "centre, fixity, stability."[21]

Royce defined loyalty as "the willing and practical and thoroughgoing devotion of a person to a cause."[22] First (and, for Royce, foremost), when people make commitments that inform their actions, they do so as *an act of will*. Although certain causes or commitments may come to us as a function of the particular communities and traditions of which we are a part, in order to become consciously loyal to a particular cause, we must choose it—or at least approve of it, when it appears as a possibility. We cooperate in the choice of cause by willingly taking it up. "My loyalty is never my mere fate," Royce argued.[23]

Loyalty marks not just the emotional attachment that one might feel for a cause, but also the work involved. Royce's definition further specifies that devotion to a cause must be *practical*. Loyalty is expressed through a sense of commitment that is enacted throughout a person's life. Moreover, commitment to a cause is precisely how a self becomes a full person—a person with purposes and plans, concerns and cares (as opposed to a mere automaton). True loyalty is *thoroughgoing*. We cannot be loyal to a cause on Tuesdays and Saturdays as it suits us, or according to our moods—loyalty implies a sustained commitment and a life of integrity informed by that commitment.[24] Without plans or purposes, individuals are not yet *persons*.

At the outset, Royce qualifies "cause" in a manner fitting with his view of the embedded, social nature of the self. The cause to which one is loyal goes beyond the individual person and cannot be merely an expression of self-love or the seeking one's own private advantage.[25] Causes bind a person to something larger than herself; causes tend to demand coordinated work and thus bind several individuals together. Moreover, worthy causes contribute to the store of loyalty in the world. They encourage and enable other worthy causes; worthy causes together form a web of activity and

---

21. Royce, *Philosophy of Loyalty*, 12.

22. Royce, *Philosophy of Loyalty*, 9.

23. Royce, *Philosophy of Loyalty*, 57.

24. For an elaboration on this ideal of the full person whose life is one of integrity, see chapter 8 of this volume.

25. Royce, *Philosophy of Loyalty*, 11.

meaning. Unworthy causes are vicious because, Royce argued, they are predatory; they impinge on someone else's opportunity to be loyal.[26]

To summarize, then, Royce's approach to loyalty features several important elements. The virtue of loyalty involves a certain aspect of reflection and willed choice rather than passive resignation or blind obedience. It is expressed in practical action rather than mere promises. Loyalty to a cause cannot be sustained by sporadic gestures of commitment; it entails (and makes possible) a sustained integrity and is necessary for full personhood. And, finally, loyalty is relational: one's chosen cause binds one to others who are also loyal to that cause. These aspects of Royce's approach figure significantly in what follows—namely, how thinking in terms of loyalty and commitment to a cause can help address some problems that arise in the vocational discernment process of young adults.

## Addressing the undergraduate conundrums

Discerning one's vocation is a difficult and fraught process, and mentoring undergraduates in that process can be challenging. In this section, I want to return to the four conundrums that arise in the vocational discernment process for young adults (as described in the first section of this chapter) and to suggest some ways in which the language of loyalty can be helpful to those who hope to accompany young people on this journey.

### "I must be true to myself": The problem of expressivism

When confronted with questions of vocation, undergraduates tend to turn inward, assuming that the answers to be found are a function of self-expression. Moreover, they feel acutely the modern pressure to "be original." Vocational discernment can founder under the weight of this seeming obligation. If the answer is to be found within, then the discernment process is in a state of suspension until the inner voice speaks and the words ring true; this in turn can lead to infinite postponement.

Here, the problem lies in part with our truncated understanding of what it means to be a self. As discussed above, Royce took seriously that the self is an ongoing process—dynamic, relational, and teleological. Identity and vocation are indeed intertwined, but young adults are mistaken when

---

26. Royce, *Philosophy of Loyalty*, 54.

they imagine that they must first sort out the former ("who am I?") before engaging the latter ("what am I called to do?"). One's calling and purpose, and the ways these are expressed in a life, are integrally related to the question of identity. It is only by setting about the task of "fulfilling our purpose," and being oriented toward this larger project, that we even become a self. Therefore it would be a mistake to imagine that we can ascertain who we are—to "find ourselves"—prior to making a commitment to undertake meaningful deeds.

In terms of the process of vocational discernment in young adults, we have to help them begin from where they are: to identify those communities of which they are a part and which inform who they are, the causes to which they are already committed, and the underlying (or overarching) loyalties that already give their lives meaning. Giving them opportunities to make these explicit and to reflect upon them provides an important starting point for vocational discernment. It helps them to see that they are already embedded in webs of relationship and meaning and to move them beyond dwelling in self-expressivism. (I will return to this point in the third part of this section.)

Examples of other people's vocational journey can be beneficial on this front. Whether it is the stories of the adults around them (on campus and beyond) or of invited guests (alumni or other campus visitors), sharing our stories exposes undergraduates to the messy, serpentine realities of vocational discernment. What often emerges in such stories and (in the chance to respond to and reflect upon them) is the recognition that a call often seems to originate in the context of a particular encounter. This means that the call comes from without as opposed from within; that it can be unexpected; and that it can re-direct the course of a person's life. Several years ago, the former nun and social activist Kathleen O'Shea visited Monmouth College to talk about her work with women on death row. In the question and answer session after her talk, an audience member marveled at the significance of the work and wondered what she could do. O'Shea's response was arresting. She told the story of how she came to know a woman on death row and how the encounter made a claim on her. But, she insisted to the student who asked the question, "I don't expect you to do what I am doing. The world is full of need, of important work. You just need to be ready to respond when the call comes for you." We need to help our students become attuned in that way—to see and hear that the answers are not necessarily or even likely to be found by cogitating upon their inner selves.

## "You can't tell me what to do": the paradox of autonomy

As suggested above, students often find the experience of college to be confusing, in part because of the many and sometimes conflicting messages that they are given about who they should be and what they should do. Helping students sort out and reflect upon this medley of voices is an important part of the discernment process. We must also help them become more attuned to the ways in which the people around them may be subtly confirming, advising, pressuring, assuaging, or dissuading them. We need to help them take these messages seriously and to engage in dialogue with the significant people in their lives about their commitments and sense of calling.

Given that we must choose our own cause—but also that we do not have direct access to any kind of internal, pure self—how can we know our own will? This question concerned Royce, but he believed that loyalty helped provide an answer:

> I can never find out what my own will is by merely brooding over my natural desires, or by following my momentary caprices. For by name I am a sort of meeting place of countless streams of ancestral tendency. From moment to moment, if you consider me apart from my training, I am a collection of impulses. There is no one desire that is always present to me. *Left to myself alone, I can never find out what my will is.*[27]

Separate from the influence that comes from their participation in a community and its traditions, individuals have no personal will of their own. "One of the principal tasks of my life," Royce asserts, "is *to learn to have a will of my own.*"[28] These demands form a paradox for moral agency, one that is relevant to the struggle for discerning vocation. I must decide in accordance with an autonomous will; yet strictly speaking, doing so is impossible. Only by recognition of external forms of authority and through training can I learn what my will is. Yet how can such training avoid becoming what Kant called *heteronomy*—the surrender of control over one's life to others?

---

27. Royce, *Philosophy of Loyalty*, 14, emphasis added.

28. Royce, *Philosophy of Loyalty*, 16, emphasis added.

For Royce, moral agency is always a process of learning, action, and reflection; and so likewise is vocational discernment. The development of our consciousness involves an ongoing dynamic between listening to our own "inner voice" and looking to others for guidance. As we face new challenges or situations that relate to our "plans of life," we must "look within, at what we call our own conscience, to find out what our duty is." Yet given how "wayward and blind" we are, we must also "look without" for guidance. This will often throw us back upon ourselves, and so the inevitable and unavoidable dynamic of inner and outer authority continues.[29]

A significant aspect of the virtue of loyalty for Royce lies precisely in its ability to address the tension between "inner and outer authority." Only loyalty can help us to move beyond this tension, precisely because it involves an oscillation *between* inner and outer authority; through reflection, the loyal self makes the cause its own. Loyalty to a cause brings stability to the otherwise chaotic mess we call the self. Offering an insight that is relevant to young adults struggling to discern their vocation, Royce asserts the following, seemingly paradoxical claim: "The only way to be practically autonomous is to be freely loyal."[30]

As mentors, we must help students ascertain what is important and of value to them at the current moment, to derive what underlying ideals and values inform their lives, and to then begin imagining what those ideals and values might look like when expressed over the longer arc of their lives. The specificity of their commitments does not curtail their choices but instead suggests pathways of where they might go.[31] Helping them through this process of reflection enables them to make their causes and commitments their own.

## "Where do I belong?": communities and commitments

If vocation is understood both in terms of discerning a call but also in terms of forming and acting upon commitments, our students need help in identifying and sorting through the communities of which they are a part and the commitments they may already hold. Many of their activities

---

29. Royce, *Philosophy of Loyalty*, 18–19.

30. Royce, *Philosophy of Loyalty*, 45.

31. On the tyranny of choice, see chapter 1 of the present volume, particularly the subsection headed by this phrase.

might be seen merely as ingredients for building a résumé; yet others are constitutive of how they see themselves and what they value. One important vehicle for helping students to sort out these commitments is that of *mentoring*. In her treatment of the role that mentoring environments play during the important transitional period of young adulthood, Sharon Daloz Parks emphasizes the need for a sense of belonging. Drawing upon the work of Piaget, Parks asserts, "everyone throughout life is dependent upon a tangible 'network of belonging.' Everyone needs a psychological home, crafted in the intricate patterns of connection and interaction between the person and his or her community."[32] She goes on to explore different forms of community, mapping them onto a developmental model as the adolescent matures into an adult; among these various forms, according to Parks, the "mentoring community" is one of the most powerful for young adults.[33] Mentoring communities are necessary for the nurturing of young adults, Parks states, because they "offer hospitality to the potential of the emerging self" and "access to worthy dreams of self and world."[34]

Both Parks and Royce see the self as embedded within different communities. These can be depicted using concentric circles, moving outward from the family, to local communities such as neighborhood, civic organizations, church or other religious institutions, to a larger sense of participation in the region, country, and world.[35] Asking young adults to create such a map can be a helpful tool for getting them to begin to think about themselves as standing within different communities, or "networks of belonging." While their sense of their communities may be limited at this stage in their life, this exercise encourages them to begin to think about themselves and their lives from a broader perspective and to think about their relationship to the world.

Royce explored the possibilities for "training for loyalty" in the sixth lecture of *The Philosophy of Loyalty*. "Training the young for a willing and thoroughgoing devotion of the self to a social cause," Royce advised, "must

32. Parks, *Big Questions, Worthy Dreams*, 89 (see chap. 2, note 18 *supra*).

33. For an extended description of the development of one form of mentoring environment—the "mentoring community"—in a specific institution's vocational exploration programming, see chapter 2, particularly the subsection headed with that phrase.

34. Parks, *Big Questions, Worthy Dreams*, 93.

35. See Parks, *Big Questions, Worthy Dreams*, 94.

be a long and manifold task."[36] His discussion of how loyalty might be encouraged during adolescence is particularly relevant to educators working in college and university settings today. He mentions two forms of loyalty that are important at this stage: athletic contests and fraternal organizations (the latter are manifested today on the college campus chiefly as fraternities and sororities, but would also include all kinds of other organizations outside the "Greek life" system). Despite their problematic excesses and "well-known abuses," Royce suggested that sports and campus organizations provide natural opportunities for loyalty. He does warn us to acknowledge, and respond to, those aspects of such organizations that are "profoundly objectionable," but otherwise to "leave wholesome youth to their natural life." His treatment of this subject in 1908 resonates even more profoundly today:

> The most unhappy features of the athletic, and in some measure of the fraternity, life in our colleges and universities are due to the false social prominence which the public opinion of those who have nothing to do with college life often forces upon our youth. The athletic evils, such as they are, of our academic world, are not due to the college students themselves nearly so much as the absurd social prominence which the newspapers and the vast modern crowds give to the contests which ought to be cheerful youthful sports.[37]

When students are asked about the communities of which they are a part, they often mention their participation in Greek life as well as their active involvement, often over many years, with certain sports. Some identify other organizations on campus, including service or religious organizations; others include the department of their major. These are all important aspects of their burgeoning identity, central to how they begin to think about vocation. However, they are also "networks of belonging"; Parks is right to encourage us to take them seriously as an important part of helping young adults ask "big questions" and ascertain their "worthy dreams."

In vocational programming, students can be asked to draw a diagram of their communities and commitments, either in a free-form style or as a set of concentric circles. How does such a diagram become a map, a basis

---

36. Royce, *Philosophy of Loyalty*, 120.

37. Royce, *Philosophy of Loyalty*, 124.

for reflecting upon one's commitments and potentially chosen causes? Part of getting young adults to think about themselves as embedded in certain communities entails getting them to think beyond their communities as simply ingredients in their identity. For example, if they have drawn their communities as a series of concentric circles, with themselves at the center, it can be helpful to have them reverse the direction of emphasis by asking, "what communities make a claim on you?" or "where do you belong?" That is, with whom are you already in relationship, to whom do you already have obligations or responsibilities? Or, borrowing a phrase from Richard Rorty, with whom are you in solidarity?[38]

Thinking in terms of communities and commitments can help young adults begin to think about themselves and their lives in terms of causes. To what principles or ideals are they committed, and how do these causes inform their vocational discernment? If prompted to reflect upon their loyalty to their fraternity or sorority, for example, a student may reveal that the meaning of their participation derives in part from their commitment to a sense of service to the community. A student who shares that he enjoys working with children may, upon reflection, realize that his enjoyment stems from a sense of wanting to invest in future generations. A young person who has been a successful athlete may, through a thoughtful conversation with a mentor, be guided to see that her athletic commitment is grounded in a desire to work with others, as a coordinated team, to accomplish a goal. If a student has had a meaningful experience with service learning or civic engagement, these can be important occasions for reflecting upon his or her commitments to forms of social justice.[39] These realizations can be extremely important for young adults as they begin the work of translating their current commitments into potential paths for their future lives. Making those commitments explicit helps them realize that they are already connected to certain communities and loyal to certain causes. As H. Richard Niebuhr put the matter in *The Responsible Self*, "the bond of loyalty" is a "double-bond, on the one hand to the companions, [and] on the other to the cause."[40]

---

38. For a different take on the issue of our multiple responsibilities stemming from the fact that we live in multiple communities simultaneously, see chapter 4.

39. For more on the fruitful connections between civic engagement and vocation discernment, see chapter 13.

40. See *The Responsible Self: An Essay in Christian Moral Philosophy* (New York: Harper & Row, 1963), 83.

## "What do I do now?": loyalty in times of crisis or change

Guiding young adults through a discernment process that draws upon the vocabulary of loyalty—the willed commitment to a chosen cause—not only frees vocation from being reduced to a job or a career; it can also help them in the future when they face moments of crisis or change. Given the probable realities of their lives—which include changes in personal relationships, changes in location, possible unemployment, the changing needs of their communities, the necessity of developing new skills, potential injury or illness, and even retirement itself—it is important that we provide them with tools that they can use in those future and inevitable moments of change. If they have a developing sense of how their vocational choices stem from a fundamental commitment to a cause, they can refer to that in those moments. There will be a capaciousness to their self-understanding about their choices that will serve them well when a change is necessary.

Royce devoted several pages in *The Philosophy of Loyalty* to describing the experience of being loyal to what comes to seem as a "lost cause."[41] In naming some causes "lost," Royce does not mean that they are wrong or not worthy of our devotion. Indeed, for Royce, the best causes in this world are often "lost causes." Loyalty to a lost cause is "attended by two comrades, grief and imagination."[42] In exploring the sorrow that attends the sense that one's cause is lost, Royce astutely observes how humans are able to reinterpret and creatively revise in the face of crisis. Grief chastens the imagination and our interpreting self begins to reform "the story of the past" and build "wonderful visions of what is yet to be."[43] Such moments of crisis are "loyalty's opportunity" because they challenge us to further reflect upon our commitments.[44]

Many of the young adults with whom we work do not yet know setback or tragedy, although sadly many already have experienced some sort of trial or personal challenge. Young people can sometimes tend to think of themselves as invulnerable or immune to crisis. Thinking in terms of their loyalties can ultimately help them when they do encounter

---

41. See Part V of Lecture 6, "Training for Loyalty" in Royce, *Philosophy of Loyalty*, 117–39.

42. Royce, *Philosophy of Loyalty*, 132.

43. Royce, *Philosophy of Loyalty*, 132.

44. Royce, *Philosophy of Loyalty*, 137.

a challenge, but this does not mean that the time of vocational discernment should be used primarily as an opportunity to warn young people
of the challenges they will face, or to put fear into them. A vague, often
unnamed fear—of failure, of going down "the wrong path," of disappointing a respected mentor or loved one—sometimes arises during the conversations. At those moments, it is helpful to name this fear and to get
them to imagine possible challenges, as well as how they might creatively
respond. Approaching such visualizations in terms of the students' most
deep-seated commitments and loyalties can help them see that they are in
the process of building up the resources that they will need when the time
comes. Causes and commitments at those moments can offer the needed
compass for negotiating difficult passages throughout their lives.

## Loyalty and vocational discernment

This essay has sought to demonstrate how the language of loyalty—
as it relates to Royce's insights about the self, the nature of commitment,
and the role of community—can be meaningfully applied in the context
of mentoring young adults through a process of vocational discernment.
Helping them ascertain their commitments is a process of realizing the
dynamic of what Royce calls "inner and outer authority." This can help
students reflect with greater subtlety about the role of various authorities
in their lives, while still authorizing their own agency in making their
decisions and in acting upon their commitments. Loyalty implies practical action, yet it also entails a sense of how ideals can operate as a compass
in one's life—even in moments of change or crisis. Finally, the language
of loyalty encourages and even challenges young adults to set about the
task of vocational discernment by starting from where they are: from the
current relationships, communities, and commitments that are the substance of their lives and their identities.

# PART FOUR

# *Vocational Discernment Beyond the Classroom*

The essays that we have presented thus far in this volume have focused on vocation and calling in the undergraduate context, broadly conceived. They have not been limited to classroom contexts, and they have not attempted to suggest that their observations about the theory and practice of vocational discernment can only be carried out within the academic divisions of colleges and universities. Nevertheless, by its very nature, higher education tends to draw our attention to academic teaching and research as its primary goal; and in the undergraduate context, this often means that the focus is on academic coursework, and on the places where that work is most commonly undertaken: the lecture hall, the seminar room, the laboratory, and the campus's various study spaces. Moreover, colleges and universities are typically structured in ways such that the size, power, and governance of its academic division tends to overshadow all the other places where education takes place.

Because of this tendency, the contributors to this volume considered it important to make sure that at least one section of the book focused specifically on vocational discernment outside the context of the traditional academic program. Anyone involved with undergraduate education is aware that much of a student's life is spent outside the classroom, and indeed outside the academic division of the institution. Residential life, athletics, co-curricular programs, and any indoor or outdoor space on campus can be, and often is, a location where education takes place. Nor need this be limited to physical boundaries of the institution; off-campus programs, community engagement, internships at local businesses and schools, and many other experiential learning opportunities are part and parcel of undergraduate education. In fact, most undergraduate institutions are very clear about this in their self-descriptions and promotional materials; college is a place where learning takes place in a variety of contexts, and in which personal and social development—both on campus and off—is as much a part of the "curriculum" as is the coursework that is often taken to be the essence of higher education.

If we are to take these claims seriously, and if we truly believe that vocation and calling are an essential element of the undergraduate experience, then we are not only advised but required to consider the ways that vocational discernment takes place beyond the classroom, beyond the traditional academic program, and even beyond the campus. Indeed, one might well argue that—given the sheer number of hours that students spend in the residence halls, on the athletic fields, attending meetings of student organizations, undertaking internships, studying abroad, or just hanging out (whether at school or in town)—we should probably have made this fourth section of the book larger than all the others. But we hope that we have at least made a start in the right direction by intentionally focusing on more of the places on campus, and beyond the campus, where vocational discernment takes place.

The authors who have contributed these final three chapters are engaged with a number of questions that seem to be of central importance to anyone who wants to encourage vocational reflection in undergraduate education today. These include:

- Are students more willing to engage in serious conversation about vocation and calling when they are in a context that strikes them as less specifically academic?
- How closely is vocational discernment related to other aspects of student development, including personal, emotional, and social development?
- What kinds of co-curricular programs most encourage vocational reflection, and what kinds might obstruct it or even devalue it?
- How does the physical layout of the campus, particularly outside the classroom, contribute to (or limit) students' ability to listen to a call and to respond to it?
- To what extent do programs of vocational discernment require that students get away from the campus and experience the world that lies outside of the structures of the college or university?
- How can the co-curricular programming and allied elements of an undergraduate institution be designed to integrate well with the academic program, so that vocational reflection and discernment can be vigorously promoted through as many channels as possible?

As has already been noted, the elements of undergraduate education that lie "beyond the classroom" are so significant in scope and number that we cannot possibly cover them in three brief chapters. We hope, however, that the very important contributions of these three scholars will inspire others to consider this question in greater depth, and to develop additional resources that will address the role of vocation and calling in these important areas of undergraduate life.

*II*

# Rituals, Contests, and Images

## VOCATIONAL DISCERNMENT BEYOND THE CLASSROOM

*Quincy D. Brown*

COLLEGES AND UNIVERSITIES have typically been interested in the development of the whole student. These institutions intentionally create environments that center on vocation and purpose, helping students reflect on such questions as: Who am I? What are my goals in life? and How do I make a difference with my life?[1] Although these questions are often addressed in the classroom, they also come to the fore in the rituals and cultural expressions of co-curricular activities. Such experiences can have positive influences on our students' quest for new images of identity; undergraduates can often develop a sense of what it means to belong to something larger than themselves, which can in turn help them address more significant questions of meaning, purpose, and faith.

Because they seek to provide a transformative experience, colleges and universities often invest in students in challenging and supportive ways[2] to help them acquire knowledge and develop a life of purpose. For some students, however, going to college is akin to moving to a new planet with

---

1. See Larry A. Braskamp, Lois Calian Trautvetter, and Kelly Ward, *Putting Students First: How Colleges Develop Students Purposefully* (Bolton: Anker Publishing Company, 2006), xvii.

2. Nevitt Sanford characterized learning as a process of challenge and response that can helpful in fostering conversations for vocational discernment. See Nevitt Sanford, *Self and Society: Social Change and Individual Development* (New York: Atherton Press, 1966).

no gravity, where they find themselves in a world in which everything is free-floating. As they begin to chart their various courses and tell their stories, students must navigate experiences of evaluation, reassessment, instability, fear, excitement, experimentation, adjustment, and risk. Such occasions might be best described as experiences of liminality.[3]

Contemporary accounts of liminality (from the Latin word *līmen*, meaning "a threshold") owe a great deal to the work of cultural anthropologist Victor W. Turner and his study of the rituals, symbols, and culture of the Ndembu tribe in Zambia. Liminal time develops within what Turner calls "an inter-structural situation," in which a person's identity is neither that of the old nor that of the new.

For the majority of college students, vocation is not an activity or event, but rather a transformative, life-long journey of liminality filled with experiences that shape the future persons they will become, and that provide opportunities for discernment, commitment, and self-expression.[4] This process of transformation can be promoted by out-of-classroom activities, where students receive support from a "holding environment"[5]—a space in which students can gather and which serve as something of a mirror, reflecting common experiences and gestures of identity formation during the time that they are pursuing an academic degree. Students need to find ways to carve out opportunities within the space and time of college life, where they can pursue numerous interests and where the goals extend beyond cognitive and skill development into values, civic responsibility, and spiritual development. Helping students in this process is essential if we are to help them ask big questions and pursue worthy dreams.[6]

This chapter begins with a general discussion of co-curricular activities, indicating some of the reasons that they provide particularly appropriate

---

3. For many young adults, college represents the liminal space between adolescence and adulthood. See Victor W. Turner, "Betwixt and Between: The Liminal Period in the Rites of Passage," *The Forest of Symbols: Aspects of Ndembu Ritual* (Ithaca, NY: Cornell University Press, 1967), 93. See also the comments on "emerging adulthood" in the Introduction.

4. John Neafsey, "Psychological Dimensions of the Discernment of Vocation," in John C. Haughey, S.J., ed., *Revisiting the Idea of Vocation: Theological Explorations* (Washington, DC: Catholic University of America Press, 2004), 163–95.

5. Borrowed from Donald Winnicott, "holding environments" are nonthreatening environments of challenge and support. See Donald W. Winnicott, *Playing and Reality* (London: Tavistock, 1971).

6. Braskamp, Trautvetter, and Ward, *Putting Students First*, 81; see also Parks, *Big Questions, Worthy Dreams* (see chap. 2, note 18 *supra*).

venues for vocational discernment. Then, in order to offer some historical perspective, it examines the life of John Wesley as an instance of how, in a time and place very different from our own, a college education that emphasized such activities helped him discern a lifelong vocation.

The second half of the essay employs the concept of a "tribe" to illumine how academic administrators, faculty, and other professional staff might guide students as they form and re-form their identities in relationship to those around them. I argue that this process has something to do with our students' "tribal identities" and that it takes place through three categories in particular: rituals, contests, and images.

## The significance of co-curricular activities for vocation

When the subject of a life's calling arises, the two most common questions students ask are: How do I know what I am being called to do? And: If I am being called to be a special sort of person, or to do something special with my life, am I capable or even willing to be the person, or accomplish the actions, to which I am being called? Questions such as these often prompt students to participate in a variety of co-curricular activities[7] in hopes of connecting with others to make meaning, better understand themselves, and begin to live into their identities. In a sense, they are testing their own provisional understandings of their various callings, recognizing that these will be played out beyond the classroom and in their broader life experiences.[8]

Following the work of Larry Braskamp, it may be helpful to differentiate between two aspects of the co-curriculum: *places* to be involved outside the classroom, and *activities* other than the kinds of cognitive work that takes place primarily in the classroom. The first relates to environments that most strongly shape students' lives (e.g., residence halls, off-campus gathering venues, faculty offices), and the second describes the kinds of activities that the co-curricular experience comprises (e.g., athletics, student government, group conversations, volunteer service). Obviously, some beyond-the-classroom experiences cross over into the academic

---

7. Braskamp, Trautvetter, and Ward, *Putting Students First*, 130.

8. Braskamp, Trautvetter, and Ward, *Putting Students First*, 125.

sphere (thus the current tendency to use the language of "co-curricular" rather than "extra-curricular" activities). In particular, activities such as service-learning opportunities, campus publications, international education opportunities, work in the fine and performing arts, and undergraduate research provide students with ways to integrate classroom and laboratory work with out-of-classroom experiences. These activities help students sharpen a wide variety of skills and can contribute to success and fulfillment following graduation.

Each of these activities helps students learn that taking a risk for something big, for something good—even, perhaps, being willing to devote one's whole life to a cause—offers a sense of worth or purpose.[9] Of course, in order for co-curricular activities to function in this way, they need to be carefully conceived and rightly implemented. Co-curricular activities of high quality can help students ask—and often answer—questions of how to live with meaning and purpose. These activities attract a large number of students across all regions of campus life; so much so, in fact, that they are sometimes perceived as being in some degree of conflict with the goals of academic life. This potential conflict can be minimized, however, when all participants recognize that both venues—the classroom and the co-curricular environment—can provide the time and space that students need to begin to ask the questions of vocation: What can I believe in? Where am I going? How can I be happy? and Will my life make a difference?[10]

These questions, when prompted by formative co-curricular activities, can be shaped by experiences of *rituals* (including rituals that are not specifically ecclesial, such as pledging into Greek life), *contests* (athletic, artistic, or academic), and *images* (the outward signs of membership in a particular campus community or culture). Although we might not think so at first, all these experiences can provide potential avenues for vocational discernment.[11]

Although co-curricular activities are not always addressed or "unpacked" in an academic setting, they can nevertheless be excellent opportunities for faculty, staff, and administrators to understand how

9. Sharon Daloz Parks, *Spirituality in Higher Education Newsletter* 4, no. 1 (November 2007): 29.

10. See James W. Fowler, *Faith Development and Pastoral Care* (Philadelphia: Fortress Press, 1987); see also Schwehn and Bass, *Leading Lives That Matter* (see Introduction, note 12 *supra*). For more on happiness and *telos*, see Chapter 8.

11. See Urban T. Holmes III, *Ministry and Imagination* (New York: The Seabury Press, 1976).

vocational discernment can take place in a challenging and supportive environment other than the classroom. Discerning a vocation requires a process of unmasking the hidden questions that students have about life, the world, and God. This "unmasking" can be a highly structured, heavily footnoted, academic venture; but it can also be a playful process in which young people seem to "stumble on" to the answers. Think of "those meddling kids" of the "Mystery Inc." gang in the old cartoon series *Scooby-Doo, Where Are You!* They are hardly deep thinkers or a well-resourced group; yet in the midst of their games and fun, they manage to find the clues that "unmask" the villain at the end of every episode. This playful example of understanding vocation fits well for beyond-the-classroom experiences, where students are given a break from class assignments and where complex issues are more readily examined through images and rituals of play, adventurous fun, and "hanging out" with friends.

Co-curricular activities are notable not just for the kind of activity that takes place, but also for their location: they take place in the library, computer labs, residence halls, chapels, recreation centers, dining halls, sports facilities, and off campus. These locations can sometimes help students lower the intellectual and personal defenses they have erected for themselves in the classroom, and thereby find the wherewithal to consider larger questions of meaning and purpose. For example, even though a religion class might focus on faith development and moral reasoning, the classroom might not provide the best atmosphere for open discussion of these matters. A co-curricular study group, however—taking place in a different kind of space and under different rules of engagement—might allow students to range more freely. In one such group, a senior in her fall term reflected on the uncertain process of deciding on a major.[12] She said,

> If you had asked me where God was leading me four years ago that would've been an easy answer. Speech pathology was the direction that I believe I was going in. If you had asked me two years ago where God was leading me, I would have said into art education, because I love art and I love children. If you ask me today where I think God is leading me, I will tell you that I just don't know.

---

12. Excerpts from students that were published, with their permission, in Quincy Durand Brown, "The Metanoia Project," D.Min. diss., The Interdenominational Theological Center, 2003, 109.

This senior's questions, which were essentially vocational in nature, prompted further discussion within the group. Several questions of identity and purpose emerged; her questions had opened the door for her peers to move from their individual perspectives to a much broader discussion of the college experience. Because of the similarities in what students had encountered during their collegiate journey, they were able to participate in a "holding environment" or *communitas*.[13]

Such communities, though relatively unstructured, encourage people to feel equal to one another, thereby creating a level of community spirit and solidarity within which everyone can ponder the kinds of issues that are part of vocational reflection and discernment. One junior education major alluded to this common experience, and to the need for community spirit, when commenting on the transitional nature of college. She observed that "college is a time you experiment with life and discern what direction God has for you. No matter what people you meet, friends you lose, experiences you have, God will always be there for you." A third student, a freshman math major, concurred with the description of college life as "experimental" in nature. She expressed this in her need to come to terms with living in a dormitory:

> College has been a big adjustment. I have been learning to live with new people who are constantly around. The people in the dorm don't just go away. I have never really and truly had to share my personal space like I do now. I believe that God has a plan for me and that everything happens for a reason, but right now I am not sure what dorm life has to do with that.

Each student's comments about struggling to "know where God is leading," "adjusting to a new environment," and "experimenting with life," suggests that the college environment serves as an important mediator of the images by which students will re-imagine themselves, their worldview, God, and their vocations. In many ways, this co-curricular study group provided these students with an experience of what Sharon Daloz

---

13. *Communitas*, the Latin term used to describe the characteristic of people experiencing liminality together, denotes intense feelings of social togetherness and belonging. In college, *communitas* can occur most readily during co-curricular activities outside the customs and expectations of the classroom. See Turner, *Forest of Symbols*, 129.

Parks refers to as a "laboratory of formation" of the young adult dream.[14] Like many co-curricular activities in colleges and universities across the country, this out-of-class experience helped students grapple with questions of vocation and how a college education helps them realize their purpose.

Of course, attending to the significance of co-curricular activities in the discernment process is hardly a new phenomenon. Throughout their history, colleges—particularly at the undergraduate level—have sought to provide spaces where students can explore these questions outside the traditional classroom environment. The collegiate system in the ancient English and Scottish universities had precisely this goal. To offer one particularly well-documented example of this process: the collegiate experience of John Wesley—Anglican priest and founder of the Methodist movement—demonstrates how co-curricular activities can help students discern a lifelong vocation. A brief look at the influences on Wesley's life will help to frame discussion of the importance of vocation beyond the classroom.

## *John Wesley's co-curriculum and vocation*

Wesley came to understand his vocation to be, broadly, to follow God's will; and, more specifically, to undertake a ministry that would have a transforming effect on the world through God's grace, a disciplined life, and the integration of personal piety and social holiness. In some ways, his life and vocation can be traced back to the profound influence of his mother's rigid approach to raising children. The spiritual heritage of Puritanism (with its emphasis on discipline and personal religious affections), and of Anglicanism (with its sacramental orientation), made its way to Wesley originally through his parents. One particular childhood event strongly marked his sense of vocation: he was saved from a fire at the Epworth rectory in 1709. After this experience, he regarded himself as providentially set apart for God; he referred to himself as a "brand plucked from the fire."[15] This event, at least in retrospect, set his entire life into the

---

14. Parks, *Big Questions, Worthy Dreams*, 139–40.

15. James W. Fowler, "John Wesley's Development in Faith," in M. Douglas Meeks, ed., *The Future of the Methodist Theological Traditions* (Nashville: Abingdon Press, 1985), 176.

framework of vocation; he understood himself as having been chosen for significant work.[16]

Wesley's education continued at Charterhouse School in London, where he struggled to understand the meaning of Christian faith. From there he moved on to pursue his undergraduate studies at Oxford. After his graduation he remained at Oxford where, as a Fellow at Lincoln College, he was appointed to supervise and tutor a group of undergraduates in both academic and spiritual progress.[17] Wesley gave leadership to a group of undergraduates (later called the "Holy Club"[18]) that met four nights weekly for study of the classics and reading the Greek New Testament. In addition to their classical studies, they practiced prayer, fasting, confession, and frequent partaking of the sacrament. Due to their extremely methodical effort of trying to serve God every hour of the day, they were mocked and disparagingly called "Methodists."[19]

The Holy Club became very influential in Wesley's adult education practices throughout his ministry. His educational theory and his pedagogical approach were being developed through these group encounters, and he demanded a balance between cognitive and intellectual stimulation—as well as the practical application of both.[20] He worked hard to make these formal groups "laboratories" for living out what had been learned in the context of education.

Attempting to provide students with a framework to discern a lifelong vocation of serving God and the church, Wesley created a co-curricular atmosphere for Oxford students that valued setting aside time for praying, spirituality, studying the Bible, meeting together, and teaching orphans how to read. To use the terminology that will be employed in the second half of this chapter: the *ritual* of meeting together weekly to study and

---

16. Compare this account to the features of the "call stories" discussed in chapter 5.

17. Martin Schmidt, *John Wesley: A Theological Biography*, vol. 1/2 (Nashville: Abingdon Press, 1966), 196–97.

18. John Wesley led what was essentially a co-curricular organization at Oxford, the Holy Club, upon his return to Oxford University in 1729 after a brief stint at Lincoln College. The organization had been started by his brother, Charles Wesley. See Richard P. Heitzenrater, *Wesley and the People Called Methodist* (Nashville: Abingdon Press, 1995).

19. Charles Wesley reported that the name of *Methodist* was given to them because of their strict conformity to the method of study prescribed by the university.

20. David Michael Henderson, *A Model of Making Disciples: John Wesley's Class Meeting* (Nappanee, IN: Evangel Publishing House, 2005), 43.

receive Holy Communion, the *contests* of answering twenty-two rigorous questions of self-examination, and the physical *images* of transforming the world through acts of mercy by visiting the prisons and orphanages of England, helped to shape the life and ministry of the Holy Club. Even with the success of the Holy Club, however, Wesley felt empty. Outwardly he acted as an ordained clergyperson serving the church, but inwardly he was searching for God's assurance by secretly asking questions about his own vocation and faith.

Years later, Wesley took a ship bound for the American colonies with the desire to "work out his own salvation," and to be a missionary to the Native Americans. During the journey across the Atlantic, the Moravian believers he met on board astounded him. At one point, a huge storm broke upon the ship during a worship service, and yet the Moravians calmly sang on, while Wesley and the other passengers were terrified. When Wesley asked one of them later if he was afraid, he responded, "I thank God, no." Wesley believed he was seeing holy living in action.

After a failed mission to the Americas, Wesley returned to England, feeling a sense of emptiness in his efforts. During what was arguably his lowest point, he met Peter Böhler, a German-born Moravian missionary. Böhler spent considerable time discussing the Christian faith with him and served as his spiritual mentor. John and his brother Charles could not help but observe the contrast between their own spiritual depression and Böhler's deep sense of Christian peace. Böhler talked to them about the necessity of prayer and faith. He urged them to focus less on what they wanted to achieve for God, and more on what God could do for them. Böhler's counsel on the nature of grace and "heart religion" was instrumental in the conversion of John Wesley that occurred one evening at a Moravian gathering on Aldersgate Street. Wesley experienced a dramatic awakening that he famously reported in his journal: "I felt my heart strangely warmed. I felt I did trust in Christ, Christ alone for salvation: And an assurance was given me that He had taken away my sins, even mine, and saved me from the law of sin and death."[21]

Through the support they offered and the challenges they presented, the members of the Holy Club and of the Moravian communities provided Wesley with a sense of belonging, spiritual guidance, and wise

---

21. John Wesley, *The Works of John Wesley*, ed. Thomas Jackson, 3rd ed. (London: Wesleyan Methodist Book Room, 1872; Franklin, TN: Providence House, 1994), 1:105.

counsel—all of which issued in an ongoing process of vocational reflection and discernment in his life. They can usefully be understood as the "co-curriculum" that found a place in his life alongside his more academic pursuits—not only during his college days, but throughout his life's journey. Or, to use different terminology, these experiences provided the "holding environments" that made space for Wesley's spiritual growth through a community mentoring process. Because he was able to receive wise counsel and positive influences from his peers, he and other students found a relatively safe space in which to share their experiences of faith, doubt, and uncertainty about both their religious beliefs and their academic studies—and to discern and prepare for their life-long vocations.

From Wesley's experience, today's colleges and universities have much to learn. They need to provide students with the time and space to undergo this kind of listening, sharing, and discernment. They also need to allow the development of rituals, contests, and images that can support this process. And they need to provide and cultivate mentors (and communities of mentors) who can inspire students for the long haul. This last-mentioned approach, which we have explored at various points in this volume,[22] is especially ripe for development within the higher education context, and has significant potential to foster and sustain vocational reflection and discernment.

## Mentoring communities

Academic communities can take many forms: a classroom or course, a laboratory, an athletic team, a section of rooms within a residence hall, or a campus ministry group (among many others). Not only can these communities become spaces where students feel that they are truly seen as whole persons, appropriately supported, challenged, and inspired; they can also help students view their calling and vocation in terms of what people do, in a responsible and personally satisfying way, to help meet the needs of society and thus to make this a better world in which to live.[23]

---

22. See especially the description of Goshen College's program in chapter 2, as well as the references to mentoring and mentoring communities in chapters 3 and 10.

23. Howard Gardner, Mihaly Csikszentmihalyi, and William Damon, *Good Work: When Excellence and Ethics Meet* (New York: Basic Books, 2001).

These reflections echo Will Campbell's understanding of "vocation as grace."[24] He emphasizes that vocational discernment is best negotiated in the community of others. For many students, such a community can be experienced through a service club, religious life group, or a Bible study group among other places and programs. In these organizations, many students engage in a process that helps them discern their gifts, needs, weaknesses and strengths.

Moreover, these experiences underscore the importance of the spiritual value of students being there for each other—even if at some point during the process, a student's desires pull her in a different direction from that of the group. These communities become spaces where students feel truly seen as whole persons—supported, challenged, and inspired to embrace worthy aspirations. Campbell's notion of vocation as grace in a community of others is comparable to what Sharon Daloz Parks calls a "mentoring community."[25] Parks argues that mentoring communities in higher education play a pivotal role in the faith and worldview formation of young adults, by

> offering a network of belonging in which young adults feel recognized as who they really are, and as who they are becoming. It offers both challenge and support and thus offers good company for both the emerging strength and the distinctive vulnerability of the young adult.[26]

A sense of community is important for students who are evaluating their journey throughout their college careers. The relationships they develop with others—fellow students, faculty, and staff—provide the social support necessary for undergraduate life. All members of the community thus need to work together and become models in a "mentoring community." As Parks illustrates, and as John Wesley discovered, college students will not make this journey alone. Like the hero character who answers the "call to adventure" in a quest story, a student does not undertake the journey without the aid of a guide.[27]

---

24. See William D. Campbell, "Vocation as Grace," in James Y. Holloway and Will D. Campbell, eds., *Callings!* (New York: Paulist Press, 1974), 279–80.

25. Parks, *Big Questions, Worthy Dreams*, 93.

26. Parks, *Big Questions, Worthy Dreams*, 95.

27. See Brown, "Metanoia Project," 75.

Mentoring communities have been explored fairly widely in the literature on vocational reflection and discernment, including in this volume. With respect to co-curricular programs, however, it may be helpful to think about a somewhat different category: that of the *tribe*. As a way of entering into this conversation, let us begin with an ancient tale of tribal identity and mentoring.

## Mentoring and the campus as "tribe"

In the biblical account given in 1 Chronicles, a new king has been named, but the previous king is still on the throne. David, the newly anointed king, is in exile; his predecessor Saul is still on the throne, but the men in Saul's army are defecting to David. As the narrative continues, David is soon installed in Jerusalem as king. In preparation for this event, the Chronicler lists the names and divisions of the troops who have joined with David, one of which is the tribe of Issachar. The members of this tribe are identified as "those who had understanding of the times, to know what Israel ought to do" (1 Chron. 12:32).

Traditionally known as a group of religious scholars, the tribe of Issachar provides us with a conceptual framework to begin a discussion on mentoring for vocation beyond the classroom.[28] In the same way that this tribe was able to provide King David with guidance by interpreting the "signs of the times" during large-scale changes, college and university administrators and professional staff members can help to provide our students with guidance in our own time of ever-hastening change. In particular, educators who work with students outside the classroom can help them identify and interpret their own "tribal" identities, and help them better understand the rituals, contests, and images of college culture. Through this process, students can better understand their own role as part of a greater whole—an essential ingredient in vocational discernment.

If we allow ourselves a somewhat broader understanding of the biblical narrative, we can consider how administration and staff members can serve as a modern equivalent of the "tribe of Issachar." They can serve as

---

28. See Stephen W. Rankin, "Faith on Campus: How an Obscure Bible Verse Sparks Thinking about our Work with College Students," chapter 2 of Bridgette D. Young and Hendrik R. Pieterse, eds., *The Promise of United Methodist Campus Ministry: Theological Explorations* (Nashville: The General Board of Higher Education and Ministry, 2010), 31.

those who have "an understanding of the times" and work with students who are engaged in various kinds of co-curricular activities on college and university campuses. Since these activities are significantly liminal—a threshold experience for students, filled with social, emotional, and spiritual change—they offer opportunities for reflection with students concerning life situations that challenge their assumptions about God, self, world, meaning, and purpose.

Educators may be able to extend the usefulness of the metaphor of the "tribe of Issachar" as a mentoring community by re-imagining their own campuses as *tribes*.[29] The concept of *tribal identity*[30] is borrowed from the academic discipline of cultural anthropology, which defines and locates an individual within it and within the larger context of the world, nature, and even the supernatural. It can provide a helpful way to interpret the stories and cultural behaviors of students and the importance of these stories in shaping their faith. In particular, a tribal identity gives an individual a place in the world, thereby providing a framework on which he or she can depend, especially when interacting with faculty, with other students, and with the whole of the college environment. In ancient cultures, tribes defined relationships; they forged social bonds, identities, and commitments; and they provided individuals with a sense of security, continuity, and well-being. Rightly understood, they can have similar community-building effects today.

When students participate in co-curricular ritual activities[31] (tailgating before the football game, pledging a fraternity or sorority, or seeking out spaces like the chapel, an open outdoor space on campus, the student

---

29. Obviously, this terminology is not meant to replicate the painful national conversation on the divisive and controversial use of Native American tribes as mascots for collegiate and professional sports. The use of "tribe" as a descriptive metaphor here comes from cultural anthropology and from the Hebrew Bible; it should in no way be read as advocating the use of names or symbols as a harmful form of stereotyping.

30. Tribal identity is closed related to the term *participation mystique* that was coined by anthropologist Lucien Lévy-Bruhl to describe a type of relationship in which the boundaries between a person and an object (thing) are blurred. Despite many flaws in his approach, it has been influential in later anthropology. See Lucien Lévy-Bruhl, *How Natives Think* (1926; Princeton, NJ: Princeton University Press, 1985).

31. See Victor W. Turner, *The Ritual Process: Structure and Anti-Structure* (Chicago: Aldine Publishing, 1969), 95–96. Executed well, ritual can help deepen college students' faith development and vocational discernment. See David Hogue, *Remembering the Future, Imagining the Past: Story, Ritual, and the Human Brain* (Cleveland: Pilgrim Press, 2003), 122–23.

union, or a local coffee house or restaurant), they are making tribal associations by constantly trying to "fit together" with others. They are building connections that will enrich their minds, stir their imaginations, satisfy their hungers, and nourish their souls. The language of *tribe* therefore provides us with an entry point for developing a better understanding of the rituals, contests, and images that are formed and shaped through co-curricular activities.[32]

## *Rituals, contests, and images*

Since the earliest of tribal associations, human beings have constructed knowledge and meaning in powerful and often unconscious ways through image, symbol, and ritual. As cultural interpreters of the big questions of meaning and purpose that students often ask and explore, it is important for educators—including faculty, staff, and administrators—to be aware of how the "symbolic processes" and the "unconscious structuring processes" of tribal identification can aim for the good. These same cultural interpreters need to keep in mind that some ritual activities can be practiced destructively.

Students frequently encounter various compelling (but largely unexamined) images and rituals that clamor for their attention and ultimately take on the power and allure of "unknown gods." As tangible and visible objects of devotion, these unknown gods show themselves in more overt community-building ways through allegiance to ritually enacted tribal activities such as Greek life, athletics, and other co-curricular programming. These new "tribes" provides a sense of power and stability during the uncertain experiences of college. Of course, there can also be dangers in the powerfully unifying features of belonging to a particular community. For instance, while fraternities and sororities may work to comply with risk-management standards of national chapters for rush and initiation rituals, they must also be aware that they enter into hazardous territory when loyalty to a group supersedes the life-giving and constructive

---

32. According to Dave Logan and his colleagues, every organization can be understood as a set of small towns. They use the language of "tribes" to describe these structures, which form naturally; because of this, they argue, one's "tribe" can seem to be almost hardwired into one's genetic code. See Dave Logan, John King, and Halle Fischer-Wright, *Tribal Leadership: Leveraging Natural Groups to Build a Thriving Organization* (New York: HarperCollins, 2008), 3–4.

practices that would otherwise help to support the process of vocational discernment. Too much emphasis on outward signs of unity—clothing, chants, and secret handshakes—can end up stripping a student of his or her identity. News organizations regularly report on the disturbing proliferation of hazing, alcohol abuse, racism, sexual harassment, and even rape in fraternity culture. These destructive and dehumanizing behaviors promote violence, blind loyalty, and the objectification of various categories of human beings. Clearly, some rituals are powerfully destructive and must be denounced and rooted out.

Apart from such depravities, however, fraternities and sororities can offer notable benefits—both to their members and to the larger college community. This is especially true when they are able to uphold the ideals upon which they were founded: sisterhood and brotherhood, scholarship, leadership, philanthropy, and civic responsibility. Many students find that joining a fraternity or sorority provides them a home away from home and a strong foundation on which to build a new and exciting future. In addition, the fraternity and sorority community can provide students with a place to "fit" that opens many doors to leadership and to academic, athletic, service, and interpersonal opportunities.[33]

## Official rituals and makeshift rituals

The word *ritual* can conjure up images of behaviors that are followed without thinking. Rubbing a rock on an athletic field before a football game, enjoying a certain snack or drink at a regular time each day, or not walking in an area on campus until one has become a senior—all are examples of ritual traditions that occur on college and university campuses across the country. In truth, the word *ritual* has its origins in the notion of "fitting together" and suggests a space where the spiritual and physical can make common cause.

Victor Turner describes ritual as an activity in which people move from their ordinary daily life across a threshold into a state of liminality. College students are often in particular need of a symbolic or ritual life, since their own liminal state can make it difficult for them to fully grasp the structures of their lives (which are in constant motion). This is a time of

---

33. See the discussion in chapter 10, especially at note 37, on the comments of Josiah Royce—made a century ago, but still relevant today—concerning the positive benefits (and possible dangers) of fraternity and athletic culture in the undergraduate setting.

life when one's former worldview is questioned and the certainties of life dissolve; what was once understood as "normal" is now just one option among many. As we suggested in chapter 1, students can find themselves overwhelmed by the apparent range of choices that they are being offered. On the positive side, however, liminal spaces can often be important venues for vocational reflection and discernment.

Rituals abound on college campuses. One of the most common and easily recognized of these rituals occurs during commencement exercises. Before the event, faculty members don their colorful academic regalia that signify their mastery of knowledge in an academic discipline, and they process into a stadium or arena. Students wear robes, stoles, or tassels, often of varying colors, to signify their manifold allegiances and honors. Certain features of the event are carefully structured by tradition: a formal procession, the awarding of honorary degrees, a major commencement address, the reading of names, and a pronouncement that the students are now graduates. All of these elements help convey the significance of the day as a rite of passage.

According to Kathleen Manning, however, college students often create their own rituals, separate from the administratively sanctioned rituals of campus life. She argues that for most students, these are the "real" rituals of campus life, the ones that are more significant in structuring the shape of life at college.[34] Needless to say, some of these makeshift rituals can be highly destructive; all the same, the fact that students engage in them is a reminder that they are often in search of spaces where the apparent chaos of this stage of life can be tamed. In one of his online blogs, Steve Rankin, university chaplain at Southern Methodist University, expands on Manning's notion. Rankin gives an example of the social ritual of drinking. He asks:

> Why does a young man drink so hard, so heavily, to the point of alcohol poisoning? One of the reasons is glory. He wants to prove that he's man enough to handle it. If he can prove that he's man enough, he'll have the approbation (glory) of his peers. He will have shown that he can rise to the challenge, that he can take it, and that he can stand with the best of them. He'll be a man among men.

---

34. See Kathleen Manning, *Rituals, Ceremonies, and Cultural Meaning in Higher Education*, Critical Studies in Education and Culture (Westport, CT: Bergin and Garvey, 2000).

He'll have respect, status, and standing. This is the benefit that they desire.[35]

Rankin explains that the "lust for glory" in the ritualistic episodic drinking culture found on many college and university campuses is not the same as a mere desire for acceptance. He points out that this lust for glory is more about setting oneself apart and proving one's distinctiveness, even if in a negative way.

In order to address the destructive nature of some of our students' makeshift rituals, we need to present them with a different vision of their better selves—which in turn requires colleges to develop a holding environment in which honesty and transparency are key features. Rankin argues that administrators and staff members should not try to *impose* the vision for bigger questions of purpose and meaning, but rather to *impart* it so that students can *catch* it. He contends that students do not readily recognize its significance through training and information distribution. Instead, they "catch" this vision through relationships—real, organic, and intentional, though not overly structured.

According to Elaine Ramshaw, rituals—such as using the mascot to form a campus identity or plastering the image of the team logo on campus—have the unique ability to order experience and communicate some type of meaning, even if the meaning is as simple as "I will act as is expected of me in this situation."[36] This is the reaction that is expected when, for example, during new student orientation, new students are encouraged to identify themselves with a college's mascot. They might be asked, for example, "Are you ready to be a Panther?" In this case, the new identity as "Panther" is frequently reinforced, both on and off campus.

Whether it involves banners with the Panther logo or seeing "Panther Paw Prints" stamped on the street on the drive to the athletic complex, informal rituals and images like these carry the core meanings of the social group performing them and provide key insights into the meanings, symbols, and images that influence that group's worldview. By aligning themselves with the "Panther" or other mascot, students are initiated,

---

35. See Stephen W. Rankin, "Choices and Inclinations 2: Imparting a Moral Vision," Rankin File: Ruminations, Fulminations and Cogitation on the Spiritual Life, entry posted July 27, 2013, http://stephenrankin.com/choices-and-inclinations-2/ (accessed 24 December 2013).

36. See Elaine Ramshaw, *Ritual and Pastoral Care* (Philadelphia: Fortress Press, 1987), 25.

even if unconsciously, into one of their first collective identities on campus. Common ground is immediately created among a diverse group of students without any additional effort on their part.

## The good life and athletic contests

As we provide spaces for students to catch a new or renewed vision of themselves, we should try to help them find their way toward Aristotle's notion of the good life: a life of happiness, a fulfilled and fulfilling life.[37] Viewed through the lens of vocation, Aristotle's ethical approach can serve as a foundation for co-curricular programs such as athletics and residential living. In these arenas, students foster the virtues of what it means to belong to a community (team), how to be accountable to the team, what it means to be a true teammate (or friend or roommate), and how to balance individual rights with one's larger responsibilities to the community.

When considering the virtues that can be cultivated through team participation and friendship, we need to remember that both athletics and residential living address the need that students feel for belonging, for being part of something larger than themselves. In athletics, in particular, the coach is the one who has the most power to impart this vision of belonging that allows students to ask bigger questions of meaning and purpose. In many cases, a coach's influence over a student-athlete is more powerful than that of a professor in the classroom. Sharon Herzberger quoted the late Miles Brand, former president of the NCAA, in a public address to Whittier University that touched on the power of the coach. "The purpose of higher education is to take teenagers and turn them into people. There are many adults on college and university campuses that play this kind of transformational role; some of them are teachers whom we call 'coach.' "[38]

Given the influence of coaches and the power that athletics have on any college or university campus, Conrad Cherry and his colleagues

---

37. A fuller description of Aristotle's understanding of the good life, and the role of virtue for obtaining it, can be found in chapters 8 through 10 of this volume. See also chapter 7 for the significance of narrative as a category for defining and exemplifying the virtues.

38. See Sharon Herzberger, "Playing to Win: Understanding the Demands of Campus Athletics," posted October 30, 2008, http://www.whittier.edu/about/presidentpen/athletics (accessed December 24, 2013).

posit that there are times where the college or university will heavily rely on its athletic images to provide students with a distinctive identity and alumni with ongoing institutional loyalty.[39] They suggest that the images of team logo and colors supplied by intercollegiate activities can actually help to provide a sense of community. These same features also promote a narrative framework within which students can develop an understanding of particular virtues and can seek to cultivate them in their own lives.

With regard to vocational discernment with students, athletic depart-ments can serve as an "out-of-class laboratory" where student-athletes learn what it means to be a good teammate. Intercollegiate athletics are a space where students learn not only about themselves, but also about how to take responsibility for their own development through principles of leadership and team-building activities.

When they are part of a team, many athletes learn cooperation by understanding their role in the group; they also discover how they might help to create a sense of purpose for themselves and for others. The importance of being a good competitor, and of recognizing that win-ning is not always possible, are among the hallmarks of sportsmanship. Athletic contests can develop a student's sense of fair play and camara-derie among teammates when they play for the love of the game.[40] The rituals and images of value, acceptance, and belonging are important for a student-athlete who consistently puts forth her or his best. And while winning isn't everything (nor even "the only thing"!), victories and awards are a part of the process—often symbolized through the conferring of trophies and medals.

Sometimes the experiences of college athletes can reverberate across the entire campus. At LaGrange College, for example, when the men's bas-ketball and golf teams both won their conference championships, a spirit of excitement swept over the student body that rivaled the more typical end-of-year rituals. Press conferences were held after the announcements of victory; the mayor of the city presented an official statement from the city to the teams, proclaiming that it was a "great day to be a Panther."

---

39. See Conrad Cherry, Betty A. DeBerg, and Amanda Porterfield, *Religion on Campus: What Religion Really Means to Today's Undergraduates* (Chapel Hill: University of North Carolina Press, 2001).

40. Braskamp, Trautvetter, and Ward, *Putting Students First*, 145–47.

This phrase became the mantra that created a new kind of *communitas*; new relationships were forged between groups of students who had not, until that point, been in much contact with one another.

Through this experience, students caught a glimpse of something larger than themselves through taking on the tribal "Panther" identity and cheering on their classmates. The championships provided an opportunity for students to participate—even as fans on the sidelines—in what it means to set goals, work hard as a team, and succeed. Faculty reported that during these two championship runs, the attention level among their students—most of whom were not athletes—was very high, and their participation in the classroom was more energetic. Some faculty used this event as an opportunity to remind students of the college's mission ("challenging minds and inspiring souls"). They pointed out that the physical stamina of the championship teams has a parallel in the mental stamina required for success in college and beyond—including the ability to keep one's focus, to think critically, and to communicate well.

## A search for a new image

For many students, the process of vocational reflection and discernment may depend, in significant measure, on access to fitting, vital *images*. Images provide the form, and sometimes the content, that help students name and embrace their own life experiences. By employing images, we are able to name self and world and conceive the ideal, the worthy, and the good—as well as avoiding those elements that are toxic and destructive.[41] Images help us to participate in the ongoing process of creation by birthing new realities into being.

Images abound around campus—statues of mascots, pictures of donors and benefactors hanging in buildings, logos of restaurant chains and athletic teams in the student union, banners that try to capture the salient features of an institution's mission and purpose, and posters plastered on kiosks. A student's quest for meaningful purpose depends upon distinguishing between destructive images and images of truth, as well as coming to terms with both negative and positive images of one's self.

---

41. Parks, *Big Questions, Worthy Dreams*, 105.

Unfortunately, as many students discover, their identities can be negatively shaped by the constant flutter of images that bombard them; they need help constructing positive images of themselves. They can often be assisted in this process by the "tribal" associations described above; sometimes, however, these images are insufficient. For example, students may find it difficult to identify with a tribe on campus due to unresolved issues stemming from their tribe of origin. Campuses must be conscious of the effect that images have on their students; they should also work to cultivate healthy and productive campus-wide images that can have a positive effect on issues of identity and attachment, while still allowing for the particular variations that will come to shape each student's vocational journey.

## A complex time, a liminal space

The varied experiences of collegiate rituals, contests, and images invariably prompt big questions during students' liminal experiences, forcing them to question unexamined assumptions about self, God, and the world. This can create an enormous range of complications in a person's life, which helps to explain why these moments are sometimes described as "shipwreck" experiences.[42] At the same time, however, these moments can be substantial opportunities for the kinds of vocational reflection and discernment that we have attempted to describe in this book: they help us understand how the open time and liminal space of undergraduate education can underwrite an ongoing process of identity formation.

Serving as "the tribe of Issachar"—a mentoring community—educators have an enormous opportunity to help students seek out new paths in their life journey.[43] Interpreting the signs of the times will mean assisting

---

42. Sharon Parks uses the metaphor of "shipwreck" to describe those moments when young adults experience something unexpected or disappointing or when they engage questions that challenge the way they make sense of the world around them. Shipwreck can take many forms—a family crisis, loss of a relationship, sickness, betrayal, or an intellectual inquiry that poses a challenge to an assumed faith or belief. See Parks, *Big Questions, Worthy Dreams*, 27. See also the comments on such experiences as one of the disconcerting features of undergraduate life in chapter 10 of the present volume, particularly in the subsection headed "'What do I do now?': loyalty in times of crisis or change."

43. Gary Miller, "Future Directions for the College Chaplaincy," *Ailanthus: The Journal of the National Association of College and University Chaplains* (Winter 2003).

students with the work of discerning and living into their callings through vocational practices, which in turn requires attention to campus rituals, contests, and images. This important work can aid students in their "tribal" quest for direction, identity, meaning, and purpose during the college years.

# *Sound and Space*

## MAKING VOCATION AUDIBLE

*Stephen H. Webb*

STUDENTS GO TO colleges and universities not just to learn skills and broaden their horizons, but also to find their vocations—or, to use its synonym (which resonates particularly strongly with the topic of this chapter): their *callings*. As noted throughout this book, the idea of a calling in Western history is rich and complex; but many callings, as suggested by this very word, are quite simply a matter of *sound*. Sonically construed, a calling requires a speaker and a listener, and the spoken word also requires a medium, like sound waves traveling through air. Of course, callings do not necessarily take an audible form, since our vocational experiences can occur through any of our senses. Recall that the narrator of Marcel Proust's *Remembrance of Things Past* is summoned to examine his memories, and thus become a writer, when he tastes a madeleine cake. And when we come to consider how we are called, we often do so in the privacy of our own thoughts. Nevertheless, the stories that we tell about our callings often include descriptions of those who have *spoken* to us.[1] Even if this is only rarely a divine voice, it is still an audible voice when it is that of a friend, a teacher, an advisor, or someone we encounter by chance. Moreover, as much as we need peace and quiet to reflect on our callings, our internal voices share some of the properties of perceptible speech;

---

1. On this point, see especially the discussion of call stories in chapter 5 of the present volume.

indeed, scientists now think that the same system involved in processing external speech also works with internal speech.[2] Our brains are able to produce a copy of the sound of our voice, so that we can hear ourselves think in ways that mimic the dynamics of sound.

Hence, whether the call is literal or figurative, exterior or interior, human or divine, we need to acknowledge a deep connection between vocation and voice. The authors of this volume (and many other authors as well) have written about the importance of *making space* for communal belonging, *being open* to the people who know us well, and *actively attending* to the opportunities and challenges of higher education. All of these claims make some use of language that relates to the human capacities for hearing and listening; yet most of us who write about vocation have rarely paused to ask how these capacities are both shaped and limited by evolving social conditions. These conditions can make an extraordinary degree of difference in our ability even to *hear* a call—and, when we have heard it, to understand its meaning and significant in our lives.

To what degree can colleges and universities consider their own physical spaces as a location where the process of vocational discernment takes acoustical form? This question is particularly relevant in the current context, since recent developments in audio technology put sound right into the heads of students—no matter where they are on campus. Universities, like churches, depend on the idea that people need to come together to hear each other; but recent technological developments give us so much control over how we hear that our physical listening environment doesn't seem to matter. If the voices that our students hear are not connected to a specific place, does it matter where they go to school—or if they go anywhere at all? Can higher learning still play a significant role in helping students find their vocation, if the voices that they hear are always, and only, the voices that they choose to hear? Colleges teach the art of public speaking, but perhaps it is time to think about the art of public *listening* as well. The time has come to stop thinking of calling in a merely

---

2. Mark Scott, "Corollary Discharge Provides the Sensory Content of Inner Speech," *Psychological Science* 24, no. 9 (September 2013): 1824–30. For a fascinating examination of the richness of inner speech and religious practices that help believers discern what inner speech comes from God, see T. M. Luhrmann, *When God Talks Back: Understanding the American Evangelical Relationship with God* (New York: Alfred A. Knopf, 2012). I am grateful to Jeremy Hustwit for inviting me to deliver the 2014 Womack Lecture at Methodist University on the topic of "The Sound of Learning." Conversations with Jeremy, his students, and his colleagues greatly contributed to clarifying my thoughts for this essay.

metaphorical sense; we need to engage in the practice of *making vocation audible*. If our institutions of higher education are to become places where vocational exploration and discernment are truly possible, then they need to think more seriously about how their campuses sound—and whether they are places in which a calling can truly be heard.

## Schools as places of hearing

The liberal arts have deep roots in speaking and hearing—more so, even, than in reading and writing. Greco-Roman culture, Judaism, and Christianity have all contributed to the central significance of speaking and hearing in education. Indeed, in the ancient world, leadership of every kind was ordinarily dependent on the strength and quality of one's voice. That is why the Greek and Roman intellectual traditions valued rhetoric, which taught these mechanical elements as part of the art of public speaking, and understood them to be among the highest educational achievements. Voices brought people together, while writing enabled people to connect across vast distances; but writing's strength was (and is) also its weakness. The use of papyrus, and later vellum and parchment, made it possible for students to learn from their teachers even when they were alone; but this was not necessarily seen as an advantage. The written word was fixed and therefore lacked the dynamic, context-specific character of speech; it was inattentive to the particularities of the moment but instead had "a hardness as of cut stone."[3] The spoken word, on the other hand, required proximity, but rather than understanding this special demand as a burden, it was celebrated; indeed, everyday life was organized in such a way as to make the spoken word audible. Spaces needed to be constructed—even outdoor spaces, like the agora, the forum, or the amphitheater—to make sure that speakers could be heard. Hearing was an inherently communal activity.

Judaism, too, was oriented more toward the ear than the eye. It has often been pointed out that God in the Hebrew Bible is primarily heard rather than seen, but less often noticed is just how important acoustics were for the Hebrew understanding of what it means to be *chosen* or *called*. When Moses spoke, community was born. "Then Moses said to Aaron,

---

3. Catherine Pickstock, *After Writing: On the Liturgical Consummation of Philosophy* (Oxford: Blackwell Publishers, 1998), 89.

'Say to the whole congregation of the Israelites, Draw near to the Lord, for he has heard your complaining'" (Exod. 16:9). This passage emphasizes that God not only speaks, but also hears. Hence the Israelites were united to each other, and bound to God, through the sound of Moses's voice.

Christianity follows suit by identifying Jesus with God's spoken word (John 1:1). Notice, too, how his followers knew him by the authority of his voice (John 7:46). Just as Jesus called his disciples, Christians began proclaiming the Gospel to anyone who would listen; thus, as the Apostle Paul said, faith came by hearing (Rom. 10:17). The Church emerged at a time when rhetoric was the keystone of public education, and it eagerly embraced the rhetorical arts, which organized and applied the other scholarly disciplines. Augustine, who before his conversion was a professor of rhetoric at Milan, solidified the connection between learning and speaking in his great work, *On Christian Doctrine*, where he urged Christians to embrace pagan learning by putting it in service to the mission of the Church.[4]

With the collapse of the Roman Empire in the West, the Church assumed responsibility for liberal learning. Christianity promoted preaching, but before the rise of cathedral and monastic schools, many clergy were uneducated. The Church responded by publishing classical sermons in collections known as homilaries. Priests were thus encouraged to become better readers in order to be good public speakers. Historically speaking, whenever the Church has emphasized preaching, education in the liberal arts has flourished. This was the case, for example, in the emergence of universities in the High Middle Ages, which coincided with renewed interest in preaching by the Franciscan and Dominican orders. Protestants joined with the humanists in rethinking education because they put preaching at the center of the liturgy. After the Council of Trent, Roman Catholics followed the same path with a commitment to seminary training for priests. Reading in Christian education was in service to

---

4. On the importance of rhetoric in theology and church history, see, inter alia, Rebecca Chopp, *The Power to Speak: Feminism, Language, God* (New York: Crossroad, 1989); David S. Cunningham, *Faithful Persuasion: In Aid of a Rhetoric of Christian Theology* (Notre Dame, IN: University of Notre Dame Press, 1991); Serene Jones, *Calvin and the Rhetoric of Piety* (Louisville: Westminster John Knox Press, 1995); Walter Jost, *Rhetorical Thought in John Henry Newman* (Columbia: University of South Carolina Press, 1989); James L. Kinneavy, *Greek Rhetorical Origins of Christian Faith: An Inquiry* (New York: Oxford University Press, 1987); and Stephen H. Webb, *Re-figuring Theology: The Rhetoric of Karl Barth* (Albany: State University of New York Press, 1991).

speaking, since textual and linguistic studies were necessary prerequisites for expounding on biblical passages. The Puritans carried this tradition to North America, where their heirs built colleges and installed classical curricula to train preachers and teachers.[5] Catholics soon followed, eager to form students in both spiritual and academic disciplines.[6]

All of this historical background is meant as evidence for this chapter's claim that colleges are, in a way, *acoustical* constructions designed to enhance, prolong, and memorialize the spoken word. Colleges in America were often built in rural areas, away from the big cities and their noisy distractions. Excessive sound—sound pollution, ugly sound, or unwanted sound—is sound that is out of place, just as dirt is soil that is out of place.[7] What dirt is to a landscape, noise is to a soundscape. Campuses were designed as acoustical as well as scenic pockets for quiet conversation and noiseless studying. Colleges, like churches, are hearing cultures; and, like churches, colleges call their students not just to listen, but to participate in the conversations it considers sacred. That is why the goal of education is sometimes described as encouraging students to "find their voice."

Indeed, the language of "finding one's voice" might serve as a good definition of vocation as well. Vocational discernment requires listening, but it also requires incorporating what we have heard into our own lives, such as that we are able to construct an account of the paths upon which we have embarked—to tell our own stories, using our own voices.[8] We listen to teachers, preachers and actors because we want to be called to something higher than ourselves; but as we make their voices part of the constitution of our own lives, we develop a voice of our own. What others say can be recorded for later use or projected on screens for broader access; still, in order for a human voice to draw us out and open us up, physical proximity is crucial. Similarly, in order for us to employ our own voices

---

5. See the discussion of the founding of early American colleges in chapter 2.

6. For the different soundscapes in Catholic and Protestant traditions, see Stephen H. Webb, "Silence, Noise, and the Voice of Jesus Christ," in *Developing Ears to Hear: Listening in Pastoral Ministry, the Spiritual Life, and Theology*, ed. Aaron Perry (Lexington, KY: Emeth Press, 2011), Ch. 2. Some of this analysis is drawn in revised form from Stephen H. Webb, *The Divine Voice: Christian Proclamation and the Theology of Sound* (Grand Rapids, MI: Brazos Press, 2004).

7. This description is drawn from Garret Keizer, *The Unwanted Sound of Everything We Want: A Book about Noise* (New York: Perseus Books, 2010), 27.

8. See the detailed discussion of narrative in chapter 7.

and communicate with others, we need to be close enough to them that not only can they hear us, but also that they can distinguish among the various voices that they hear. Without a suitably limited space, sound can never become much more than mere noise.

## Sound and space in higher education

Precisely because sound leaves no visible physical trace in its wake, its transient nature shapes the shared space of communal living. Before the power of electricity was harnessed to transmit, amplify, and manipulate the human voice, the appropriate size of an educational community was limited by the physical properties of sound. It is relatively easy to design a space to make a speaker or singer visible; sight lines should not be blocked by any obstacles. But to make a space where voices are audible is an incredibly complex task. No surprise, then, that all forms of listening involve not only attending to the other, but also caring about the built environment where we study, work, and live.

Because sound cannot be seen, we need to be immersed in its production in order to make the most of its meaning. Simply put, we hear better and listen more carefully when we are not only close to the source of sound but also able to connect a voice with a body. Few people understand this better than teachers, preachers, and actors. The classroom, sanctuary, and stage are compelling places because they acknowledge the fact that voices travel only so far. They also depend on the hearers' capacity to understand the relationship between the voice and the body, including posture, gestures, and facial expressions. When the spaces for these interactions get too large, we are forced to rely on acoustical technologies that diminish the subtleties of the human voice and separate the hearer from the visual cues that would provide a more nuanced context for the sound.

It is all too easy for educators to think about learning in abstract ways and thus to bypass the physical realities of how education takes place. This abstract approach is encouraged by the longstanding tradition of connecting knowledge with sight—an association with Platonic roots. This perspective was especially popular during the Enlightenment, when advances in the making of glass lenses enabled philosopher-scientists to break through the assumptions of ancient cosmology. Visual metaphors for knowing, when taken seriously (even if not always literally), tend to suggest an isolated, impassive observer; after all, one can see something without being seen and correlatively, know something without being known. Thus conceived, knowers are like inspectors (to look into, from the Latin *in-specere*); they can carry out an examination without revealing anything about themselves.

Clarity of thought occurs as an illumination of the mind, but the vocal word originates inside the body of the speaker. It travels on waves that agitate the air until it enters the body of the hearer in an unbelievably precarious process. Sound waves literally strike the eardrum, which sends the resulting vibrations through a passageway occupied by the body's smallest bones. They transfer their motion to the fluids in the labyrinthine canals of the cochlea. This hydraulic energy brushes against thousands of hair cells that respond by sending chemical signals along neural pathways to the brain. And only then does the brain begin to interpret what the sound means! All of this suggests that hearing is more *physical* and *relational* than is the case for seeing. Voices bring human beings together in ways that make our physical presence to each other important, even when we use technology to overcome the distance that would otherwise so starkly limit all oral/aural communication.

Exploring the auditory dimension of learning gives us an opportunity to bring together our specialized pursuits of knowledge with our desire to help students find their vocation. Reflection on hearing and its relation to seeing reminds us that learning is a local, relational, and vulnerable activity. We process information so quickly with our eyes, but hearing takes time; moreover, in our visually stimulated culture, listening increasingly requires patience and discipline. And because sound waves dissipate so quickly, hearing also requires careful attention to space.

## *The severing of sound from space*

For better and worse, the laborious and highly social process of listening has been abbreviated and individualized by technology that permits people to inhabit their own personalized sound cocoons.[9] The history of any social

---

9. Two books that were ahead of their time and are still important are David Seamon, *A Geography of the Lifeworld: Movement, Rest, and Encounter* (New York: Palgrave Macmillan, 1979) and Joshua Meyrowitz, *No Sense of Place: The Impact of Electronic Media on Social Behavior* (New York: Oxford University Press, 1985). See also Lori Kendall, *Hanging Out at the Virtual Pub: Masculinities and Relationships Online* (Berkeley: University of California Press, 2002); Robert Glenn Howard, *Digital Jesus: The Making of a New Christian Fundamentalist Community on the Internet* (New York: New York University Press, 2011); Paul Dourish and Genevieve Bell, *Divining a Digital Future: Mess and Mythology in Ubiquitous Computing*

transformation often has a beginning that impresses itself upon all subsequent developments, and that was true in this case. The story of how sound and space fell apart begins in 1979, when Sony marketed the Walkman as the world's first wearable stereo. With no external speaker, it was designed to create a totally individual listening environment—although, as evidence that the designers had not yet grasped the revolution they were initiating, the first model came with a second earphone jack so that two people could listen to it at once. That model also had a "talk" button that, when pressed, lowered the volume so that users could have a conversation without removing their headphones; needless to say, that button was soon discontinued, since the success of the Walkman was its ability to insulate its user from all other sonic input. For the first time in history, people who otherwise had no hearing problems could participate in the world—walk, shop, run—without being a part of its acoustical properties. Social scientists call this phenomenon the "Walkman Effect."[10] It could also be considered a voluntary form of deafness, since headphones eliminate ambient feedback from the body's movement through space. People could now exercise complete control over how they experience their sonic connection to a particular place. They still have to look where they are going, but they are no longer subject to environmental "noise."

This means, however, that we can easily lose touch with the world around us. Ears, because they are lidless, cannot close like eyes; loud or intrusive sounds, unlike unpleasant sights, cannot be avoided by simply turning one's head. Any environment, but especially an urban one, is noisy, if noise is defined as sounds that are not intended to convey useful information. Because we are not protected from noise, we have to be constantly on the alert to distinguish between sonic 'junk' and the signals we need to try to understand. By surrounding ourselves with our own soundtrack, we effectively silence our interaction with our environment's soundscape. We are located somewhere, but we could be anywhere. We

---

(Cambridge, MA: MIT Press, 2011); Brett T. Robinson, *Appletopia: Media Technology and the Religious Imagination of Steve Jobs* (Waco, TX: Baylor University Press, 2013); and Jonathan Sterne, *MP3: The Meaning of a Format* (Durham, NC: Duke University Press, 2012).

10. For excellent social scientific approaches, see Shing-Ling S. Chen, "Electronic Narcissism: College Students' Experience of Walkman Listening," in *Qualitative Sociology* 21, no. 3 (1998): 255–76 and Michael Bull, "The Seduction of Sound in Consumer Culture: Investigating Walkman Desires," *Journal of Consumer Culture* 2, no. 1 (March 2002): 81–101.

thus avoid all the ways in which our environment can interrupt us, but we also miss out on all of the serendipitous ways that our environment signals its presence to us. We miss, that is, voices that can call us out of ourselves and into future possibilities we cannot imagine on our own.

Because it is uncontrollable, noise keeps us grounded. Even our visual input is changed when it is silenced by earphones. In "auditized looking," our eyes are not drawn to the sounds that are all around us; moreover, when we do look at something, we gaze as one unaffected by what we see. Sound is a serendipitous element, and living with the unpredictable gives the social world much of its excitement and meaning. Sound cocoons eliminate not only unpredictable and chance encounters, but also opportunities for others to reach out to us in friendly ways. To those who happen to be near the person who is listening with headphones, that person does not really seem to be there. Yet he or she is there, even if the social rules of reciprocity no longer apply. The Walkman and its many successor devices create an acoustical bubble that nobody else can pop.

After the Walkman, it was only a short step to enable individuals to control not only their environments but their music as well. Soundtracks could be mixed at will, so that everyone could be his or her own DJ. The Walkman disconnected songs from space, but MP3 players dematerialized sound altogether. Think about how records had to be cared for by protecting them from dust, coffee spills, and the sun. The grooves on the vinyl had the physical appearance of the information they conveyed, and they could be easily scratched or even destroyed. They were objects meant to be handled, and they were also enclosed in covers that appealed to the eye. The digital format changed all of that. While previous generations were defined by what music they loved, recent generations have been defined by how they listen to music. Audiophiles in the sixties and seventies were committed to acoustical fidelity; they wanted stereo speakers that reproduced as closely as possible the experience of a "live" concert. Today, digital compression alters and, in the minds of many audiophiles, diminishes the quality of music by limiting its dynamic range; but young people seem to be more interested in the convenience of having control over their listening environments than in the authenticity of the music's reproduction.

Music that has no physical form can be manufactured and consumed on demand, which heightens the way popular taste chases after the contemporary and the new. Albums and records were just that: audio documents that functioned like scrapbooks in preserving the history and literary creativity of musical groups. The digital format abstracts music from its traditional role of expressing a shared passage through time. Indeed, the whole notion of a "generation" has diminished in sociological importance as the musical industry became global and musical cultures extremely local. People increasingly identify their friends as those with whom they share *their* music—rather than those in whose presence they want to be, as they listen to the music they share. Increasingly sophisticated websites help customers build on what they already hear, rather than help them learn to enjoy new sounds. Overuse of these technologies runs the risk of producing what critics have called "electronic narcissism"; social connections increasingly take place in a virtual space that is interior to each individual.

How do these trends impact education and vocation? All teachers have experienced the disruptive consequences of multi-listening (the auditory equivalent of multitasking) practices. Students can surf sound waves of their own choosing while pretending to be engaged with classroom activities. As a result, microprocessing technology can turn the average classroom of sleepy, mute students into a beach party with separate bands playing in everyone's heads. The problem, however, goes much deeper than this. When people carry their sound with them, they do not need to go to specific places to be able to hear what others have to say. When anything can be heard at any time, we lose the way that voices summon us to explore common themes in a common setting. The human voice, freed (or severed, depending how one chooses to look at it) from bodies, carries less weight than it once did, which makes listening to teachers a less formative learning experience. Rather than calling us out of ourselves, voices disconnected from particular spaces merely echo what we think we already know. Sound, when dematerialized, traps us in the immaterial space of our minds.

The separation of sound and place is thus an important rubric for examining worries about the future of face-to-face education. If distance no longer poses a limit to sound's dissemination—remember when people used to worry about the charges for *long distance* phone calls?— then why would students need to come to a residential campus to learn? Experts already are debating the future of television networks, since they rely on the notion that certain programs must be watched at certain times. Educators should be equally worried about the future of classrooms that are similarly constrained. Why go to college if everything you want to hear comes calling right in your ears?

These reflections have profound implications for vocational exploration and discernment. As it becomes easier for students to make their own decisions concerning which voices they will listen to and which voices they will tune out, they are less likely to hear a calling that comes from outside their ordinary range of experiences. Students are increasingly able to control and reduce the number of encounters that they have with anyone other than those whom they choose to encounter. As a result, vocation seems likely to be reduced to a mere matter of choice (with all the associated problems of that tendency, as described in chapter 1 of this book). If the idea of a calling depends to some extent on a caller (see chapter 6), doesn't this caller need some degree of access to our ears? If we can always tune out the caller by plugging into our favorite tunes, will we ever hear the call?

## *Trying to hear what the future will sound like*

This is not to say that students need to be totally unplugged before colleges can draw them out into a world of new ideas and challenging perspectives—or prepare them to hear their callings. Indeed, it is important not to exaggerate the negative consequences of the Walkman and its progeny, especially since it has become so pervasive that most people no longer respond to it with negative feelings; indeed, users often report increases in confidence and calmness. Teenagers can be sonic islands, but the world is also quieter—and public places less contested—without boomboxes. At airports and in prisons, where the visual field is limited and the place one inhabits is imposed and enforced, MP3 players can deliver something close to liberation. As these examples show, technology is not the problem; human nature is. Thoughtful hearing is hard work, and its difficulties are compounded if we are trying to hear something as complex and nuanced as the call to a particular way of life. Indeed, the problem with listening has been the same throughout human history: how to listen intentionally, with focus and discernment, to voices that surprise, inspire, and challenge. What technology has severed, it can also repair—if we think creatively enough about the social conditions that make vocational discernment possible.

Technology can sever sound from space, but it can also alter space to make room for the delicate dispersion of sound. Amplifying voices, for example, is as old as the megaphone; even the masks actors wore in ancient Greek tragedies had important acoustical functions. There is nothing inherently wrong, then, with efforts to reconfigure the classroom to expand its acoustical range. The phrase "long-distance learning" is treated with derision by many educators, but in some respects, it is a misnomer, since teachers have always worked to close the gap between spoken words and far-off ears. What is truly new is that advances in audio technology can function to bring the voice of the teacher directly into the student's brain, almost bypassing sound waves altogether. Technological progress might eventually "solve" the problem of the acoustical design of open spaces by making space itself irrelevant to learning; if so, "long-distance learning" will be better described as "no-distance learning." In any case, education seems to be heading in a direction where it will increasingly occur "in the ear" rather than in a classroom. Though many studies show that distance learning on its own cannot compete in quality with "real space" instruction, hybrid or blended courses are another matter and surely will become more common in the not-so-distant future. No teachers want their students to learn only in the classroom, and integrating audio technology into their courses can be one way of expanding the space of teaching—even if it means making that space as mobile as the student herself. What would it mean to make use of technology such that students are "assigned" to hear things outside the classroom, and to make sure that some of the things that they hear are related to questions of calling and vocation?

We cannot predict future developments in technology, except to say that the changes seem to be coming faster than ever before. Educators need to be imaginative to an array of possibilities rather than resistant to trends that many think are inevitable. Churches and universities are lagging far behind other sectors, like entertainment and business, in experimenting with audio advances. Such resistance can be positive, of course, when it seeks to preserve that significance of the spoken word. Nonetheless, there are new opportunities to think about how technology can expand the space of vocation and how instruction can reach these multiple niches.

Those who are severely hard of hearing are completely dependent on auditory technology. They are particularly aware of the need to improve the acoustical environments; they should serve as reminders to everyone else that we still need better accommodations on campus for teachers, students, staff and others who are hearing challenged. Hearing aids are not like glasses. They penetrate the body with incredibly complex technology in ways that make a person aware of the need for a battery-powered machine to facilitate even one's most personal and private connections with others. And hearing aids do not correct deficiencies in the ear like glasses correct the weakness of the eye; they simply amplify sound. But sound is more fragile than light, and its amplification can just as easily make hearing harder rather than easier. When students walk around with their ear buds, they might be damaging their hearing; but they are also engaging in fulfilling a basic human need, and it is one that those who are hard of hearing immediately recognize: they, too, long to be where the sound is.

Those who depend on hearing aids never feel close enough to speakers to understand everything they say. Nearly every single act of communication is fraught with an increased possibility of misunderstanding. The hard of hearing cannot take acoustics for granted, which can put them in a position to have something important to say about how campuses structure vocal exchanges. Colleges work hard to beautify their landscapes, but they only rarely take the same kind of responsibility for their soundscapes. How can sound and space be reconfigured in ways that help our students not only to listen better, but also to reflect more carefully on what they will need to be able to hear, in order to find their callings?

## *Toward a sonic audit*

Sensitivity to sound can open up new ways of thinking about how colleges create environments for students to both find and practice their callings. This will require new ways of thinking about how students learn. So much of what students hear from us is, to them, merely noise. We have to give them words worth listening to, but we also have to learn from them how they best like to hear.

Colleges are usually very effective in using their landscapes and architecture to convey the significance and history of their sacred ambitions. When alumni return or high school students visit, campus representatives show them the sights that give their school its identity. The soundscape of a school, however, is often neglected or ignored altogether. If students "hear" their way into learning (and, even more, into the process of vocational reflection and discernment), and if colleges want them to seek their callings and find their voices while at school, then a "sonic audit" would be a good place to begin considering ways to reconnect sound and space.

A sonic audit might begin by constructing a map of the various sound zones on campus with the goal of reconsidering how technology has altered the relationship between sound and space. Consider, for example, libraries, chapels, stadiums, auditoriums, and open space. Libraries were once oases of silence in the midst of campus chatter and noise. Most libraries are adapting to the fact that students can find silence on their own by listening to music or wearing noise reduction headphones. If libraries need not be silent, what are their auditory possibilities?[11]

Many colleges, even those that are not (or are no longer) church-related, often have a chapel where important addresses take place, and these chapels often have a bell tower. In the medieval era, church bells defined the boundaries of village identity. If you could not hear the village bell, you were not a part of the village life. A bell (or other kinds prerecorded music broadcast from a bell tower) that can be heard from any spot on campus has the same unifying purpose. Bells summon the community to gather for important announcements, speeches, and other auditory events.[12]

One of the presidents of Wabash College, where I taught for twenty-five years, was fond of saying that the institution should never get so large that all of the students cannot fit in the largest space on campus, which in that instance was the chapel (and he meant "comfortably" fit). Do colleges still need spaces like that? Probably so, but such restrictions are not practical for many educational institutions. Thus, it is important to think about the many ways today that students can participate in all-campus addresses. Campuses that have outgrown their chapels can still have auditory centers, but their physical configuration will have to be reconceived. Auditory technologies can create new "chapels in space" where speakers and listeners can be connected beyond the reach of enclosed architecture. Walls need not limit the human voice.

Stadiums are usually the loudest sound zone on any campus. Many people take delight in testing their lungs to see how much noise they can make for their team. Sports and noise go together, but especially when

---

11. Libraries are a principal site for vigorous discussions about sound and learning in the modern academy. See, for example, Kathryn Zickuhr, "Should Libraries Shush?" Pew Internet and American Life Project, February 6, 2013, http://libraries.pewinternet.org/2013/02/06/should-libraries-shush (accessed July 14, 2014).

12. Bells can also be the source of intense discussion about the rights of communities to regulate public sound. See Isaac Weiner, *Religion Out Loud: Religious Sound, Public Space, and American Pluralism* (New York: New York University Press, 2014).

alcohol enters into the mix, noise can get out of hand. Colleges have always confronted very practical problems with noise: complaints about roommates, debates about regulations and penalties, and anger from campus neighbors over noisy parties. Rules need to be put in the context of a wider campus conversation about sound. Without asking what sound is for—including, of course, the role of listening in education—regulations will amount to nothing more than entangling bureaucratic procedures and political compromises among the various constituencies. Rules about loud noises are important, but so are ritualized acts of transgression that permit people to channel their energy and anxiety into harmless but energizing blasts of sound. Even in the era of ear buds, some students are used to music played loudly; and although this can have damaging consequences for their ears, the cranked-up decibels do not have to be deafening. Campuses that do not accommodate the zeal for noise in a variety of forms do a disservice to students and set themselves up for constant conflicts. For college students, loudness can be as important as silence; could the occasional loudness of a campus be a vehicle through which some students might hear a calling?

Auditoriums, of course, are constructed for performances, but theater and music departments are also in privileged positions to explore how actors and musicians can be heard in unconventional ways. Sound can be subjected to the standards of artistic design just like space, and the performing arts can lead the way. Public art does not have to be three-dimensional. Put students in a theater class in charge of making a campus come acoustically alive and who knows what will happen. Pair them with students from courses in religion or literature or history who have been studying the language of vocation, and let them try their hands at making vocation audible.

Even open spaces like pedestrian malls or greenways need to be appreciated for their acoustical features. By being expansive and wide open to the sky, malls let people laugh and shout without disturbing others. A counterpart to the mall is the wooded areas that many campuses have. These park-like areas invite playful behavior but they can also encourage meditative walks where people can listen to the sounds of nature. Woods near campuses are not wilderness, of course; they are managed, and this can be done in ways that enhance the natural noises and provide places for rest and quiet. Are there callings that are more likely to be heard, and responded to, if they are heard—really, actually, physically *heard*—in such settings?

The list could go on. Not only are there places like cafeterias that are obviously designed for conversation, but what about areas that appear on the surface to be beyond sonic exploration? Most people know what a science laboratory looks like, but how many faculty and students outside the natural sciences have any idea what a lab *sounds* like? We need to pay more attention to the auditory qualities of the spaces within which our students are exploring and discerning their vocations. We have no real justification for relying only a purely figurative interpretation of the language of "hearing one's calling."

## *Sound experiments*

After conducting a sonic audit, a college could begin experimenting with ways to reconnect sound and space. One obvious way to "clear the air" about sound is to set aside time for a sound-fast, which would be similar to fasting from food, or from "screen time." All religions promote ascetic practices that teach believers the importance of restricting their ordinary interactions with the world. These practices are meant to make people mindful of how distractions eat away at their time, and the possibilities for distractions on today's campuses are endless. Faculty, staff, coaches, and administrators are not only very busy people, but sometimes it seems as if they are busy plotting various ways to keep students even busier than they already are! Moreover, every new device that promises to improve our connectedness to the world ends up distracting us from each other and from our common tasks. Colleges can put sound on the campus agenda by treating unwanted noise as a problem for the physical and spiritual well-being of students. A constant bombardment of noise can be a form of torture, as any military knows. Just as colleges promote good dietary choices by educating students about their eating options, colleges can promote "good hearing" by asking students to be thoughtful about how they listen.

A sound-fast does not mean asking students to be heroic in the face of silence; indeed, we should remember that silence can be destructive as well as creative. Too much silence for some people is an indication or cause of social isolation and emotional depression. Indeed, absolute silence is a physical impossibility; for some, it may be a theological problem as well.[13]

---

13. Consider, for example, the Christian doctrine of the eternity of the Word of God.

Still, some degree of relative silence is a fundamentally important entry into self-reflection and personal growth.[14] Because silence can be experienced in threatening ways, a sound-fast obviously needs preparation and contextualization. Communicative sounds are meant to be shared, but so are intentional practices of silence. Silence is not the "default mode" of sound; it too must have its own constructed space and thus should be shared in creative ways. Moreover, before students are asked to unplug their ears, the value of music needs to be directly addressed. The point of a sound-fast is not to prevent students from listening to what they enjoy, like Odysseus plugging the ears of his sailors so that they would not be seduced by the songs of the Sirens. The point is to encourage students to listen to the world around them in new ways.

A sound-fast can create a communal experience of new hearing opportunities by clearing away the background noise that clutters the local soundscape. To give up audio technology is to invite conversations that might not otherwise occur. Students could be encouraged to keep "sound journals" where they reflect on their personal listening journeys and how their campuses shape what they hear. In silence we learn to listen to our own hearts, so that we can do a better job of speaking to each other. In prayerful silence we also learn to listen for the promptings, invitations, and perhaps even the voice of God. Absolute silence may be a fearsome thing, but shared silence is not. Educators have much to learn from monastic practices that promote peace and quiet without treating silence as an end in itself. In many monastic traditions, for example, monks eat without speaking, but they do not eat in total silence, since they take turns reading out loud so that souls will be nourished as well as bodies.

There are other ways to test the limits and possibilities of sound in education. Can students really learn as much from their ear buds as from a personal encounter with an embodied voice? Perhaps not, but why not let them try? Why not let students listen to lectures while taking a walk? It is often the case that one has to experience something in order to learn its limits. Better yet, why not have prerecorded lectures with specific campus places in mind? What would a lecture on Romantic poetry sound like if

---

14. See George Michelsen Foy, *Zero Decibels: My Quest for Absolute Silence* (New York: Scribner, 2010). Also see the excellent blog entry, "Silence on a College Campus," by Albert S. Rossi, who teaches pastoral theology at Saint Vladimir's Seminary, posted March 15, 2012, http://ocawonder.com/2012/03/15/silence-on-a-college-campus/ (accessed June 10, 2013).

it were heard by someone taking a walk in the woods? Colleges can give incentives for courses to become hybrids of sonic dissemination, so that classes offer some kind of out-of-the-classroom sonic experience. After all, students do some of their best thinking (and talking) late at night, when most professors are soundly asleep. How can we synchronize those schedules? Do we need to limit our voices solely to the classroom, or could we use the classroom as the *primary* site of speech but also branch out from there? More classes could require students to utilize the methods of oral history in order to treat voices as seriously as texts. All of this might strike some teachers as a case of "if you can't beat them, join them," but it is also a matter of extending the reach of the professorial voice. The first rule of rhetoric is to meet one's audience where it is, and our students are all ears.

Another experiment would set aside a portion of a day so that everyone could listen to the same piece of music all over campus. Colleges use shared space to shape learning, but what about shared sound? Do campuses have a place where students can sing together, outside of formal musical organizations? Singing together is one of the most powerful ways to create community, but in an age when musical choices are so diverse and individual, commonly known songs are increasingly rare.[15] Colleges have musical groups of all kinds, of course, but more could be done to promote shared song in public places. College radio stations, for example, could take the lead in shaping student listening habits and making listening an aspect of community again. Many campuses have days when large numbers of students read the same book or attend the same lecture; why not have days when everyone hears the same piece of music? What might it be like, for example, for the whole campus to listen simultaneously to a particular singer, perhaps one who spans the generations, and to think about what the music means, as well as what kind of community that experience created?[16] Teachers can be intimidated by their students' knowledge of music, but that just means there is a great deal that they

---

15. See T. David Gordon, *Why Johnny Can't Sing Hymns: How Pop Culture Rewrote the Hymnal* (Phillipsburg, NJ: P & R Publishing, 2010).

16. Bob Dylan would be an obvious choice. For further reflections on his relevance, see Stephen H. Webb, *Dylan Redeemed: From Highway 61 to Saved* (New York: Continuum, 2006); Stephen H. Webb, "The Sound of One Voice Writing inside Your Head," in "Montague Street," ed. Nina Goss, special issue, *Montague Street: The Art of Bob Dylan* 1, no. 1 (Winter 2009): 18–23; and Stephen H. Webb, "Twenty Musings on Bob Dylan and the Future of Sound," *Dylan at Play*, ed. Nick Smart and Nina Goss (Newcastle upon Tyne: Cambridge Scholars Publishing, 2011), 111–18.

can learn. Educators need to find ways to share music with students more often—inside and outside of the classroom—in order to interact with what are, for many young people, their most passionate auditory experiences.

Perhaps most importantly, colleges need to find ways to let their campuses speak, if only because that is how students are used to experiencing any particular place. While being intentional about sound might seem like yet one more way for administrators to enhance their control over campus environments, the fact of the matter is that such regulations are already taking place. Go to any online guide to colleges and universities and you will find discussions of the management of noise related to dorm life, town–gown relations, and extracurricular activities. Significantly, personal listening devices are making campuses less noisy, since it used to be the case that every dorm room was its own concert hall. Still, the mere existence of devices that limit their listeners to one or two persons is hardly a solution to the problem of sound and place. The public square is quieter, but personal experience is still constricted by immersive audio technologies; this has dramatically reduced the range of shared acoustical spaces, whether loud, quiet, or silent.

There are many ways that colleges can give their campuses a voice. Campus soundscapes can become as attractive and creative as their landscapes. Picture, for example, listening stations, like works of art, positioned at various significant places. These stations can tell the story of the college, but they can also be works of art that demonstrate the beauty of sound for its own sake. Sonic sculptures can function as audio-hotspots by giving students a private experience that they can nonetheless share and discuss. Sound can also be a medium of publicity and promotion. Although every college has a symbol that it reproduces in its promotional materials, and is very eager to show photos of what it looks like, does any college send out a digital compression of what it *sounds* like?

Colleges can tell stories with sound in ways that invite interaction and reflection. Janet Cardiff is an auditory artist who is known for works that create narrative links in particular places through the use of portable audio players.[17] She has made these audio walks in cities and museums around the world. Her tapes bring out hidden dimensions of places by requiring the listener to slow down and see things in a new way. Her art

---

17. See the discussion in Seth Kim-Cohen, *In the Blink of an Ear: Toward a Non-Cochlear Sonic Art* (New York: Continuum, 2009), 222–29.

puts into play the lesson that hearing often takes shape as a physical act of following, since nearness is a crucial ingredient in understanding what someone says. She makes use of the distancing effect of the Walkman and its kind, turning it against itself.

The invisibility of sound allows it to be associated quite readily with spirituality; however, just as the spiritual always needs to be grounded in the material, sound needs to be connected to bodies and places. Hearing the voices of others is an essential ingredient in finding one's own voice and hearing one's calling. By making vocation audible, colleges can invite students to reconfigure their relationship to popular culture and the world at large. A campus can take the shape of a call-and-response, thereby illustrating how higher education is itself a certain kind of acoustical space. If colleges and universities choose to do so, they can become places where students can practice patient listening, genuinely hear their callings, and develop their own unique voices so that others may hear as well.

## 13

# Self, World, and the Space Between

### COMMUNITY ENGAGEMENT AS
### VOCATIONAL DISCERNMENT

*Darby Kathleen Ray*

IF VOCATION IS, in Frederick Buechner's iconic definition, "the place where your deep gladness and the world's deep hunger meet,"[1] then the task of discerning one's vocation is no simple matter. To find that place to which Buechner here refers, we need to attend to two important aspects of our work—a point made in the Introduction to this book and sustained throughout its chapters. To give these two aspects a slightly different nuance, we might call the first of these "self-work": efforts to discover and cultivate one's authentic self, as well as everything that brings it alive. The second, equally important aspect, we can name "world-work": efforts to understand and transform the systems of thought and practice that contest and undermine the world's goodness and integrity. Vocation's wager is that these two labors are rightly conjoined—self and world are constituted by one another and are only and always in relationship. The world's deep hunger can be met by gifts gladly offered, and the self is rightly formed in this crucible.

The promise of such symbiosis is compelling. Even so, we might press Buechner's insight toward an even more thoroughgoing reciprocity; it is not only the world, the "other," that is deeply needful, but the self as well. And perhaps more often than we like to admit, it is the apparently needy "other" who becomes the giver in this relationship, offering us healing

---

1. Buechner, *Wishful Thinking*, 95 (see Introduction, note 7 *supra*).

balm, meeting us where we are, contesting our misdirected desires and inflated or diminished selves, and drawing us into life-giving relationship.

This reciprocally edifying intersection of self and world, self and other, can be cultivated by practices of civic or community engagement. As a vocational discernment practice, civic engagement invites self-work, world-work, and their mutually transformative meeting. This essay offers a thick description of this tripartite dynamic and considers the potential of civic engagement to expand and deepen vocational exploration and discernment practices by bringing the world—the vulnerable and gifted other—into full view as a necessary and vital dimension of vocation.

## *From service to engagement*

Over the last several decades, community service has become a hallmark of undergraduate education. One finds it featured to one degree or another in institutional mission statements and strategic plans; in recruitment and public-relations materials; in athletic, residential, and student life programming; and, increasingly, in the academic program. In the last of these, it may play a minor role—for example, as one assignment in a single course—or may serve as a unifying commitment or methodology for an entire department, division, or institution. Many colleges and universities have established offices, centers, or institutes charged with administering broad-ranging programs of campus–community partnership.[2] Others have certificate programs, general education requirements, or majors and minors designed to nurture and build capacity for civic knowledge and action.[3] A growing number of institutions recognize publicly engaged teaching and research as assets within faculty hiring and review processes.[4] Multi-institutional networks and consortia such as

---

2. For recent work on centers, see Carole A. Beere, James C. Votruba, and Gail W. Wells, *Becoming an Engaged Campus: A Practical Guide for Institutionalizing Public Engagement* (San Francisco: Jossey-Bass, 2011) and Ariane Hoy and Mathew Johnson, eds., *Deepening Community Engagement in Higher Education* (New York: Palgrave Macmillan, 2013).

3. According to the Center for Engaged Democracy at Merrimack College, there are over fifty such academic programs scattered across higher education. See Dan Butin, *The Engaged Campus: Majors, Minors and Certificates as the New Community Engagement* (New York: Palgrave Macmillan, 2012).

4. While many institutions recognize such work as "service" and as "teaching," far fewer have policies that reward publicly engaged research as "scholarship." Over twenty years ago, former U.S. Commissioner of Education Ernest Boyer, writing in *Scholarship*

Campus Compact, Imagining America, and Project Pericles host conferences, peer-reviewed journals, and other professional development and collaborative research opportunities focused on public engagement.[5] At the national level, the Carnegie Foundation for the Advancement of Teaching—the education and policy research center that, among other things, has developed the classification system for U.S. institutions of higher learning—established its only elective classification in 2005: the Carnegie Classification for Community Engagement.[6] More recently, in 2012, the U.S. Department of Education and the Association of American Colleges and Universities joined forces to issue *A Crucible Moment*—a call to action to make civic learning and democratic engagement part of every student's college education.[7]

What, exactly, are these and other such efforts attempting to institutionalize, and toward what end? While there is a clear family resemblance among them—what we might describe as an outward focus or an externally directed beneficence—there are nevertheless important distinctions at work. One way to illuminate these distinctions is to consider an important semantic shift that has been underway in higher education in recent years. It is a shift from the language of community "service" toward the language of community "engagement." While these terms are sometimes used interchangeably and should not be set in rigid opposition to one another, they can nevertheless signal fundamentally different philosophies of identity and relationship. Attending to this semantic shift can

*Reconsidered* (see chap. 2, note 49 *supra*), called for the inclusion of the "scholarship of engagement" in definitions of scholarship. Since then, many colleges and universities have reconsidered faculty reward structures and rewritten tenure and/or promotion policies to recognize publicly engaged faculty work as scholarship. Leaders include Portland State University, the University of Washington School of Public Health and Community Medicine, Community-Campus Partnerships for Health, and Tulane University.

5. For more on the programs of these consortia, see www.compact.org, www.imaginingamerica.org, and www.projectpericles.org (all accessed October 8, 2014).

6. As of 2014, 311 institutions were listed in this classification.

7. The full text of *A Crucible Moment*, along with related materials, is available at https://www.aacu.org/crucible (accessed October 8, 2014). In the introduction to the report we learn that "*A Crucible Moment* was prepared at the invitation of the U.S. Department of Education under the leadership of the Global Perspective Institute, Inc. (GPI) and the Association of American Colleges and Universities. The publication was developed with input from a series of national roundtables involving leaders from all parts of the higher education and civic renewal communities." We are also told that "the report pushes back against a prevailing national dialogue that limits the mission of higher education to workforce preparation and training while marginalizing disciplines basic to democracy."

shed light on important conceptual and practical changes underway on many campuses and in many communities today—changes with notable implications for how students understand themselves and their current and future work.

Within the higher education context, community-*service* programs predated *engagement* programs. They were typically housed in campus ministry or chaplain's offices and were motivated in large part by a desire to enact theologically rooted practices such as showing compassion for the suffering or oppressed, or concern for "the least, the lost, and the last."[8] Campuses without religious affiliations or identities embraced similar commitments and programs, though with humanistic rather than theological justification. Such community-service programs continue to have a vital presence on many campuses and are major forces for student moral and vocational formation and for community impact. Within these programmatic contexts, college or university members are typically encouraged to participate in acts of service out of a sense of social responsibility or moral obligation, with the plight of the needy or the realities of suffering and injustice functioning as the primary motivating factor. Importantly, the ultimate goal of such action is the service itself—the offering of assistance and care to one (or to a world) in need. It is the gift of service that matters or should matter, not the recipient's response (e.g., gratitude, satisfaction, or indifference) to the service. The primary point of the service is not to accomplish this or that, nor to get something in return, but simply to serve—to respond with compassion to one in need. Thus, the flow of intention and labor moves from the volunteer to the one(s) being served. It is, ideally, a one-way flow. The volunteer may, and often does, get some benefit from the service experience, but that benefit is not a priority; it is not sought after and is, in fact, typically downplayed. The point of service is to serve, not to receive.

Religious and quasi-religious narratives, warrants, and concepts are frequently embedded in this community-service model of the campus–community relationship, functioning as motivating or explanatory factors for such work. For example, one might be motivated to serve others by a sense of moral obligation rooted in the awareness that "there but for the grace of God go I" or "from those to whom much has been given,

---

8. This phrase is a favorite among United Methodists. See, for example, www.umc.org/news-and-media/finding-god-in-unexpected-places and www.umc.org/news-and-media/what-can-ethnic-caucuses-teach-the-church (both accessed October 8, 2014).

much is to be expected."[9] As a model for service, Buddhists may hearken to the *bodhisattva* ideal[10]—the one who sacrifices or delays his or her own enlightenment in order to help others toward enlightenment. Many Jews take inspiration from stories of God's activist compassion for the suffering and marginalized. For Muslims, *zakat* or charitable giving is one of the five pillars of the faith;[11] and for Christians, *agape* or self-emptying love is often understood to be the essence or primary modality of God and Jesus. For Martin Luther, William Perkins, and other pioneers of the modern concept of vocation, service to one's neighbor was a necessary ingredient of one's calling, and that service was to be rendered freely and without expectation of reward or recognition.[12] A vocation, according to this tradition, is work in response to God's call to serve others; our work is a vocation if, and only if, we use it to serve our neighbor. In this tradition, service is not a reciprocal or two-way affair; it is, rather, a freely offered and unilateral gift to one in need—a gift that mirrors God's self-gift in creation and in the person and work of Jesus the Christ.

This language of service, with its rich theological provenance, has been a powerful motivator of individual and communal acts and traditions of charity and social justice, and it continues to function as such for many people and institutions today. With the development of the field of "service learning," however, the purpose and aim of service underwent a marked redefinition. In service learning, service is undertaken not only to respond compassionately to the needs of another but also to enhance student learning and develop students' civic awareness and capacities. With this development, service becomes a "win-win" proposition—good for both the recipient *and* the bestower of service. In addition to addressing a real need in the off-campus community, service-learning projects have clear learning goals for students that connect to course content. In order to insure the student's potential gain from this process, service is often prescribed rather than purely voluntary; its completion (or lack thereof) is typically reflected in the student's grade. Many schools make

---

9. The first aphorism is of unknown origin but is often attributed to English reformer John Bradford. The second is attributed to Jesus (Luke 12:48).

10. See, for example, *The Oxford Dictionary of World Religions*, ed. John Bowker (Oxford: Oxford University Press, 1997), s.v. "bodhisattva," 155–56.

11. Bowker, *Oxford Dictionary of World Religions*, 1064.

12. See the discussion in Darby Ray, *Working* (Minneapolis: Fortress Press, 2011), 68–83.

community service a graduation requirement, mandating its completion for all students. Others have incentive and reward systems to motivate participation.

Clearly, service learning and service requirements mark a departure from earlier notions of service. On most college and university campuses today, community service is no longer practiced primarily as a unilateral offering or unconditional gift; it is increasingly embraced as a two-way street, with both parties receiving clear benefits. Interestingly, many would argue that with the widespread institutionalization of community-service requirements, incentives and rewards, majors, and centers on our college and university campuses, the pendulum may have swung too far. Whereas the older version of community service may have ensconced a romanticized ideal of the ego-free volunteer who works selflessly and unilaterally on behalf of the suffering other, the more recent service-learning version has the opposite problem: it threatens to subsume the needs of the other under pedagogical and institutional priorities that can run at cross-purposes to the genuine good of that other.[13] Here, the desire to engage in service—whether to advance student learning and citizenship, develop work-relevant skills, fulfill a requirement, enact an institutional commitment, or bring distinction to one's organization or school—can be surprisingly self-referential and self-aggrandizing.

In spite of good intentions, heroic models of service of the sort found on many campuses may wind up serving narrower interests than intended. Sometimes, in our hurry to do good through service, we do a disservice to others—and, ultimately, to ourselves. For instance, many institutions herald annual "days of service" and other one-off events designed to encourage and celebrate the institution's commitment to service. Unfortunately, these institutions often fail to appreciate the toll such events can take on off-campus partners, who have to scramble to come up with projects and work sites and who often wind up working extra hours to open their agency's doors for these events. Students may well grow their awareness of community issues and their own civic agency in relation to such issues during these kinds of service experiences, but what the community often experiences is a "service dump" that may be only tangentially related to its self-defined needs and aspirations. Thus, the "two-way street" model of

---

13. For a discussion of the unintended harm produced by some service-learning efforts, see Randy Stoecker and Elizabeth A. Tryon, *The Unheard Voices: Community Organizations and Service Learning* (Philadelphia: Temple University Press, 2009).

service heralded by many in higher education can at times be surprisingly unilateral and self-serving.

As awareness of this reality has sunk in at the campus level, it has generated a desire for more authentic reciprocity in college–community relations. As a result, many institutions and leaders in this area have begun to use the discourse of "civic engagement" or "community engagement" as an alternative. Unlike community *service*, with its implied bifurcation of servant and served and its unilateral flow of agency and labor, the language of *engagement* has come to signal full partnership and co-created work. In keeping with the priorities of the service-learning movement, community engagement acknowledges that service should, ideally, benefit all who participate in it—not only the recipients (nor only the providers) of service. It also emphasizes the positive learning outcomes typically associated with community-engaged or service learning. Connecting classroom learning to real-world situations and challenges has been shown, time and again, to increase students' investment in their learning, enhance their mastery of course concepts, build their awareness of themselves as public actors, and contribute to their psychosocial well-being. Community engagement has also proved to be an important ingredient in the retention and flourishing of historically underrepresented students.[14]

While affirming these benefits, the discourse of community engagement offers three important friendly amendments to the service-learning field. First, engagement aims for an assets-based or strengths-based approach to the off-campus community—which is to say that it recognizes the community, the "other," as an equal partner whose perspective, knowledge, and expertise are vitally important. Second, the engagement model challenges colleges and universities to acknowledge and mitigate the social, economic, and political power they tend to hold relative to the off-campus community members and organizations with which they seek to collaborate. Third, and somewhat paradoxically, engagement involves an awareness of the neediness of the college or university—an acknowledgment that its knowledge and expertise are necessary but not sufficient for community transformation. These recognitions have profound implications for both the method and content of engaged work, as well as for civic engagement as a vocational discernment practice.

---

14. See, for example, the essays in *Diversity & Democracy* 15, no. 3 (2012). See also Christine Cress et al., *A Promising Connection: Increasing College Access and Success through Civic Engagement* (Boston: Campus Compact, 2010).

## *From patronage to partnership*

In order for community engagement to play a role in vocational exploration and discernment, the off-campus community needs to be recognized as having valuable experience, expertise, knowledge, and skills of its own. Only then can it become a genuine "other" with whom students can carry out a conversation and through whom they might begin to hear a call. This requires an awareness of the community as a mature, full-bodied entity, instead of a victim in need of rescue by external actors. As Paulo Freire argued over four decades ago in *Pedagogy of the Oppressed*, transformation does not happen without the participation and self-determination of the oppressed; they must be allowed to live into their vocation for true humanization in order for those who serve them to live into theirs.[15] Community-engaged learning embraces Freire's dialogical model by acknowledging and privileging the voices and choices of the community whose well-being is in question and by encouraging interrogations of power disparities in practices of engagement. Conversations about vocation are likely to be most productive when a range of voices is included; in programs of community engagement, this means that the college and the community need to share power and strive for co-created knowledge and collaborative problem-solving. In reality, such equity and reciprocity are difficult to achieve, but since the process of engagement is at least as important as its products, the effort is worthwhile.[16]

When colleges recognize that the community is not merely the inert object of engaged work but an active subject with invaluable expertise and skills to contribute, a great many exciting, and sometimes unnerving, possibilities begin to emerge. Foremost among them is an equalizing or democratizing effect within college–community relations. If university and community are equal citizens, then the model for their relationship can no longer be one of "patron and client," in which intellectual resources and moral purpose flow unilaterally from one to the other. Instead, the model is of partnership or collaboration, where each party brings both assets and needs to the relationship and where responsibility for the partnership and its work is shared.[17]

---

15. See the remarks on Freire in chapter 3 of the present volume.

16. The complexities of community research are explored in Lisa Goodman and Jenny Phillimore, eds., *Community Research for Participation* (Bristol: Policy Press, 2012).

17. The language of service can certainly be used to articulate such commitments and practices. What the language of engagement enacts, then, is not so much a rejection of the

Thus, in engagement-rooted practices such as community-engaged learning, community-based research, and community organizing, the purposes, goals, methods, and outcomes of proposed work are negotiated *with* members of the community instead of being developed *for* them or imposed *on* them. In a similar fashion, vocational discernment involves opening the self to the claims of the world beyond the self. Instead of imposing the self's desires onto the world unilaterally, vocational discernment involves a kind of negotiation or reciprocity between self and world—a process in which the self allows its own desires to be re-formed by the needs of those beyond the self. In a culture in which self-gratification is a foundation of economic and social life, the recognition and affirmation of self-transcendent goods is downright countercultural. Thus, vocational discernment as the interplay of self and world requires courage; it requires the abdication of assumptions of a heroic, insular self—a self that is unmoved by the world beyond the self. In practices of community engagement, the courage to transcend narrow conceptions of the self and the good can be affirmed and practiced. Old dualisms such as town versus gown can be contested and more nuanced relationships embraced.

When prospective work and service projects are being designed to address genuine community needs, those needs should be identified or affirmed by community members. Similarly, the community should play a defining role in identifying the methods or processes for undertaking the work, determining how results will be shared, and agreeing on how to attribute the knowledge and materials that are produced. In the higher education setting, this might be facilitated by professional staff in conjunction with a standing community-engagement advisory committee of faculty, staff, students, and community members, which might function in tandem with smaller (and more nimble) project-specific teams. When community-based research projects merit institutional review, review boards will ideally include one or more community members who can help consider the potential impacts of projects on the community. Many projects will benefit from a "cultural broker" who can assist faculty and students in navigating cross-cultural or language differences in informed and sensitive ways. As a project unfolds, consultations and negotiations will ideally continue so that community members have sustained

---

language of service as a refinement of its meaning by emphasizing reciprocal, assets-based relationships instead of unilateral or deficit-based models of relationship.

opportunities to shape their own futures, and college/university players can adjust methods and strategies as needed.[18] As these and other practices suggest, the all-important foundation and ongoing framework for community-engaged work is relationship; the more authentic, sustained, and flexible that relationship, the better. This kind of work involves lots of moving parts; it is challenging and complex but also enormously gratifying in the growth, insight, and joy it cultivates. For students seeking to explore or discern purpose or direction in life, community-engaged projects and partnerships can be important opportunities for learning about both self and world.

An engagement model of college–community relations means that faculty, staff, and students will want to educate themselves about the community with which they hope to engage: its history, defining moments, shared narratives, debates and challenges, points of pride, assets and resources, and hopes and plans for the future. Incorporating community voices and assets into orientation programs for new employees and new students is an important step in this direction. These voices and assets can also be integrated into academic courses through guest panels or as "learning associates" whose expertise is invited to stand alongside the faculty member's. At Bates College in Lewiston, Maine, the Learning Associates program allows community partners to serve as "co-teachers" of courses, integrating their knowledge into the curriculum and contributing notably to student learning. In addition to enhancing students' knowledge of the course topic, Learning Associates also embody an implicit challenge to what some call the "epistemology of knowledge"— that is, the dominant assumptions about who has knowledge and what should count *as* knowledge. In a college–community partnership, college or university members can be expected to contribute important academic expertise, volunteer labor, material resources, and social capital to community-engaged work. Often overlooked, but foregrounded in an engagement model, are the considerable assets of the off-campus community, which might include local or "inside" knowledge of a particular community or issue, access to opinion leaders within the community,

---

18. For recommended engagement practices such as those discussed in this paragraph, see Kerry J. Strand, et al., *Community-Based Research in Higher Education: Principles and Practices* (San Francisco: Jossey-Bass, 2003); Catherine Etmanski, Budd L. Hall, and Teresa Dawson, eds., *Learning and Teaching Community-Based Research: Linking Pedagogy to Practice* (Toronto: University of Toronto Press, 2014), and Goodman and Phillimore, *Community Research for Participation*.

cross-cultural communication skills, organizing skills, and wisdom gained from past attempts to address issues of concern. Taken together, assets from a diverse partnership can constitute a formidable toolkit for co-created work. As a partnership or collaborative model is embodied over time, increasingly complex or challenging projects can be undertaken, thanks to the trust and shared resources that develop among partners and the wealth of assets available for use. Where a traditional model of service might be able to address only the symptoms of a problem—a hungry belly, a lack of shelter, or low reading scores—an engaged relationship can take aim also at root causes by mobilizing diverse citizens over time in collaborative work.

Students who want to navigate a course for the future that is informed and enriched by the gifts and needs of both self and world can find in community engagement a treasure trove of partners and mentors, knowledge and avenues for growth. One of the primary benefits of community-engaged work, both for community members and students, is the practice it offers in civic agency and democratic participation. Practices of shared work across differences such as age, income, status, race, and ethnicity build the capacity of individuals and communities for responsible citizenship in a democratic society. Working with diverse others for the common good is both an aim and a method of civic engagement. It is work that both enacts and expands democracy. Community members stand to gain something quite important from the profoundly humanizing and empowering experiences of having one's voice heard, being recognized by others as an asset instead of a liability, and experiencing oneself as a worthy colleague of those with more social, economic, or institutional power—in short, by being welcomed as an *equal*. These experiences are important not only for those accustomed to being treated as less than equal, but also for those with relative power and privilege. Such persons are confronted with the revelation of the full humanity, irreducible dignity, and skilled intelligence of the other—a realization that can disrupt long-held assumptions about both self and world. The effects of such experiences ripple out across one's entire life.

## *The call of the world*

Community-engaged work invites a wide range of transformations and challenges; as such, it can be a highly effective framework for vocational discernment and exploration. If vocation is a call to a life of magnanimity and to a life lived not only for one's own benefit, then we can understand community engagement as a world of practice that cultivates ears that can hear and respond to that call. Community or civic engagement is sustained, shared work for the common good; as such, it can be habit-forming and character-shaping. It is generative of virtues such as practical wisdom, attentiveness, and generosity; it encourages practices such as deep listening, gratitude, and empathy. It is also an important crucible for the development of skills, capacities, and relationships that can serve participants well throughout their lives, including in their work lives. Perhaps most importantly (at least with respect to vocation), community engagement exposes participants to diverse worlds of experience and possibility and nurtures in them an awareness of the world and the other as gift—an awareness that can pull the self away from distraction, egocentrism, and consumerist or instrumentalist relationships, freeing the self for virtuous living and meaningful work.

Of the virtues cultivated by community engagement, one of the most important in today's world is surely attentiveness.[19] Most of our students live thoroughly "connected" lives. They are virtually connected to others and physically connected to their electronic gadgets around the clock, constantly accessing and being accessed by news, images, products, and "friends." While this kind of connected living certainly has its benefits, joys, and opportunities, its cultivation of habits of cognitive and emotional "surfing" can undermine or derail processes of vocational discernment. Like a hungry hummingbird, screen-focused minds are often frenetically mobile, always on the lookout for the next tweet, text, status update, or image. Flitting almost involuntarily from message to message, post to post, or image to image, the mind eventually loses its ability to dwell contentedly in one place for any length of time. Unless counteracted by disciplines of attentiveness, this habit portends a life of distraction and superficiality.

And yet, such attentiveness is absolutely essential to the vocational discernment process, as are the practices that help us cultivate it. It requires deep listening—to the self's innermost needs and hopes, to the world's brokenness and beauty, and to what many would regard as God's desire for the entire creation: life abundant for all.[20] As sustained, shared work

---

19. See the comments in chapter 5, particularly the section headed "Open to a call."

20. For a book-length reflection, see Sallie McFague, *Life Abundant* (Minneapolis: Fortress Press, 2000).

for the common good, community engagement at its best cultivates habits of attentiveness and deep listening. Such habits, though clearly countercultural in important respects, lead not to withdrawal or escape from the world but, instead, to new levels of understanding and connection. For those in search of their place in the world, learning to listen deeply to that world is a valuable lesson indeed. Such listening does not come easily, which is why we speak of vocational *discernment* instead of vocational achievement. Discernment is an ongoing process that takes time and courage. It is an attempt to see things as they really are—to discern the truth of the matter—while also opening one-self to new possible truths. Vocational discernment involves an assessment of who one is, on the one hand, and of who one feels called or created to be, on the other. It involves the world as it currently is and the world as it could be. While most of us in the West are fairly accustomed to self-examination (Who am I? What do I desire or hope for? What should I do with my life?), we tend to be far less practiced in world-assessment (What is the state of the world today? Where is the flourishing? Where is the suffering? How can we move toward life abundant for all?) Practices of community engagement help us become attuned to the world. They challenge us to listen to the voices we too often fail to hear, to see the truths and ask the questions we might otherwise neglect. In community engagement we find ourselves stretched, often uncomfortably so. As we listen deeply not only to ourselves but also to our world, we realize the inseparability of these two spheres—their co-constitution and shared future. We become aware that there is no inde-pendent, isolated self, just as there is no world, no other "out there." Self and world are always and already co-defining each other. To discern our way forward in life requires careful and sustained listening to both.

In an essay entitled "In the Beginning Is the Listening," theologian Jay McDaniel explores listening as "the receptive side of love: a side that listens to others on their own terms and for their own sakes and that is transformed in the listening without trying to change them according to preconceived purposes."[21] This kind of mutually transforming receptivity is exactly what is at work in community engagement at its best.[22] We meet

---

21. Jay McDaniel, "In the Beginning Is the Listening," in *Theology That Matters: Ecology, Economy, and God*, ed. Darby Kathleen Ray (Minneapolis: Fortress Press, 2008), 26–27.

22. While I am using listening as a metaphor for exploring the dynamics and bene-fits of community engagement as a vocational discernment practice, in a recent article Deborah Dunn of Westmont College considers "Seeing as a Form of Service." Deborah

others where they are, on their own terms. With discipline and practice we find ourselves opening to their story, their experience, their hope for their own lives—which is to say, we learn to listen. And we need to keep listening, attending with discipline and care to the perspective of our community partner, so that the relationship does not slip from partnership back into patronage, from mutuality into mastery.

Especially for those who are accustomed to asserting themselves and being heard or attended to by others, listening does not come easily. As McDaniel notes, "it requires education in the art of vulnerability," a "willingness to be changed by others."[23] Millsaps College in Jackson, Mississippi, put this kind of vulnerability to practice when it launched its "1 Campus 1 Community" engagement program with a "Shut Up and Listen" luncheon. Over 100 opinion leaders from faculty, staff, administration, and student body "shut up" and listened to the experiences, aspirations, and admonishments of a diverse group of community members representing the adjacent neighborhood that the college had been (or thought it had been) "serving" for decades. After these guests voiced their experiences of past practices and challenged the college to re-imagine itself as a more sincere partner of the neighborhood, campus members gathered in small groups to reflect on what they had heard and what a truly responsive and reciprocal relationship might look like. A commitment to deep listening as a formative practice for college–community relations emerged; nearly a decade later, the listening continues as a foundation of what has become a mutually transformative partnership.

An engaged community is a community that listens deeply and creates sustained practices of attentiveness. It continually asks: Whose voice is not being heard? Whose experiences are being overlooked or excluded? To whom do we need to listen, and how can we change our systems so that more voices can be heard? An engaged community might think of assessment as a listening practice, an opportunity to consider one's work from the vantage point of another, to attend with care to the voices of others.

For those trying to discern a call for their life or work, habits of deep listening are enormously important. They draw us away from the frenetic pace and superficial distractions of screen living and consumer culture and

---

Dunn, "Bearing Witness: Seeing as a Form of Service," *Liberal Education* 100, no. 2 (Spring 2014): 36–41.

23. McDaniel, "In the Beginning," 27.

toward attention to the needs and gifts of both self and other. Reflecting on the community-engaged dimension of a course on Wabanaki (Native American) History, a Bates College student wrote, "Listening to Wabanaki people tell their stories, their struggles, and their hopes, was an incredibly enlightening experience. Hearing from them in person made them real, as weird as that might sound, not just an abstract concept of a person."[24] In this course, community-engaged learning primarily took the form of listening to the stories, experiences, and wisdom of those whom the dominant culture has largely forgotten. In spite of terminological changes, we still tend to think of engagement in terms of community service, in which students give of themselves to underprivileged others; but as this example highlights, the gifts often flow in the other direction.

Learning to listen with care and openness to the other, to the world beyond the individual self and its most immediate concerns, is a key dimension of vocational discernment. The self's aspirations and passions never occur in a vacuum; rather, they are shaped by, and ideally responsive to, the world in which the self is situated. Community engagement is an ideal way for students not only to act in and on the wider world but to listen deeply to that world in order to discern which actions hold the most promise for the flourishing of self and world. A key question for the individual who is in discernment is not only "What do I want to do with my life?" but also "What does the world offer or ask of me?" In practices of community engagement, this latter question is probed by seeking out and being attentive to the distinctive strengths and needs of community partners.

## *Unlikely role models*

If a lack of attentiveness to the world beyond the self is a major obstacle to vocational discernment and clarity, another challenge for college or university students comes in the form of today's collegiate culture of achievement. With a four-year degree now considered practically a necessity for decent employment, and more and more people earning degrees, the pressure is on for students not only to complete a degree program but also to distinguish themselves from their degree-earning peers. For

---

24. Anonymous student response to an online survey conducted by the Harward Center for Community Partnerships at Bates College, Lewiston, Maine, May 2014.

many, this means striving to achieve as many accolades and "extras" as possible, often while holding down a part-time or full-time job. Days and nights crammed with school work, co-curricular activities, jobs, and social events leave precious little time or energy for the sustained reflection of vocational discernment or the rejuvenation of deep rest.

Although civic or community engagement depends in part on activist dispositions of hard work, commitment, and a passion for problem-solving, it nevertheless prioritizes relationship as the bedrock value. Hence, its non-negotiable feature—more important than productivity, achievement, or "success"—is sustained attention to the other and to the integrity of the relationship. Where an achievement culture tends to incentivize the formation of instrumentalized relationships that can move one's personal goal-set or career forward, the relationships established with community partners through community-engaged work are rarely of this sort. Despite the fact that career-relevant skills are routinely developed in a community-engagement context, it is rarely beset by the instrumentalism that characterizes so many other relationships and pursuits. Thus, even though it involves time and effort, community-engaged work often functions for students as a kind of psychic and emotional break from the pressures and busyness of the rest of their lives. By dwelling in a space of authenticity and mutual regard, even if only for a few hours a week, students can experience a rejuvenation of spirit and an opportunity to recalibrate. Under such circumstances, one can remember who one is and what truly matters.

In the face of relentless cultural messages endorsing materialist and individualistic notions of self-worth and success, community-engaged work nurtures alternative perspectives in which success is measured not by income, status, or possession but by the depth and quality of one's character, relationships, and commitments. By spending extended time with those who have "failed" (according to the dominant culture's assessment), we come to recognize the perversity and arbitrariness of that system and to nurture an appreciation for alternative virtues such as thrift, solidarity, and loyalty. No longer limited by normative notions of success, students' vocational imaginations can fly free. As they experience the intelligence and ingenuity of the "unsuccessful," students often begin to question myths of merit and presumptions of self-making and individual success. They come to appreciate the importance of networks of care and opportunity for individual and communal thriving, and many find themselves asking how their own future work might nurture such networks. Students also learn from community members the importance of resilience in the face of failure. We hear a lot these days about the virtue of "grit," often defined as "perseverance and passion for long-term goals," and identified by researchers as a predictor of academic and professional achievement.[25] In community-engaged work, students routinely rub shoulders with women and men of grit—people whose resourcefulness and perseverance in the face of adversity or challenge have been essential to their survival and flourishing. Such persons serve as exemplars, modeling for students an important ingredient of purposeful work and life.

Community engagement as a context for vocational discernment also cultivates another countercultural capacity: long-term thinking and commitment. In their community-engaged work, students often experience the complexities of entrenched social challenges such as intergenerational poverty, domestic violence, and climate change. In the process, they come to understand that problems such as these will not be solved anytime soon; such transformations will take time, tenacity, and imagination. In his classic study *The Corrosion of Character*, sociologist Richard Sennett describes short-term thinking as endemic to late capitalism, where the hypermobility of capital, information, products, and jobs and the enthronement of novelty, flexibility, just-in-time production, and incessant consumer desire undermine long-term relationships and virtues such as loyalty and sustained commitment.[26] He argues that a "no long term" mentality pervades our personal relationships and practices, dissuading us from putting down real roots by, for example, meeting our neighbors, becoming active citizens, and maintaining deep, lifelong friendships. This mentality affects our relationships to work as well, where loyalty, artistry and craft, and moral integrity are increasingly sacrificed on the altar of corporate profit and self-advancement. After extensive interviews with a range of workers, Sennett concludes that "the qualities of good work" as defined by corporate capitalism—things like flexibility, mobility, short-term profitability, productivity, efficiency, competition, and unfettered growth—simply "are not the qualities of good character."[27]

---

25. Angela L. Duckworth et al., "Grit: Perseverance and Passion for Long-Term Goals," *Journal of Personality and Social Psychology* 92, no. 6 (2007): 1087–1101; Tim Clydesdale, "Holy Grit!" *Liberal Education* 100, no. 1 (2014): 14–19.

26. Richard Sennett, *The Corrosion of Character: The Personal Consequences of Work in the New Capitalism* (New York: W.W. Norton & Company, 1996), especially chap. 1.

27. Sennett, *Corrosion of Character*, 21.

What does it mean, in such a context, to undertake vocational exploration and discernment? How can we help students find the time and space, and to develop the attentiveness and stamina, that such work requires? As they ponder and prepare for their futures, community-engaged work and partnerships offer them meaningful opportunities and role models for developing and appreciating countercultural capacities like long-term thinking and commitment. Such experiences school their participants in patience, persistence, and stubborn imagination; it requires and rewards loyalty and sustained partnerships; and it focuses one's attention on both the challenges immediately at hand and the possibilities and hope for their eventual transformation. Community members who embody these values—while living and working with dignity and purpose in an often hostile world—serve as exemplars for students: unexpected role models, perhaps, but role models nonetheless.

In the face of intransigent challenges of the sort students routinely encounter in community-engaged work, expectations of easy victory or ultimate triumph are quickly shattered. Ethicist Sharon Welch suggests that this kind of shattering is all for the better because it prepares one for the complex realities of authentic living and moral struggle.[28] She argues that expectations of quick success can lead to an "ethic of control" in which we assume we are entitled or equipped to shape the future as we see fit. Such assumptions can feed despair and undermine courage and conviction when things don't go our way or when a problem is too complex to be easily solved; they also encourage us to act only when success is guaranteed. As students listen for a call to meaningful work, positive experiences of patience and persistence in the face of complex and ongoing challenges can whet their appetite for work whose success is not guaranteed—which is to say, for any kind of work that demands courage and conviction. For students who do not hear a clear call to a particular vocational pathway and who, as a result, are struggling with fear, frustration, and uncertainty about their future, community-engaged experiences of tolerating uncertain or ambiguous outcomes may provide some comfort. These encounters can remind them that meaningful work does not require absolute certainty, predictability, or control; in fact, it typically occurs in situations of risk, vulnerability, and external constraint. Here again, community partners

28. Sharon Welch, *A Feminist Ethic of Risk* (Minneapolis: Fortress Press, 1990).

become mentors for students, exemplifying courage and ingenuity in the face of uncertainty and setback.

## *Called to community*

Community-engaged experiences can be surprisingly unsettling, calling into question long-held assumptions about both self and world. As we have seen, these experiences challenge us to become radically open to those whose life stories are often dramatically different than our own and to allow our own story to be re-made under the impress of that connection. There is a kind of paradox here, as we find ourselves both diminished and enlarged. Disabused of illusions of self-reliance and meritocracy, we become aware of our profound neediness, our dependence on the goodness and graces of others, and the absurdity (and danger) of our presumptions of knowledge, self-efficacy, and moral certitude. Even as the self is powerfully relativized, however, it is also enriched and empowered by being placed—or rather, by becoming aware of its place—within a world of expanded relationships and multitudinous gifts. Community engagement at its best cultivates a twofold realization for students: The world is decidedly *not* all about me, and yet I do have something worthwhile to contribute to it.

According to sociologist Tim Clydesdale, today's most-well-adjusted college graduates are those who have cultivated this combination of humbling self-transcendence and honest self-knowledge.[29] Asked what was most valuable about a Spring 2014 community-engaged learning project, one student responded, "Knowing that I am contributing to something bigger than simply worrying about myself." A student who took a different course, reflecting on the "amazing and life-changing experience" of engagement, offered the opinion that "There should be more community-engaged learning courses. . . . Getting students out in the community teaches them about the community that they are part of and increases their appreciation for [that community]. It also humbles students in an invaluable way and helps them adjust to college life by forcing them to explore and meet people outside of [the college]." Still another student

---

29. Plenary presentations at the "Called and Equipped" conference hosted by the Network for Vocation in Undergraduate Education, Gordon College, Wenham, MA, March 21–22, 2014. See also Clydesdale's *The Purposeful Graduate* (see Introduction, note 3 *supra*).

from another course characterized the community-engaged learning experience as "a life-changing door-opener."[30]

As students seek to discern a call to purposeful work, community engagement offers them a taste of such work. Despite the complexities, unpredictability, vulnerability, and struggle that frequently characterize this work, students nevertheless find it powerfully compelling. In it they find themselves not only pushed and challenged but also encouraged and grown. Simultaneously humbled and empowered by their community engagement experiences, students gain fresh perspective on their own lives and on the complex world in which they live. As they work alongside off-campus community members and are supervised, taught, and mentored by them, students develop skills and capacities that will serve them well—no matter what field of work they eventually pursue. Realizing this, students gain the confidence they need to pursue their aspirations, as well as the self-awareness necessary to identify and articulate their skills and capacities in, for example, a job application or graduate school interview.

Instead of supplanting more traditional forms of learning and support (such as that provided by parents, professors, coaches, and other college or university staff), community engagement complements and extends the learning and mentoring environment by bringing the world into full view as a vitally important dimension of vocation. Nurturing an awareness of the world as gift rather than threat or burden, community engagement invites students into practices of self-awareness, self-transcendence, and radical empathy. It expands their options for meaningful work and life by developing students' skills and capacities and exposing them to diverse worlds of work and unexpected role models and mentors. Perhaps most importantly, community engagement functions as a counterweight to the tendency for vocation to be exclusively or primarily focused on the self, with the world considered merely a convenient backdrop for one's personal odyssey. When students truly engage the world in its exquisite beauty, heartbreaking suffering, and mind-boggling complexity, they often find themselves desiring not just their own flourishing, but that of the whole world. Self and world are, after all, hopelessly, hopefully entangled.

---

30. Anonymous student responses to an online survey conducted by the Harward Center for Community Partnerships at Bates College, Lewiston, Maine, May 2014.

## Epilogue

# In Various Times and Sundry Places

PEDAGOGIES OF VOCATION / VOCATION AS PEDAGOGY

*David S. Cunningham*

THE LANGUAGE OF vocation has a remarkably wide scope. In some ways, it continues to bear the marks of its historical origins—in both its narrower version, focusing on the specialized and particular callings of those of whom something rather extraordinary is expected, and the broadened account in which it applies to the manifold stations in life of all human beings. Its theological aspects can be brought to the fore, such that God is identified as the caller and a decision to answer the call is closely aligned with religious faith; but the incipiently theological elements of the vocation can also be minimized or ignored. Vocation seems particularly relevant for emerging adults who are making decisions about how they will live and what they will do with their lives; and yet, because one's direction in life is never irreversible, it continues to be important across the lifespan. Individual and universal, sacred and profane, specific to a time yet relevant throughout life: vocation seems to play an important role at all times and in all places, a constant presence in our increasingly episodic existence.

The scope of vocation may help to explain why it seems to be making such a significant impact on undergraduate life at the present moment. College life is similarly marked by a degree of breadth and capaciousness that has been difficult to maintain in a culture that increasingly rewards narrow specialization. Undergraduate education focuses on and rewards individual talent, yet it is increasingly seen as something to which everyone should have access. The roots of most colleges and universities are deeply intertwined with those of the church, yet many educational institutions struggle to discern the appropriate level of attention to religious faith within their academic contexts. Most undergraduates are emerging adults, in their late teens and early twenties, and so it can be tempting to identify college as nothing more than a passing phase; yet all evidence suggests that what happens during these years has an outsized impact on the shape and direction of a person's future. Moreover, the important questions that an undergraduate student must face do not simply vanish after graduation; they retain their profound significance throughout one's life.

The essays in this volume have sought to trace the outlines of vocation and to show how it variously aligns with, points toward, and maps onto undergraduate education. The contributors have identified how the language of vocation can respond to certain persistent features of contemporary culture, from the overabundance of choices that we have to make, to the complex and often conflicting narratives that vie for our attention, to the presence (or absence) and quality of the sounds that surround us. These authors have shown how vocational exploration and discernment can be relevant to undergraduate students in all their diversity—including not only the forms of diversity that they bring with them (race, class, gender, sexuality, and other elements of personal identity), but also the manifold ways that they experience college: lecture hall and playing field, residence hall and seminar room, professor's office and community agency. These essays have also been attentive to shared goals of vocational discernment and undergraduate education: helping students to become more self-reflective, to recognize how deeply they are shaped by their own particular practices, and to understand their own lives as situated within a much broader horizon of times, places, and cultures.

## *Pedagogies of vocation / vocation as pedagogy*

From early in the genesis of this volume, a key term of conversation was *pedagogy*. The authors understood and discussed this term as related to vocation and undergraduate education in two ways. First, we were interested in asking whether we might be able to propose various *pedagogies of vocation*. This involved a consideration, at the outset, of whether vocation is something that can be taught. Can it enter the undergraduate curriculum, like mathematics or foreign language—something that can become an object of study and underwrite a specific region of ongoing practice? Might it even be its own interdisciplinary field of study, with its own methods, sources, and norms? We recognized that such pedagogical questions are complicated by the description of vocation as something that comes to us from outside ourselves, such that inquiry cannot really be initiated by the student but must be waited upon, listened for, and discerned. Still, the contributors to this volume have come to agree that appropriate "pedagogies of vocation" can and should be developed: we need ways of teaching the theory and practice of vocational reflection and discernment in the undergraduate context. The chapters of this book are filled with suggestions, examples, and theoretical accounts of such pedagogies, which we believe can be implemented in a variety of educational settings.

At the same time, however, we also have been engaged in a line of inquiry that moves in the opposite direction. Could vocational discernment become something more than merely an object of study—more than just a set of specific practices that we hope to introduce to colleagues and to our students? Might it function as a kind of organizing principle for undergraduate education, which otherwise seems to have become unmoored from its original anchor-points and now sometimes tries to be all things to all people? Could it help answer the question that seems to surface in practically all discussions of higher education today, namely: what is the *purpose* of undergraduate education? We want to offer, as a general response to these kinds of questions, the notion that vocation might itself be a kind of pedagogy. It can be deployed in ways that turn the focus of inquiry outward—away from the usual subject-driven, empirical study of discrete objects in the external world, but also away from the tendency to collapse knowledge back into the interior emotional world of the subject (in which the value of external objects is reduced to their ability to satisfy felt needs and desires). In short, *vocation* also names an approach to learning that avoids various forms of reductionism, whether of the objectivist or the subjectivist variety.

## *Five themes*

Beyond these two broader rubrics—pedagogies of vocation, and vocation as pedagogy—a number of significant themes emerged as we undertook the development of this volume. While a great many of these could be listed, five such themes seem worth holding up for further investigation.

They are themes that mark the enterprise of vocational reflection and discernment, but they also point us toward key elements of undergraduate education. The remainder of this epilogue offers brief reflections on the relevance of these five themes, both for vocation and for higher education.

## Narrative

Vocation is a story-shaped reality. The writers of this volume were aware of this from the outset, but its significance became more and more salient as we carried out our work of conversation, writing, and commentary. Narrative appeared everywhere: in the stories that are told about a moment when someone senses a call; among our students, as they try to make sense of their experience of college life; and even in our own accounts of the historical, theological, and educational sojourns of the concept of vocation. Of course, narrative is given extensive treatment in chapter 7, making it the "central" essay of this volume in more than just a numerical sense; but just as that chapter points out how much our framing narratives shape our understanding of the good, so the three chapters that follow remind us that, in order to understand and live into the virtues, we need to consider the narratives in which they are ensconced. In fact, the close relationship between narrative and vocation is announced in the very first chapter of this volume, which concludes by suggesting that answering a call means, in part, learning to tell the story of our lives in a way that substantiates and underscores our callings. In light of the claims presented in the rest of the book, one might go so far as to say that our vocations *are* our narratives: to tell the story of our lives is to narrate the ways that we have been called, as well as the ways that we have responded to those calls.

Narrative is also a key component in higher education. Again this was noted most clearly in chapter 7, particularly in its discussion of the three archetypical narratives of our culture and the tendency of colleges and universities to align themselves with one or another of these. Beyond that specific analysis, however, the role of narrative in higher education is implicit throughout the book. For example, the stories that academic institutions tell about themselves affect the degree to which they create space for students to listen for, and actually to hear, their callings. Moreover, the various framing narratives of our institutions can be evaluated by considering whether, or to what degree, they allow for the cultivation of the virtues. Even the account offered in chapter 2 might profitably be read as a survey of the stories that are being told about higher education in the present cultural moment—told by experts in the field, by the institutions themselves, and by the various constituencies that inhabit them. Colleges and universities are story-shaped institutions, much like vocation itself.

## Habit

A closely related element of our analysis focuses on the surprising degree to which vocation is a matter of our habits—including not only the stories that we tell, but also the practices that permeate our lives. These are practices in which we engage regularly, often without giving them much thought or consideration; as a result, they become so much a part of our existence that we don't even notice them. Every chapter of this volume documents certain habits of our culture—some of which facilitate vocational reflection and discernment, and some of which create obstacles to that process. For example, we have become so accustomed to having a myriad of choices that we no longer think about whether this situation is actually *good* for us. We make habitual assumptions about others that may prevent them from hearing a particular calling, or from imagining that they might be able to respond to it. Cultivating particular habits among our students—whether in or beyond the classroom, whether on- or off-campus—can either facilitate or obstruct vocational reflection and discernment. And of course, the chapters in part three are very specifically about those habits known in the ethical tradition as virtues and vices. The particular virtues examined in those chapters—magnanimity, prudence, and loyalty—are integrally related to vocation, in two ways: they prepare the ground for vocational discernment by making us attentive to the needs of those around us; and they serve as markers of the called life, since our vocations lead us into a more engaged relationship with others.

Habit is also one of the primary (and too seldom remarked-upon) features of higher education. This fact is known to every faculty member; one need not spend a great deal of time working at a college or university to discover how thoroughly many of its practices depend upon the seductive rationale that "we've always done it that way." Several chapters in this volume highlight many of the most formative habits at work within higher education—not only those of longstanding importance, but also a number of newly developing habits that demand our attention. Similarly, the habits of college students are discussed in most of the chapters of the book; even the narratives that frame our educational institutions are developed largely as a result of the habitual practices in which these institutions are engaged. By their very nature, habits are often overlooked; but they provide an important key both for making sense of the current state of higher education, and for understanding why pedagogies of vocational exploration and discernment have so much to offer.

## Relationship

A certain romanticized account of vocation might picture the solitary wanderer, having taken leave of the influence of others, mulling over her or his potential callings with no conversation-partner other than God, the gods, or some incorporeal muse. But as we have seen throughout this book, vocation is most often discerned through our relationships with others: we read others' stories, and we compare our own accounts of a fulfilled and fulfilling life with similar accounts of the lives of others. We have suggested that the very grammar of vocation seems to demand a "caller" who issues the call; even when this being is understood to be God, the call is often described as being delivered through the words and actions of a human being in which we are in some kind of ongoing relationship. Stories of a call require, at the very least, someone to tell the story and someone to listen to it; lives of virtue require exemplars to be followed; athletic training requires a coach; the classroom requires a teacher. As many of these essays have suggested, some of the most poignant and consequential moments of vocational discernment take place when a friend, teacher, or even a mere acquaintance taps a person on the shoulder and says something along the lines of, "you know, you're very good at this." Vocation is often born in the midst of relationship.

Colleges and universities face a similar situation: their historical origins lie in the efforts of medieval religious orders to train scholars in theology and related disciplines; this was, quite literally, a monastic enterprise. But despite the etymology of this word (relating to the solitary life), most monasteries depend very heavily on relationships that make possible the induction, training, mentoring, and assessment of the person who is leading this supposedly solitary life. Early forms of higher education adopted this relational approach quite directly, beginning with the Oxbridge model of one-to-one relationship between students and teachers. Thus, while higher education has often accented the individual work and achievement that academic success requires, this does not occur in a vacuum. Any particular individual's academic achievements are always, to some extent, the product of his or her relationships to others. The ability of higher education to single out the work of the individual, while still bearing in mind its dependence on these relationships, makes it particularly fertile ground for the work of vocational discernment—which similarly understands particularity and difference as grounded in a person's relationship to others.

## Community

Still, "relationship" does not tell the whole story; vocational discernment is not usually exhausted by one mentor speaking words of wisdom to one seeker. Rather, finding one's calling typically involves immersion in various communities—familial, ecclesial, civic, educational, or simply a gathering of friends. These groups help to provide the context within which vocational judgments can be made. This book refers to a wide range of such communities: mentoring communities that support students within the academic environment; groups that hold up various virtues as key elements of a life well lived; and the community of fellow readers who find themselves immersed in the same, or similar, narrative worlds. As noted in chapter 4 and elsewhere, most of us belong to multiple and overlapping communities that shape our outlook; these communities may even espouse positions that are in tension with one another. This, too, is the work of vocational discernment; to sort out the varying and sometimes conflicting signals that we receive from the communities of which we are a part, as we attempt to understand the lives to which we are being called.

Again, this theme helps us understand the close fit between vocational discernment and undergraduate education. A college is a community; its members work and play (and often live) together over the course of a substantial and formative period of their lives. An academic institution also includes a wider range of smaller communities, in which students have varying levels of membership at various times during their undergraduate careers. Some of these communities may come to play a very important role in the process of formation that is described in the previous paragraph. In short, undergraduate life creates communities, and communities shape the contours of the vocational landscape for their members; thus, the collegiate years are a time when a person's understanding of his or her callings are being shaped by powerful forces. In order for students to move through this process in ways that are confidence-building and productive (rather than frustrating and overwhelming), they need to be offered the kinds of theoretical frameworks and practical opportunities that the chapters of this book describe.

## Provisionality

A final theme that has emerged in these essays is the importance of an appropriate degree of humility and reserve, both in vocational discernment and in higher education more broadly. Both are provisional enterprises—never complete, never encapsulated in a single moment. They are journeys, not just destinations. Therefore, it is wise (and indeed, invoking the language of chapter 9, *prudent*) to avoid the temptation to press for definitive conclusions or to describe the state of a person's life and learning with too much confidence. Both vocation and higher education are ever-evolving realities; therefore, the work of vocational discernment in the academic setting needs to be flexible and resilient. It needs to be able to adapt to the very different degrees of attention to vocation that students will bring to their undergraduate experience, and it needs to guide them with a certain degree of gentleness, recognizing how quickly their lives can evolve. Students can also be helped in this process when they learn that their own teachers' vocational journeys have seen a certain amount of evolution and change, and that the apparent certainties to which vocational discernment leads can often be displaced by new opportunities, sudden changes of scenery, or events that are completely out of one's control. Students will be better able to face the provisional nature of their own vocational reflections if they are aware that those who are farther along in the journey have had to do the same.

## *Various times and sundry places*

Vocational reflection and discernment, we believe, is a very appropriate undertaking within the higher education context. We have suggested throughout this book that the undergraduate years provide the appropriate degree of relatively unfettered time, and a "free and ordered space," within which students can listen for their callings and discern the shape that their future lives might take. Of course, this can be a complex and time-consuming process, involving a great many people; it demands attention to all the nuances surrounding the concept of vocation, both in theory and practice. Hence, when academic institutions recognize the importance of vocational reflection and choose to implement programs that will support it, they are embarking on a journey that will require much of them. While such programs need not be extraordinarily expensive, they do require sustained institutional and individual commitment.

Fortunately, however, help can be found at every turn. A significant number of institutions have already embarked upon this path; together, they offer an enormous panoply of best practices (and a few failed experiments as well!) that can help others along the way. Much of this wisdom has been collected and made accessible through the Network for Vocation in Undergraduate Education.[1] Scholarly interest in vocation continues to increase; this book is one contribution to this field, and more will follow. In short, the work of vocational reflection and discernment is already occurring, at various times and in sundry places, within the educational enterprise. The challenge before us is to ensure its place as a standard and thoroughgoing feature of undergraduate life, such that all students are given the opportunity to consider the kind of life to which they are being called.

---

1. The Network's website is located at www.cic.edu/netvue.

# Index of Proper Names

# Subject Index

academic major. *See* major field of study

acedia, 195, 207, 209–210, 213

action: calling as, 144–47, 150–52; civic and social, xix, 51, 115, 302–4; in response to a call, 42, 49, 109, 121, 134, 140, 153, 167, 267; product of the will, 159, 167; relationship to character, 166–67, 181, 200, 208, 212, 217–21, 224–26, 234, 240, 246. *See also* agency

adversity, facing, 207, 218, 317. *See also* crisis

advertising, 36, 302

advising, advisors, 62, 64, 68–69, 75, 80, 83, 87, 147–48, 163, 171, 235, 248, 281. *See also* counseling, mentoring

agency: human, 106–7, 114–15; moral, 193, 223–26, 248–49, 254; of the called, 45, 254, 306–7, 311; of the caller, 17, 144–54, 159, 163–64, 167. *See also* action

alcohol abuse, 273–75, 295

ambiguity, 107–9, 117, 318. *See also* uncertainty

Anglicanism, 28, 92, 265

anti-clericalism, 8, 99

anxiety, about one's calling, 26, 33, 153, 159, 237, 254; about wrong choices, 35, 237, 254; among students, 16, 39, 77, 230, 237, 295; moral and religious, 27, 102, 222

apathy, 209, 230. *See also* acedia

asceticism, ascetic practices, 27, 296–297

athletics, 64, 170, 200, 239, 251–52, 255–56, 261, 268, 272, 276–77, 294–95, 302

attention, attentiveness, 128–30, 136–39, 312

authenticity, 218, 238, 244, 301

authority, 86, 107–8, 114, 137, 155, 225, 227, 238, 248–49, 254, 284

autobiography, 177, 186–187, 231, 235. *See also* call stories

autonomy, 22, 195, 238–39, 242, 248–49

Baptist (Christian denomination), xviii, 92–93, 228

Bible: reading, 266; narratives of, 153, 168. *See also* call stories

"big questions" (Parks), ix, xviii, 47, 66–68. *See also* meaning and purpose

Buddhism, 305

built environment, 286, 293–95

undergraduate research, 262

undergraduate students, ix–xi, xiii–xiv, xix–xxi, 1–3, 6, 9–12, 14–16, 18–19, 21–23, 26, 40, 44, 47, 52–63, 66–71, 73–76, 80, 82–83, 85–95, 101–2, 113–21, 151–59, 165–66, 169–72, 175–76, 180, 185–88, 189–91, 193–94, 197, 201–14, 227–32, 235–39, 246–54, 259–65, 268–80, 281–85, 290–300, 304–20, 321–29. *See also* academic major; athletics; Greek life; residential life; undergraduate education

universality of vocation. *See* vocation, universality of

universals. *See* particulars and universals

vice(s), 43, 195–96, 200, 207, 222, 231, 246

virtue(s), 7, 17–18, 42–43, 67, 117, 128, 142, 169, 181–87, 189–91, 194–206, 211–15, 216–34, 241–44, 246, 249, 276–77, 312, 316–17, 324–27; cardinal or classical, 216–219, 221–223, 232–33; theological, 216, 218, 222–23, 232–33. *See also* habit(s); vice(s); and entries under specific virtues, e.g. attentiveness, charity, faith, fortitude, hope, humility, justice, loyalty, prudence, temperance

virtue ethics, 166–69, 195–97, 241. *See also* narrative

vision: in calling. *See* call(ing), vision and visual images in; moral, 166, 181, 185, 275; visual representations of virtue, 232–34

vocabulary (for discussing vocation), ix, 57–58, 65, 70, 190–91, 217, 253; theological, ix, 7, 11–15, 97–98, 152–53,

236–37, 240, 321–22. *See also* vocation, journey metaphor for; vocation, theatrical analogy for

vocation: ambiguity and uncertainty in, 153, 156–57, 162–64, 263, 273–74, 328; assumed singularity of, 237–38, 254; history of, 7–8, 16, 26–27, 61, 99–100, 135, 149, 321; instrumental accounts of, 56–58, 62–63, 115–16, 149–50, 190, 198, 237,316; integrative nature of, 57–58, 61–62, 66–68; journey metaphor for, 8, 202–4, 207, 210–12, 260, 328–29; mysteriousness of, 8, 142, 152–53, 155–56; ongoing quality of, 201–3, 207; pedagogies for, xii, 110–11, 193–94, 197, 210 (*See also* pedagogy); provisionality of, 162–64, 328–29; role of faith and theology in, ix, 7, 10–15, 97–100, 151–53, 187, 236–37, 240, 304, 321–22; secularization of , 28, 100, 135; as service, 305; tendency to reinforce the status quo, 8, 107–10, 149; theatrical analogy for, 45–46, 154–57, 159–61, 286, 291–92, 295; universality of, 7–8, 159, 162. *See also* vocational exploration and discernment

vocation of the institution. *See* institutional vocation and mission

vocational exploration and discernment: as an academic enterprise, ix–x, xiii–xv, 6, 14, 60–61, 64–71, 285, 322–29; communal nature of, 44, 148–50, 164, 248; cultural context for, 21–23, 76; definitions of, 97; as humanizing force, 73–74, 80–82, 86–89, 92–95; moral nature of, 189–91, 193, 197, 201–2, 223–25, 241, 315; out-of-classroom contexts for, 260–65, 268–71; 273–79, 281–83, 307–18; potential